ANCIENT INDIAN TRADITION & MYTHOLOGY

Translated by

A BOARD OF SCHOLARS

Edited by

Prof. J. L. SHASTRI

VOLUME 22

ANCIENT INDIAN TRADITION AND MYTHOLOGY

Mahāpurāṇas *Translated into English*
Gen. Ed. Dr. G.C. Tripathi
Founder Eds. Late J.L. Shastri and Late G.P. Bhatt

PUBLISHED VOLUMES

Vols. 1-4	ŚIVA PURĀṆA *Tr.* J.L. Shastri
Vols. 5-6	LIṄGA PURĀṆA *Tr.* J.L. Shastri
Vols. 7-11	BHĀGAVATA PURĀṆA *Tr.* G.V. Tagare
Vols. 12-14	GARUḌA PURĀṆA *Tr.* J.L. Shastri
Vols. 15-19	NĀRADA PURĀṆA *Tr.* G.V. Tagare
Vols. 20-21	KŪRMA PURĀṆA *Tr.* G.V. Tagare
Vols. 22-26	BRAHMĀṆḌA PURĀṆA *Tr.* G.V. Tagare
Vols. 27-30	AGNI PURĀṆA *Tr.* N. Gangadharan
Vols. 31-32	VARĀHA PURĀṆA *Tr.* S. Venkitasubramonia Iyer
Vols. 33-36	BRAHMA PURĀṆA *Tr.* J.L. Shastri
Vols. 37-38	VĀYU PURĀṆA *Tr.* G.V. Tagare
Vols. 39-48	PADMA PURĀṆA *Tr.* N.A. Deshpande
Vols. 49-71	SKANDA PURĀṆA *Ed.* G.P. Bhatt, *Tr. & Annot.* Shridhar Balooni & Pratosh Panda
Vols. 72-73	VĀMANA PURĀṆA *Tr. & Annot.* R.S. Shiva Ganesha Murthy
Vols. 74-76	GAṆEŚA PURĀṆA *Tr. & Annot.* Greg Bailey
Vols. 77-82	BRAHMAVAIVARTA PURĀṆA *Tr. & Annot.* G.P. Bhatt

PURĀṆAS UNDER PREPARATION

Viṣṇu Purāṇa • Harivaṁśa Purāṇa • Bhaviṣya Purāṇa • Matsya Purāṇa • Devī Bhāgavata Purāṇa • Kālika Purāṇa • Mārkaṇḍeya Purāṇa • Viṣṇudharmottara Purāṇa

THE
BRAHMĀṆḌA PURĀṆA

Translated and Annotated by
DR. G.V. TAGARE

PART I

MOTILAL BANARSIDASS PUBLISHERS
PRIVATE LIMITED • DELHI

2nd Reprint: Delhi, 2017
First Edition: Delhi, 1983

ISBN: 978-81-208-0354-1

Also available at

MOTILAL BANARSIDASS

41 U.A. Bungalow Road, Jawahar Nagar, Delhi 110 007
8 Mahalaxmi Chamber, 22 Bhulabhai Desai Road, Mumbai 400 026
203 Royapettah High Road, Mylapore, Chennai 600 004
236, 9th Main III Block, Jayanagar, Bengaluru 560 011
8 Camac Street, Kolkata 700 017
Ashok Rajpath, Patna 800 004
Chowk, Varanasi 221 001

UNESCO COLLECTION OF REPRESENTATIVE WORKS—*Indian Series*
This book has been accepted in the Indian Translation Series of the UNESCO Collection of Representative Works, jointly sponsored by the United Nations Educational, Scientific and Cultural Organization (UNESCO) and the Government of India

MLBD Cataloging-in-Publication Data
Brahmāṇḍa Purāṇa
Translated and Annotated by Dr. G. V. Tagare
Edited by Prof. J.L. Shastri
Includes Detailed Introduction
ISBN: 978-81-208-0354-1
I. Hinduism II. Purāṇa III. Brahmāṇḍa
IV. Prakriyā V. Anuṣaṅga
VI. Tagare, G.V. VII. Shastri, J.L.

Printed in India

by RP Jain at NAB Printing Unit,
A-44, Naraina Industrial Area, Phase I, New Delhi–110028
and published by JP Jain for Motilal Banarsidass Publishers (P) Ltd,
41 U.A. Bungalow Road, Jawahar Nagar, Delhi-110007

PUBLISHER'S NOTE

The purest gems lie hidden in the bottom of the ocean or in the depth of rocks. One has to dive into the ocean or delve into the rocks to find them out. Similarly, truth lies concealed in the language which with the passage of time has become obsolete. Man has to learn that language before he discovers that truth.

But he has neither the means nor the leisure to embark on that course. We have, therefore, planned to help him acquire knowledge by an easier course. We have started the series of *Ancient Indian Tradition and Mythology* in English Translation. Our goal is to universalize knowledge through the most popular international medium of expression. The publication of the Purāṇas in English translation is a step towards that goal.

PREFACE

The present volume contains the *Brahmāṇḍa Purāṇa*, Part I (Chapters 1-38) completing the first-two sections (*Prakriyā* and *Anuṣaṅga*) of the text *in English Translation*. This is the Twenty-second volume in the series which we have planned on *Ancient Indian Tradition and Mythology*.

The project of the Series was envisaged and financed in 1970 by Lala Sundar Lal Jain of Messrs Motilal Banarsidass. Hitherto twentyone volumes of the Series (comprising English translation of *Śiva, Liṅga, Bhāgavata, Garuḍa, Nārada* and *Kūrma Purāṇas*) have been published and released for sale.

This Purāṇa, like all other Purāṇas, is encyclopaedic in character. It deals with miscellaneous topics such as Cosmogony, Religion, Philosophy History, Geography and Astronomy. It is called *Brahmāṇḍa* since it gives explanation of the real state of affairs about the universe. It is divided into four sections : *Prakriyā, Anuṣaṅga, Upodghāta* and *Upasaṁhāra*. It is accompanied by *Lalitā-Māhātmya* (the glorification of the Goddess Lalitā) in 40 chapters.

The present volume consists of two Sections viz. *Prakriyā* and *Anuṣaṅga*. Section I *Prakriyā* consists of five chapters which deal with the creation of the universe in the light of the Vedic metaphysics which it expounds in detail in the Purānic manner. This section describes the original state of equilibrium of guṇas (qualities), the laying of the Golden Egg, the emergence of the creator lord Brahmā from it. The second section *Anuṣaṅga*, which this volume includes, contains 33 chapters (6-38). It is a connected continuation of the theme of *Prakriyā pāda* inasmuch as it recounts the account of the birth as well as the genealogies of Brahmarṣis (Brahmanical sages), Devarṣis (Celestial sages) and Rājarṣis (Royal sages). The two sections which complete this volume illustrate the two characteristics of a Mahāpurāṇa viz., *Sarga* (Creation) and *Vaṁśa* (genealogy), although the latter trait is resumed in the third section, namely the *Upodghāta* of the next volume.

The aim of this series is to universalize knowledge through the most popular international medium of expression, namely English. Old Sanskrit Text has been rendered into English as precisely as possible. *The translation is based on the standard edition of the Veṅkaṭeśvara Press.* The text is well edited, still it presents problems, hard to be overcome by mere translation. The need of annotations is evident therefore. The learned translator has added ample materials in the footnotes which facilitate correct interpretation of the text. He has put elaborate comments in these notes on each and every problem of importance and discussed textual variations in the verses common to other Purāṇas. His critical Introduction needs no comment in the preface. The comparative study of the Javanese text of Brahmāṇḍa Purāṇa in Kavi language with the Sanskrit text of the present Purāṇa is a feature that shall be most welcomed by the reader.

We have included Abbreviations in this part. They will be repeated in the succeeding parts too with such additions as are made in the notes of those parts. The general Index will be appended to the last part.

Acknowledgement of Obligations

It is our pleasant duty to put on record our sincere thanks to Dr. R. N. Dandekar and the UNESCO authorities for their kind encouragement and valuable help which render this work more useful than it would otherwise have been. We are extremely grateful to Dr. G. V. Tagare who has meticulously and delightfully accomplished this onerous task. The critical Introduction, the lucid translation and comprehensive annotations are, in fact, his monumental contributions to the studies in Indology. We must thank Shri T. V. Parameshwar Iyer for his valuable assistance in the preparation of this work. We should also express our gratitude to all those persons who have offered suggestions for improving the same.

—Editor

CONTENTS

PART I

ABBREVIATIONS

Common and self-evident abbreviations such as ch(s)—chapter(s), p—page, pp—pages, v—verse, vv—verses, Ftn—footnote, Hist. Ind. Philo—History of Indian Philosophy are not included in this list.

ABORI	*Annals of the Bhandarkar Oriental Research Institute*, Poona.
AGP	S. M. Ali's *The Geography of Purāṇas*, PPH, New Delhi, 1973.
AIHT	*Ancient Indian Historical Tradition*, F. E. Pargiter, Motilal Banarsidass (MLBD), Delhi.
AITM	*Ancient Indian Tradition and Mythology* Series, MLBD, Delhi, 1972 onwards.
AP	*Agni Purāṇa*, Guru Mandal Edition (GM), Calcutta, 1957.
Arch. S. Rep.	Archaeological Survey Report.
AV	*Atharva Veda*, Svadhyaya Mandal, Aundh.
Bd. P.	*Brahmāṇḍa Purāṇa*, MLBD, Delhi 1973.
BG	*Bhagavadgītā*.
Bh. P.	*Bhāgavata Purāṇa*, Bhagavat, Vidyapeeth, Ahmedabad.
Br.	*Brāhmaṇa* (preceded by name such as *Śatapatha*).
Bs. P.	*Bhaviṣya Purāṇa*, Vishnu Shastri Bapat, Wai.
Bv. P.	*Brahma Vaivarta Purāṇa*, GM, 1955-57.
CC	*Caturvarga Cintāmaṇi* by Hemādri.
CVS	*Caraṇa Vyūha Sūtra* by Śaunaka; Com. by Mahidāsa.
DB	*Devī Bhāgavata*, GM, 1960-61.

De or GDAMI	*The Geographical Dictionary of Ancient and Mediaeval India*, N. L. De, Orienta Reprint, Delhi, 1971.
Dh. S.	*Dharma Sūtra* (preceded by the author's name such as Gautama).
ERE	*Encyclopaedia of Religion and Ethics*—Hastings.
GP	*Garuḍa Purāṇa*, Ed. R. S. Bhattacharya, Chowkhamba, Varanasi, 1964.
GS	*Gṛhya Sūtra* (Preceded by the name of the author such as Āpastamba)
HD	*History of Dharma Śāstra* by P. V. Kane, G.O.S.
IA	*The Indian Antiquary*.
IHQ	*The Indian Historical Quarterly*.
KA	*Kauṭilīya Arthaśāstra*.
KP	*Kūrma Purāṇa*, Venkateshwara Press Edt. Bombay, also Kashiraj Trust Edt., Varanasi 1971.
LP	*Liṅga Purāṇa*, GM, 1960; also MLBD, Delhi, 1981.
Manu	*Manu Smṛti*.
Mbh.	*Mahābhārata*, Gītā Press, Gorakhpur, VS 2014.
MKP	*Mārkaṇḍeya Purāṇa*.
MN	*Mahābhārata Nāmānukramaṇi*, Gītā Press, Gorakhpur, VS 2016.
Mt. P.	*Matsya Purāṇa*, GM, 1954.
MW	*Monier Williams* Sk. English Dictionary MLBD, Delhi, 1976.
NP	*Nāradiya or Nārada Purāṇa*, Venkateshwar Press, Bombay.
PCK	*Bhāratavarṣiya Prācina Caritra kośa*, Siddheshwar Shastri, Poona, 1968.
Pd. P.	*Padma Purāṇa*, GM., 1957-59.
PE	*Puranic Encyclopaedia* by V. Mani, English, MLBD, Delhi, 1975.

PJ.	*Purāṇa* (Journal of the Kashirāj Trust), Varanasi.
PR or PRHRC	*Puranic Records on Hindu Rites and Customs* R. C. Hazra, Calcutta, 1948.
ṚV	*Ṛg Veda*, Svadhyaya Mandal, Aundh
Śat. Br	*Śatapatha Brāhmaṇa.*
SC or SMC	*Smṛti Candrikā*—Devanna Bhatta.
SEP	*Studies in Epics and Purāṇas* by A. D. Pusalkar Bharatiya Vidya Bhavan(BVB), Bombay.

INTRODUCTION

1. *The Title Brahmāṇḍa*

This Purāṇa is called 'Brahmāṇḍa', as god Brahmā narrated it with special emphasis on the description of the Brahmāṇḍa (the Cosmic Egg) and deals with the future Kalpa-periods.[1] KP. states that this Purāṇa, sanctified by the description of the Brahman was recounted by Brahmā to Sages engaged in a Sattra in Naimiṣa forest.[2] The NP (Nārada Purāṇa) calls it 'an ancient treatise dealing with the events of the Ādi-Kalpa.[3] The Bd.P.[4] (Brahmāṇḍa Purāṇa) repeatedly declares its main object to give 'the explanation of the real state of affairs or the reality about the Universe or the world (*loka-tattva*). The term Brahmāṇḍa connotes a mix of ancient Indian concepts about cosmography, cosmology and cosmogony.

Traditionally[5] the Purāṇa is divided into four parts (Pādas) of unequal length as follows :

1) Prakriyā Pāda (No. of Chs. 5)
2) Anuṣaṅga Pāda (No. of Chs. 33)
3) Upodghāta Pāda (No. of Chs. 74)
4) Upasaṁhāra Pāda (No. of Chs. 4)

---

1. Brahmā brahmāṇḍa-māhātmyam adhikṛtyā'bravit punaḥ /
tacca dvādaśa-sāhaśraṁ Brahmāṇḍaṁ dviśatādhikam //
Bhaviṣyāṇāṁ ca kalpānāṁ śrūyate yatra vistaraḥ /
tad Brahmāṇḍa-purāṇaṁ ca Brahmaṇā samudāhṛtam //
Mt.P. 53.54-55.

2 *KP*. II. 43.4.
atra pūrvaṁ sa Bhagavān ṛṣiṇāṁ sattram āsatām /
sa vai provāca Brahmāṇḍam Purāṇam Brahma-bhāvitam //
AP. 272.22 repeats *Mt. P*. 53.54a, b.c.

3. NP. 109.1

4. loka-tattvārtham akhilaṁ Veda-sammatam /
—*Bd.P*.I.I.1.1-8.
loka-tattva-vidhānārtham—*ibid*. 12

5. *Bd.P*. I.I.1.39 : Evam pādāstu catvāraḥ
NP. 109.29 calles *Bd. P*. 'catuṣpāda'

This seems to be the original division as followed in the Pūrva Saṁhitā (*Vā. P.* II.61.58-59), but later on, Pādas 1 and 2 were included under *Pūrva bhāga*, Pāda 3 under the middle part (*Madhya Bhāga*) and Pāda 4 as *Uttara-bhāga* (the latter part).

The original Bd. P. ended with the 4th Ch. of the *Upasaṁhāra Pāda* as its concluding verses (III IV.4.41-73) state that all the sages of Naimiṣāraṇya, the performers of the sacrificial session, went to heaven. It further gives the genealogy of the teachers of *Bd. P.* who handed down the Text (and it—the Genealogy—is much more comprehensive than that in the beginning—I.i.1.8-12).

Moreover, we find that the Lalitā Māhātmya starts with a fresh Maṅgalācaraṇa and has a new pair of interlocutors. Its contents—manifestation of goddess Lalitā to kill Bhaṇḍāsura, her marriage with Kāmeśvara, (Śiva) and glorification of Mahāpadmā etc.—show that it is an independent work and not an integral part of the *Bd. P.*

Lalitā Māhātmya of 40 chapters is thus a later accretion or an Appendix, as it is not mentioned in the NP. Ch. 109 nor in the Javanese version of the *Bd. P.*

2. *Extent* :

As to the extent of the Purāṇa, majority of the Purāṇas[1] regard "*Bd. P.* as consisting of 12000 verses" (*dvādaśa-sāhasraṁ Brahmāṇḍam*). Though *Mt. P.* 53.54 gives 12,200 as the number of verses in *Bd.P.*, the Venkateshwar Press edition of this Purāṇa, however, contains 14286 verses. Obviously Venk. Press edition is inflated with an interpolation of 2286 verses. The absence of Lalitā māhātmya in the *NP.* and that of the so-called 'Prophetic history of future dynasties' in the Indonesian edition of the Bd.P. show that the original *Bd. P.* was smaller.

3. *Position*

All Purāṇas, however, agree about the 18th position of *Bd. P.* in the list of Purāṇas (*vide VP.*III.6.21-24, *Bh. P.* XII. 13. 4-8, *LP.* I.39.61-63, *Mt. P.* 53.12ff, *SK.* P.VII.2.5-7).

---

1. e.g. *Bh.P.* XII. 13.8., *AP.* 272.23.

4. *Transmission*

The Bd.P. records the following two lines of transmission of this Purāṇa :

I. God Brahmā→Sage Vasiṣṭha→Parāśara→Jātukarṇya Dvaipāyana (Vyāsa)—Sūta Ro (Lo) maharṣaṇa (*Bd.P.* I.I.1 8-17). *NP.* (109.33-36) substitutes Śakti for Parāśara and adds Vāyu (the Wind-god) between Jātukarṇya and Vyāsa. II. This is much longer than the I above, and is given in the concluding portion of the Purāṇa (*Bd.P.* III.iv.4.58-66).

It is as follows :

God Brahmā→Mātariśvan (The Wind-god)→ Uśanas→ Bṛhaspati→The Sun-god→The God of death→Indra→Vasiṣṭha →Sārasvata→Tridhāman →Śaradvata→ Triviṣṭa→antarīkṣa→ Trayyāruṇi→Dhanañjaya → Kṛtañjaya → Bharadvāja → Gautama→Niryyantara→Vājaśravas→Somaśuṣma → Tṛṇabindu→ Dakṣa→Śakti→Parāśara (while in womb)→Jātukarṇya→Dvaipāyana (Vyāsa)→Sūta Ro (Lo)maharṣaṇa.

One wonders why Vasiṣṭha did not transmit this Purāṇa directly to his son Śakti and why fifteen generations of teachers or contemporary teachers had to intervene between the father (Vasiṣṭha) and the son (Śakti).

The *Vā.P.* 103.58-66 gives this very list of teachers who transmitted the text of that Purāṇa.

It must however be conceded that all the teachers in the list are accommodated in the longer II list.

5. *The Place of Composition*

It is difficult to pin-point the place of the composition of *Bd.P.* In *Bd.P.* I.ii.16.43-44 the author states :

"The region towards the northern extremity of the Sahya mountain where the Godāvarī flows is the most fascinating realm in the whole of the earth. A city named Govardhana was built there by Rāma. Heavenly trees and divine medicinal herbs were planted there by sage Bharadvāja to please Rāma. Hence the region of that excellent city is charming".

In my note on Govardhana,* I have noted that Govardhana

*Note 1 on p. 157.

was an important centre of learning and was mentioned several times in the famous inscription of Uṣavadāta (100 B.C.)—*Epi. Ind.* VIII, p. 78. Brahmins hailing from that area are known as Govardhana Brāhmaṇas. Some of the details of the Śrāddha ritual (*Śrāddha Kalpa*) in *Bd.P.* (II.iii. Chs. 10 to 20) are common to those of the Mādhyandin Brahmins (Mādhyandin Brahmins seem to have colonised the Godāvarī valley right from its source at Tryambakeshwar).

Kane regards this area as the place of composition of *Bd. P.* (HD.V.ii.895 and IV. 710 Footnote 1618), I still think that some more clinching evidence is necessary to support this claim, for in Ch. 16 under reference and elsewhere a number of places in India are mentioned in glowing terms.

II. *Text-Criticism* : *Materials*

II. i. Chapter Concordance of the Brahmāṇḍa and Vāyupurāṇa

Brahmāṇḍa	*Vāyu*	*Brahmāṇḍa*	*Vāyu*
		7	8
Prakriyāpāda		(195)	(209)
		8	9.1-84
1.1	1	(66)	(64)
(174)	(205)	9	10.1-67
2	2	(92)	(67)
(48)	(45)	10	27
3	4	(88)	(60)
(38)	(92)	11	28
4	5	(45a)	(39)
(34)	(54)	12	29
5	6	(53)	(49)
(141)	(79)	13.1-86	30.1-78
		(86)	(78)
Anuṣaṅgapāda		13.87-151	31
		(65)	(61)
6	7	14	33
(77)	(80)	(75)	(65)

Brahmāṇḍa	*Vāyu*	*Bd.P.*	*Vā.P.*
15.1-51a	34.1-57	32	59.1-106a
(50)	(57)	(122)	(106)
15.51a-61b	43.1-9	34	60.1-62
	(9)	(68)	(62)
15.61b-80	45.1-20a	35.1.4a	60.63-66a
(20)	(20)	(4)	(4)
16	45.67-137	35.4b-215	61
(69)	(71)	(211)	(186)
17	46	36	62
(37)	(37)	(227)	(193)
18	47	37	63
(84)	(80)	(60)	(56)
19	49	38	64
(197)	(186)	(33)	(31)
20	50.1-57a		
(58)	(57)		
21	50.57b-224	*Upodghātapāda*	
(176)	(167)		
22	51	II.1	65.1a-120
(84)	(76)	(125)	(120)
23	52	2	65.120b-159
(108)	(99)	(32)	(39)
24	53	3	66
(152)	(123)	(131)	(152)
25	54	4	67.1-47
(117)	(117)	(37)	(47)
26	55	5	67.68-135
(65)	(68)	(106)	(88)
28	56	6	68
(100)	(94)	(39)	(39)
29	57.1-85	7.	69
(92)	(85)	(479)	(355)
30	57.86-125	8.	70
(48)	(40)	(162)	(91)
31	58	9	71
(127)	(126)	(76)	(79)

Bd.P.	*Vā.P.*	*Bd.P.*	*Vā.P.*
10.1-52a (52)	72 (50)	19 (74)	83.1-107 (107)
10.52b-120 (68)	73 (73)	20 (23)	83.108-129 (22)
11.1-35a (35)	74 (32)	59 (86)	84 (86)
11.35b-116 (81)	75 (77)	60 (28)	85 (28)
12 (46)	76 (43)	61 (53)	86 (69)
13 (143)	77 (135)		
14 (117)	78 (28)	*Upasaṁhārapāda*	
15 (68)	79 (95)	III.1 (243)	100 (246)
16 (59)	80 (62)	2 (316)	101 (355)
17 (22)	81 (26)	3 (113)	102 (135)
18 (15)	82 (15)	4 (73)	103 (73)

It is due to this close correspondence between the texts of Bd. P. and Vā P. that I referred to the reading in the corresponding verse in the Vā.P. in case the reading in Bd.P. is corrupt, incorrect or doubtful.

II. ii. The Brahmāṇḍa and the Nārada Purāṇas

The NP., in Ch. 109, briefly gives a list of topics in the Bd. P. They are not 'a Table of contents' in the modern sense of the term but are found described at various places in the Bd.P.

Below is a comparative table of the topics in the Bd. P. as recorded in the NP.

NP.Ch. 109		*Bd.P.* *Pūrva bhāga* *Prakriyā pāda*
V.4	Stipulation of duties	I.1.1.
	Story of the Naimiṣa forest	I.1.2.
	The origin of Hiraṇyagarbha	I.1.3.
	The conception of different worlds.	I.1.4

N.P. Ch. 109		*Bd. P.* *Pūrva-Bhāga-Anu-ṣaṅga Pāda*
V.5	Narration of Kalpas and Manvantaras,	I.ii.6
	Krowledge about worlds	I.ii.7.
V.6	Narration of mental creation	I.ii.8.
	Rudra's offspring	I.ii.9.
	Prowess of Mahādeva	I.ii.10.
	Creation by Sages	I.ii.11.
V.7	Agnivaṁśa	I.ii.12
	The wheel of Time	I.ii.13.
	Dynasty of Priyavrata	I.ii.14
	The extent of the earth	I.ii.15
V.8	Description of Bhārata	I.ii.16
	Review of other sub-continents	I.ii.17
	Description of Jambūdvīpa and other continents	I.ii.18 & 19.
	The description of the nether-worlds	I.ii.20
V.9	Enumeration of the upper worlds	I.ii.21.20 ff.
	The movements of planets	I.ii.23.
	Planetary system	I.ii.21, 22

	NP	*Bd.P.*
	Enumeration of Divine plants	I.ii.24
V.10	Explanation of the name Nīlakaṇṭha	I.ii.25
	Prowess of Mahādeva	I.ii.26, 27
	Description of the New Moon day	I.ii.28
	Review of the Principles of Yuga	I.ii.29.
V.11	The Institution of Yajñas	I.ii.30.
	The last two Yugas described	I.ii.31
	Characteristics of human beings in different Yugas	I.ii.32.
	Spiritual lineage of Sages	I.ii.32
V.12	The classification of the Vedas	I.ii.34.
	Svāyambhuva Manu and his Manvantara	I.ii.35.
	Enumeration of remaining Manu epochs	I.ii.36.
	Milking of the Earth	I.ii.36.
V.13	The Cākṣuṣa Manvantara	I.ii.37.

	NP.	*Bd.P. III Upodghāta Pāda*
	The creation of Seven Sages	II.iii.1.
V.14	The family of Prajāpati and the birth of Devas	II.iii.2, 3
	Birth of Maruts	II.iii.5
V.15	The race of Kaśyapa	II.iii.7
	The families of Sages	II.iii.8
	Pitṛ-Kalpa	II.iii.9
	Śrāddha-Kalpa	II.iii. Chs.10-20.

	NP.	*Bd.P.*
V.16	The origin of Vaivasvata Manu and his creation	II.iii.59
	The family of Manu's sons	II.iii.60
	The review of Gandharvas (Science of Music)	II.iii.61.
V.17	The race of Ikṣvāku	II.iii.63.
	The race of Atri	II.iii.8
	The race of Amāvasu	II.iii.66
	The story of Raji	II.iii.66
V.18	The story of Yayāti	II.iii.68
	The race of Yadu	
	The story of Kārttavīrya	II.iii.69
	The story of Jamadagni and Paraśurāma	II.iii.21-46.
V.19	The race of Vṛṣṇi	II.iii.71.
	The birth of Sagara	II.iii.47.75-100.
	The story of Bhārgava and the killing of Kārttavīrya	II.iii.37-46.
V.20	The story of Sagara	II.iii.45-56
	The story of Bhārgava again	II.iii.57-58.
	Battle between Devas and Asuras	II.iii.72.67-195 and 73.1-68.
	Birth of Kṛṣṇa	II.iii.71.195-241.
V.21	Indra's (Prob-Śiva's) prayer by Śukra	II.iii.72.163ff
	Greatness of Viṣṇu	II.iii.73.
	The race of Bali	II.iii.74.26 ff.
V.22	The future kings of Kali Age	II.iii.74
		Bd. P. *Uttara Bhāga-Upasaṁhāra Pāda*
V.23	Description of Vaivasvata Manvantara	III.iv.5 ff.
V.24	Stories of future Manus	III.iv.1.7 ff.

	NP	*Bd.P.*
V.25	Kalpa and Pralaya	III.iv.1 & 3.
	Measures of Time	III.iv.2.90 ff.
	14 Worlds and their character	III.iv.2.-8-89.
V.26	Description of Hells	III.iv.2.145-195.
	Prakritic Pralaya	IV.3.
V.27	Description of Śiva's city Threefold goals	IV.iv.2.
V.28.	Description of Brahman	IV.iv.iv.4.

It will be seen from the above comparative Table that *Lalitā-Māhātmya* does not form a part of Bd.P. according to Nārada.

*II. (iii) The Old-Javanese Brahmāṇḍa Purāṇa**

The first scholar to invite attention to the old-Javanese (OJ.) Bd. P. was R. Friederich who, in A.D. 1847, noted it in his 'Provisional Report of the Isle of Bali'. But that Purāṇa in *Kavi* language came to be edited and translated in Dutch by the great scholar Prof. Dr. J. Gonda of Utrecht in 1932-33. (Het oud-javaansche Brahmāṇḍa Purāṇa Edited and annotated, Bandung 1932 and II translated, Bandung 1933).

Like other OJ. texts (e.g. many Parvans of the Mbh.) the Bd. P. in Kavi Language is an abridged prose translation of the SK. Bd. P. or was a translation of an abridged form of the original SK. written in the Śloka style. It prunes superfluous adjectives and other trammels and succinctly presents the story. It follows SK. passages which were borrowed and translated very closely. Although it is much shorter, it does not generally speaking, omit, from the chapters what is essential. What is especially

*Based on Prof. Dr. J. Gonda's paper : *Einige Mitteilungen über das alt-jāvānische Brahmāṇḍa Purāṇa* in *Acta Orientalia* XI. 218-259. I am grateful to Dr. Gonda for inviting my attention to this article (His letter dated 1.12.82).

interesting is that many Ślokas, double or single *pādas* are literally borrowed and interspersed at irregular intervals. These SK. quotations constitute fragments of an independent tradition of these texts. The Javanese Bd. P. is closely related to the Brahmāṇḍa-Vāyu recension though different in many respects from it and is a valuable source of knowledge for studying the textual tradition of the Purāṇas. Dr. Gonda examines the structure of the Javanese Bd. P. and draws attention to the following particulars which shed light on its relation with SK. Bd. P. and the inter-relation between the SK. Purāṇas themselves:

1. The introduction mainly agrees with SK.Vā.P., with the sacrifice of King Adhisīma-Kṛṣṇa. Among Brāhmaṇas and Sages who attended was Bhagavān Romaharṣaṇa. He, at their request, proceeds to narrate the *Manuvaṁśakrama* including Puranic stories. OJ. (Old-Javanese) Bd. P. p. 48.5—p, 53.30 correspond to Vā.P. 1.8-28. Vā. P. 1.1-9 are completely missing.

2. Romaharṣaṇa commences his narration by describing the creation of the universe Bd.P.1, 3, 8. After describing Pradhāna, the OJ. text informs about the creator : Rudra, Kāla adding some notices of (originally Sāṅkhya but Puranised concepts like) mahān, ahaṁkāra, ekādaśendriya, tanmātras and the origin of the cosmic egg. Then the creation of nine devarṣis, the birth of Rudra (cf. Bd.P. Ch.10), the origin of Saṅkalpa and Dharma (Cf. Vā. P. 9.7 ff), the creation of gods, Asuras, pitṛs. The first quotation in OJ. Bd. p. corresponds to Bd. P. 1.3.8 and the last to 1.8.54-55.

3. After some details about the chronology of creation and origin of four Varṇas, the OJ. text treats the birth of Svāyambhuva Manu and Śatarūpā, their marriage and birth of Rati etc. The narrative runs parallel to Bd. P. 1.9.32 ff (Vā. P. 10.8ff) but the OJ. version is shorter and presents the topics in different order. While dealing with Dakṣa's wife Prasūti and her twenty-four children (OJ. Bd.P. p. 58.1.21 ff) the text agrees with KP. 8.15 rather than with the more detailed Bd.P. 1.9.47-49 (Vā.P. 10.23-24) showing that the Javanese author had a shorter SK. redaction of the Bd. P.

The text Bd. P. ch. 11 (Vā. P. ch. 28) and OJ. Bd. P. run parallel but OJ. version drops *Agnivaṁśa-varṇana*. The short note on Pitṛs (Bd. P. 1.13.1 ff. Vā. P. 30.1 ff) is also missing.

4. OJ. Bd. P. is silent on *Deva-vaṁśa Varṇana* (Bd. P. 1.13.87-151, Vā. P. 31).

5. *Kṣattriya-Sarga* i.e. the genealogy of Manu Svāyambhuva in OJ. Bd. P. p. 68.1.2 ff corresponds to Bd. P. 1.14 and Vā. P. 33. In SK. Bd. P. and Vā. P. the description of Jambūdvipa (Bd. P. 1.15, Vā. P. 34. 1-57, 53.1-9, 45.1.20a) follows rationally and chronologically after narrating the appointment of Manu's seven grandsons to seven *dvipas*, but Chs. Bd. P. 15-31, Vā. P. 34-58 are not found in OJ. Bd. P. It gives the geography of Jambūdvīpa at a later place.

6. The OJ. Bd.P. p.72.1,ff. containing *yuga-prajā-lakṣaṇam* and *Ṛṣi-pravaravarṇanam* corresponds to Bd. P. 1.32.1 ff). The duration of life of gods, demons, men, dharma, āśramas etc. are discussed to some length.

7. Bd. P. Ch. 33 containing sages and sacred formula (ṛṣ-ṇāṁ nāmāni, mantra-lakṣaṇam, mantrāṇāṁ *nānāvidhatvam* etc.) is missing in OJ. Bd. P., though the contents are to follow later on (p. 14 ff.). Though the subject matter of Bd. P. 34 is generally speaking adequately represented in the OJ. text, there is much diversity in details (so in Vā.P. as well).

8. The episode of the pupils of Devamitra Śākalya and Śākapūṇi are common to OJ. and SK. Bd.P. (Ch. 35 of Bd. P.); so are the next subjects such as division of Yajurveda, Vaiśampāyana's *brahma-hatyā*, behaviour of Yājñavalkya who, after 'vomitting' old Yajurveda, acquires a new (white) Yajurveda and names of 86 pupils of Vaiśampāyana etc. The OJ. text spells many names differently. There is a curious statement in OJ. Bd. P. p. 90.1 where Yājñavalkya is shown to refuse Vaiśampāyana's request to observe penance to atone for his Brahmahatyā. But both SK. Bd.P. 1.35.20 and Vā. P. 61.17 state the willingness of Yājñavalkya to obey:

aham ekaś cariṣyāmi tiṣṭhantu munayas tvime

9. The next section on the *ṛṣis* of four Vedas, the *mantras*, their use differs considerably in details from SK. Bd. P. Ch. 33 but Vā. P. too differs and so the origin of deviation is Indian and not Indonesian.

10. When OJ. text (p. 112.30) reaches SK. Bd. P. 1.35.201 and Vā. P. 61.172, it (OJ.Bd.p. p. 112.30) observes : "Like that the narrative goes in the *Prakriyāpāda* of Brahmāṇḍa-saṁhitā as told by the revered Vyāsa"). But the *Prakriyā-pāda* in SK. Purāṇas ends much earlier viz. at the end of Ch. 5 in Bd. P. and 6 in Vā. P. It is puzzling how the term *Prakriyāpāda* is used in the OJ. Text which shows no knowledge of the four-fold division (viz. *Prakriyā*, *Anuṣaṅga*, *Upodghāta* and *Upasaṁhāra*) of the *mūla-purāṇa*.

11. The long section dealing with other Manus and the descendants of Svāyambhuva Manu esp. the Vena-Pṛthu episode runs parallel in general with Bd. P.,Vā.P. Kirfel points out the difference between redaction of the Vena-Pṛthu episode in Bd. P., Vā. P. and in other Purāṇas like Brahma, Harivaṁśa and concludes that the OJ. text betrays the activity of the same redactor who arranged the Indian Bd. P.-Vā. P. texts. Hereafter OJ. text treats the description of Jambūdvīpa, *Bhuvana-vinyāsa* and a part of *Jyotiḥpracāra* which constitute Bd. P. Ch. 1.15 and Vā. P. Ch. 34. The harmonization of this remarkable transposition of the topics is a problem.

12. Bd. P. 1.15-24, Vā. P. 34-54 and Mt.P. 112-128 constitute a large coherent treatise of geography and cosmography. OJ. text (p. 128.22 ff) refers to Bhaṭṭāra Bāyu "The Lord Vāyu" as an authority (cf. the beginning of Bd.P. 1.15, Vā. 34) and deals with Jambūdvīpa, its mountains (esp. Meru) the Saptavarṣa of Jambūdvīpa and closes with Kuruvarṣa.

13. Next OJ. text (p. 136, 30-143, 4) gives the description of Bhāratavarṣa. The order of Stanzas in Bd. P., Vā. P. is similar to OJ. text but curiously enough the line Bd. P. 1.16.8 and Vā. P. 45, 78 regarding the mutual unapproachability of the nine regions of Bhārata-Varṣa is untraced in OJ. text and SK. Mt. P.

14. The next section deals with other *varṣas* of Jambūdvīpa (Kimpuruṣa etc.), the penance of Bhagīratha, the descent of Gaṅgā, lakes, rivers and Vaḍavāmukha or Aurvāgni. The OJ. shows the influence of Mt. P. and the quotation in OJ. text p. 152.12 (yasyāṁ jambūnadaḥ smṛtaḥ) has more in common with Mt. P. 120.67 rather than Bd. P. 1.18.69a and Vā. P. 47.66b.

15. The next section deals with other *dvipas*, Śaka, Kuśa etc. On this cosmographic topic SK. Purāṇas resolve into three groups (1) Bd. P., Vā. P. etc. (2) Mt. P., Varāha (3) Pd. P. and Mbh. The Javanese version joins the *Matsya* recension of this cosmography.

16. The last section deals with astronomy. Bd. P. 20, Vā. P. 50.1-57 give the description of the nether-worlds. But OJ. deletes this and goes with Mt. P. As to the description of stars, planets, division of stratosphere, the Solar car (Bd.P. 1.22), the OJ. text follows more closely Mt. P. In Mt. P., Bd. P, Vā. P. the narration (of the stars etc.) continues but the OJ. text abruptly comes to a close where the above Indian parallel texts do not even finish the chapter.

From this Prof. Dr. Gonda concludes that the OJ. text is incomplete.

The *Vaṁśānucarita* traditionally dealt with in the Purāṇa is completely absent as it was of little importance to Javanese readers*

A part of this OJ. text containing the Vena-Pṛthu episode, the geography and part of cosmography has come down to us in a metrical adaptation in a MS called Pṛthuvijaya, the name of the poet being Aṣṭa-guṇa.

III. The Brahmāṇḍa as a Mahā-Purāṇa

It may be due to the interpolatory nature of Ch. 1 of our Purāṇa, that the ancient division of this Purāṇa in four parts-*Pādas*) follows the *Pañca-lakṣaṇa*-list characterising Mahā-purāṇas, as the former is given in VV. 38b-39 and the latter in VV. 37b-38b of the opening chapter. Be it as it may, the latter—the *Pañca-lakṣaṇa* definition of a Purāṇa is very popular as it is repeated in a number of Purāṇas e.g. AP. 1.14, KP. I.1.12, MK. P.134.13-14, Varāha P. 2.4, Vā. P. 4.10-11.

It is interesting to note how this ancient Purāṇa of "four feet" (*Catuṣpāda*) adapts itself to the *Pañca-lakṣaṇa* formula

*It is equally possible that the MS of SK.Bd.P. taken to Java might have been at a period before the so-called 'future kings'. Hence their non-mention.

adopted by it. The five characteristics (*lakṣaṇas*) of a Purāṇa given by it, are : (1) *Sarga* (creation of the Universe), (2) *Pratisarga* (Dissolution and re-creation of the world), (3) *Manvantaras* (Periods of Time presided over by Manus), (4) *Vaṁśa* (Genealogies of gods, the Patriarchs, The Sun and The Moon) and (5) *Vaṁśānucarita* (accounts of dynasties of different ruling families).

(1) *Sarga—Creation of the Universe*

The Purāṇa gives the following theories of the creation of the Universe :

(1) *Creation from the Brahman*

The eternal Brahman, the source of the Universe is beginningless and endless. It is the source of the beginning and the place of ultimate merging and rest (of the Universe). It is incomprehensible and beyond *Sat* and *Asat*. It pervaded the entire universe which was dark (unmanifested), as the *guṇas* were in a state of equilibrium. At the time of creation, *Kṣetrajña* presided over *Pradhāna* and agitated the *guṇas* which thereby became uneven (due to loss of their equilibrium) and the great principle *Mahat* was evolved. As the *Sattva-guṇa* predominated in the *Mahat*, the *liṅga śarira* psychic-subtle-body) was evolved and was presided over by the *Kṣetrajña*. *Saṅkalpa* (thought-power) and *Adhyavasāya* (determination) are remembered to be his functions. With a desire to create, he created this great creation (I.1.3.10-24).

(*II*) *The Purāṇic Theory**

The *Kṣetrajña* called Brahmā who awoke in the egg of *Prakṛti* (Cosmic Egg) is the first embodied being and he is called *Puruṣa* (One lying in the abode of the cosmic egg). This god Brahmā, the first creator of *Bhūtas* (elements or beings) existed first. This four-faced Hiraṇyagarbha appeared at first in this (Cosmic Egg). Both at the time of creation and re-creation (after destruction), he is the *Kṣetrajña* called Brahmā.

*A few verses in the text of Bd. P. are corrupt and unintelligible. So this theory is given on the basis of the corresponding verses of the Vā. P. 4. 76-79 as both these Purāṇas have identical verse

In the Vedic tradition, Hiraṇya is the Light-Life principle. He in whom this principle vibrates is *Hiraṇyagarbha**. Our Purāṇa states that the Cosmic Egg contains seven worlds, the earth along with Seven continents, oceans—nay everything including the Sun, the Moon, Stars, Planets and the mountain Lokāloka (I.1.3.26-31). The egg is enveloped from outside with seven sheaths of the four elements (water, fire, wind and the ether), of the *Bhūtādi*, *Mahat* and *Pradhāna* each sheath ten times bigger than the former. Sāṅkhya influence is obvious here.

This is the *Prākṛta* creation, a *vivarta* of the Brahman presided over by *Kṣetrajña* (Brahma). It takes place without preplanning (*abuddhipūrva*) like the flash of a lightening (I. 1.3.24-37).

(*III*) *Prākṛta Sarga*

Our Purāṇa presents the Sāṅkhya Theory of Creation as follows :

Before the creation of the Universe, the Unmanifest was stationed in itself and the product (the Universe) was withdrawn. The *Pradhāna* and *Puruṣa* remained with their characteristics Tamas and Sattva respectively. *Laya* means equilibrium of *Guṇas* and Creation means dis-equilibrium of these *Guṇas*. Three divinities viz. Brahmā, Viṣṇu and Rudra were born out of the qualities Rajas, Sattva and Tamas respectively. But it is Viṣṇu who, as the enlightener and revealer of the Rajas, becomes Brahmā and that of the Tamas adopts the form of Kāla (Rudra) and of these Sattva assumes the form of Viṣṇu. Thus, the trinity of gods, though separate with separate functions, are but one entity. "The self-born deity has three states. He has four faces as Brahmā and possessing Rajas exclusively, creates the worlds; as Kāla, he has the guṇas—Rajas and Tamas, and he annihilates. As Puruṣa with a thousand heads, he is exclusively Sāttvika. This is the position of Guṇas in the case of the Self-born deity" (I.i.4.17-19) That Deity is *Om*, Omniscient, *Ādya*, (first), *Aja* (Unborn) *Hiraṇyagarbha*, Kāla and eternal. (ibid.26-34).

---

*The Purāṇas amplify Vedic tradition. For the concept 'Hiraṇyagarbha' vide V. S. Agrawala—*Hiraṇyagarbha* (Purāṇa II i.ii.285-306).

(*IV*) *The Nine Creations of Brahmā*

At the beginning, there was one vast ocean (Ekārṇava, also called Mahārṇava, *Stabdha-Salila* or *Yugānta-Toya* 'Water at the end of Yugas' in other Purāṇas). This primeval watery flood expresses the infinite unmanifest cause of the Universe (called the *Kāraṇa Brahman* by Nīlakaṇṭha on HV.P.3.9.1-4). Brahmā named Nārāyaṇa with a thousand heads slept there. He remained meditating for a thousand Yugas. He moved alone in waters and knew that the Universe had sunk into that vast expanse of water and thought of the other eight-fold cosmic body (evolved by) Oṁkāra in the beginning of Kalpas as before (I.i.5.1-9).

He assumed the form of a boar and lifted up the earth* and re-arranged the mountains, oceans etc. on the earth as before 'again and again at the beginning of every Kalpa' (ibid 9-27). With a desire to create, he meditated and as he was meditating *Avidyā* with its five 'knots' (*parvans*) viz. Tamas (ignorance), Moha (Delusion) Mahāmoha (great Delusion and) others (These are the *Kleśas* in the *Yogaśāstra*) unfolded itself and immobile (*mukhya* or *sthāvara*) creation took place. Brahmā was not satisfied with this meditated (Vaikṛta) creation and created the animal world called *Tiryak-srotas* as it functioned obliquely. This second creation was Tāmasika and Brahmā being dissatisfied with it created the Third divine—Sāttvika—of gods (called *Urddhvasrotas*).

These are the three 'meditated' and Primary creations (ibid. 28-46). Later, god Brahmā desired to create another set of beings and Lo ! a 'down-currented' category of mortal beings full of Rajas and Tamas yet capable of achieving these goals was created (*ibid* 47-50).

The fifth creation is called *Anugraha Sarga* (favoured creation) as it was created through the favour of *Avyakta* or *Prakṛti*. It consists of four classes and they are born again and again (VV.51-52 and VV. 100-104).

---

*The beautiful allegoric description of Yajña-Varāha should be read in the original VV.11 ff.

The sixth creation is the *Bhūta-Sarga* (creation of elements, Tanmātras).

There seems to be some confusion (probably due to the uncritical nature of the Text). But to recapitulating the names of these sargas:

I. Primary Creation :

(1) Creation of *Mahat*

(2) Creation of *Tanmātras*, (called Bhūta sarga here again)

(3) *Vaikārika* (Creation of *Aindriya Sarga*)

These are the *Prākṛta* (created from *Prakṛti*) Primary creations and

II. Secondary Creation :

(4) *Mukhya Sarga* (Creation of insentients or *of immobiles*).

(5) *Tiryak-Srotas* (Creation of lower creatures and animals).

(6) *Ūrddhva Srotas* (Creation of gods and divine beings).

(7) *Arvāksrotas* (Creation of human beings)

(8) *Anugraha-Sarga* (Both Sāttvika and Tāmasika)

These five (4-8) are called *Vaikṛta* (Secondary) creations and these function without consciousness or fore-knowledge (*a-buddhi-pūrvaka*).

III. Primary-Cum-Secondary (?)

(9) The *Kaumāra Creation*—Creation by mind-born sons. But when Sanat-Kumāra and others became Yogins and did not procreate, Brahmā created mind-born sons viz. Bhṛgu, Aṅgiras, Marīci, Pulastya, Pulaha, Kratu, Dakṣa, Atri and Vasiṣṭha from various parts of his body (I.i.5.70-76). These are termed as nine Brahmās as they participated in creation. but his mental sons Sanat-Kumāra and Kratu became Yogins. Later on (VV.107-108), the Ṛgvedic idea about the creation of four Varṇas from different parts of the Lord's body, is stated. In spite of the overlapping of these theories, they represent a metaphorical amplification and continuation of Vedic concepts with a strong admixture of Sāṅkhya (e.g. the concept of the

Trinity of gods—Brahmā, Viṣṇu and Rudra). The corner-stone of Purāṇic lore, is a mix of the Vedic Brahman and the Sāṅkhya concept of three *guṇas* etc.

PRATI-SARGA (DISSOLUTION AND RE-CREATION)*

The *Pralaya* is of four types :

(1) *Nitya*—usual

(2) *Naimittika* (Periodical).

(3) *Prākṛtika* (of Prakṛti, the primordial nature)

(4) *Ātyantika* (Absolute or final).

(1) The *Nitya Pralaya* is what goes on every day e.g. deaths of beings.

(2) *The Naimittika* Pralaya takes place at the completion of a Kalpa i.e. at the end of one thousand sets of (*Catur*) Yugas. God Brahmā begins to absorb the subjects in him. A continuous drought for hundred years, the Sun with his seven rays burns up everything and evaporates the oceans. The Saṁvartaka fire burns down the four worlds viz. Bhū, Bhuvar, Svar and Mahar. Thereafter, Saṁvartaka clouds pour down torrential rains and everything mobile and immobile is destroyed and dissolved into one vast expanse of water and god Brahmā becomes a thousand-eyed, thousand-headed entity and goes to sleep for a period of one thousand sets of four Yugas (God Brahmā's night) (II.iv. 132-190).

At the end of Brahmā's night, he wakes up and recreates. The day and night of Brahmā i.e. the complete day of Brahmā is called Viśeṣa Kalpa (ibid. 190-210)

(3) *The Prākṛtika Pralaya* takes place at the end of Brahmā's period. When the Pratyāhāra' (withdrawal of the Universe) is imminent, Bhūtas (elements, both gross and subtle) are annihilated, evolutes of *Prakṛti* beginning with *Mahat* and ending with *Viśeṣas* are destroyed. The waters swallow the special quality—smell—of the earth, the fire that of the water upto *Ākāśa* which merges into *Bhūtādi*. In this way the higher evolute of *Prakṛti* "swallows up" the lower one, till at last the *Mahat* dissolves itself into *Guṇa-sāmya* (equilibrium of *Guṇas*). Only, the

*Cf. KP.II.45. 1-10. VP.1.7.41-43, VI.3.2 ff.

Ātman remains. This process of reabsorption of Principles (*Tattva-Sāmya*) is recurrent (II.iv.3-1-24).

(4) *Ātyantika Pralaya* takes place when one becomes liberated through spiritual knowledge. He does not take up another body just as a sprout (never comes out) when the seed is burnt. (ibid. 80-84).

This is called "dissolution due to dawning of knowledge (II.iv.1.131).

Manvantaras

Purāṇas look upon Time as a form of God.[1] His power to create the universe by disturbing the equilibrium of *guṇas* of Prakṛti, the destroyer of all beings[2] and the empirical time-sequence. The Bd. P. is committed to the description of all Manvantaras and Kalpa-periods[3] and it describes Time figuratively in terms of units of time : "The Sun is his source and the period of *nimeṣa*[4] (twinkling of an eye or utterance of a short vowel) is his beginning. Day and night constitute his form and *nimeṣa*-unit his limbs. The year is his essence. This lord of subjects (Prajāpati) is of the nature of the present, past and future".[5]

The main division of time are the day, the fortnight, the month, the season and Ayanas.[6]

The Manvantaras are based on the concept of Yuga periods. Originally a Yuga consisted of five years called (1) Saṁvatsara, (2) Parivatsara, (3) Iḍ or-Iḍāvatsara, (4) Anuvatsara and (5) Vatsara[7]. We find the same duration of Yuga in Mbh. Sabhā 11.37-38) Kauṭilya[8] and Vedāṅga-jyotiṣa.[9]

1. *Yugābhimānī Kālātmā-Rudraḥ* / I.ii.13.139
2. I.ii.13.109. *Sarva-bhūtāpahārakaḥ* / also see V. 149.
3. I.i.1.46
4. It means either 'winking of the eye' or 'time required to utter a short letter. (*laghvakṣaram*) vide Bd. P. I.ii.29.5.

   nimeṣakāla-tulyaṁ hi vidyāllaghvakṣaraṁ ca yat
5. I.ii.13.III-113a.
6. Ibid. 113b-114a.
7. Ibid. 114b-115.
8. *Pañca-saṁvatsare yugam—Artha-śāstra* II.20 p. 109.
9. *Pañca-saṁvatsara-mayaṁ Yugādhyakṣam Prajāpatim* V. 1.

   Hence Kane conjectures that 'yuga' in ṚV.III.26.3,III.55.18 means 'a period of 5 years'.

Later on, the period of Yuga came to be extended to 12000 years e.g. Bd. P.I.ii.29.25-29, state 12,000 years as the total number of years of four Yugas (including the 'twilight' years)—a period endorsed by Manu[1] and Mbh.[2]. Nowhere is there a hint that these are not human years but divine ones.

But later on, the concept of 'divine' or super-human years developed as can be seen from units of time given as follows[3].

15 nimeṣa = Kāṣṭhā; 30 Kāṣṭhā = Kalā

30 Kalās = Muhūrta;

30 Muhūrtas = Day and night (24 hours)

30 days = A month = One day and night of Pitṛs

30 human months = 1 year of Pitṛs

360 human months = 1 year of Pitṛs

Human Uttarāyaṇa = 1 day of the Devas

Human Dākṣiṇāyana = 1 night of the Devas

1 human year = A complete day and night of Devas

30 Human years = A month of Devas

360 Human years = One year of Devas

3030 Human years = 1 Saptarṣi year

9090 Human years = 1 Dhruva year

360,000 Human years = 1,000 years of gods.

Thus the Yuga periods with the twilight period (*Sandhyāṁśa*) of each Yuga is as follows:

	Period years'	*Sandhyā*	*Sandhyāṁśa*		*Total*
1. Kṛta-yuga :	4000	400	400	=	4800
2. Tretā-yuga :	3000	300	300	=	3600
3. Dvāpara-yuga:	2000	200	200	=	2400
4. Kali-yuga :	1000	100	100	=	1200

Total period of four yugas (*Catur-yugi* or *Mahā-yūga*) = 12,000 years.

1. Manu 1.71.
2. Vana. 188.27.
3. Bd. P. I.ii.29.5.-21.

But these are 'divine' years. And our Purāṇa converts them into human years as 4320,000. This new concept of Yugas is adopted in Purāṇas *vide* KP.I.Chs.51,53 NP. I. Ch. 41, Mbh. Vana, Chs. 149, 188, VP. I.3, Vā.P. Chs. 21, 22, 57, 58.

The day of god Brahmā consists of 1000 *catur-yugis* in which fourteen Manus ruled. It means a manvantara $= \frac{1000 \text{ catur-}yugis}{14}$ or $71\frac{6}{14}$ *catur-yugas* or $12000 \times 360 \times 71 + 17{,}28000)$, or 30,67,20,000 human years[1]. Strangely enough, this yuga-theory is limited to Bhārata-varṣa.[2]

The theory of Yugas and Kalpas began to take shape in 300 B.C. and was fully developed in the first centuries of the Christian Era.[3]

The Characteristics of Yugas :

Our Purāṇa offers a few remarks about the state of society in Kṛta-yuga : There was social equality. People were ever young, equal in beauty and longevity. They were without malice and had no conflicts. The institution of *Varṇāśrama-dharma* (classification of Society into *Varṇas* and Stages in life) was yet to be established. People lived in natural surroundings as the climate was pleasant. Strangely enough, birds, beasts and reptiles were non-existant. Knowledge was valued the most.[4]

The Tretā-Yuga : Though Dharma lost 'one leg' Vedic mantras and Siddhis which were 'lost' at the end of the (last) Kalpa, manifested themselves to sages. The belief in the eternal nature of *mantras* and their disappearance at the end of a Kalpa only to manifest themselves at the beginning of another Kalpa is peculiar to Purāṇas. In Tretā Yuga, there was only one Vedic Saṁhitā.[5]

The beginning of this Yuga was marked with rainfall and luxuriant vegetations. People gave up their previous nomadic

---

1. Bd. P. 38, 39; also VP. I. 3.19-21.
2. *Catvāri Bhārate varṣe yugāni kavayo'bruvan* / Ibid. 23
3. Kane—HD.III.888-890.
4. Bd. P. I.ii.7.45-59.
5. Ibid 74-195 and Ch. 29.52-92.

habits and settled by constructing houses in mountains, along the rivers and also establishing villages, townships etc. They maintained themselves by products from the trees but due to some climatic change, the vegetation was 'swallowed up' by the earth and the earth had to be 'milched' as per god Brahmā's direction (i.e. Agriculture was developed). The Social structure based on fixed prescribed duties (*Varṇāśrama-dharma*) came to be established. The *Saptarṣis* (Seven sages) laid down *Śrauta* and *Smārta dharmas*. The institution of Kingship and of Law and order (*Daṇḍanīti*) became established. Ritualistic sacrifice came in vogue in Tretā.

The Dvāpara-Yuga :[1] With two 'legs' of Dharma lost, this Yuga shows the deterioration and confusion of social, religious and other conditions providing the background for the chaos of Kali Yuga. It is in every Dvāpara that a Vyāsa is born to arrange the floating Vedic hymns into four Saṁhitās. This idea of an incarnation of a Vyāsa is found in other Purāṇas such as VP. III. 3, Bh. P. I.4. 24-25, KP. I. 52, Vā. P. 23.107-213.

The list of the Vyāsa per each Dvāpara is as follows:[2]

1. Svayambhū (Self-born god Brahmā), 2. Prajāpati, 3.Uśanas, 4. Bṛhaspati, 5. Savitṛ, 6. Mṛtyu, 7. Indra, 8.Vasiṣṭha, 9. Sārasvata, 10. Tridhāman, 11. Trivarṣa, 12. Sanadvāja 13. Antarīkṣa, 14. Dharma, 15. Traiyyāruṇi, 16. Dhanañjaya, 17. Kṛtañjaya, 18. Ṛjīṣa, 19. Bharadvāja, 20. Gautama, 21. Uttama, 22. Haryavaṁśa, 23. Vena, 24. Vājaśravasa, 25. Somamukhyāyana, 26. Tṛṇabindu, 27. Tataja, 28. Śakti, 29. Parāśara. 30. Jātukarṇa, 31. Dvaipāyana. 32. Future Vyāsa, Droṇi (Aśvatthāman).

So here we have a bonus of three more Vyāsas in addition to the prescribed twenty-eight.[3]

Kali Yuga :[4] Almost all Purāṇas depict a gloomy picture of the Kali Age e.g. Mbh. Vana. Chs. 188, 190, Śānti 69.80-97,

---

1. Bh. P. Ch. 31.
2. Ibid. Ch. 35.116-126.
3. There are different names in the list of Vyāsas in KP. I. 52 viz. 11. Ṛṣabha, 12 Sutejas 14. Sucakṣus 18. Ṛtañjaya 22. Nārāyaṇa, 24. Vālmīki.
4. Ibid. Ch. 31.33-101.

Bh. P. XII. 1-2, VP. VI. 1, Vāyu 58 and 99. 391-428, Mt. P. 143.32-78. It appears that that was the actual state of the society when Purāṇas were written, though they prophesise it as a future state of society.[1]

In a prophetic tone, our Purāṇa says : The Dharma will be on the last leg. Men and women will be character-less. Kṣattriya and Vaiśya classes will be practically eliminated. Brahmins will be fallen and associate with Śūdras in eating etc. and bow to them. Śūdras will be kings and act as Brāhmaṇas. Kings instead of protecting subjects will act like robbers.

Predominance of Buddhists, Jains, Kāpālikas and atheists is predicted.

The only relieving feature is that a person gets the fruit of his good act immediately in Kali-yuga.[2]

At last god Viṣṇu incarnates and puts an end to the chaotic conditions.

Seventyone such groups of four Yugas constitute a *manvantara*. A Manu presides over the world for this period of seventy-one cycles of four yugas. Each Manu has his separate set of Indra, gods, *saptarṣis* (seven sages) etc. All Manus and their paraphernalia (Indra etc.) have the same powers, function etc. as those of the previous ones. The number of Manus is fourteen. Out of them six have already ruled and retired. The present Manu is Vaivasvata. The names of the Manus are as follows:—

(1) Svāyambhuva, (2) Svārociṣa, (3) Uttama, (4) Tāmasa, (5) Raivata, (6) Cākṣuṣa, (7) Vaivasvata (8) Manu Meru (?) Sāvarṇi, (9) Dakṣa Sāvarṇi (10) Brahma Sāvarṇi, (11) Dharma-Sāvarṇi, (12) Rudra-Sāvarṇi, (13) Raucya (14) Bhautya.

The following example of one Manu Svāyambhuva[3] will illustrate the personnel attending upon a Manu.

---

1. R. C. Hazra points out that such was the actual condition of the Hindu Society after Aśoka and before 200 A.D. (*Puranic Records on Hindu Rites and Customs II* Ch. 1).

2. Bd. P. I. ii. 31. 31-72b.

3. Vide Bd. P. I.ii.36 and III. iv.1.

I Manu—Svāyambhuva:

(1) Gods—Yāmas, (2) Incarnation of Viṣṇu, Yajña, officiated as Indra (3) Seven Sages—Marīci, Atri, Aṅgiras, Pulaha, Kratu, Pulastya, Vasiṣṭha.

II Manu—*Svārociṣa*

(1) Gods—12 Tuṣitas and 12 Pārāvatas (2) Indra—Vipaścit (3) Seven Sages (the descendants of the Saptarṣis of the previous Manvantara)—Ūrja, Stamba, Prāṇa, Ṛṣabha, Datta, Niścala, Arvārivan. (4) Sons—Nine sons such as Caitra, Kimpuruṣa and others.

Fourteen Manvantaras complete the day of god Brahmā. At the end of god Brahmā's day, there is a deluge. After taking rest 'at night' of an equal duration as that of the day, god Brahmā creates the Universe as he did in the previous Kalpa[1] —a fact hammered by the author of the Purāṇa every now and then. As noted above, the *Pralaya* after the completion of a day of Brahmā is called *Naimittika* while that at the end of life of Brahmā is called *Prākṛtika Pralaya.*

(4 & 5) *Vaṁśa and Vaṁśānucarita*

Genealogies of ancient dynasties are the chief data for reconstructing history of ancient India. The disbelief of early scholars in Purāṇic accounts of these dynasties is now much modified by the works of F.E. Pargiter,[2] S. N. Pradhan,[3] H. C. Raychaudhary,[4] A.D. Pusalkar[5] and others. Scholars like M. K. Acharya[6] D. R. Mankad[7] and others have tried to reconstruct the chronology of these ancient events. Pusalkar, in the *Vedic Age* takes 3102 B.C.—the usual date for Deluge or Flood

1. *Vide* for example *Op. cit.* 31:118-119. Cf. Dhātā yathā-pūrvam akalpayat / *Mahānārāyaṇīya* 5.7
2. Ancient Indian Historical Tradition.
3. Chronology of Ancient India.
4. Political History of Ancient India.
5. Vedic Age (Bharatiya Vidya Bhavan, Bombay).
6. Dates of Ancient Indian History.
7. Purāṇic Chronology.

in Mesopotamia—as the definite starting point for the date of Manu Vaivasvata and divides the ancient Indian historical periods as follows :

(1) Manu Vaivasvata period 3102 B.C.
(2) Yayāti Period (C. 3000—2750 B.C.)
(3) Māndhātā Period (C. 2750—2550 B.C.)
(4) Paraśurāma Period (C. 2550—2350 B.C.)
(5) (Dāśarathi) Rāmacandra period (C. 2350-1950 B.C.)
(6) Kṛṣṇa period (C. 1950—1400 B.C.)

Tentatively, I accept this chronological frame work.

Our Purāṇa describes the dynasties of Vaivasvata Manu (I.ii.chs. 36, 38, II.iii. 59, 60). The dynasties of sages like Kāśyapa, Atri, Vasiṣṭha (II.iii.Chs. 5-8), Dynasties of Ikṣvāku, Nimi (*Ibid* Chs. 63, 64), of Amāvasu and Dhanvantari (*Ibid* Chs. 66-67), the Lunar dynasty (*Ibid* Chs. 65, 68-71).

Despite these attempts in fixing period frames and determination of contemporary kings (for example Daśaratha of Ayodhyā and Divodāsa of Vārāṇasī), the chronology of these kings is comparative and a sort of rational guess work !

We are on firmer grounds from the time of Megasthenes. Although Sandrocottus mentioned by Megasthenes is showed to be Candragupta I of the Gupta dynasty and not Candragupta Maurya, according to K. D. Sethna.[1] I, however, still believe that Megasthenes refers to Candragupta Maurya.

Our Purāṇa has given the following dynasties of the Kali age (i) Pauravas (Parīkṣit to Kṣemaka), (ii) Aikṣvākus (Bṛhadbala to Sumitra), (iii) Bārhadrathas (Sahadeva to Ripuñjaya) Bd.P.II.iii 74-107b—122a. (iv) Pradyotas, (v) Śiśunāgas (vi) Nandas 74.139-143. (*ibid.* 74.122b-127a.) (74.127b-135a) (vii) Mauryas (74.144-1449) (viii) Śuṅgas (74.150-156a.) (ix) Kāṇvāyanas (74.156b-160a.) and (x) Āndhras (74.160b-170.)

1. Troyer in A.D. 1858 advocated this identity in his *Rājataraṅgiṇī*. This is confirmed by K.D. Sethna, G. C. Bose and others (*Purāṇa* Jan. & July 1966).

The various periods of these genealogies given in this Purāṇa are roughly correct.[1]

Thus, our Purāṇa supplies important material on the history of ancient india and stands the test of the Pañcalakṣaṇa criterion.

Pañca-Lakṣaṇa and Four Pādas

So the problem arises : What is the relation between the four *Pādas* of the Bd. P. to these *Pañca-lakṣaṇas* ? Our Purāṇa positively states: 'This Purāṇa as recognised by people consists of four *Pādas* viz. (1) *Prakriyā*, (2) *Anuṣaṅga*, (3) *Upodghāta* and (4) *Upa-Saṁhāra*[2], (III.iv.4.43-44). Roughly these four divisions have accommodated the five *Lakṣaṇas* of a Purāṇa as follows:

(1) *Prakriyā*—It means the creation of the Universe and corresponds to *Sarga*. Our Purāṇa describes the Vedic metaphysics of creation in a Purāṇic manner in Chs. 3, 4 and 5 of *Prakriyā pāda* when it deals with the original state of equilibrium of *guṇas*, the laying of the Golden egg and emergence of Hiraṇyagarbha (Lord Brahmā, the creator from it).

(2) *Anuṣaṅga-pāda* : As its name suggests it is a connected continuation of the previous *pāda* and includes the birth and genealogies of Brahmarṣis (Brahmanical Sages), Devarṣis (celestial sages) and Rājarṣis (Royal Sages as in Chs. 8-38.

(3) *Upodghāta Pāda* : This seems to have combined in itself the Manvantara and Vaṁśānukīrtana. A sort of overlaping and mixing up of topics seems to have taken place as the Dynasty of Manu and the topic of Manvantaras is given in Chs. 36-38 of the previous section. The lineages of Sages which should have formed a part of the previous section are given in the III Section Chs. 1-7. The topic of *Śrāddha* and an inflated version of Paraśurāma legend (which are probably accretions of a later date) have occupied Chs. 12-58. The topic of Vaivas-

---

1. For the details of these dynasties see the annotations on that chapter (II.iii.74). And *infra* '*Historical Tradition in Bd. P.*'

2. *Prakriyā prathamaḥ pādaḥ kathāyās tu parigrahaḥ* |
Anuṣaṅga upodghāta upasaṁhāra eva ca ||
evam eva catuḥ-pādam purāṇaṁ loka-sammatam |

vata Manu is repeated in Chs. 59-60. And the real Vaṁśānukrama dealing with the dynasties of Ikṣvāku, Nimi etc. are crammed in Chs. 63-71 (which was probably the older portion in the original Purāṇa) and Ch. 74 which deals with the dynasties in Kali age in a prophetic vein.

(4) *Upasaṁhāra Pāda* : It deals with the dissolution of the Universe and corresponds to the *Pratisarga lakṣaṇa.*

Although I have discussed the Mūla Purāṇa theory in my introduction to the Nārada Purāṇa (pp. 2-9), it is difficult to state which topics formed the parts of the original *catuṣ-pāda* Brahmāṇḍa Purāṇa in the absence of a critical edition.

IV. *Religious Sects in the Bd. P.*

Although the Bd. P. believes in the Para Brahman as the ultimate principle and the trinity of gods—Brahmā, Viṣṇu, Śiva as His manifestation on a lower plane, it testifies to the existence of the following religious sects at that time.

1. *Śaivism*

Rudra or Śiva as Maheśvara is the Supreme deity. Śiva on a lower plane is born of god Brahmā as Nīla-lohita and was given the following eight names : (along with the explanation of their significence) Rudra, Bhava, Śarva, Īśāna, Paśupati (*Paśūnām patiḥ* in the text), Bhīma, Ugra and Mahādeva[1]. From the Brāhmaṇa period where (as in the *Śatapatha* VI. I.3.1-18) Rudra was regarded as born from Prajāpati and was given the same list of names (except *Aśani* for *Bhīma* in Bd. P.). The names Śarva, Bhīma, Ugra indicate the terrific or destructive aspect of Rudra, while the rest, his auspicious nature. He is credited to have created all the Universe including god Brahmā and Viṣṇu.[2] Śiva's four faces create functions of guardians of quarters such as Indra, Kubera and Varuṇa.

Mythological legends

The most outstanding feat ascribed to Rudra in all the Purāṇas (e.g. Bh. P. IV. 5, LP. I. 99 & 100, NP. II.66.5-16,

---

1. Bd. P. I.ii.10.
2. Op. Cit. I. 2.26.9.
Śukra's eulogy of Nīlalohita II.iii.72.163-195.

Śiva II.1.1-36 Vā. P. I.30.122-160) is the destruction of Dakṣa's sacrifice. The legend dates back to the Brāhmaṇa period where (as in Śatapatha and Kauṣītaki) Dakṣa's moral turpitude is given as the cause of destruction. The Mbh. (Śānti 283.26-33) attributes the destruction of Dakṣa's sacrifice to his denial to give Rudra his due sacrificial share. But in the next chapter (284) sage Dadhīci is said to have condemned Dakṣa for not inviting Śiva and cursed that it would not be completed (*ibid* 284.12-21). But in our Purāṇa (I.II.13.45 ff) Dakṣa insults his eldest daughter Satī, the wife of Śiva. Satī immolates herself in Yogic fire. Rudra and Dakṣa mutually curse each other.

Another miracle attributed to Śiva is the drinking of Halāhala poison which emerged while churning the milky ocean. He was requested by god Brahmā to save the world from it. Śiva drank it and became blue-throated as the effect of that deadly poison (I.ii. 24.7-98). The Mbh. (Śānti 342.114-115) attributes it to the strangling of Śiva's throat by Viṣṇu in a fight. Bd.P. takes every opportunity to glorify Śiva. Paraśurāma, an incarnation of Viṣṇu, is advised by his forbear Aurva to perform penance for propitiation of Śiva and secure from him his secret missiles. Paraśurāma performs penance, is tested by Śiva and granted the missiles (II.iii.Chs. 22-24). For avenging his father's death by killing Sahasrārjuna, Paraśurāma approaches Brahmā for guidance and is directed to propitiate Śiva by penance (II.iii. Chs. 31-32). As a contrast, Mbh. Śānti, disposes of this episode in a few verses, even though it is a 'Bhṛguised' version.

The Śiva-liṅga

Modern scholars hold that the symbol (*Liṅga*) of Śiva is his phallus. As in KP (I.26.66-99) the Liṅga of Śiva is the manifestation of a column of fire (the *Skaṁbha* in A.V.) the beginning and end of which were untraceable and hence incomprehensible to gods Brahmā and Viṣṇu (I.2.25.18-28). They jointly prayed that Liṅga in terms attributable to the Supreme-most power who creates, permeates, protects, destroys everything. It is called *para Brahman*, the highest abode (*paramaṁ padam*) etc. (Ibid. VV. 31-54). It is as it were a garland of the epithets of Śiva.

The identification of Rudra and sacrificial fire is found in Vedic literature (e.g. *Tait. Saṁ.* V.iv.3.1). The similarity in Liṅga-worship and fire-worship is significant. Here the phallus-aspect has no place.

As in KP. II. 38-39, Śiva P. IV.12.4-54, our Purāṇa describes the falling of the Phallus of Śiva in Dāruvana (I.ii.27). God Śiva came to bless the sages of Dāruvana and demonstrated to them the Pāśupata way of reducing sins by inviting public censure, technically called '*Dvāra*' which includes outward acts of courting (*śṛṅgāraṇa*), irrelevant speech (*avitad-bhāṣaṇa* etc.)*. The sages were aghast as the behaviour was against *dharma* as they understood it. They requested him to drop his phallus; clothe himself and speak gently. Śiva of his own accord dropped it and disappeared. God Brahmā advised them to prepare its replica and worship him. The words are :

> dṛṣṭaṁ vai yādṛśaṁ tasya liṅgam āsīn mahātmanaḥ /
> Tādṛk-pratikṛtiṁ kṛtvā Śūlapāṇim prapadyata //

'After making the replica of the Liṅga of the great soul in the same form as seen by you, resort to Lord with the trident in his hand.'

Strictly speaking, this is not the direct advocacy of phallus-worship. Nor the Liṅga-replica prepared by them could include *Yoni*. But the hint of phallus-worship is clear, though the two panegyrics of Lord Śiva, one by God Brahmā (VV. 47-55) and the other by the sages of Dāruvana (VV. 63-91) show that our Purāṇa pays the greatest respect to Lord Śiva.

The remaining chapter is a glorification and explanation of the elements of Pāśupatism as follows:

(i) The Pāśupata vow is based on Yoga and was chronologically promulgated at first. The *Varṇāśrama-dharma* is a later creation by god Brahmā (VV. 116-117).

(i) Bath in holy ashes is essential. Holy ashes are the semen of god Śiva and they reduce to ashes all the sins of him who besmears himself with it. It has

*For details vide Bhāsarvajña's *Ratnaṭīkā* on Haradatta's *Gaṇakārikā* pp. 18-19. cf. KP. II.39.15-17.

a protective influence against all evils. A person whose self is purified by applying the ashes and is self controlled is liberated (VV. 106-115).

Skanda—Kārttikeya

The Purāṇa does not explain the Kumāra-Vidyā and the yogic significance of the legend of the Śaivite god Skanda-Kārttikeya. Bd. P. (II.iii.9.22-51) gives the legend as follows:

Indra being afraid of the child that would be born of Śiva and Umā requested Agni (the omnipresent Fire-god) to disturb their sexual intercourse. At the appearance of Agni, Umā naturally got up and the Semen of Rudra was spilt on the ground. Being enraged, Umā, as a punishment for his disturbance at such a juncture, forced Agni to carry the semen as foetus in his belly. Finding it unbearable, he requested the river Gaṅgā to carry it. Gaṅgā also was too much tormented to bear it and discharged it. His birth was welcomed with joy by all divine beings. The wives of six *Saptarṣis* (except Vasiṣṭha's wife Arundhatī) fed him and the god manifested six mouths to suck them and came to be known as *Ṣaṇmukha* (Six-mouthed). He is the defeater of the enemies of gods and hence is called *Skanda*. He was brought up by six Kṛttikās (Pleids) and hence was known as *Kārttikeya*. When he yawned, a javeline (*Śakti*) came out of his mouth. God Viṣṇu gave him two birds, a cock and a pea-cock. It is noteworthy that Kushan seals from the 1st to 3rd cent A.D. represent Kārttikeya holding a javeline and a cock. He was anointed as the commander-in-chief of the army of Devas. A seal of the 5th Cent A.D. from Mathura represents him as seated on a peacock and being installed by god Brahmā and Śiva (?) as the leader of Deva army. Our Purāṇa does not record his marriage with a girl called Devasenā as in Mbh. *Vana* 229. Being a destroyer of the army of enemies of gods he is called *Skanda*. Another remarkable factor is that his army consists of goblins and evil spirits (*Pramathas* and *Vināyakas*) in addition to Devas. This supports the tradition which explains his names Mahāsena and Kumāra associated with diseases like demon-cough (as in *Pāraskara Gṛhya Sūtra*) and his permission to the Mothers to be evil spirits (Mbh. *Vana* 220.22).

Skanda's inability to intervene in the scuffle between

Paraśurāma and Gaṇeśa in which Paraśurāma smashed the tusk of Gaṇeśa and his performance of the role of a reporter of the incident to Pārvatī (Bd.P.II.3.41.32-55 and *ibid* 42.1-10) is not creditable to the commander-in-chief of the Deva army.

A cult worshipping the image of Skanda, was in vogue at the time of Patañjali (1st Cent A.D.) and the names of Skanda were adopted by the rulers of the Gupta dynasty. The name Subrahmaṇya is not applied to Skanda in our Purāṇa (and also in the Mbh.)

Gaṇeśa

Gaṇeśa, the elephant-headed god whose images are found all over Eastern Asia has an honourable place even among the Buddhists as a later development of the Vedic Brahmaṇaspati. Our Purāṇa notes two exploits of this leader of the Gaṇas of god Śiva. The benevolent Gaṇeśa is the son of Umā. When Paraśurāma went to Lord Śiva to report his exploit (the killing of Sahasrārjuna) Śiva and Umā were in their privacy. Gaṇeśa and Skanda were guarding the door of that private apartment. Gaṇeśa prohibited Paraśurāma from immediate entrance. When he was forcing his way in, Gaṇeśa lifted up Paraśurāma, whirled him in all the different worlds and placed him on the ground again. Being over-powered thus by Gaṇeśa, Paraśurāma hurled the axe given to him by Lord Śaṅkara. In order to respect the axe of god Śiva, Gaṇeśa allowed a tusk of his to be cut down (II.iii.42.1-5). Pārvatī became offended at this act of Paraśrāma and remonstrated with lord Śiva for his favouritism to Paraśurāma as against his son Gaṇeśa and wanted to leave Śiva's house with her children. Ultimately Lord Kṛṣṇa and Rādhā consoled her and brought about a *rapproachment* between Pārvatī and Paraśurāma (*ibid.* 2.3.43.28-54).

The second episode (Bd. P. II. 3.67) is not creditable both to Śiva and Gaṇeśa. Śiva's mother-in-law did not approve of his unconventional ways. Umā, Śiva's spouse felt insulted and straightway urged Śiva to seek residence elsewhere. Śiva selected Vārāṇasī, the capital of Divodāsa. Śiva commissioned Gaṇeśa named Nikumbha or Kṣema or Kṣemaka) to get Vārāṇasī vacated for his (Śiva's) residence. Gaṇeśa (i.e. Nikumbha) appeared in a dream to a Brahmin Maṅkaṇa and asked him to instal his image at the outskirt of the city (*nagaryante*). Maṅkaṇa obeyed and Gaṇeśa went on giving munificent gifts according to the wishes of all his worshippers.

At last the fame of the deity as a dispenser of all desires including sons, gold, longevity—in fact everything reached king Sudās. King Sudās who was issueless directed his senior queen Suyaśā to worship Gaṇeśa and pray him to grant her a son. In spite of her repeated services, Nikumbha purposely did not grant her the boon. "The god is benevolent and munificent to my subjects but is ungrateful enough to grant me nothing in spite of our rich worship, meals etc. This is no god but an evil spirit (*Bhūta*). I shall destroy the shrine of this Gaṇapati". (*ibid.* VV. 51-54). In his desperation the king destroyed the shrine of Nikumbha-Gaṇeśa. Nikumbha got a fine excuse and he cursed that the city of Vārāṇasī be totally deserted. When Vārāṇasī became vacant Nikumbha reported the matter to god Śiva who came to live there with his spouse. (*ibid* VV. 55-62)

God Śiva alone knows the moral justification of this act.

Kṣemaka alias Nikumbha was really a Rākṣasa. At the end of the period of the curse, king Mahābāhu killed demon Kṣemaka and rehabilitated the beautiful city of Vārāṇasī. The curse motif for the desertion of Vārāṇasī by Divodāsa is used in the Harivaṁśa, Brahma and Vā P. but it records it as a phase in the conflict between Haihayas and the kings of Vārāṇasī (Pargiter AIHT., p. 263).

Epithets of Gaṇeśa

During reconciliation of Pārvatī, Kṛṣṇa explains the significance of various names of Gaṇeśa:

(1) *Gaṇeśa*—The commander-in-chief of the various powerful tribes (groups) of Pramathas.

(2) *Lambodara* : He contains within his belly all the past, present and future Brahmāṇḍas.

(3) *Gajānana* : When beheaded, the head of an elephant was substituted on his torso in its place.

(4) *Bhālacandra* : When the moon was cursed on the 4th day of a fortnight he held the moon on his forehead.

(5) *Śūrpakarṇaka*—When the fire-god, being cursed by *Saptarṣis* (Seven Sages), was on the point of extinction, he rekindled it by (the flapping of) his ears.

(6) *Vighna-nāśa*—Before the battle with Asuras, gods worshipped him and he warded off all their impediments.

(7) *Ekadanta*—Due to chopping off one tusk by Paraśurāma.

(8) *Vakra-tuṇḍa* : In the future creation his snout will be bent.

Since the Tenth Kalpa, Gaṇeśa got priority of worship before all gods. Kṛṣṇa further gives the boon that all auspicious rites such as *Jātakarma* (consecratory rites after birth), *Garbhādhāna*, in proceeding on a journey to holy places or on trade or business missions or military expedition, Gaṇeśa will be worshipped first and the undertaking will be successful*.

The Paraśurāma episode is revised and enlarged. The above 'boons' show that the cult of Gaṇeśa was well-established and the eminent position given to him in Hindu Pantheon dates prior to the final redaction of this Purāṇa.

Vaiṣṇavism

Our Purāṇa identifies Viṣṇu with the Brahman. As the enlightener and revealer of the Guṇa Rajas he becomes Brahmā, the creator, and of the Tamas, he becomes Kāla, the destroyer, and that of Sattva, he stands separate as a sustainer of the universe (Bd. P. I. i. 4-7). It means that on the Lower Plane Brahmā, Viṣṇu and Rudra are the representatives of the guṇas Rajas, Sattva and Tamas (*Ibid.* I.i.4.6-8). They are the three states of the Brahman (*ibid* VV. 17-19). Viṣṇu is called a thousand-headed Puruṣa who is threefold according to guṇas, fourfold according to *Vyūhas* (manifestations). He is *Ādya* (First), *Aja* (unborn), *Nārāyaṇa* (causing sleep i.e. perfect rest of *Naras*), omniscient, the divine *Om* (*ibid* VV. 20-30).

It is this great god who incarnates for the sake of gods to destroy *Adharma* and to establish *Dharma* (II.iii.72.64., 73.69-70). Another reason attributed to Viṣṇu's descent is the curse of Sage Bhṛgu. When the Asuras took shelter in the hermitage of Bhṛgu,

*Bd. P. II. iii. 42.30-44.

Indra, Viṣṇu and other gods attacked them. Bhṛgu's wife rushed forward and ordered Indra and others to get out, otherwise she would burn them down by her power of Penance. At the instigation of Indra, Viṣṇu killed her. The sage Bhṛgu cursed Viṣṇu to take birth as a human being seven times and in their presence restored his wife back to life (*ibid* 72.VV 116-147).

The original Purāṇa had ten incarnations of Viṣṇu, three divine and seven human. But later accretions added two more to the divine incarnations and one more (that of Pramati) to the human incarnations. The serial Nos. in Roman figures in the table below indicate the original numbering of the Purāṇa.

Incarnation No.	*Period*	*Name of the incarnation*	*Name of his Preceptor and other details*
—	Cākṣuṣa Manvantara	Nārāyaṇa	Son of Dharma
—	Vaivasvata Manvantara	Pṛthu the Son of Vena	God Brahmā himself became the sacrificial priest of Pṛthu's yajña.
—		Varāha (?)	Born within the Ocean when gods were in distress.
II—	—	Narasiṁha	For slaying Hiraṇya-Kaśipu.
III—	—	Vāmana	Begged of Bali, while he was performing a sacrifice, three paces of land. Bali gladly donated it when Vāmana assumed a refulgent Trivikrama form, deprived Bali of his kingdom of the three worlds, bound down Bali and confined Bali and his tribe to Pātāla. And gave the kingdom of three worlds to Indra. (*Bd.P.*II.iii.73.70-86.

He enumerates the following seven incarnations of Viṣṇu among human beings.

Incarnation No.	*Period*	*Name*	*Details*
IV	10th Tretāyuga	Dattātreya	His preceptor's name Mārkaṇḍeya.
V	15th Tretā Yuga	King Māndhātā	His preceptor, Utathya.
VI	19th Tretā Yuga	Paraśurāma Son of Jamadagni	Preceptor Viśvāmitra, Annihilated Kṣattriyas.
VII	24th Tretā Yuga	Rāma, Son of Daśaratha	Preceptor Vasiṣṭha Exploit : Killing of Rāvaṇa.
VIII	28th Dvāpara Yuga	Veda-Vyāsa son of Parāśara	Preceptor Jātukarṇya
IX	28th Dvāpara —end period	Kṛṣṇa (Vāmana) son of Devakī (Aditi) and Vasudeva (Kaśyapa) in Vṛṣṇi family	Preceptor Gārgya and Sāndīpani. Killed Daityas Kaṁsa, Śālva, Jarāsandha, Naraka, cut off Bāṇa's 1000 arms. Annihilated Kurus, established Dharma.
X	Future Incarnation: Kalki or Viṣṇuyaśas	Will be born in the Family of Parāśara, son of Devasena.	Preceptor Yājñavalkya; with his army he will conquer and exterminate Mlecchas.
	In the 25th Kalpa at the end of Kali-Yuga.	Viṣṇu formerly called Pramati in Candramas Gotra.	Exterminating living beings for 25 years. People also will kill each other, usurp properties of others and in the twilight of Kali age the number of people will dwindle down; with the dawn of Kṛta age happy period will prevail (cf. *Mt. P.* 143.61-65).

This list of Viṣṇu's incarnation shows a fluid state when new accretions were made to our Text. That the number of incarnations is ten is the firm belief of the author who enumerates them as 2nd, 5th etc. But some additions were made later as in the case of Pramati, the so-called tenth Incarnation of Viṣṇu. The verses are obviously adapted from Mt. P.143.61-65, even when the 10th incarnation Kalki alias Viṣṇuyaśas is already described.

The standard list of ten incarnations of Viṣṇu now-a-days does not include King Pṛthu, Māndhātā, Dattātreya, Vyāsa.

The cause of non-mention of the Boar-incarnation is perhaps due to its detailed treatment in I.i.5.1-27. There too, Viṣṇu whose abode is waters (Nārāyaṇa) is described as sleeping on the vast expanse of Cosmic Waters and he wished to lift up the submerged earth and assumed the form of Yajña-Varāha. As the notes on that chapter (I.i.5) show, the concept of Yajña Varāha is a continuation of the Vedic tradition presented here in Purāṇic form.

Rāma, the son of Daśaratha, the 7th incarnation of Viṣṇu is cursorily treated in a few verses (II.iii.64. 192-197) recording his killing of Rāvaṇa and good government for 10000 years. Not a word about his defeat of Paraśurāma though Kṛṣṇa is made to predict it formerly (II.iii.36.30-33).

The author of our Purāṇa is an ardent devotee of Kṛṣṇa or rather of the Rādhā cult. Even when Paraśurāma got the secret missiles from god Śiva, he is made to go to Agastya and learn from him Kṛṣṇa's eulogy called *Kṛṣṇa-Premāmṛta* (the nectar in the form of Kṛṣṇa's love).* When Paraśurāma recited the hymn, Kṛṣṇa, the pastoral god with a flute, manifested himself to Paraśurāma** (The IX incarnation of Viṣṇu favouring an audiance to the VI incarnation of the same god !) Paraśurāma glorified Kṛṣṇa in Vedantic terms applied to the Brahman (VV. 15-24). Kṛṣṇa blessed him with success in his mission to kill Sahasrārjuna who is an incarnation of his disc Sudarśana and the slaughter of Kṣattriyas. He disappears promising him

---

*Bd. P. II.iii.36. The hymn is a list of 108 epithets (VV.16-41) of Kṛṣṇa.
**Op. Cit. Ch. 37.

to deprive of his martial power in his incarnation as Dāśarathi Rāma*

Kṛṣṇa and Rādhā are shown to be greater than god Śiva and Pārvatī. When Pārvatī threatened to leave the house due to Śiva's inaction against Paraśurāma, Śiva meditates and invokes Lord Kṛṣṇa who comes with Rādhā. Rādhā is shown to have brought about a *reconciliation* between Pārvatī and Paraśurāma.** Rādhā is not known to the authors of Harivaṁśa and the Bhāgavata Purāṇa. But the pastoral Kṛṣṇa, the Lord of Go-loka (Cow's heaven) and of Gopīs (Cowherdesses) manifests himself with Rādhā and Sudāman. Paraśurāma's eulogy of Rādhā (*Op. Cit.* 43.8-9) especially the epithets used: *Rāseśi* (the chief figure, sovereign of Rāsa dance), *rasikeśvari* (Goddess of the aesthetes) and the mother of *Ativirāṭ* (extremely Superior being), the mother of the great Being in whose pores of body the cosmic eggs shine.

These show that Rādhā has attained the status of the highest deity in public mind. Buddha is not regarded as Viṣṇu's incarnation. The epithet is applied to god Śiva (II.iii.72.177). More important is the declaration of the identity of Śiva and Viṣṇu, Rādhā and Umā by Rādhā herself: "You (Umā) and I are one. There is no difference between us. You (Umā) are Viṣṇu and I am Śiva who has duplicated in forms.

In the heart of Śiva, Viṣṇu has assumed your form and in the heart of Viṣṇu, Śiva has assumed my form". (*Op. cit.* 42. 48-49.)

The Synthesis of Śaiva and Vaiṣṇava cults was the mission of the Purāṇas and Bd. P. is not an exception.

As compared with the passages, Kṛṣṇa's biography in the description of Vṛṣṇi dynasty (II.iii.71.195-265) is practically the same as in the Bh. P., but our Purāṇa notes one good act of Kaṁsa—He did not kill Nanda's daughter who was brought as a substitute for Kṛṣṇa. He magnanimously says to Vasudeva, "Just as she is your daughter, she is mine too. I won't kill her". And the girl grew up in Vṛṣṇi family (II.3.72.219-220).

*Op. Cit. 37.26-33.

***Op. Cit.* 42.18-56.

One more point is the mention of the Vyūha theory. The four manifestations of Saṅkarṣaṇa, Vāsudeva, Pradyumna and Aniruddha.*

---

*Closely connected with the incarnations of Viṣṇu is the struggle between Suras and Asuras. 'Suras' were so called as they accepted Surā (goddess wine) when she emerged while churning the ocean, 'Asuras' preferred to be dry teatotaller and did not accept her. Hence *A-sura*. Suras (gods) committed ungodly acts and Asuras showed super-human magnanimity. The first three common rulers of both Suras and Asuras were Hiraṇyakaśipu, Bali and Prahlāda and they ruled for ten yugas (II.iii.72.88-92). Our Purāṇa indicates that Devas and Asuras were cousin-tribes. "There was great friendship between the Devas and Asuras. For a full period of ten yugas, the universe was uninterrupted. The Devas and Asuras abided by the behest of Asura Indras (II.iii. 72.69). Hiraṇyakaśipu, Bali and Prahlāda were the three Asura Indras (Note the order of succession in Bd. P. (*Op. Cit.* 72.68-92). But due to the mischief, fraud or aggression of Devas, twelve battles were fought between them in the Varāha Kalpa and Viṣṇu's incarnation was involved in some.

Sr. No. of the battle.	*Cause*
I	Narasiṁha and Hiraṇyakaśipu.
II	Vāmana's fraud—Bali was cheated and deprived of his empire and confined to Pātāla.
III	Varāha.
IV	Churning of the nectar, Daityas cheated by Viṣṇu as Mohinī. Prahlāda was defeated by Indra.
V	Tārakāmaya battle—Abduction of Bṛhaspati's wife Tārā by Candra. As Bṛhaspati's cause was espoused by Devas, Asuras supported Candra—Indra killed Virocana.
VI	*Āḍi-baka*. The conflict between Vasiṣṭha and Viśvāmitra (But the sages only fought in the form of birds).
VII	The fight for Tripura—Śiva massacred Asuras.
VIII	Andhakāra—Devas and men jointly defeated Daitya, Asura and Rākṣasa alliance.
IX	Vṛtra—Viṣṇu joined Indra and killed Vṛtra and his allies.
X	Dhvaja—Vipracitti and his younger brother assumed Dhvaja form by Māyā—Indra penetrated a hundred thousand Dhvajas and killed him.
XI	Hālāhala—No apparent cause.
XII	King Raji surrounded by the gods defeated Daityas (II.iii.72.72-88).

Śāktism

Although there is a big section of 40 chapters (IV.iii.5-44) called *Lalitā Māhātmya* appended to the Bd. P., it is apocryphal. The concluding verses of Ch. 4 of the *Upasaṁhāra pāda* (III.iv.4. 41-73) state that all the sages of Naimiṣāraṇya, the performers of the sacrificial sessions, went to heaven, gives the genealogy of the teachers of the Bd. P. who handed down the Text and the *Phala-Śruti* —the merit accruing from listening to the Bd.P.— That clearly shows that the Bd. P. ended here.

The section on *Lalitā Māhātmya* starts with a new *Maṅgalācaraṇa* (benedictory verses) and a new pair of interlocutors, and the contents—manifestation of Goddess Lalitā to kill the Asura Bhaṇḍa, her marriage with Kāmeśvara (Śiva), glorification of the goddess Mahāpadmā and Kāmākṣī etc.—show that it is an independent work.

If *Lalitā-māhātmya* is treated as an integral part of the Bd. P., Śakti-worship with all its Tāntric details must have been prevalent at the time of the inclusion of the Lalitā-Māhātmya in Bd. P. It is not so much of Rādhā but rather Kṛṣṇa cult (with its Tantric aspect as in NP. Chs. 82-83) that is emphasized in Bd.P. (e.g. It is Bhakti in Rādhā's eulogy by Paraśurāma II. iii. 43.8.ff). [See Tantrism also].

The Sun-worship

There are references to the Sun-worship or propitiation of the Sun-god. Thus Yājñavalkya returns—"vomits back"—Yajurveda to his teacher Vaiśampāyana, propitiates the Sun-god who confers on Brahma-rāti (Yājñavalkya) Yajur-mantras, after assuming the form of a horse (I.ii.35. 23-26). Hence white Yajurveda is called *Vājasaneyī Saṁhitā*. The story of Satrājit receiving Syamantaka gem from the Sun-god (II.iii.71.21-33) shows how generous the Sun-god is to his devotees.

As in other Purāṇas, in the *Bhuvana-Kośa* portion—in Bd.P. there is mythical astronomy describing the position, dimensions of the Sun-god, his chariot and paraphernalia of gods, sages, Gandharvas, celestial damsels, serpents, demons, the twelve sun-gods presiding over each month, the different colours he assumes in each season, his function to burn down the Universe at the end of Kalpa. Can we regard this mythical astronomy as a part of the Sun-worship, as we can say about it in the *Bhaviṣya Purāṇa* where Maga Brahmins are found worshipping the Sun ?

An Obscure cult

There is an obscure cult called *Godharma* or the Cult of the Bull.

In II.iii.74.53-58 the Bull of god Śiva explains to sage Dīrghatamas : "We do not distinguish between what should or should not be eaten or drunk or with whom one should go (cohabit). No sin is committed by us". Dīrghatamas followed it and was cured of his blindness and fear of Age and death by Surabhi, the Divine Cow. He came to be known as Gautama as his Tamas (blindness) was removed by a Cow.* This is a crude description of the Vrata poetically described by Kālidāsa in Raghuvaṁśạ. (II.1.25.)

Non-Vedic religions

There are indirect references to Jainism, Buddhism Kāpālikas and Ājīvakas (called Ājīvas). They are all called *nagnas* 'nudes' as they are not covered by the Trinity of Vedas (II.iii.14.34-36, 39-40). In the description of Kali Age, the ochre-coloured (Buddhists), the *nirgranthas* (Jains) and Kāpālikas are bracketed with the "merchants" of the Veda and holy places (I.2.31.65-66).

The Purāṇa strongly opposes animal sacrifices. In the Tretā Yuga sages declared to Indra that the slaughter of animals in a sacrifice was not *dharma*. *Hiṁsā* (Injury to animals) can never be *dharma*. Sacrifices are to be performed with Seeds which are three years old (unproductive)". When king 'Uparicara' (Heaven-moving) Vasu disagreed with this principle of non-injury, he fell down and sank to Pātāla (I.2.30.9-32). This is the Upaniṣadic thought-current and need not be traced to Jainism or Buddhism.

The institution of Bhikṣus is not limited to Jains or Buddhists so the *daśalakṣaṇaka dharma* 'Dharma characterised by Ten

*gavā hṛta-tamāḥ so'tha Gautamaḥ samapadyata / II.iii.74.94

rules of discipline' in I.27.177-179 are meant for Brahmanical forest-hermits.

It is not certain whether the *aniścitatā-vāda* in I.ii.8.64 should be attributed to Sañjaya Belaṭṭhiputra, although it can be taken as a brief unscientific statement of Syādvāda.

The classification of living beings as *Aupapattika, Nāraka* (III.iv.2.192-93) is common to Jainism and Brahmanism.

But much more convincing evidence is regarding the derivation of the name Bhārata from Bharata[1] the son of (Jain Tīrthaṅkara) Ṛṣabha born of Nābhi and Merudevī (I.2.14.59-62).

Vedyardha (I.2.15) is a hypersanskritisation of mount Veyaḍḍha met in Jain Pkt. literature. But very little information is preserved about non-Vedic Section of this Purāṇa.

V. *Dharma-Śāstra—Ancient Lores—Science of Music*

The mention of a Bhaviṣyat Purāṇa and quotations from Purāṇas on matters pertaining to Dharma Śāstra in the *Āpastamba Gṛhya Sūtra* (II.9.24.6; I.6.19.13; II.9.23.3-6) show that materials of Dharma Śāstra came to be incorporated in Purāṇas since the 5th Cent. B.C.[2] In my introductions to KP.p.xliv, NP. pp.52-53, I pointed out how Purāṇas were looked upon as authorities on Dharma Śāstra by mediaeval Nibandha writers. Though the special feature of Dharma Śāstra in Bd. P. may appear to be Śrāddha to which 879 verses (II.iii.Chs. 9-20) have been devoted, there are some more topics like the duties of different Varṇas and Āśramas (I.ii.7.132-185; I.ii.29.89.90 I.ii.31), the denunciation of animal sacrifices (I.ii.30-16-48). One, however, wonders how this attitude to *ahiṁsā* is to be reconciled with the promised fruits for non-vegetarian articles of food to be served at Śrāddha (Bd.P.19.2-11). But Bd.P. is not the only work which prescribes such diet in Śrāddha. Manu III.267-72, Yājñavalkya I.258-60, Mbh. *Anuśāsana* Ch. 88, *Kātyāyana Śrāddha-Sūtra* (Kaṇḍikā 7-8), KP.II.20.40-42, Mt. P.17.31-35 do the same and specify the period Pitṛs are gratified with the flesh of a particular animal.

1. *Tasmāt tu Bhāratam varṣam tasya nāmnā vidur budhāḥ* / I.ii.14.62a.
2. Intro. to NP. pp. 6-8.

The topic of Śrāddha is so comprehensively discussed that it covers the following topics of Dharma-Śāstra viz. Holy places of Pilgrimage (II.iii.Ch.13), *Dāna* (*ibid.*Ch.16), *Tithis* and *Nakṣattras* (ibid. Chs. 17 & 18), though the emphasis is on its suitability to Śrāddha.

As I have discussed these topics in details in my annotations giving cross references to various works on Dharma Śāstra I do not repeat them here. But I may state that all the details of Śrāddha such as relative superiority of people partaking of the feast in Śrāddha (II.iii.9.66-76) among whom Yogins have a special place of honour (19.29, 49-52, II.iii.9.70; metal pots to be used in Śrāddha, offering of *Piṇḍas*, *Agni karaṇa* 'establishment of fire' (*ibid.*ch.11) rites of purification, distinguishing features of appropriate and inappropriate features in the ritual of Śrāddha; eschewing the sight of naked ascetics, atheists etc. (*Op. Cit.* Ch.14) the test of Brahmins attending Śrāddha (*ibid* ch. 15) etc. are found practically the same in Smṛti and Purāṇa works (see notes on the various chapters).

The classification of Pitṛs into seven as in Vā.P.73, Pd.P. Sṛṣṭi 9.2-4 shows a later accretion. The superstition of food-pollution by the sight of non-Vedic ascetics Sāṅkhyas, Śaivas like Kāruṣas etc. (19.43-44) is found in *Gautama Dh.S.* 15.25-28, Manu III.239-42, KP.II.22.34-35 VP.III.16.12-14 to mention a few.

There is some contradiction in the tests of the Brāhmaṇa invited for Śrāddha (ch. 15) where Bd.P. instructs that Brahmins should not be tested (V.7) and also gives qualifications of invitation-worthy Brahmins.

It is not understood why Orissa, Telaṅgana and North Sindh were regarded as unfit for performing Śrāddha (14.31-33). Not that the contradictions mentioned above are limited to Bd.P. (*vide* annotations on the relevant topics). That is a characteristic of literature of growth (like Purāṇas) where, due to lack of critical editing, both old and new portions are allowed to remain despite their non-agreement.

In spite of these, Bd.P. was looked upon as an authority on Dharma Śāstra. For example, *Mitākṣarā* on Yājñavalkya III.309 and *Smṛticandrikā* I.p.118 quote Bd.P. to support the purificatory rite of bathing along with one's dress if one happens to touch Śaiva, Pāśupata or Lokāyata (Materialists). Aparārka quotes 75 verses from Bd.P. (out of them 43 are on Śrāddha.) *Smṛti Candrikā* quotes about 50 verses on Āhnika and Śrāddha.

Ancient Lores in Bd.P.

The author of the Bd.P. is not exact in information about our ancient works: Thus (i) there is a difference in the total number of Mantras in different Vedas as stated in Bd.P. I.ii.35-70-81 and the actual Vedic Texts.

	Name of the Veda	*Total No. as per Bd.P.*	*Total No. in the Svādhyāya Maṇḍala (Satavalekar) edition.*
1.	Ṛgveda	8635	10552 (The same in CVS [*Caraṇa Vyūha Sūtra*]
2.	Sāmaveda	8014 (CVS supports this)	1810 (The only 75 Sāman) in these
3.	Ādhvaryava (Black Yajurveda)	12000	12330
4.	Vājasaneyī (White Yajurveda)	1900 (Kātyāyana supports this) 8880 when Śukriya and Khila Mantras are added).	3988
5.	Atharva Veda	6026	5977

2. In statements about Ṛṣis (Sages), their lineage, the Śākhās (Branches of the Vedas), there are a number of discrepancies between Bd.P. and CVS. (vide annotations on Chapters 32-35). The uncritical nature of the text can be a cause for some, but the number of discrepancies is too large to be explained that way.

3. *Brāhmaṇa Texts*

Out of the ten different characteristics of the Brāhmaṇa Texts, Bd.P. I.ii.34.63-64 explains *Purākṛti*—'a precedent, an instance where another did something of the same kind', and *Purā-kalpa* 'what happened in the past ages, changing the meaning after considering the context.'

4. *Mīmāṁsā*

On Pūrvamīmāṁsā Sūtra II.1.33, Śabara quotes Bd.P. I.ii.33.47-48 as the characteristics or function of Brāhmaṇas*. In Bd.P. I.2.32.31.22 we find mention of Āyurveda, Jyotiṣa, Arthaśāstra, Hetu-Śāstra (Science of Logic.)

Science of Music[1]

There are seven notes (Svaras) viz. *Ṣaḍja* (*Sa*), *Ṛṣabha* (*Ri*), *Gāndhāra* (*Ga*), *Madhyama* (*Ma*), *Pañcama* (*Pa*), *Dhaivata* (*Dha*) and *Niṣāda* (*Ni*). There are three *Grāmas* (basic scales). *Grāma* means the group of seven notes. The Purāṇas mention three *Grāmas viz. Ṣaḍja-grāma*, *Madhyama-grāma* and *Gandhāra-grāma*—The *Sa-scale*, the *Ma-scale* and the *Ga-scale*. These have *Sa*, *Ma* and *Ga* as the starting notes. Thus the *Sa-scale* would have notes : *Sa*, *Ri*, *Dha*, *Ni*. The *Ma*-scale would have the notes *Ma*, *Pa*, *Dha*, *Ni*, *Sa*, *Ri*, *Ga*. The *Ga*-scale which fell into disuse —"went to heaven"—would have *Ga*, *Ma*, *Pa*, *Dha*, *Ni*, *Sa*, *Ri*. The number of Śrutis (the Micro-tones) in the *Saptaka* fixed by Bharata is 22. The *Śruti*-intervals were distributed in the notes as follows :

Sa scale : 4 *Sa*, 3 *Ri*, 2 *Ga*, 4 *Ma*, 4 *Pa*, 3 *Dha*, 2 *Ni*—22

Ma scale : 4 *Ma*, 3 *Pa*, 4 *Dha*, 2*Ni*, 4 *Sa*, 3 *Ri*, 2 *Ga*—22

---

* *Hetur nirvacanaṁ nindā praśaṁśā saṁśayo vidhiḥ* /
Parakriyā Parākalpo Vyavadhāraṇa-Kalpanā
Upamānaṁ daśaite vai vidhayo Brāhmaṇasya tu //

1. The note is based on the translation and annotations of Ch. 61.29-35 and Ch. 62 by Prof. Dr. G. H. Tarlekar. The Sk. text of Bd.P. is extremely corrupt. Prof Tarlekar has devoted his life to the study of ancient Indian music. With the help of Vā.P. and other texts on ancient Indian Music he has tried to emend and translate these verses. I am grateful to Prof. Tarlekar for his help in the matter.

Mūrchanā was the gradual ascent and descent of the seven notes of the basic scale. As the *Mūrchanās* started from each note of the scale, there were seven *Mūrchanās* of each scale. Thus the *mūrchanās* of the three *grāmas* numbered twentyone.

Tāna is like *Mūrchanā* in which one or two specific notes are dropped. When one specific *svara* (note) is dropped it is called *Ṣaḍava Tāna* (one consisting of six notes) and when two specific notes are dropped, it is called *Auḍuva Tāna* (One consisting of five notes). According to Purāṇas, there were twenty *Tānas* of *Madhyama-grāma*, fourteen of *Ṣaḍja-grāma* and fifteen of *Gandhāra grāma*. Thus the number of *Tānas* of three *grāmas* is fortynine—in Pre-Bharata (*Nāṭya Śāstra*) State of Indian Music. The Puranic concept of *Tāna* is different from that of the present day.

The Text enumerates the names of 31 *Tānas* only in their corrupt forms, but they do not throw any light on their nature. But they disclose the names of two ancient authors on Music. Bhīmasena (with reference to the *Tāna Nāgarapriyā*—a form reconstructed from the obscure form *Nāgarātānayapriyāḥ* in the text, and Nārada.

Very obscure names of *mūrchanās* and their presiding deities are given (in 61.43b-53b). Only a critical edition of the text will help to clarify it.

Alaṅkāras in Music[1]

As the whole chapter on Alaṅkāras (Ch.62) is full of corrupt readings and obscurities, readings from Ch. 87 of Vā.P. are taken as the basis and *Saṅgita Ratnākara*, though much later in date than Bd.P. or Vā.P., is used as it preserved some of the Purāṇic traditions (But it was found to be of little use).

Alaṅkāras are to be spoken of along with the *Varṇas* (movements of notes such 'steady', 'ascending' etc.). The *Varṇas* are (1) *Sthāyin* (*Sa, Sa, Sa*), (2) *Ārohin* (*Sa, ri, ga etc.*) (3) *Avarohin* (*Ni, dha, pa*) and (4) *Sañcārin* (*Sa ri sa ri ga etc.*) The author enumerates four *alaṅkāras* such as *Sthāpanī*, *Pramāda*, *Apramāda*, promises to explain them but the explanations are not found in the text. The treatment is very scrappy and obscure. He is however right when he emphasizes the use of the right *Alaṅkāra*

1. Based on II.iii.62.

at the right place (62.24-26). The author gives the local varieties of songs such as Madraka, Aparāntika (62.31-36).

About *Tālas*, Bd.P. gives two even measures (*caturasra*—of four beats and eight *Mātrās*) and *Tryasra*—of four beats and six *Mātrās*).

Lastly, he mentions three *Vṛttis* viz. *Citrā*, *Vṛtti* and *Dakṣiṇā*. The *Vṛttis* are styles of rendering songs with accompaniment. In *Citrā*, the music of stringed instrument was prominent and the song subservient. In *Dakṣiṇā*, the song was prominent and instrumentation subservient and in the *Vṛtti*, both were employed equally (*vide Nāṭya śāstra* (Baroda) Vol. IV, pp. 100-101, *Saṅgita Ratnākara* V.10-16 and VI.165-167).

VI. *Religion and Philosophy in Bd. P.*

Vedānta :

In the *Maṅgalācaraṇa* (benedictory verses at the beginning of the Bd.P.), the author pays obeisance to the omnipresent Self-born Deity called Lord Hari who in his threefold form representing *rajas*, *sattva* and *tamas*, creates, sustains and annihilates the Universe.[1] He possesses three *guṇas* and is yet devoid of them. He is endowed with unparalleled knowledge, detachment, superhuman power and dharma. Resorting to Yoga he created the world of mobile and immobile beings (I.i.1.1-7). Later the creation of the Universe from Prakṛti is called a *Vivarta* (of Brahman) and not *Pariṇāma* of the Sāṅkhya (I.i.3.24). The Brahman has neither beginning nor end. It is unborn, subtle, incomprehensible, beyond both *Sat* and *A-sat* (existence and non-existence) (I.i.3.9-11). It is the source of the world.

In concluding the Purāṇa (III.iv.4.71-73) he pays homage to that Primordial Deity whose description is like that of the Puruṣa in the *Puruṣa-Sūkta* (ṚV.X-90). It is the Puranic way of presenting the Vedānta.

Śāṅkhya :

Kapila, the founder of the Sāṅkhya school is said to be one of the Seven Sons of god Brahmā and a brother of Āsuri and

1. Viṣṇu assumes these forms. I.i.4.6-8.

Pañcaśikha—other ancient teachers of this school and Kapila's followers (III.iv.2.272-274). He is called *Paramarṣi* (I.ii.32.86) as intellectually he comprehends what is still unmanifest, simultaneously with its manifestation. This epithet is preceded by the description of the evolution of the Universe (*ibid* VV. 71-76) which is the same as in I.i.Ch.s 3, 4 & 5. Bd.P. uses Īśvarakṛṣṇa's terms and process of evolution of the Universe in the *Sāṅkhya Kārikā* e.g. the state of equilibrium of Guṇas, the creation of *Mahat*, *Ahaṁkāra* (Cosmic Ego), the elements (*Bhūtas* , Sense-Organs but it posits the presence and power of Viṣṇu for this, while Īśvarakṛṣṇa is an atheist. The Guṇas—Sattva, Rajas and Tamas are personified by Viṣṇu, Brahman and Rudra. This is Theistic Sāṅkhya probably posterior to Īśvarakṛṣṇa (circa 300 A.D.).

Yoga

Yoga as a philosophy is not directly discussed in the Bd. P., but the importance of Yoga is stressed everywhere. Viṣṇu created the world through his power of Yoga (I.i.1.1-7 . In inviting Brāhmaṇas for Śrāddha, a Yogī has a precedence over learned Brāhmaṇas (II.iii.9.70; 15-25). A guest at the time of Śrāddha should be received as 'masters of Yoga move in different forms to guide people in Dharma' (*ibid* V. 9). The path of Yoga through Prāṇāyāma, Pratyāhāra etc. is regarded as 'undoubtedly the means to Mokṣa' (II.iii.13.138-139)

Bhakti

In Bd.P.II.iii.34.37-41, we are told that due to lack of Bhakti, Paraśurāma was unable to master the Kṛṣṇa-Kavaca. There Bhakti is classified as follows:

(i) *Uttamā*— The best one. The devotees in this class are Śiva, Nārada, Śuka, Ambarīṣa, Rantideva, Māruti, Bali, Bibhīṣaṇa, Prahlāda, Uddhava and last but not the least Gopīs of Braj. Many of these Bhaktas are included in *Nārada-Bhakti-Sūtra* 83 but that *Bhakti-Sūtra* rates the Bhakti of Gopīs as the Sinceremost.

(ii) *Madhyamā*: The middle class. Vasiṣṭha and other sages, Manu and the like of him and Paraśurāma.

(iii) *Prākṛta*—Common. Of ordinary people.
or
Kaniṣṭhā (lowest)

Tantra

The anachronism of bringing in Kṛṣṇa (and Rādhā) in Paraśurāma legend shows its interpolatory nature. But it is the Tantric cult in which Kṛṣṇa and Rādhā are used for *Mantra*, *Kavaca* etc. that is important here. God Brahmā advises Paraśurāma to secure them from god Śiva (II.iii.32.37-39).

The whole chapter (ibid 33) is Tantric. The Mantra is the core of Tantra-Śāstra and Kṛṣṇa-Mantra of 10 syllables given to Paraśurāma is :

Gopījanavallabhāya Svāhā

The sage of this Mantra is Sadāśiva; *Paṅkti* is the metre; Kṛṣṇa is the deity. And its utilization is for the achievement of everything (33.3-4).

The Mantra is followed by *Kavaca* (Protective charm with mystical syllables) called *Trailokya-Vijaya* (33.6-27) imploring Lord Kṛṣṇa to protect different parts of the body everywhere, under all circumstances. Accompanied with mystic syllables like *Oṁ Hrīṁ* a number of epithets of Kṛṣṇa express his close association with Rādhā.

Later, a Stotra, called *Kṛṣṇāmṛta Stotra*, a series of 108 epithets of Kṛṣṇa reported to have been recited by Śeṣa, is narrated by Agastya to Paraśurāma (36.16-50). The epithets cover all the episodes in the life of Kṛṣṇa and the importance of this Stotra is described at the end of that Chapter.

Paraśurāma recited the *Stotra* and when Kṛṣṇa manifested himself, he devoutly prayed him with another *Stotra* (37. 15-24).

When Lord Śiva implored Kṛṣṇa to appease the wrath of goddess Umā at hacking down the tusk of Gaṇeśa by Paraśurāma, both Rādhā and Kṛṣṇa appear and bring about a peace, Paraśurāma is shown to praise them in Vedantic terms intermixed with Purāṇic episodes (II.ii.43, VV.8-10). These Stotras may not be Tantric, but they show the influence of Rādhā cult. Cf. NP.I.Chs. 80, 81, 82.

The section on *Lalitā Māhātmya* starts with a new *Maṅgalācaraṇa* (benedictory verses) and a new pair of interlocutors, and the contents—manifestation of Goddess Lalitā to kill the Asura Bhaṇḍa, her marriage with Kāmeśvara (Śiva), glorification of the goddess Mahāpadmā and Kāmākṣī etc.—show that it is an independent work. But if *Lalitā-Māhātmya* is treated as an integral part of the Bd.P., Śakti-worship with all its Tantric details must have been prevalent at the time of inclusion of the Lalitā-Māhātmya in Bd.P.

Other points

A few more points are remarkable :

(i) *Ahiṁsā*—Though animal sacrifices are condemned on the ground of *Ahiṁsā* (non-injury) which is regarded as 'The gate-way to Dharma' (I.ii.30.35) and though non-retaliation is recommended for sages aspiring for Mokṣa (II.iii.32.9.-12) it is not a blind *Ahiṁsā*. For Bd.P. (I.ii.36.188) states "If by killing one, many can lead a happy life, there is no sin, major or minor, in killing him".

(ii) *Non-covetousness* : The tirade against *Tṛṣṇā* (covetousness) in the traditional verses ascribed to King Yayāti (II.iii. 68.96-103) need not be attributed to Buddhism as this revulsion is expressed inMbh. *Vaṅa* 2.36, *Śānti* 174-46 and in other Purāṇas.

(iii) *Free-Will and determination* : Bd.P. (I.ii.8.61-62) raises the point whether one succeeds in one's efforts due to his *Daiva* (destiny), effort or *Svabhāva* and decides that a combination of *Daiva* and human efforts yields fruit. Cf. Mbh. *Śānti* 238.4-5 and Mt.P. 220.8 for similar views.

VII The Paraśurāma Legend

The Legend of Paraśurāma and his exploits in killing 'the thousand-armed' Kārttavīrya Arjuna and 'de-Kṣattrising the earth' twentyone times, is a favourite topic of Purāṇa-writers as can be seen from the Bh.P.IX.15 & 16, Pd. P. VI. 241, Mt.

P. 43, 44 Sk. P. (Revā Khaṇḍa 218). The legend deserves special attention as our Purāṇa has devoted 37 chapters (chs. 21-58) of the *Upodghāta Pāda* and shown his connection with Sagara, King of Ayodhyā and encounter with Rāma, the son of Daśaratha of the same Ayodhyā house (though both Sagara and Rāma (circa 2350 B.C.)[1] were born many generations later) and with the reclamation of land from the Sea from Gokarṇa (in Karnatak) to Cape Comorin, in the South.

The basic incident of the legend took place in the hoary antiquity (circa B.C. 2550)[2] and there is no unanimity in the account of the Purāṇas.[3] The bare facts of the case appear as follows:

(1) Jamadagni's royal reception to King Kārttavīrya.

(2) Raid on Jamadagni's hermitage and manhandling him by officers of Kārttavīrya.

(3) Paraśurāma's killing Kārttavīrya in retaliation.

(4) As a revenge, Kārttavīrya's sons killed Jamadagni.

(5) Twentyone battles in which Paraśurāma defeated Haihaya allies.

Our Purāṇa magnifies Paraśurāma as an epic hero. The story begins after the *Śrāddha-Kalpa* (procedure of performing Śrāddha) as follows :

With the permission of his father, Paraśurāma visits his grandfather Ṛcīka and then his great-grandfather and so on till he visits Bhṛgu the founder of his family. Bhṛgu advises him to propitiate Lord Śiva and obtain from him his missiles (Ch. 21). Accordingly Paraśurāma performs penance on the Himalayas to propitiate Śiva (Ch. 22). Śiva, disguised as a hunter tests Paraśurāma and is satisfied. He imparts the knowledge of secret missiles to Paraśurāma for killing demons, but advişes him to go on pilgrimage and perform penance to attain ability to handle these weapons (Chs. 23 and 24) Paraśurāma kills a tiger in a Himalayan cave and saves a Brahmin boy safe and uninjured

1. Vedic Age, p. 292.
2. Ibid, p. 283.
3 See below : Was Kārttavīrya a villain ?

and hence the boy is named 'Akṛtavraṇa'. He becomes his permanent companion. Both of them return to Jamadagni's hermitage (Rāma's home) (Ch. 25).

Kārttavīrya of Haihaya dynasty visits Jamadagni's hermitage and gets a royal reception and comfortable night-halt to all his men and officers due to the power of Jamadagni's cow (Kāmadhenu). On his departure, the Haihaya king is instigated by his minister Candragupta to confiscate the Kāmadhenu. While Paraśurāma is away, Candragupta returns and in the scuffle that follows Jamadagni is killed. The Kāmadhenu flies away in the sky. Candragupta returns with the calf to the king (Chs. 26-29).

Paraśurāma's return and Reṇukā's lamentation beating her breast twenty-one times. Parasurāma's vow to annihilate Kṣattriyas twentyone times. Bhṛgu visits the hermitage and revives Jamadagni. (From Bhṛgu's visit and resuscitation of Jamadagni to the end of Ch. 39, the Bd. P. adds new material (out of which some is anachronistic, not found in older Purāṇas).

Paraśurāma consults god Brahmā and discusses the strategy to kill Haihaya. Brahmā directs him to god Śiva. Paraśurāma approaches Śiva, propitiates him and gets the secret of the perfect missile (Chs. 31-32).

The protective mantra (*Kavaca*) is called *Trailokya-Vijaya* (conquest of the three worlds) (Ch. 33). The story of the male and female deer illustrating the fruit of the hymn called *Kṛṣṇa-premāmṛta* (Ch. 34), Paraśurāma goes to Agastya's hermitage and listens from him the hymn *Kṛṣṇa-Premāmṛta* (Chs. 35-36). Kṛṣṇa, the future 8th incarnation of Viṣṇu, manifests himself to Paraśurāma (the 6th incarnation of Viṣṇu, and orders him to annihilate Kṣattriyas 21 times and in the 24th Tretā Yuga, Kṛṣṇa will incarnate as Rāma (the 7th incarnation of Viṣṇu) in Raghu family with his 4 *Vyūhas* and deprive Paraśurāma of his divine power. Bhārgava sends a challenge to Kārttavīrya and kills him but he, being an incarnation of the Sudarśana discus of Viṣṇu, reassumes his original form (Chs. 36-40).

After carrying out his vow Paraśurāma goes to Śiva to report his exploits but is prevented by Gaṇeśa to enter, as Śiva and Pārvatī were taking rest. Paraśurāma strikes Gaṇeśa with his axe and cuts his tusk. Pārvatī strongly complains against this to Śiva and wants to leave for her father's house but is conciliated by Rādhā. Rādhā is eulogised by Paraśurāma. (This shows the predominance of Rādhā-cult when this part of the Bd. P. was interpolated despite its anachronic import). Returning to his father's hermitage, Paraśurāma reportes his revenge on Kārttavīrya. Jamadagni advises him to perform penance for twelve years in atonement for his blood-shed. Paraśurāma departs and in his absence sons of Kārttavīrya kill Jamadagni and Reṇukā too dies heart-broken. After completing his penance for Twelve Years Paraśurāma learns how his father was killed. He recalls his divine charioteer and advances against Haihayas, Kārttavīrya's son Vītihotra hides and saves his life. Paraśurāma repeats the slaughter of Kṣattriyas twenty-one times. In Kurukṣetra, he fills five tanks with Kṣattriya blood and performs Śrāddha of his Pitṛs. His manes appear in the sky, command him to desist from blood-shed and perform penance. Paraśurāma (though unmarried and unanointed as a king) performs a Horse-Sacrifice (*Haya-medha* II.iii.47.45-53) and gives to Kaśyapa all the earth except Mahendra Mountain reserved for his residence. Thereafter, he quietly performs penance there (Chs. 41-43).

The Sagara episode (Chs. 44-50) intervenes here as follows:

After Paraśurāma's retirement, Haihayas organise themselves and in alliance with warlike tribes like Śakas, Hūṇas and others they assail Bāhu the king of Ayodhyā, the ally of Bhārgavas. Bāhu flies and dies near Aurva's (Bhārgava's) hermitage* This intervention of Sagara episode is for explaining why Paraśurāma returns to active life and reclaims the land from the Sea.

Paraśurāma is approached by Brāhmaṇas of Gokarṇa as, due to the excavation of the earth by Sagara's sons, the Sea engulfed and drowned the holy place. Paraśurāma accompanies them and requests the Sea-god to recede and vacate the holy place Gokarṇa. Varuṇa, the Sea-god, does not respond. Paraśurāma angrily fixes an arrow to his bow to evaporate the whole ocean. Then only Varuṇa appears and concedes to vacate.

---

*In fact it was a fight for the control of Indo-Gangetic plain between kings of the north, the allies of Bhārgavas and the Haihaya kings.

Paraśurāma takes his ladle and facing the north throws it and it goes and forms the śūrpāraka Tīrtha (Nālā-Sopārā in Thana District of Maharashtra). Thus Paraśurāma reclaims a strip of land six hundred Yojanas in length (Chs. 57-58).[1]

As compared with older Purāṇas, this legend of Paraśurāma brings in many new elements (as recorded above). The sources of these new extra episodes are obscure. But the legend of Paraśurāma as amplified in the Bd. P. becomes the source of newer versions in later Purāṇic works like the *Sahyādri Khaṇḍa, Datta Purāṇa, Kerala-Māhātmya* and the like.

Some works like *Paraśurāma-Kalpasūtra, Jāmadagnya-dhanurveda* are attributed to him.

The Paraśurāma legend raises a few problems of historical importance. We have to grope for the answer, as Paraśurāma probably belongs to the 3rd millenium B.C.[2] We shall try to ascertain the facts which could be deduced from the conflicting Purāṇic evidence:

(1) *Who were the Bhārgavas?*

The name Bhṛgu (GK. Phrugus) leads one to believe that they came from Phrygia in West Asia.[3] This migration must have taken place before the Vedic period. The Vedas credit the Bhṛgus to have brought the fire from the heaven and that they were performers of Soma-Sacrifice.[4] They seem to be a martial people who participated in the famous Dāśarājña war (ṚV. VII.18.6). They explored the technique of the use of fire in war, as a Bhārgava sage Aurva is said to have been dissuaded by his Pitṛs (probably elderly people of his clan) to desist from perfecting his fire-missile.[5] They were advanced in medicine and

1. Vide Pargiter AIHT (Ancient Indian Historical tradition), pp. 197-200.

2. C. 2550—2350 B.C. is regarded as Paraśurāma period in *Vedic Age*, pp. 283-288.

3. A. J. Karandikar states that Romans were a Bhārgava people who migrated to the West after the fall of Troy—vide *Mahābhāratācī Pārśvabhūmi*), Intro. pp. 2-6.

4. Macdonnel—Keith—*Vedic Index*, vide reference to Bhṛgu and other Bhārgavas.

5. Mbh. Ādi. 178.14-22.

surgery and hence the *Sañjīvani Vidyā* (The lore of re-suscitating the dead) is attributed to them. Śukra, a Bhārgava preceptor of Asuras, is credited to have been restoring the 'dead' Asuras to life and gods sent Kaca, the son of their preceptor Bṛhaspati, to learn that lore from him.[1] Our text (Bd.P.) records that Bhṛgu brought back to life Jamadagni (II.iii.30.57-58). Some of them were Atharvan priests. Manu, a Bhārgava was a law-giver. They were experts in arts and crafts as they are mentioned as chariot-builders[2]. The word 'Bhārgava' came to mean a handicraftsman, a potter,[3] archer, architect—And we can't presume that all of them could be Brāhmaṇas.

They were on the coast of Gujarat at the time of Paraśurāma, as his father is associated with Bhṛgukaccha (Broach) from which they migrated to Madhya-deśa due to the pressure of Haihayas[4].

(2) *Was Paraśurāma a Brāhmaṇa* ?

Nobody has raised this point. But in Mbh.Ādi.58.5-6, we are told that when all Kṣattriyas were slaughtered by Paraśurāma, Kṣattriya ladies went to Brāhmaṇas and the children born from them were the Kṣattriyas of the new generation.[5] If this matriarchical system was then the accepted custom, Jamadagni, the son of a Kṣattriya Princess must be regarded as a Kṣattriya. He married Reṇukā, a Kṣattriya Princess of Ayodhyā and Paraśurāma is a full-blooded Kṣattriya and not a Brāhmaṇa at all. The story of Ṛcīka's wife (Jamadagni's Kṣattriya mother) eating up a portion of *Caru* charged with a specific *mantra*

1. *Op. Cit.* 76.12-18.
2. RV.IV.16.20,X-39.141.
3. Mbh. Ādi. 190.47,191.1.
4. Pargiter, AIHT. ch. XVII.
5. tadā niḥkṣattriye loke Bhārgaveṇa kṛte sati /
Brāhmaṇān Kṣattriyā rājan sutārthinyo' bhicakramuḥ"
tebhyaśca lebhire garbhaṁ Kṣattriyās tāḥ Sahasraśaḥ /
tataḥ suṣuvire rājan Kṣattriyān vīravattarān //
—Mbh. Ādi. 58.5-6.

meant for Ṛcīka's mother-in-law, the queen of Kanouj[1], is obviously intended as an apologetic explanation of the martial character of Paraśurāma, though a Brahmin. The fact is that the Patriarchical system was well-established in the days of Mbh. But to justify the refrain in the old ballad on Paraśurāma (which the Mbh—a Bhārgava version—assimilated)

tri-sapta-kṛtvaḥ vasudhāṁ
kṛtvā niḥkṣattriyām Prabhuḥ /

—Mbh. Śānti 49.63.

the Kṣattriya ladies were said to have been constrained to adopt the Niyoga method for the continuation of their families. To credit a man with span of active military leadership for twenty-one generations is historically absurd. And it shows the hollowness of the refrain, if it is taken literally to be true. And a complete genocide of Kṣattriyas is not implied by the Purāṇas as shown below :

The main point is that Paraśurāma was regarded as a Brāhmaṇa by the Mbh. and Purāṇas which took for granted the patriarchical system.

(3) *Was Kārttavīrya Arjuna a Villain* ?

No. He was the greatest King of the Narmadā region. Even the Mbh. which is supposed to have been influenced (revised ?) by Bhārgavas[2] states that he was a pious king, respectful and friendly to Brāhmaṇas, full of compassion to the needy—a thoroughly religious prince"[3]. The NP. Ch. 76 & 77 deify him and his *Mantra* and *Kavaca* are regarded as very effective. Purāṇas tell us that he was blessed with a thousand arms by Dattātreya. He was the sovereign ruler who conquered the earth and donated it as *dakṣiṇā*.

The only fault committed by him was the raid on Jamadagni's hermitage when he and his entourage were given a royal

1. *Op. Cit.* Śānti 49.9-28, also Anuśāsana, Ch. 4.

2. V. S. Sukthankar—"The Bhṛgus and the Bhārata, A Text historic study" ABORI.XVIII.1-76. (1936)

3. *Arjunas tu mahātejā balī nityaṁ śamātmakaḥ* /
Brahmaṇyaśca śaraṇyaśca dātā Śūraśca Bhārata //
—Mbh.-Śānti. 49-44.

reception by Jamadagni. Arjuna was a king of Māhiṣmatī. Jamadagni was a prominent Bhārgava whose hermitage was either in or on the border of Arjuna's kingdom. He knew how powerful was the Bhārgava clan, their matrimonial relations with his rival kings of Ayodhyā, Kanauj (Kānyakubja) etc. Politically it was not desirable to allow such an inimical centre either in or near the borders of his kingdom. For many years Bhārgavas turned inimical since when his tax-collectors harassed them and many fled for life, though they were on friendly terms during his father's reign. No sane ruler should allow such an economically powerful inimical centre near his kingdom even though he be given a rousing reception and treated with sumptuous banquets etc.

But he did not raid the Āśrama. Even the pro-Bhārgava Mbh.—an *Itihāsa* (Record of facts)—does not hold him responsible for taking away the calf of Jamadagni's cow (not the cow as stated in other Purāṇas) *but his sons did it without his knowledge.* This is the oldest pro-Bhārgava account of the cause of Paraśurāma's action. Our Purāṇa attributes consent of the king to his minister Candragupta's plan of carrying away the cow, but Mbh. recognizes Arjuna's ignorance and not even his assent on the matter, though that was the cause of his death. The Mbh. however attributes his death to Āpava Vasiṣṭha's curse which turned the heads of his sons.

Other Purāṇas offer different versions: The Bh. P., a Vaiṣṇava Purāṇa, attributes the order of taking away the cow to king Kārttavīrya (IX.15.26). Pd. P. (VI.241.30-38) tells us that when king Kārttavīrya attempted to seize the cow, she by the dint of her power defeated his army, went out of sight and approached Indra. The frustrated king, mad with rage, killed the sage by the blows of his fist.[1] SK.P. V (Revā Khaṇḍa) Ch. 218

---

continued

tasya putrā. . . .Jamadagni—dhenvas te vatsam āninyuḥ /
ajñātaṁ Kārtavīryeṇa Haihayendreṇa dhimatā //
tannimittamabhūd yuddhaṁ Jāmadagner mahātmanaḥ //
—Mbh. Śānti 49.45-47.

1. *sva-sainyaṁ nihataṁ dṛṣṭvā so'rjunaḥ Krodha-mūrchitaḥ /*
muṣṭinā tāḍayāmāsa Bhārgavaṁ dvijasattamam //
tāḍitas tena bahuśo (. . . . . .) *vikalāṅgaḥ prakalpitaḥ /*
Papāta sahasā bhumau mamāra dvija-sattamaḥ //
—*Pd.P.* VI.241. 37-38.

describes the scuffle between Jamadagni and Kārttavīrya for the cow (Kāmadhenu) in which Jamadagni is killed (26).

The lack of unanimity in the account of the Purāṇas is significant.

VIII *Historical Tradition in Bd.P.*

Although as a Mahā-purāṇa, Bd.P. has treated the dynasties of Vaivasvata Manu, the Solar and Lunar races etc., this Purāṇa like the Mt. (50.57-89, 271-273), Vā.99.250-435 and Bs.P. (Bhaviṣya 3.1.3 & 6) Purāṇas, presents eight successive dynasties of the rulers of Magadha since the Bhārata War.*" It mentions not only the total number of years covered by each dynasty but also the number of years each king (of every dynasty) reigned—details not given for any other kingdom. It is obviously due to the political importance of Magadha as a seat of imperial power while the Purāṇas were in the formative stage. The author of Bd.P. assumes that he writes the Purāṇa in the reign of Senajit of the Bṛhadratha dynasty of Magadha (a contemporary of Adhisīmakṛṣṇa of the Paurava dynasty and Divākara of the Solar dynasty of Ayodhyā and uses future tense to all the kings of all the dynasties who ruled after them. The details of dynasties that ruled over Magadha since the beginning of the Kali Age are as follows:

*I The Bārhadratha Dynasty**
(Bd.P.II.iii.74.107-121)

Jarāsandha→Sahadeva (killed in the Bhārata War)→ Somāpi (58)→Śrutaśravas (67)**→Ayutāya (26)→Nirāmitra*** (100)→Sukṣatra (56) → Bṛhatkarmā (23) → Senajit (The 'Present ruler' for Bd.P.)

---

*Although Bh.P. IX.12.9-16; 22.34-49; XII.1.2-36 VP.IV.21; 22, 23, 24 deal with the same topic. Bd., Vā. and to some extent Mt.P. form a group. Hence I have taken them together. Bs.P. is probably their Chief source.

*The Arabic figures in brackets after the name of the king denote the number of years of the reign of that king.

***As such a long period is not normally possible, some petty or insignificant rulers preceding him are not mentioned and a consolidated period is probably alloted to his reign.

Future rulers : Śrutañjaya (40)→Ripuñjaya (35)→ Śuci (58)→Kṣema (28)→Suvrata (64)→Dharmanetra* (58)→Suśarma (38)→Dṛḍhasena (58)→Sumati (33)→Sunetra (40)→Satyajit (83)→Viśvajit (25)→Ariñjaya (50).

These 22 Bārhadratha kings ruled for 1000 years.

II *Pradyota Dynasty*

(*Op.Cit.* VV.122-127a)

According to Bd.P., Śunaka (Pulaka in Mt.P.) a minister of King Ariñjaya (V.L. Ripuñjaya) killed his master and installed his son Pradyoti on the Magadhan throne. The following is the list of rulers of Pradyota dynasty:

Pradyota (23)→Pālaka (24)→Viśākhayūpa (50)→Ajaka (21)→Nandivardhana (20).

Thus the five kings of Pradyota dynasty ruled over Magadha for 138 years.

This account in the Purāṇa is misleading. Pradyota or Caṇḍa Pradyota, Vāsavadattā's father and Udayana's father-in-law ruled from Ujjayinī as has been attested by Bhāsa in his plays and also in the Mt.P., while describing future kings.[1] This Pradyota was a contemporary of Bimbisāra of Magadha according to Pāli records and there is no reliable evidence to presume a Pradyotad ynasty in Magadha.[2]

III *Śiśunāga Dynasty*

(*Op.Cit.* 127b-135a)

Śiśunāga of Vārāṇasī vanquished the Pradyota rulers and his son shifted his capital to Girivraja. The following were the rulers :

Śiśunāga (40)→Kākavarṇa, shifts his capital to Girivraja (63)→Kṣemadharman (20)→Kṣattraujas (40) →Vidhisāra

---

*Installed as a king when he was only five years old.

1. *Bṛhadratheṣvatīteṣu vītihotreṣvavantiṣu* |
   Pulakaḥ Svaminaṁ hatvā svaputram abhiṣekṣyati ||

   —Mt.P. 271.1

2. *The Vedic Age*, p. 329.

(Bimbisāra) (38)→Ajātaśatru (25)→Darbhaka (Darśaka) (35) →Udāyin, the founder of Kusumapura (modern-Patna) to the south of the Gaṅgā (33)→Nandivardhana (40)→Mahānandi (43).

There is a discrepancy in the total period of this dynasty viz. 360 years (V. 134)—actually it amounts to 377 years.

The Purāṇas (including Bd.P). have distorted history. Vidhisāra i.e. Bimbisāra (Seṇiya in the AMg canon) occupied the throne of Magadha immediately after Ariñjaya and that Śiśunāga came a few generations (*after* and *not before* Bimbisāra[1].

IV *Nanda Dynasty*
(*Op.Cit.* VV.139-143)

Mahāpadma (Nanda), The son of Mahānandi from a Śūdra woman, exterminator of all Kṣattriyas, the sole emperor (*ekarāṭ*, *ekachattra*) ruled 88 years—8 sons one after another ruled for 12 years.

Total period of Nanda dynasty 100 years.

V *Maurya Dynasty*
(*Op.Cit.* VV. 144-149)

A Brahmin Kauṭilya 'will' uproot Nandas and instal Candragupta Maurya as the king.

Candragupta (24)→Bhadra-Sāra (Bindusāra) (25)→ Aśoka (36)→Kulāla (Kuṇāla) (8)→Bandhupālita (8)→Indra-Pālita (10)→Devavarmā (7 →Śatadhanu (8)→Bṛhadratha (7).

The number of regnal years of Bandhupālita and Śatadhanu are given as per emendation in DKAP. 29.Though Bd.P. records 9 Mauryan kings, Mt.P., VP. and Bh.P. state that the total number of these kings as 10.

VI *Śuṅga Dynasty*
(*Op.Cit.* VV.149-156a)

Puṣpa-mitra (Puṣya—0), (60 years)→Agnimitra (8)→ Sujyeṣṭha (7)→Vasumitra (10)→Bhadra (2)→Pulindaka (3) →Ghoṣa (3)→Vajramitra (7)→Bhāgavata (32)→Devabhūmi (10).

1. *The Vedic Age* (BVB), p. 328 and *The Age of Imperial Unity*, pp. 18-22

Other Purāṇas agree that Puṣyamitra, the commander of the army of Bṛhadratha Maurya uprooted him but credit him with a rule of 36 years and not 60. Thus 10 Śuṅga kings are said to have ruled for 112 (*Śatam pūrṇaṁ daśa dve ca*) years in Bd.P. V. 156a but actually the total amounts to 142 years.

VII *Kāṇva Dynasty*
(*Op.Cit.* VV. 156b-159)

As the last Śuṅga king Devamitra was dissolute, his minister Vasudeva overthrew him and killed him. There were five kings in his dynasty as follows : Vasudeva (5)→Bhumimitra (24)→Nārāyaṇa (12)→Suśarman (4).

These Kaṇvāyana kings ruled for 45 years.

VIII *Āndhra Dynasty*
(*Op.Cit.* VV.160-170)

Bd., Vā, Bh. and V. Purāṇas agree that there were 30 kings in this dynasty but actually give only 16, 25, 23 and 24 names. The fullest list of 30 kings is in the Mt. P. Bd. P. gives the rulers in this dynasty as follows :

Sindhuka (Simuka) (23)→Kṛṣṇa, brother of Sindhuka (10)→Śāntakarṇi (56)→Apolava (12)→Paṭumān (24)→Aniṣṭakarmā (25)→Hāla (1) (5 according to the text adopted in DKA.p.41)→Pattallaka (5)→Purīṣabhīru (v.l. 1. Purikaṣeṇa) (21)→Śātakarṇi (1)→Śivasvāti (28)→Gautamīputra (21)→Śātakarṇi (1) →Śivasvāti (28)→Gautamī-putra (21)→Yajñaśrī → Śātakarṇi (29) → Vijaya (6) → Daṇḍaśrīśātakarṇ (3) →Pulomāri (v.l. Pulomāvi) (7).

Bd.P. states that the 30 kings of this dynasty will rule for 456 years (*Samāḥ śatāni catvāri pañcāśat ṣaṭ tathaiva ca*) V. 170. The number of kings enumerated is 16 and the total years of their rule amounts to 262.

The total span of these dynasties of Kali age is given as follows :

1050 years : From the birth of Parīkṣit to the coronation of Mahāpadma Nanda*

836 years : From Mahāpadma Nanda to the end of the Āndhra Dynasty.

The period is re-stated with reference to Saptarṣi era years.

---

*That means the Bhārata War took place in the 15th Cent. B.C.

814 years :	From Pratīpa to Parīkṣit
1050 years :	From Parīkṣit to Mahāpadma Nanda
836 years :	Mahāpadma to the last of Āndhras.
2700 years.	

Thus from Pratīpa to the end of the Āndhras comprised a complete cycle of the Saptarṣis (Great Bear).

Our Purāṇa presents this much historical data from the beginning of the Kali Age to the end of the Āndhra dynasty. Other great dynasties like the Solar race and the Lunar race are not adequately treated.

After the description of the Āndhra dynasty, Bd.P. enumerates some local dynasties with the total number of Kings per dynasty :

No. of Kings in the Dynasty	*Total No. years of the dynastic rule*
7 Āndhras (Prob. Āndhrabhṛtyas)	300 years.
10 Ābhīras	67 years.
7 Gardabhins	72 years.
10 Śakas	380 years.
8 Yavanas	160 years.
14 Tuṣāras	500 years.
13 Guruṇḍas (Mlecchas)	300 years.
11 Maunas	300 years.

After these, Kilakila clan will rule, after whom Vindhyaśakti (300 A.D.) will rule for 96 years(?) Vindhyaśakti, the founder of Vākāṭaka dynasty was a Brāhmaṇa of Viṣṇu-vṛddha *gotra* and 96 years is probably not the reign-period but his life-span*. Vindhya-Śakti's son Pravīra i.e. Mahārāja Pravara-Sena I (death circa A.D. 325) who is credited to have performed not only Vājapeya sacrifices but four Aśvamedhas.**

It shows that on the back-drop of Mleccha rule he championed the cause of Brahmanism.

---

*The Age of Imperial Unity, p. 219.

**Op., cit. p. 220.

The Nāga dynasty of Vidiśā

The Nāga dynasty of Vidiśā is recorded only in Bd.P. and Vā.P. but not in Mt.P.

The following is the line of kings—

Sadācandra Son of Śeṣa Nāga)→Candrāṁśu→Nakhavān →Dhanadharman→Bhūtimān.

Bd.P. does not mention the Gupta dynasty. Bd.P.II.iii.74. 195 which corresponds to Vā.P.99.383 reads *Sapta-vaṁśajāḥ* instead of *Gupta-vaṁśajāḥ** as in Vā P.

IX. *The Date of the Bd. P.*

Like the Mbh. and other Purāṇas, Bd.P. has assimilated a number of modifications, interpolations etc. during the course of its transmission from the days of Kṛṣṇa Dvaipāyana Vyāsa. We can fix the date (s) of the different parts of the text, the general date being that of its last redaction.

Bd.P. states that it was composed during the reign of Bārhadratha king Senajit (II.iii.74.113)—a contemporary of Paurava king Adhisīma Kṛṣṇa and king Divākara of Ayodhyā. Adhisīmakṛṣṇa was the fourth in descent from Parīkṣit. Bd.P. states that a period of 1050 years elapsed from the birth of Parīkṣit (the Bhārata War) to the coronation of Mahānanda (*ibid* V.227). The coronation of Mahāpadma Nanda took place in 382 B.C. This means the Birth of Parīkṣit took place in 1432 B.C.**. Pargiter's assumption of 950 B.C. as the date of the Bhārata war (AIHT, pp. 179-183) is not acceptable in view of the unanimous tradition of the Purāṇas. The *Vedic Age* (p. 273) accepts 1400 B.C. as the date of the Bhārata War. Now Adhisīmakṛṣṇa was the fourth in descent from Parīkṣit***. If 1432 B.C. be the date of the birth of Parīkṣit, a period of 100 or 125

*I however believe (in the absence of MSS. evidence) that it should be regarded as an open question.

**or in 1397 B.C. if the reading in the Purāṇa be taken as 1015 as is done in the Vedic Age, p. 273. S.K. Chatterji. Selected writings, p. 140 (Vikas, Delhi 1978) locates Parīkṣit in the middle of the 10th Cent. B.C. and Ray Choudhari in 900 B.C. *Political History of India from the Accession of Parīkṣit to the extinction of the Gupta Dynasty*, p. 9.

***Parīkṣit →Janamejaya→Śatānīka →Aśvamedhadatta→Adhisīmakṛṣṇa.

years must have elapsed between Parīkṣit and Adhisīmakṛṣṇa. Thus the narration of Bd.P. in the Naimiṣa forest in the reign of Bārhadratha king Senajit took place circa 1300 B.C. according to the Bd.P.

As a Purāṇa is mentioned in the *Atharva Veda* XI.7.24; XV.6.10-11 and in *Āpastamba Dharma Sūtra* I.6.19.13; II.9.23.3-6, we need not doubt the existence of the nucleus of Bd.P. in that early period.

But the present text is definitely later both in language and contents as can be seen from the following :

(1) The Sk. language of the text is much more modern than *Atharvaveda* and *Āpastamba Dharma Sūtra*. As the various etymologies* (noted in annotations) show, people have forgotten the root-sense of the words. It means Sk. has ceased to be a language of common parlance.

(2) The list of "future kings" in Bd.P. II.iii.74 describes the Āndhra dynasty (3rd cent A.D.). The evidence given by Pargiter in DK, p. 53 is sufficient to show that Gupta dynasty is mentioned in Bd.P. II.iii.74.195 though the printed edition records the reading: *Sapta-vaṁśajāḥ* instead of *Gupta-vaṁśajāḥ* in the corresponding verses in Vā.P. 99.383. The following verse is the verse in question.

anu-Gaṅgā Prayāgaṁ ca Sāketam Magadhāṁś tathā |
etān jānapadān sarvān bhokṣyante Gupta- (Sapta-Bd.P.) Vaṁśajāḥ|
Bd.P.II.iii.74.195 and Vā.P.99.383.

The verse describes correctly the region ruled by Guptas. But now the mention of Guptas in Bd.P. is accepted and Pargiter's claim (DKA 53-54) that contemporary dynasties of the early fourth Century A.D. in Vā.P. and Bd.P. is not that controversial.

(3) The mention of Bhīmasena and Nārada on Chs. on Music shows that this portion may be located between 400-600 A.D. The same applies to the mention of Vararuci and Nāṭya sāstra.

(4) Chapters on Paraśurāma legend show the strong influence of Rādhā-Kṛṣṇa cult in its Tāntric aspect (vide *Supra*

*Vide the Appendix to this note.

Tantrism in Bd.P.). Tāntrism was very popular between 8th to 11th Cent. A.D. in East India. And it was during that period that Rādhā cult flourished in that region. NP. 109.19 mentions the legend of Paraśurāma in its table of contents of Bd.P. But we cannot say definitely whether the anachronic Rādhā-Kṛṣṇa element is implied in NP. As NP. itself contains the Tantric worship etc. of Rādhā-Kṛṣṇa (Chs. 80, 81 and 82), Bd.P. might have these chapters even before the NP and the NP. may be presumed to imply the existence of these chapters before it. As most of the contents of Bd.P. (except those on Lalitā Māhātmya) are recorded in NP. 109, Bd.P. definitely belongs to the pre-NP. period (700-1000 A.D.)

(5) The Javanese version of the Bd.P. does not contain the chapter on Vaṁśānucarita section of the Bd.P. Prof. J. Gonda attributes this to the lack of interest of the Indonesian translator in Indian dynasties. But when the Indonesian translator summarises or translates the major portion of the Bd.P., he would not have disregarded the Vaṁśānucarita portion had it existed in his Sk.Ms. It must have been an incomplete copy which reached Indonesia in the early centuries of the Christian era.

In spite of the interpolatory portion, the Bd.P. is one of the oldest Purāṇas as it follows the old *Catuṣpāḍa* structure and its main body belongs to the pre-NP. period (700-1000 A.D.).

Appendix to the date of the Bd. P.

Some etymologies

The author of the Bd.P. takes pleasure in etymologies just to serve his purpose and pleasure. Although most of them are discussed in the annotations, here are a few specimens :

1. *nara* 'a man' <na+√śṛ—I.1.5.135; 1.2.6.56-57
2. *ambhas* 'water'<√bhā 'tos hine'—I.1.5.133
3. Rudra from √*ru*—and √*dru* (i.2.9.78). Normally it is derived from √*rud*—'to cry'
4. Deva √*div*—to play I.2.8.10; also √div—to shine 'a god'
5. *rakṣas* 'a demon' √*rakṣ*—to protect I.2.8.33
6. Gandharva √*dhi*<*dhay* 'to drink' I.ii.8.41

7. Pulaha : 'Keśair lavaiḥ samudbhūtaḥ /
'Born of hair'—II.iii.1.45
8. Vasiṣṭha—'possessor of *Vasu*' (wealth) or
'*Vaśī*' self-controller II.iii.1.46.
9. Medinī 'The earth'—*medas* 'fat'
'overspread with the fat of Madhu and Kaiṭabha'
I.ii.37.2
10. Kubera<*Ku* (bad)+*bera* (body) II.iii.8.44.'ugly' De-
God of wealth form-bodied
11. *Hetu*√*han*<to kill (the argument)
'cause', 'the middle Term in Logic'
√ *hi* — to go (meaning arrived at) I.ii.33.49.
12. Caraka · 'A Class of Brāhmaṇas' < √ *car* — (performed atonement for Guru's Brahmahatyā) I, ii.35.27.

PART I

SECTION I

PŪRVA-BHĀGA-PRAKRIYĀPĀDA

CHAPTER ONE

Contents of the Brahmāṇḍa Purāṇa[1]

[Arrival of Sūta Romaharṣaṇa at the sacrificial session at Kurukṣetra—Requested by sages thereof, to recite the Purāṇa-Sūta recites the *Brahmāṇḍa Purāṇa* beginning with its Contents.]

1. Obeisance, obeisance to the Self-born deity consisting of the quality of *sattva* on (the occasions of) annihilation, creation or sustenance (of the universe). Obeisance to the self-born deity of three-fold forms viz. *Sattva, Rajas* and *Tamas.*

2. Victorious is Lord Hari who sustains the worlds, who is unborn, who is omnipresent and possessed of the (three) qualities yet is (also) devoid of them.

---

1. 'The present Purāṇa is called the Brahmāṇḍa (Bd.P.), as god Brahmā narrated it with special reference to Brahmāṇḍa'. The term Brahmāṇḍa connotes a mixture of ancient Indian concepts about Cosmography, Cosmology and Cosmogony. In the *Nārada Purāṇa* (NP.) 109.1, it is said to be an ancient Purāṇa dealing with the events of the *Ādi-Kalpa.* It contains a number of verses and chapters common to the *Vāyu Purāṇa* (Vā.P.) which led Kirfel to propose a theory of common origin of the Bd.P. and Vā.P. (*Purāṇa Pañca-Lakṣaṇa*). Perhaps the wording of the *Kūrma Purāṇa* (K.P.) I.1.15 might have led him to think so, but it misled M. Ali to believe that 'The geographical section of this Purāṇa (Bd.P.) appears to be a late copy (about 1030 A.D.) of the Vāyu with slight alterations and modifications introduced by the copyist.' (*Geography of the Purāṇas* P.8.) But the statement in the Bd.P. and the N.P. about the oral transmission of the Bd.P. makes it clear that this is an independent work with Vāyu as a narrator of this Purāṇa and it need not be confused with the Vā.P.

The problem however will be discussed in the Introduction. But I must acknowledge that the text of the identical and similar verses in Vā.P. and Bd.P., helped me to emend or correct a number of printing mistakes in the Bd.P. which would have otherwise remained obscure.

3. (I seek refuge in god) Brahmā, the creator of the world, who is omniscient, unvanquished, who is the lord of (everything) past, present and future and who is the real Master of all.

4. Four things are to be resorted to by the good—namely, the unparalleled knowledge and detachment, and super-human power and virtue (found in full form in case) of the lord of the universe.

5. The Lord (knowing) that these human dispositions always consist of the good and the evil, (created) them again, indeed, without hesitation (*aviśaṅkaḥ*) for the sake of performance of (religious) actions.

6. The creator of the world who knows full well the reality about the world and is conversant with Yoga, resorted to Yoga and created all living beings mobile and immobile.

7. I am desirous of knowing the Purāṇic narrative and so I seek refuge in the mighty Lord (the creator of the universe), the witness of the worlds and the supreme all-pervading Ruler.

8. That Prajāpati (Lord of all creatures), Lord (Brahmā) recounted to Vasiṣṭha[1], the entire Purāṇa that is on a par with the Vedas and the main theme of which is the real state of the universe.

9. The holy sage Vasiṣṭha taught to his grandson, Parāś-ara, the son of Śakti, this sacred (Purāṇa) which is the nectar of the knowledge of reality.

10. The holy lord Parāśara, at first, taught sage Jātu-karṇya this divine Purāṇa that is on a par with the Vedas.

---

1. VV.8-17 give the line of transmission of the Bd.P. as follows : God Brahmā—sage Vasiṣṭha—Parāśara—Jātukarṇya — Dvaipāyana (Vyāsa)—Sūta Lo(Ro)maharṣaṇa. An important point to note is the missing link of *Vāyu* here. N.P. 109.35 states :

Vyāso labdhvā tataś'caitat,
Prabhañjana-mukhodgatam

That is according to N.P. *Jātukarṇya*—Vāyu or Prabhañjana—Vyāsa, is the proper *Paramparā* (line of oral transmission.). This lacuna is however indirectly supplied in V.36b below where the Windgod (Mātariśvan) is stated to be a narrator. Another point is the emphatic claim of the Purāṇa to a status equal to the Veda. And the third point is about the main object of the Purāṇa viz. to explain the real state or reality of the world (*Loka-tattva*, VV 1-8, 12 etc.).

11. After learning the Purāṇa, the learned Jātukarṇya[1] transferred the knowledge of the supreme, eternal Brahman to Dvaipāyana[2].

12. Dvaipāyana was delighted thereby. That self-controlled sage passed on the kuowledge of that extremely wonderful Purāṇa the content of which was the knowledge of the real state of the world.

13-14. For the sake of propagating it in the worlds, he taught this Purāṇa which is (highly esteemed) like the Vedas and which contains many topics, to Jaimini, Sumantu, Vaiśampāyana, Pailava who was the fourth among them and Lomaharṣaṇa the fifth.[3] He (Lomaharṣaṇa) was (otherwise called) Sūta. He was humble, righteous and pure. His modes of narration were extremely wonderful.

15-17. After learning the purāṇa, Lomaharṣaṇa became humbler. He became extremely intelligent and virtuous. He was approached and questioned by a sage like you (?) (regarding matters of mythology etc.) He had the most excellent self-control. Along with (the other) sages, he used to bow down to the sages after circumambulating them. He was endowed with great devotion. After acquiring learning, he became satisfied

---

1. Jātukarṇya or Jātūkarṇa was a self-controlled sage—a member of Yudhiṣṭhira's Court (Mbh.Sabhā.4.14). One wonders why the Mbh. and other Purāṇas do not furnish more details about him who taught this Purāṇa to Dvaipāyana Vyāsa. Secondly, Parāśara teaches this Purāṇa to Jātukarṇya and *not* to his own son Vyāsa.

2. Dvaipāyana—The son of Parāśara and Satyavatī, popularly known as Vyāsa (the arranger) due to his classification of the floating traditional Mantras into four Vedas. He was named Dvaipāyana as he was kept in an island in the Yamunā.

nyasto dvīpe sa yad bālas
tasmād Dvaipāyanaḥ smṛtaḥ
—Mbh. Ādi 63.86

In the Pāli canon also, we are told that one of the eight ways of naming a person is his geographical residence.

3. Vyāsa seems to have taught this Purāṇa (presumably others also) to his five disciples but Jaimini, Sumantu, Vaiśampāyana and Pailava (Paila) took interest in the Veda, leaving the preservation of the Purāṇic Lore to Sūta Lo(Ro)maharṣaṇa. According to Vā.P.1.16, he is called Romaharṣaṇa as he made the hair of his audience bristle by his eloquent narration.

and went to Kurukṣetra.[1] He (humbly) approached the pure sages who were performing the elaborate-sacrificial session.

18. The performers of the *Satra* met Romaharṣaṇa (i.e. Lomaharṣaṇa) with great humility. He excelled them in intellect (but) as laid down in the scriptures[2], (he bowed down) duly to them.

19. On seeing Romaharṣaṇa then, all those sages were extremely pleased. They were glad and their minds became happy.

20. They worshipped him with all necessary requisites of hospitality, such as *Arghya* (Materials of worship), *Pādya* (water for washing the feet) etc. He paid respects to all the sages. He received the permission of the king (?).

21. After permitting him, the sages enquired him of his health. He approached all those sages (individually) (considering them to be) the eternal Brahman, the great splendour. When the assembled persons indicated their consent, he sat on a beautiful well-covered seat.

22-23. When he had taken his seat, all the sages of praiseworthy, holy vows, well-disciplined according to (religious) rules, and of calm and concentrated minds, became delighted and surrounded him who was an observer of great (religious) vows. With deep love (and reverence), they spoke to him (as follows) :

24. "Welcome to you, O highly fortunate one. How glad are we, the residents of this place, to see you, the best of sages, of excellent vows, hale and hearty, O intelligent one !

---

1. This Purāṇa is (re-)narrated at Kurukṣetra where sages held a sacrificial session.

2. This Sūta is not a Brahmin. He is the Pratiloma offspring of a Kṣattriya father and a Brahmin mother vide Gaut.Dh.S.4.15, Baudhāyana (1.9.9) and *Smṛtis* of Manu (10-11), Yājñavalkya (1.93). Hence this formality on his part. In V.21, the term of greeting him is *anāmaya* and not *kuśala* used in the case of Brāhmaṇas. According to *Gautama Dharma Sūtra* (Gaut. Dh.S.) VV. 37-38, guests of Brāhmaṇa, Kṣattriya, Vaiśya castes should be respectively greeted with the words *Kuśala, anāmaya* and *ārogya.* Manu also (II.127) prescribes :

Brāhmaṇaṁ kuśalam pṛcchet Kṣattra-bandhum anāmayam

25. Thanks to you the performer of meritorious holy rites. I no longer consider this earth a void, O Sūta, you are the disciple of that noble-souled sage Vyāsa.

26. You are intelligent and you are always worthy of his blessings. You are fully epuipped with the good qualities of a genuine disciple. You are learned and educated. Since you are worthy of being blessed, O holy lord, you have understood the principles.

27. After having attained vast knowledge, you are free from doubts in every respect. O wise one, it always behoves you to recount to us, everything that we ask you.

28. We wish to hear the divine story of the Purāṇa that is on a par with the Śrutis and that is full of righteous topics. This has already been heard by you from Vyāsa."

29. On being requested thus by the sages then, the excessively intelligent Sūta, endowed with humility, offered an excellent reply full of modesty thus :

30. "Whatever intellect I possess is due to the service I rendered to the sage. It is certainly true that my (intellect) should be utilised for serving (others).

31. That being the situation, O excellent Brāhmaṇas (I shall recount) whatever is possible for me. It behoves you to ask questions on any topic which you desire to know."

32. On hearing his sweet utterance, the sages again replied to Sūta whose eyes welled with tears (of joy).

33. "You are particularly well-versed in the details (of this topic). You have seen Vyāsa personally. Hence you explain the origin of the world completely.[1]

34. We wish to know who was born in which family. (We wish to know the details of the family and ancestry of the kings, sages etc). Kindly recount the wonderfully diversified creative activity of Prajāpati during the days of yore".

Thus was the excellent and noble-souled Romaharṣaṇa requested after offering him due hospitable reception.

35-37a. That excellent-most Sūta narrated everything in detail and in due order.

1. This is indicative of the title 'Brahmāṇḍa Purāṇa'.

Sūta said :—

"O excellent Brāhmaṇas, I shall recount in due order that sacred story which Dvaipāyana, who was pleased with me, had narrated to me. O Brāhmaṇas, I shall expound the Purāṇa that had been related by Mātariśvan[1] (the wind-god) on being asked by the noble-souled sages of Naimiṣa forest.[2]

37b-39. A Purāṇa is characterised by five topics[3], Viz. *Sarga*(Primary creation), *Pratisarga* (Dissolution and Recreation), *Vaṁśa* (Lineage of Kings etc.), *Manvantaras* (the regions of Manus or Manu-periods) and *Vaṁśānucarita* (chronological description of kings and sages).

The first *pāda* (section) (of this Purāṇa) is called *Prakriyā-Pāda* (section on rites). In this section there is the summing

1. It means the Wind-god did not teach it to Dvaipāyana. Secondly the present text is a rehash of the Purāṇa narrated at Naimiṣāraṇya.

2. This is modern Nimsar at a distance of 20 miles from Sitapur and 45 miles to the NW. of Lucknow. The word *Naimiṣa* is derived from two different words (1) *Nimiṣa* 'the twinkling of the eye' and (2) *Nemi*—'the felly of a wheel'. According to (1), this place came to be called Naimiṣa as Viṣṇu killed an army of Asuras within the twinkling of an eye at this place (vide Śrīdhara on Bh.P.I.1.4 where he quotes V.R.P. as his authority). According to (2) which is accepted here in *infra* I.1.2.8, god Brahmā, to ensure a sacred place for a sacrifice for sages created mentally a wheel which went on running till it reached the vicinity of the Gomatī river near which its felly broke down and it stopped. The sages who followed it to that place accepted it for their sacrificial session. This popular etymology from *Nemi* is endorsed by Vā.-P.I.2.8, Devī Bh.P.1.2.28-32 where it adds that Kali cannot enter that place.

It was at this place that Rāma performed his horse-sacrifice (V.R. 7.91.15).

Although there was another Naimiṣāraṇya in Kurukṣetra (vide *Chāndogya Upa.* 1.2.13 and *Kāṭhaka Saṁhitā* 10.6) and although the Aryan expansion was from the West to the East, the Naimiṣāraṇya on the Gomatī appears to be the 'birth-place' of Purāṇas.

3. The five characteristics of a Purāṇa as found in V.37b and 38a (which should have formed one continuous verse as is found in other Purāṇas) are mentioned in AP.1.14, BS.P.I.2.4-5 BV.P.IV.133.6, GP.I.215.14, KP.I.1.12, SK.P.VII.2.84 and VP.III.6.25. Amara Siṁha (5th Cent. A.D.) has recorded this verse in his *Amara Kośa* I.6.5. Although these characteristics have been unanimously accepted as essential parts of the Purāṇas, 'The Purāṇa Texts that have come down to us hardly conform to this definition" (*The Hist. and Culture of the Indian People* Vol.III P.292). If the original Purāṇa texts conformed to this description, the present texts of the Purāṇas must have been revised or mutilated during their transmission.

up of the story; the other sections are *Anuṣaṅga* (Consequence), *Upodghāta* (Introduction) and *Upasaṁhāra* (Conclusion). Thus the four sections are briefly mentioned by me.

40. I shall narrate them in detail later on and in the proper order. At the outset, the Purāṇa among the sacred scriptures, was heard by Brahmā.[1]

41. Thereafter, the Vedas came out of his mouths. Similarly, the Vedāṅgas (ancillary subjects), the Dharmaśāstras (Law codes), the sacred rites and holy observances (also came out).

42. Then the decision[2] "I will create (the entire universe) beginning with *Mahat* (the Great Principle) and ending with *Viśeṣa* (the particular creations of worldly objects)" by the unmanifest cause which is eternal and of the nature of *Sat* (Existent) and *Asat* (Non-existent).

43-44. The golden (Cosmic) Egg and the excellent birth of Brahmā. The *Āvaraṇa* (The covering 'sheath') of the Egg (was) the ocean. The (covering) of the waters by the *Tejas* (the fiery element). The (enclosure of the *Tejas*) by the gaseous element. Then the encircling of the gaseous element by the Ether. Its covering by *Bhūtādi* (Ego). The *Bhūtādi* is encircled by *Mahat* (The Great Principle) and the *Mahat* is encircled by *Avyakta* (The unmanifest one).

45. The Egg itself has been described as situated within the (enclosure of the) elements. The appearance of the rivers and the mountains is described here.

46. There is the description of all the Manvantaras and the Kalpas. The narration of the tree of Brahman. The birth of Brahmā is then recounted.

47. After this is the description of the creation of the

1. The Purāṇa-writers claim their priority in creation and hence superiority to the Vedas. That some tract of literature called *Purāṇa* existed at the time of the Atharva Veda is clear from AV.XI.7.24, XV.1.6, but the tall claim of being heard by god Brahmā before he heard any *śāstras* before the creation of the Veda is historically hardly justifiable.

2. VV.42-44 treat briefly the evolution of the universe obviously on the basis of Sāṅkhya system. As the following topics are given as table of contents their special explanations will be given in their respective chapters.

subjects by Brahmā. Here the *Avasthās* (situations) are described, of god Brahmā whose birth is unmanifest.

48. The occurrence of the Kalpas; the stabilisation of the Universe; Hari's lying down in the waters and the uplift of the Earth.

49-50. The particular (description) of the cities etc., the classification of castes and stages of life. The positions of the stars and the planets and their transit from one Zodaical sign to another and the abode of the Siddhas and their distance in yojanas in details and the allocation of places in the heaven to men of auspicious conduct.

51. The narration of (the different species of) trees, medicinal herbs and creepers. The two paths viz. of the Devatās (deities) and of the sages are (then) described.

52. The creation and manifestation of Mango and other trees. The origin of animals and human beings is (then) narrated.

53. The definition as well as its total components of Kalpa are mentioned. Then the nine types of intentional creations by god Brahmā are described.

54. Three of the intentional creations (are mentioned in details). The arrangement of the worlds. The origin of Dharma etc. from the limbs of Brahmā.

55. (The description of) the twelve that are born again and again in the Prajākalpa; *Pratisandhi* (the period of transition) between two Kalpas is mentioned.

56. The origin of Adharma due to god Brahmā's envelopment by Tamas and the creation .of Puruṣa from his (Brahma's) body with preponderance of Sattva guṇa.

57. Similarly, (the birth of Śatarūpā) and the birth of the two sons, viz. Priyavrata, Uttānapāda as well as that of the auspicious Prasūti and Ākṛti (Ākūti).

58. Those who had rid themselves of sins and are well established themselves in the three worlds are glorified. Afterwards the birth of twins in Ākūti from Ruci, the Prajāpati.

59-60. The auspicious births of Dakṣa's daughters from Prasūti. Then the procreation by the great-souled Dharma from Dakṣa's daughters like Śabdā (rather Śraddhā as in

Vāyu P.), a race characterised by Sattva-guṇa and was (as if) the dawn (?) of happiness : As well as the race of Adharma (Evil) from Hiṁsā (Violence) characterised by Tamo-guṇa and inauspiciousness.

61. The description of the creation of subjects by Bhṛgu and other sages, where-in the lineage of the Brāhmaṇa sage Vasiṣṭha is recounted.

62. The birth of the progeny of Agni from Svāhā is recounted there. Thereafter, the birth of subjects of the two types of Pitṛs in Svadhā (is also mentioned).

63-64. In the context of the description of the line of the Pitṛs, the curse of Dakṣa by Maheśvara, Satī and Bhṛgu and other intelligent ones, (is mentioned). So also the return curse uttered by Dakṣa. The protest against the enmity by Rudra of wonderful feats, because defects were seen is described.

65. In the context of Manvantaras, Time (with its units) is recounted in detail. The auspicious characteristics of the daugher of Kardama, the Prajāpati.

66. The details of the sons of Priyavrata are described there. Their appointment on different continents and lands severally (are recounted).

67. The narration of the creation of Svāyambhuva (Manu). So also the description of the Varṣas (sub-continents) and rivers and their different types.

68. How thousands of the different continents comprise the group of seven Dvīpas. The detailed description of the Maṇḍala (Encircling zone) of Jambūdvīpa and the ocean.

69. The magnitude and extent of the Jambūdvīpa, the ocean and the mountains, is mentioned in the form of Yojanas ('Yojana = 12 Kms). The following seven mountains,[1] viz.

---

1. The mountain system of the Purāṇas as recorded here is represented under the following names today:

(i) Himavān—The great Himalayan Range.

(ii) Hemakūṭa—Ladakh—Kailash—Trans-Himalayan chain.

(iii) Niṣadha—Hindukush—Kunlun chain.

(iv) Meru—The Pamirs.

(v) Nīla.

Himavān, Hemakūṭa, Niṣadha, Meru, Nīla, Śveta and Śṛṅgin, are glorified.

70-73. The distance between pairs of these, the girth, height and extent of these mountains, all these are mentioned is so many Yojanas. The inhabitants of these mountains are recounted. Bhārata and other sub-continents are described, alongwith the rivers and mountains therein. How they are inhabited by the mobile and the immobile living beings. Jambūdvīpa and other islands (continents) are surrounded by seven oceans. Thereafter the golden earth and Lokāloka (mountain) is described. These worlds have definite extents and magnitudes, consist of seven continents.

74. Rūpa (form, colour) etc. are described because they are also made alongwith the Prākṛtas (effects of the Prakṛti). All these are partial transformation of the Pradhāna.

75. The movement, extent etc. of the sun, the moon and the earth are succinctly yet completely stated (without leaving out anything of importance).

76-77. The dimentions are mentioned. The extent of these is mentioned in so many Yojanas. Mahendra and other splendid and sacred (mountains) on the summit north of the Mānasa lake (are described) along with the present beings that are in possession of them and that identify themselves with them.

The sun's movement above these, like a firebrand moving in a circle, has been mentioned. The characteristics of Nāgavīthi and Akṣavīthi are mentioned.

78. The description of the two kāṣṭhās (*koṣṭha*—a misprint) quarters (or courses of winds), the two Lekhas, horizons (or Lekhas—deities) and the zones in Yojanas; of the Lokāloka (mountain) of the twilight, of the day and of the Viṣuvat (Equinox).

(vi) Śveta—Nura Tau—Turkistan-Atbashi chain

(vii) Śṛṅgin or Śṛṅgavān—Kara Tau—Kirghiz-Ketman chain. (For details vide M.Ali—*Geog. of the Purāṇas* Ch.III)

The progressive contraction of Bhārata up to 1947 A.D. blinds us to the fact that a large part of what is Central Asia today was an integral part of the Bhārata of the Puranic world.

79. The Lokapālas (guardians of the quarters) who stay on it in the four quarters are described. The southern and the northern path-ways of the Pitṛs (manes) and gods (are described).

80. (The goal) of householders and those who renounce (i.e. *sannyāsins*) dependent on *Rajas* and *Sattva* (is mentioned). The region of Viṣṇu where Dharma and others are stationed is mentioned.

81. The movement of the sun and the moon as well as that of the planets and luminaries is described. It has the efficacy of according auspiciousness as well as inauspiciousness to the subjects.

82-83. The chariot of the sun built by Brahmā himself for the sake of a dwelling unto the sun is mentioned. The chariot whereby the lord goes to his abode from the heaven is presided over by the Devas, the Ādityas, the sages, the Gandharvas, the Apsaras, the Grāmaṇīs, the serpents and the Rākṣasas.

84. The *Rasa* (juice) that exudes from the chariot evolved out of the essence of the waters, is mentioned : The waxing and the waning of the moon caused by Soma are mentioned.

85. The movement of the chariots of the sun and others begins from Dhruva (the pole star). The heavenly porpoise at the tail end of which the pole star is stationed is also described.

86. All the constellations of stars along with the planets wherein the gods of meritorious acts have their abodes are described.

87. The thousand rays of the sun, the asylum of rain, chillness and heat, the different classes of rays with reference to names, functions and places of operation—(all these are mentioned).

88. The magnitude and the movement of the planets depending on the sun are mentioned. The origin of the *Mahat* (Great Principle) from the *Pradhāna*, the characteristics of which are compared to a dancing girl.

89. The narration of the greatness of Pururavas, the son of Ilā. The greatness of the *Pitṛs* of two types as well as that of the dead.

90-91. Then the *Parvans* (important days in the transit of the moon such as first quarter, full moon, last quarter, New moon) as well as the *Sandhis* (junctions), of the *Parvans* are narrated. The great blessing of the two types of *Pitṛs* by means of *Śrāddha*; the *Pitṛs* who have gone to the heaven and those who have had a downfall. Their number and extent of Yugas as well as the Yuga called Kṛta are described.

92. The introduction and commencement of agricultural activities etc. as means of livelihood in the Tretāyuga as a result of the lowering of standards; the establishment of castes and stages of life based on Dharma (duty).

93. Establishment of the institution of Yajña*. The conversation of Vasu and the sages; the downfall of Vasu—all these are recounted**.

94. The penance is praised and so also the situations of the Yugas entirely. The succinct description of the Dvāpara and Kali ages.

95. Manvantara is recounted and its number (of years) is narrated according to human calculation. This alone is the characteristic feature of all Manvantaras.

96. The past, present and future Manvantaras are recounted. So also is the definition of *Pratisandhāna* (Period of transition between two Manvantaras).

97. The past and the future (reigning members) in the Svāyambhuva (Manvantara) are recounted. The movement of the sages is mentioned. So also the way of the knowledge of Kāla (Time).

98. The extent of the number of Durgas (fortresses) and the commencement and the different professions for livelihood in the Yugas ; the birth and characteristic features of the emperors in the Tretā.

---

* This verse=Vā.P. (Vāyu Purāṇa) 1.111, but it reads *Yajña-Pravartana*. This is the proper reading and hence accepted, as *Vajra-Pravartana* is baseless and hence probably a misprint.

** The text translated above: *Śabdatvaṁ ca Pradhānāt tu Svāyambhuvam ṛte Manum* is confusing. This verse=Vā.P. 1.112 which however gives a better reading:

Praśnānāṁ durvacastvaṁ ca svāyambhuvam ṛte Manum |

99. The birth of Pramati; the diminution by Aṅgulas of the living beings in the Kaliyuga—these are mentioned.

100. The enumeration of the different Śākhās (Branches) of the Vedas; the importance of the disciples ; the seven types of *Vākyas* (sentences) and narration of the spiritual lines of the sages.

101. The characteristic features of the sons of charioteers and those of the Brāhmaṇas (are described) in full. The classification of the Vedas by the noble-souled Vedavyāsa (is also given).

102. The narration of the Devas and the lords of subjects in the Manvantaras ; the due order of the Manvantaras and the knowledge of Kāla (Time): all these are recounted.

103-104. The grandsons of Dakṣa ; the splendid progeny of his beloved daughter; the children procreated by Brahmā and others and the children begot by the intelligent Dakṣa; the Sāvarṇa Manus who had resorted to Meru are also recounted here. The description of the creation of subjects by Dhruva, the son of Uttānapāda.

105. The creative activity of Cākṣuṣa Manu, the description of the prowess of the subjects; the act of milking the earth by the lord (King Pṛthu), the son of Vena.

106. The special mention of the vessels, milks and calves; (the fact) that this earth had already been milked by Brahmā and others.

107. The birth of Dakṣa the intelligent Prajāpati from the ten Pracetasas in Māriṣā as occurring through equal part of everyone of them is described.

108. The lordship over the past, present and future things of Mahendras is recounted. The Manus and others who are covered with Manu narratives will be described.

109. The detailed creative activity of Vaivasvata Manu is recounted. The origin of Bhṛgu and others in the Vestures* of Brahmā and others is narrated.

110. As distinguished from the splendid Prajāsarga (creation of the subjects) of Cākṣuṣa Manu, the creation through

* Vā.P.1.128 reads *Brahma-Śukrāt* 'from the semen of god Brahmā'.

meditation by Dakṣa in the Vaivasvata Manvantara is recounted.

111. Nārada, the mental son of Brahmā, engaged the extremely powerful sons of Dakṣa in conversation and destroyed them and was cursed (as a result).

112. Thereupon Dakṣa begot the well-known daughters named Vairiṇās.* The birth of Marut in the noble lady Diti in the course of the continuous blowing of the wind.**

113. The seven times seven (49) groups of Maruts are recounted here. They acquired *Devatva* (state of being Devas) because of their staying along with Indra. Their residence is the shoulders (?) of Vāyu (?).

114-115. The origin of the Daityas, Dānavas, Yakṣas, Gandharvas, Rākṣasas, ghosts and evil spirits, of the Yakṣas, birds, creepers etc. is recounted. The origin of the Apsaras is narrated in great details. The entire sphere of the sun is described and also the birth of the elephant Airāvata.

116. The birth of Vainateya (Garuḍa) as well as his installation as a K ng (of birds). The detailed narratives of the (races of) Bhṛgus and the Aṅgiras are recounted.

117. The detailed description of the progeny of Kāśyapa, Pulastya, noble-souled Atri and sage Parāśara.

118. Three girls in whom the worlds are stabilised are glorified. The detailed description of Icchā*** of Āditya (is found) thereafter.

119. The story of Kinkuvit† is mentioned. The annihilation of Bṛhadbalas by Dhruva‡ is mentioned. Ikṣvāku and others are glorified briefly.

120. The creation of the king Niśi etc. is mentioned in detail along with Palāṇḍuharaṇa etc; the story of the king Yayāti's race:

---

* begot from Vīriṇi—Vā.P.1.131.

** Vā.P. 1.133, reads: *Marut-Prasāda*.

***To be amended as *Ilā* as in Vā.P.1.141 as there is no person called Icchā in this context in the Purāṇas.

† (Viṅkukṣi in Vā.P.)

‡ Vā.P.I.141b-142a reads: 'The destruction of Dhundhu, Ikṣvāku and others ending with Bṛhadbala are described ? Dhruva is not credited with destroying Bṛhadbalas, vide PE. (*Puranic encyclopaedia* on Dhruva & Bṛhadbala.)

121. The description of Yadu's race and the detailed narration of Haihaya after Krodha.* Afterwards the details of the race are mentioned.

122. The greatness of Jyāmagha and his creation of subjects is recounted. So also of Devavṛdha, Andhaka and noble-souled Dhṛṣṭi.

123-124. The lineage of Animitra; the false accusation of the two Vaiśyas;** The ascertainment and the acquisition of the jewel by the intelligent Satrājit; in the course of the creation of progeny by the saintly King Devamīḍhvan, the birth and story of the noble-souled Śūra is mentioned.

125. The wickedness of Kaṁsa and the birth of Vāsudeva Viṣṇu of unmeasured splendour in Devakī, due to the unification of the families (?)***

126-127. Afterwards the creative activity of the sages; the description of the creation of the subjects; when the war of the Devas and the Asuras started; a woman was slain by Viṣṇu while protecting Śakra from death and a curse was obtained by him from Bhṛgu. Bhṛgu resuscitated the divine mother of Śukra.

128. Due to the concurrence of the Devas and the sages twelve battles were conducted.[1] Narasiṃha and others, the destroyers of sins are glorified.

129. The propitiation of Sthāṇu (Śiva) by Śukra by means of severe penance. Śarva eulogised by him who was cut off (*kṛtta*) for boons.[2]

130-131. Afterwards the material activity of the Devas and the Asuras is recounted. When the noble-souled Śukra was attached to Jayantī, the intelligent Bṛhaspati, assuming the form of Śukra deluded Asuras for which act Śukra cursed Bṛhaspati.†

* This should be Kroṣṭu and *not* Krodha vide Vā.P.I.144.

** Vā P. 1.146. (in identical verse) reads: *Viṣṇor divyābhiśaṁsanam*, 'The divine eulogy of god Viṣṇu'.

*** Vā.P.1.148 reads: 'ekāntena'.

1. Vā.P.1.151 (identical with this verse) reads: Twelve wonderful battles between gods and demons.

2. Vā.P.1.152 reads: *Varadānaugha-lubdhena* 'extremely desirous of getting boons).

† The corrupt text has resulted in this confused version. It should be as Vā.P.1.153-154 reads:

132-34. The greatness of Viṣṇu is narrated. It is expressed at the birth (i.e. incarnation) of lord Viṣṇu. Turvasu who was the younger brother of Yadu was the grandson (of Śukra). Anu, Druhyu and others as well as their sons (who were) the kings are described. The descendants of Anu were noble-souled. Excellent kings among them are fully described. They had plenty of wealth and their splendour was much. *Ātithya* (hospitality) to a Brahmanical sage is classified into seven as resorting to Dharma.

135. There the curse of Bṛhaspati by the poets[1](?) is described. The fame of Hara's (Hari's) family is slightly touched. Śantanu's prowess is explained.

136. In the concluding portion, the future kings are recounted. The description of the groups of lords, yet to come, is given in detail.

137. The description of the annihilation of all, when Kaliyuga expires at the end of the Bhautya manvantara (?). The annihilation is divided into *Naimittika* (at the end of a Kalpa) *Prākṛtika* (after two *parārdha* years when Brahmā dies and *Ātyantika* (when the individual soul merges in the Brahman.)

138. The re-absorption and dissolution of all living beings in various ways is described. *Anāvṛṣṭi* (absence of rain) and the terrible Saṁvartaka fire of the sun (are mentioned).

139. (The description of *Prākṛtika Pralaya* is described in the Sāṃkhya system of philosophy. Then Brahman (is ex-

---

Jayantyā saha sakte tu yatra Śukre mahātmani |
Asurān mohayāmāsa Śukrarūpeṇa buddhimān ||
Bṛhaspatis tu taṁ Śukraḥ śaśāpa sumahādyutiḥ ||

'When the noble-souled Śukra was attached to Jayantī, the clever Bṛhaspati, assuming the form of Śukra, deluded Asuras for which act Śukra cursed Bṛhaspati'

The story of the love-affair between Śukra and Jayantī and her subsequent marriage with him are mentioned in other Purāṇas vide PE p. 355, PCK p. 365.

1. The corresponding verse in Vā. P.1.158 is as follows:
Bārhaspatyaṁ tu surabhir yatra śāpam ihānudat |
Kīrtanaṁ Jahnu-vaṁśasya Śantanor vīrya-sabdanam ||

plained) particularly. The description of the seven worlds beginning with Bhū.

140. The definition is explained by means of Para, Parārdha and Apara (?) of the Brahman. The fixation of the extent and magnitude of Brahmā(?) in so many Yojanas.

141. Here the hells of the sinners such as Raurava etc. are mentioned. The ultimate sequel of all living beings is decisively fixed.

142. The description of the worldly existence through the *Pratisaṁsarga* (secondary creation) of Brahmā. The movement upwards or downwards as dependent on virtue or evil has been mentioned.

143. The annihilation of great Bhūtas (elements) in every Kalpa. The miseries are innumerable. Even god Brahmā is not eternal.

144. The wickedness of worldly pleasures, the pain in the course of worldly existence.[1] The inaccessibility of salvation (except) through *Vairāgya* (absence of passion) because defects are seen.

145. (One) abandons the Sattva (living beings) whether manifest or unmanifest and is established in the Brahman. Since multiplicity is seen, the idea of purity (of the world) recedes.

146. Then (the devotee) becomes afraid of the three types of *Tāpa* (distresses) arising from *Rūpa* and *Artha* (forms and objects).[2] He then becomes *Nirañjana* (unsullied). After obtaining the bliss of Brahman, he is not afraid of anything.

147. Again the creation by another Brahmā as before, is recounted. The *Vikriyās* (changes) of the universe such as creation and annihilation are described.

It was Surabhi (the heavenly cow) which uttered the curse; the family of king Jahnu is glorified.

1. *Saṁhāra* emended as *Saṁsāra*, otherwise it would mean 'Pain of annihilation'.

2. The corresponding verse in Vā.P. 1.171 gives a better reading: *tatas tāpatrayātīto nirūpākhyo nirañjanaḥ* / 'Then he transcends three types of miseries and he is called formless and free from blemishes (pure)'.

148. The activities of the living beings that are born and the fruits (they obtain) are described. Then the creation of the groups of sages is described. It is destructive of sins.

149-150. The appearance of Vasiṣṭha and the birth of Śakti. His grasping of the bone of Śaudāsa[1] as brought about by Viśvāmitra. The birth of the eminent Parāśara from Adṛśyantī. The holy lord, the great sage was born of Pitṛkanyā and the holy sage (Parāśara).

151. The birth of Śuka. The hatred towards sage Viśvāmitra of the intelligent Parāśara along with his son.

152-154. The collection of Agni (fire) by Vasiṣṭha with a desire to kill Viśvāmitra. The (hindrance to it) by lord vidhi (Brahmā) who was the well-wisher of Viśvāmitra as well as by the intelligent lord Gīrṇaskandha[2] (?) for the sake of a child.

With the blessings of Śarva (Śiva), the saintly lord Vyāsa split one Veda of four quarters into four Vedas. Many branches of the Vedas were evolved by his disciples and their disciples.

155-159a. (Defective text) They did not tremble in making practical use of the Vedas. When they were seen by Svayambhu (Brahmā) those excellent sages desirous of Dharma and wishing to get a holy place, asked him. The lord who wished for their welfare told them like this : "The nave of this wheel is excellent. Its beauty and splendour is divine. It has seven spokes. It is incomparable and praise-worthy. As it rolls down, all of you follow it alertly, watchfully. Then you will reach a place where this is broken. That place where the rim of this wheel is broken is a holy land. It should be considered sacred."[3]

---

1. *Saudāsāsthi-grahaścāsya* in this text is contrary to facts. It was Saudāsa (King Kalmāṣapāda as a demon) who devoured Śakti (Vasiṣṭha's eldest son) at the instigation of Viśvāmitra. Hence the better reading is in Vā.P. in the corresponding verse 1-175a viz. *Saudāsān nigrahas tasya Viśvāmitrakṛtena ca* /

2. Vā.P. 1.178a reads: *Cīrṇā Skandena dhīmatā* 'It (The Veda ?) was divided by the intelligent Lord Skanda for the sake of its continuity'.

3. A popular etymology of *Naimiṣāraṇya vide* note 2 p. 8.

After saying this to all those sages, he became invisible.

159b-160. The sages of Naimiṣa forest performed a Satra there taking only *Yava* (barley) as their food along with the water of Gaṅgā.

161. When Śaradvān died, he was resuscitated, as the sages of Naimiṣa forest were endowed with great kindness.

162. They made this earth boundless. They brought Kṛṣṇa as king. With great pleasure, and hospitality, the king was received and honoured duly.

163. Svarbhānu, the cruel Asura, came within the Satra and abducted the king. When the king vanished, the sages followed him.

164. They saw him protected by a Gandharva and abiding in the village named Kalāpa.[1] Again the Yajña was begun by the great sages.

165. On seeing everything golden, he had an argument with them in the Satra that lasted for twelve years and performed by the sages of Naimiṣa.

166-167. Yadu was installed by them even as they were arguing. After the son of Yadu, Ayuta was born in the forest. They concluded the Satra and began to worship Vāyu.

This is the *Kṛtyasamuddeśa* (enumeration of contents of the Purāṇa). The part of the Purāṇa has been described.

168. The Purāṇa comes to light in this order alone. Even a great topic is understood easily if mentioned briefly.

169-170a. After mentioning the brief outline, I shall now narrate the details to you. If a person, after conquering the sense organs, learns this first *Pāda* (section) very well, there is no doubt about it that the entire Purāṇa has been understood by him.

170b-171. O Brāhmaṇas, he who knows the four Vedas with their ancillary subjects and the Upaniṣads must increase his knowledge of Veda through Itihāsas and Purāṇas. The

1. A village in the Himalayas near Badarikāśrama where Maru and Devāpi, the last kings of the Solar and Lunar races respectively performed penance to reappear again as kings of Ayodhyā and Hastinapur after Kalki. —De, p. 74.

Veda is afraid of a man of incomplete knowledge saying "O this man will strike me."[1]

172-174. Repeatedly learning this chapter that had been directly mentioned by the self-born lord Brahmā one shall never lose sense after getting into an adversity. He will attain such a goal (hereafter) as is desired by him.

Since this had been (in existence) before also (*Purā api*), it is remembered as Purāṇam.[2] He who understands the etymological interpretation of this, is rid of all sins.

Hence, listen to this summary. Nārāyaṇa creates the world. It is on that occasion of creation when he makes this entire Purāṇa. It does not remain at the time of annihilation.

CHAPTER TWO

The Legend of Naimiṣāraṇya

[Greedy King Pururavas killed while confiscating the Golden altar : Prince Āyu installed as King: sages conciliated]

1-3. Those sages who considered the austerities as their wealth asked Sūta once again:—"Where did that *Sattra* (sacrificial session) of those persons of miraculous deeds take place ? How long did it continue ? How was it performed ? How did Prabhañjana (the Windgod) recount the Purāṇa ? Recount it in detail as we have great eagerness to hear it".

Thus urged, Sūta replied the following auspicious words (narrative) :

---

1. =Mbh. Ādi. 1.267b-268a. This is the traditional stand of Purāṇas regarding their indispensability. It is justifiable to some extent as they preserve the unbroken Brahmanical tradition from the Vedas and are some-times useful in interpretation as in *Ahalyāyai jāraḥ* (*Śatapatha* 3.3.4.18) or *Viśvarūpaṁ jaghānendraḥ* (*Śatapatha* 1.2.3.2 etc.).

2. A popular etymology of the word *Purāṇa*.

4. "Listen to the narration as to where those self-possessed ones performed the excellent *Sattra*, how long it continued and how it was performed.

5-7. Desirous of creating the universe formerly, he (Brahmā) discharged (everything) to those who performed the *Yajña*. They performed the highly meritorious Sattra for a thousand years.

Brahmā himself became the *Tapogṛhapati* (Lord of the penance house). Iḍā accepted the status of the *Patnī* (wife of the sponsor of the sacrifice). The intelligent Mṛtyu of great splendour performed the *Śāmitra* rite (the act of killing the sacrificial animal) in that *Sattra* of those noble souls. The *Vibudhas* (Devas) stayed there for a thousand years.

8. The place where the rim of the whirling *Dharmacakra* (wheel of righteousness) broke down became well known as *Naimiṣa*[1] on account of that event. It is a place well-worshipped by the sages.

9-10. It is the place where the holy Gomatī river is resorted to by Siddhas and Cāraṇas. The Gomatī had a daughter in a trice and that is the Rohiṇī.

Śakti became the eldest son of the noble-souled Vasiṣṭha and Arundhatī of excellent brilliance* (?)

11. It is the place where King Kalmāṣapāda and Śakra** met Śakti. It is the place where enmity broke out between Viśvāmitra and Vasiṣṭha.

12. It is the place where sage Parāśara was born of Adṛśyantī. Against his knowledge, Vasiṣṭha had to court discomfiture.[2]

---

1. Vide Ch. 1, p. 8 note 2. It appears that the Bd.P. regards Nimsar near the Gomatī as the original Naimiṣāraṇya.

* The text: *Sutāyātrādānam uttamatejasaḥ* is confusing. Vā.P.2.10 in identical verse reads:

Śakti-jyeṣṭhāḥ samabhavan Vasiṣṭhasya mahātmanaḥ /
Arundhyatyāḥ sutā yatra śatam uttama-tejasaḥ //

'There a hundred sons of excellent brilliance of whom Śakti was the eldest, were born of the noble-souled Vasiṣṭha from Arundhati"

** Vā.P. 2.11 (identical with this No. 11—verse) reads: '*śaptaḥ*' for *Śakraḥ*. It means: It is a place where king Kalmāṣapāda was cursed by Śakti.

2. Parāśara, while in his mother's (Adṛśyantī's) womb, was such a great Vedic scholar that he surpassed his grandfather Vasiṣṭha (Mbh. Ādi-176.12-15.)

13. The expounders of Brahman thought of a mountain in Naimiṣa at that spot. Since they were born (rather—performed sacrifice—Vā.P.2.13) in Naimiṣa, they are remembered as Naimiṣīyas.

14. The *Sattra* of those intelligent persons lasted for twelve years, when the Valorous Pururavas was ruling over the earth.

15. We have heard the report that, even when he enjoyed eighteen islands over the ocean, Pururavas was never contented with the jewels, due to his covetousness.

16. Urged by a divine messenger, Urvaśī made love to him. He sponsored this *Sattra* in the company of Urvaśī.

17-19. While King Pururavas ruled, the sages of the Naimiṣa forest performed the sacrificial session.* The Gaṅgā conceived a brilliant foetus from the Fire-god. She deposited it on the mountain and it was transformed into gold. God Viśvakarmā himself, the god of great imagination who evolved the world, entered that sacrificial session of those sages of unbounded (immense) lustre (and) transformed the premises and enclosure of the sacrifice into a golden one.

20-21. Pururavas, the son of Iḍā came a-hunting to that region. Seeing that extremely wonderful enclosed place of the sacrifice made of gold, his wisdom was overcome (lit. struck down) by avarice and he began to seize it. Thereupon the residents of Naimiṣa became very much infuriated against the king.

22-23. The angry learned ascetics (who were devoted to penance) urged by the Devas hit him with Kuśa grasses, charged with thunderbolt. Pounded by the adamantine Kuśa grasses that king cast off his mortal body.[1] The son of Urvaśī,

---

* *satre* emended as *satram* (as in Vā.P. 2.17, an identical verse).

1. This account of Pururavas' death recorded here appears to be correct historically. Pururavas was a chief from trans-Himalayan region—*Ilāvṛta varṣa,* the region round Mt. Meru bounded by Mt. Gandhamādana on the west and Mālyavān on the east. He established his kingdom at Pratiṣṭhāna (modern Jhusi near Allahabad) and founded the famous Lunar dynasty. His greed for wealth and his attempt to plunder the sacrificial session is recorded in the Mbh. Ādi.75.20-23. As he came there a-hunting (and not with an army

fought there on the ground.[1]

24-26. Āyus, the righteous ruler of the earth whom they call the noblesouled father of Nahuṣa, obtained a high priority among those who got purificatory bath in the principal sacrifice of that sacrificial session. Having pacified the King that way, the sages, the knowers of Brahman, who themselves were the mūrtis (idols) of the calves of the cow in the form of the earth[2] (?), began to perform the sacrificial session. In this *sattra*, the noble-souled ones observed celibacy.

27-31. They observed *Brahmacarya* as in the case of *Viśvasṛjs* (creators of the universe) formerly, when they were desirous of creating the universe. The king became endowed with the lustre of the sun and the fire. He shone like Indra with the sages and others around him, such as the anchorites Vālakhilyas fond of their friends, Marīcis; the unborn sages[3], They worshipped the Devas with hymns of praise and houses (?) and the Pitṛs by means of the holy rites befitting the Pitṛs.

---

for conquest), it is more probable that he was overwhelmed by the sages and got killed in the scuffle. The sages' curse and the bringing of fire from the heaven etc. described in the Mbh. is obviously a white-wash by its author as the episode concerned the founder of the Lunar dynasty to which Pāṇḍavas belonged. The sages wisely installed his son Āyus who, like a farsighted statesman trying to consolidate the newly-founded kingdom, extended his patronage to the sacrificial session. The Bd.P. version is supported by Vā.P.

1. The text: *aurvaśeyais tatas tasya yuddhaṁ cakre nṛpo bhuvi*, is syntactically not correct. Moreover Āyu, the son of Pururavas and Urvaśī who succeeded him is not known to have fought with the sages.

Vā.P.2.23b (a corresponding verse reads:)

aurvaśeyaṁ tatas tasya putraṁ cakrur nṛpaṁ bhuvi 'Then they made his son born of Urvaśī the king over the earth'.

2. For *Pṛthvī vatsātma-mūrtayaḥ* in this text, cp. Vā.P.2.26 (a corresponding verse reads): (*satram ārebhire kartuṁ*) *yathāvad dharma-bhūtaye* 'according to prescribed rites for the prosperity of Dharma'.

3. The reading of these stanzas in Vā.P.2.27/29a. :

Vaikhānasaiḥ priya-sakhair Vālakhilyair marīcikaiḥ /
anyaiśca munibhir juṣṭaṁ sūrya-vaiśvānara-prabhaiḥ //

(28b—the same as 28b in Vā.P.)

Sambhārais tu Śubhair juṣṭaṁ tair evendra-sado yathā //

(The sacrificial session) was attended by Vālakhilyas and other sages brilliant like the sun, the fire and by auspicious (holy) multitudes of Pitṛs, Cāraṇas, as in the assembly of Indra).

They duly worshipped the Gandharvas and others in accordance with their species. While propitiating, he remembered the Gandharvas and others. Thereafter, in other holy rites the Gandharvas sang *Sāman* hymns; the groups of Apsaras danced; the sages spoke words of wonderfully variegated letters and of splendid form.

32. The learned scholars chanted Mantras etc. They defeated their opponents by means of copious objections.

33-34. The sages were great erudite scholars. They were experts in words, meanings and logical arguments. Nothing was seized from them. No Brahmarākṣasas entered the place and spoiled the *Yajña*. Neither the Daityas nor those with weapons with feather attached to them came there. There was no occasion for expiatory acts and there was no poverty.

35. Due to the combination of efficiency, intellect and steady activity, the injunctions were duly carried out resulting in blessings. Thus the *Sattra* (sacrificial session) of those learned persons continued for twelve years.

36-38. That sacrifice of the sages residing in Naimiṣa was like that of the thunderbolt-bearing Indra. The elderly heroic and other Ṛtviks[1] performed the Jyotiṣṭoma sacrifices separately. Riding on the backs[2] (of horses?), they concluded all the sacrifices after distributing ten thousand (coins) as monetary gifts. After concluding their Yajña, all of them asked Vāyudeva (the wind god) the great lord of unmeasured vitality, O Brāhmaṇas, what I have been asked by you all. Urged (by them) the lord mentioned to them, the matter of his own race.

39. (Lord Wind) was the disciple of the self-born deity. He has perfect control over the sense organs. He sees every thing directly. He is endowed with the eight powers—*Āṇimā* (minuteness) and others. He is equipped with subtle limbs.

40. He sustains all the worlds by means of rains along with the winds blowing obliquely. The branches, the seven

---

1. Vā.P.2.36 reads: *Bhṛgvādyā ṛṣayo dhiyā*: 'intelligent & self possessed sages like Bhṛgu & others.

2. Vā.P.2.36 reads: Pṛṣṭhagamanam 'who went after them'.

boughs, have been borne by him. (? the seven types of wind are probably alluded to). He protects the mobile and the immobile beings all round.

41-43. In his realm the seven times seven (fortynine) Maruts are stationed.

He is extremely powerful and he performs the *Sattra* of the Sūtas with three Vyūhas[1] (circular or other types of arrays)

He holds the remedies of the fiery embodied beings. The five functional organ airs, viz., Prāṇa and others sustain the body filling it with its innate activities. The wind has ether (*ākāśa*) as its source of origin. It has two qualities. It is endowed with the qualities of *Śabda* (sound) and *Sparśa* (touch).

44. He has been called Vācoraṇi (source of origin of speech like the *Araṇi* which is the source of fire) by persons who are clever in the science of sound and phonetics. With soft and gentle speech, he appeared to delight the sages.

45. O learned ones, conversant with the Purāṇas, O Brāhmaṇas, well disciplined in the knowledge of the Purāṇas, the lord (wind) recounted the story in a speech befitting the basis which is the Purāṇa.

46-48. All these narrations, O excellent Brāhmaṇas, are in accordance with what had transpired. This is an excellent great principle of the world of the sages. This Purāṇa has been formerly recounted by Brahmā. It contains excellent wisdom of the deities and the sages. It destroys all sins. I shall narrate it in detail its contents in due order.[2]

1. Vā.P.2.41 reads: Vyūhāśrayāṇāṁ bhūtānāṁ 'Bhūtas (beings) who depend on the Vyūha (body)'.

2. VV. 36-48 show that this Purāṇa (Bd.P.) was formerly narrated by god Brahmā originally. His disciple, the Windgod recounted it to sages of Naimiṣāraṇya on the occasion of the *Sattra* of twelve years duration.

CHAPTER THREE

Description of Evolution of the Universe : The Creation of Hiraṇyagarbha

Sūta narrated :

1. Listen to their divine story that rids one of all sins. It is being narrated by me. It is wonderfully variegated. It has many topics (under discussion) ; it is esteemed by the Vedas.

2. He who retains this (in mind) permanently or listens to this frequently maintains his family (or propagates his race) and he is honoured in the heavenly world.

3. Listen to the topic being recounted in the manner it had been heard and it had occurred. Listen to the five *Tārās* (stars)* that are five in number. Listen to this narrative that is conducive to the increase of the fame of the ancestors.

4. The glorification of all these persons of meritorious deeds and of everlasting fame is conducive to wealth, fame, longevity and heaven. It destroys enemies.

5-7. I bow down to Hiraṇyagarbha, the lordly Puruṣa who is unborn, who is the first creator of subjects, who is the most excellent one, through whom the Kalpa has been competent to have its characteristics; through whom the fire has been capable of being a purifying factor; and who is the self-born Brahmā administering all the worlds. After bowing down to Brahmā, I shall recount the excellent creation of living beings, that begins with *Mahat* (the great First Principle) and ends with *Viśeṣa* (special created things),[1] that has its own characteristic features and diversities, that has five authorities (testimonies) ; that calmly rests in the six ones (?) and that which is presided over by Puruṣa.

8-9. Through concentration of mind, I shall describe to you the excellent creation of Bhūtas. *Avyakta* (the unmanifest

---

* For the above reading (*Viśva-tārā ca yā pañca*), Vā.P.4.7a (a corresponding verse) reads : *vistārāvayavaṁ teṣām* '(Listen to the narration of) the detailed parts (of the Purāṇa).

1. The Sāṅkhya theory of evolution of the universe is accepted in Purāṇas. Compare the account of creation of the Brahmāṇḍa in NP. I.3. 1-45; 42.1-115; Bh.P. III.20.12-53; KP.I.2.3 ff.; AP. 17.2-16.

one) which is of the nature of *Sat* and *Asat* (Existent and non-existent) is the eternal cause. Persons who discuss and ponder over the Principles (reality) call it Pradhāna and Prakṛti. It is devoid of odour, colour and taste; it is without the qualities of sound and touch.

10. It is the source of origin of the universe; it is the great *Bhūta* (living entity); the supreme and eternal Brahman. It is the (cosmic) body of all living beings; the unmanifest one has become so.

11. The Brahman has neither beginning nor end; it is unborn and subtle; it has three *Guṇas*, it is the source of origin and place of ultimate merging and rest. It is *Asāmpratika* (does not belong to the present time), it is *Ajñeya* (i.e. cannot be comprehended. It is the Brahman which is beyond *Sat* and *Asat*.

12. This entire dark world was pervaded by his Ātman (soul). As the Guṇas were in a state of equilibrium, this world full of darkness had not yet been evolved.

13. At the time of creation, *Pradhāna* is presided over by *Kṣetrajña* and since the Guṇas become uneven (due to loss of their equilibrium), the great Principle (*Mahat*) was evolved.

14. That *Mahat* (Great Principle) is subtle and at the outset it was enveloped by *Avyakta*. The *Mahat* wherein there is a predominance of *Sattva Guṇa* displays *Sattva guṇa* alone.

15. It should be known as Mahat on account of its Sattva quality. That is remembered as its sole reason. The *Liṅga* (*Śarira*) (i.e. the internal body or the psychic mechanism) alone is evolved and it is presided over by *Kṣetrajña* (individual soul).

16. *Saṁkalpa* (Wishful thought) and *Adhyavasāya* (Determination) are remembered as its two functions. With a desire to create he who is beyond measures, creates the great creation.

17-18. (Defective Text)[1] Virtue etc. and the elements are the causes of the principles of the worlds. The mind in the

1. The text from verse 17-28 is corrupt and the corresponding text of the Vā.P. Ch.4 has little in common with these verses and is of no help in interpretation. Hence reconstruction of emendations could not be hazarded. But Vā.P. 4.76b-79 bear some correspondence to Bd.P.I.i.3.24-27. The Vā.

great Ātman is Brahman. The discrimination of wicked knowledge is through Īśvara (Lord). The Prajñāsandhi (the junction of intellect) is everything that is under possession. He considers all living beings through *Saṅkhyāyatanaraśmis* (?) (the rays that are the abode of the number ?). Therefore the lord attains the desired fruit.

19-20. The *Manas* (Mind) is called *Bhoktṛ* (Enjoyer) and *Trātṛ* (Protector) and it remains as separated soul. (The *Mahat* is so called) because it falls within the collection of principles and it is great in magnitude. The Mahat principle is remembered as one having physical body that is greater than the remaining *Guṇas* and *Tattvas* (Principles). The mind is called Manas because it thinks or considers the division (or separateness) or it is thought of as a part.

21-22. The (individual soul) is remembered as Puruṣa because of its relationship with *Sat* (the Existent i.e. the Brahman) by way of enjoyment of worldly pleasures. Also the supreme soul is called Brahman because it is *Bṛhat* (very huge) and because it causes all the living beings to increase in size (Bṛṁhaṇatva). (It is possible) because it is the basis of everything. It is defined as Brahmā because it causes the living beings to increase in size and because it fills all the bodies with blessings.

23. The Puruṣa understands all the *Bhavas* (beings and things) separately. It is through it (i.e. Puruṣa) that the Brahman achieves all its tasks (lit. doing of the work) at the outset.

24. Know that the *Prākṛta* (the creation of Prakṛti) is the *Vivarta* (transformation) (of *Brahman*).[1] The *Kṣetrajña* is on a par with Brahman. Indeed it is called the first embodied being and *Purāpuruṣa* (the ancient person).

P. verses may be summarised here as follows: 'The Kṣetrajña called Brahmā who awoke in the egg of Prakṛti (Cosmic egg) is the first embodied being and he is called Puruṣa (one lying in the abode of the cosmic egg.) This god Brahmā, the first creator of *Bhūtas* (elements or beings) existed first. This four-faced Hiraṇya-garbha appeared at first in this (cosmic egg). Both at the time of creation and re-creation (after destruction), he is the Kṣetrajña called Brahmā.

1. This purāṇa supports *Vivarta-vāda* as distinguished from *Pariṇāma-vāda* in explaining the Brahma-world relation.

25. That Brahmā is the primordial creator of the living beings, that existed at the outset.[1]

26-27. That Hiraṇyagarbha with four faces appeared in the *Aṇḍa* (Cosmic egg). In the primary creation as well as in the secondary creation, the Kṣetrajña is on a par with Brahman. The (Individual souls) are asked alongwith the *Karaṇas* (sense organs). They abandon (them) alongwith the dissolutions. Again they assume physical bodies during the junctions of the *yugas*.

28. (Defective text) Those five (?) who are enlightened may take away the water of the depression (pit) of that noble-souled one who uplifts the golden Meru. (?)

29-31. These seven worlds are well established in this cosmic egg; the whole earth along with the seven continents, the seven oceans, the great mountains and thousands of rivers are established in the very same cosmic egg. These worlds are situated within (the cosmic egg). This universe is within the cosmos. Everything is established in that cosmic egg—viz. the moon and the sun along with the stars, planets and the wind as well as the mountain Lokāloka.

32.* The waters are externally surrounded by the *Tejas* (fiery element) ten times as big as themselves. The Tejas is externally surrounded by *Vāyu* (wind) ten times as big as itself.

33. Vāyu is externally surrounded by the *Nabhas* (Ether) ten times as big as itself. In the same manner the entire ether is externally surrounded by Bhūtādi (the Ahaṁkāra or ego).

---

1. From this verse onwards the *Prākṛta sarga*, the first creation of god Brahmā, is described. It takes place without pre-planning or is unpremeditated (*abuddhipūrva*)' like the sudden flash of lightning' as the Bd.P. puts it. While the *Vaikṛta* creations (five in number) are planned—*buddhipūrvaka.*

* From this verse the elemental sheaths that envelop the cosmic egg are enumerated. As verses 29-38 in Bd.P. here and Vā.P.4.81-91 are identical, we can substitute the missing line in Bd.P.32. by Vā.P. 84a as follows:

adbhir daśa-guṇābhis tu bāhyato' ṇḍaṁ samāvṛtam /

'The cosmic egg is enveloped from outside with (the sheath of) ten times (larger) water'.

This additional line is essential to make up the number seven of these Prākṛtic sheaths mentioned below in verse 34 as:

ebhir āvaraṇair aṇḍaṁ saptabhiḥ prākṛtair vṛtam /

34. The *Bhūtādi* is enveloped by *Mahat* and the *Mahat* is enveloped by *Pradhāna*. The cosmic egg is thus enveloped by the seven *Āvaraṇas* (coverings) pertaining to the Prakṛti.

35-37. Thus willingly these Prakṛtis (evolutes of Prakṛti) are stationed ready in destroying mutually. They stand ready at the time of creation; they sustain mutually and they devour mutually. Those *Vikāras* (effects) abide in the *Vikārins* (causes) by way of the supporter-supported relationship. The *Avyakta* (the unmanifest one) is called *Kṣetra* and Brahman is called *Kṣetrajña*.

Thus the Prākṛta Sarga (creation of the Prakṛti) (has been explained). It is presided by Kṣetrajña.

38. This is the first creation and it is unpremedited. It appeared just like the lightning. Undoubtedly he who factually understands this birth of Hiraṇyagarbha shall become long-lived, famous, blessed and intelligent.

CHAPTER FOUR

Constitution of the world (The Cosmic Egg)

[The creation due to disequilibrium of *guṇas*—the three states of the self-born god Brahmā—Description of Kalpas]

Sūta said :

1. When the unmanifest one is stationed within itself and when the effect (universe) had been withdrawn, the Pradhāna and Puruṣa remain with their similarity of characteristics (retained).

2. These two have Tamas and Sattva guṇas. They are stationed on a par with each other. Hence they are said to be mutual pursuers. They are not excessive (in the manifestation of the Guṇas).

3. *Laya* (Dissolution) should be understood to occur when Guṇas are in equilibrium. It is called creation when there is predominance (of one Guṇa over the other.)

The *Sthiti* (Sustenance) was at the time when Sattva was predominant. Certainly, the lotus is stationed at the top (?)

4. When Rajas closely follows and stations itself in Tamas and Sattva, it is the Rajas that causes the other things to function in the same way as in the case of the water causing the seeds to function.

5. The Guṇas assume inequality and they become stabilized casually. It should be known that three (divinities) were born out of the Guṇas which are agitated.[1]

6. They are eternal, extremely mysterious; the souls of everyone and embodied; the Sattva qualily is Viṣṇu; the Rajas is Brahmā and the Tamas is Rudra, the Prajāpati.

7. Viṣṇu the enlightener and revealer of the Rajas becomes Brahmā, and attains the status of the creator. It is from him that being of great vitality that the variety of creation of the worlds, takes its origin.

8. Viṣṇu as the enlightener and revealer of the Tamas stands separate in the from of Kāla (Time).

Viṣṇu as the enlightener and revealer of the Sattva stands separate as sustenance (i.e. one who sustains).

9. These alone are the three worlds; these alone are the three Guṇas; these alone are the three Vedas; these alone are the three sacred fires.

10. These have mutual inter-association; these are mutually attached; they exist by mutual help and they impel inter se.

11. These are mutually coupled; these are mutually interdependent; these do not become separated even for a moment; they do not abandon each other.

---

1. Though this Purāṇa accepts the Sāṅkhya theory regarding the creation of the universe being due to the imbalance of the three Guṇas, the personification of the Guṇas in Brahmā (Rajas), Viṣṇu (Sattva) and Rudra (Tamas) is the puranic way of presentation for the understanding of the process by the masses.

12. As a result of the unevenness of the Guṇas, the Pradhāna begins to function at the time of creation. At the outset it begins to function (from that *Avyakta*) of the nature of *Sat* and *Asat* and presided over by *Adṛṣṭa* (the unmanifest).

13. The pair Brahmā and *Buddhi* (Cosmic intellect) took their origin simultaneously from that (Pradhāna) of the nature of Tamas and unmanifestness*. The Kṣetrajña (and) that which is (also) named Brahmā (was born from that pair).

14. Fully equipped with *Kārya* (effect?) and *Karaṇa* (the instruments; the sense-organs) Brahmā appeared (existed) at the outset. He was unparalleled in lustre, intelligent, unmanifest but excellent enlightener (revealer).

15. (Defective text). He is the first embodied being stabilised in retention. He is endowed with unequalled knowledge and absence of passionate attachment.

16. On account of his being unmanifest and because he had kept (everything) under control, since these are three Guṇas and because all evolved beings are interdependent, (Brahmā attains) whatever he desires mentally.

17. The self-born deity has three states : He has four faces as Brahmā; as Kāla (God of Death) he is Bhava, the destroyer; (as Viṣṇu) he is the Puruṣa with thousand heads.

18. As Brahmā, he creates the worlds; as Kāla, he annihilates them; as Puruṣa, he is indifferent : these are the three states of the selfborn deity.[1]

19. As Brahmā, he possesses Rajas exclusively; as Kāla he has Rajas and Tamas and as Puruṣa (i.e. Viṣṇu) he is exclusively Sāttvika;—this is the position of the Guṇas in the case of the self-born deity.

20. Brahmā has eyes like lotus-petals*; Kāla has the lustre of collyrium ever since his origin. Puruṣa is lotuseyed with the form of the supreme Ātman.

---

* Vā.P.5.23: From that (Pair of Brahmā & *Buddhi*) was born Kṣetrajña designated as Brahmā, full of tamas and unmanifestness.

1. The trinity of gods carrying out the functions of creation, sustenance and destruction of the universe but the three states of one and the same self-born deity.

* *Kamalapatrākṣa* should be emended as *Kamalapatrābha* as in Vā.P.5. 31b, as it is the description of the complexions of three deities.

21. He is single. He is two-fold. He is three-fold. Again he is multifold. The lord of Yogins makes and un-makes the physical bodies.

22. The physical bodies adopt different kinds of shapes, activities, colours and features. Since he has the pastime of remaining threefold in the world, he is called *Triguṇa*[1] (one that has three Guṇas).

23-24. Since he is divided into four, he is glorified as *Caturvyūha* (one with four arrays). Since at the end of a Parārdha, the lord lies down (sleeps); since the lord enjoys the pleasures of the world, since all living beings always take rest (lie down) normally and comfortably in him, he is defined as Ātman, He is *Ṛṣi* because he goes everywhere and since the lord enters the physical body.

25. He is Sarva (all), because he is the master of all; he is Viṣṇu because he permeates everything. He is Bhagavān, (since) he devoured the Bhāvas (living beings). He is *Nāga* because no Āgas (i.e. sin) abides in him.

26. He is *Parama*, because he is extremely delighted. Since he has Devatva (state of being God), he is remembered as OM. He is Sarvajña (omniscient) because he knows everything perfectly. He is Sarva because everything originates from him.

27. Brahmā causes the sleep (i.e. perfect rest) of *Naras* (men), hence he is remembered as Nārāyaṇa. He functions after dividing himself into three. He is *Sakala* (having the full complement of digits and parts).

28. By means of the three (Guṇas), he himself creates, devours and protects. The *Prabhu* (Lord) himself became Hiraṇyagarbha at the outset and manifested himself.

29. Indeed he is *Ādya* (First, foremost) and *Svavaśa* (having himself under control). He is remembered as *Aja* because he is not born. Hence he is defined as *Hiraṇyagarbha* in the Purāṇas.

---

1. The author of Bd.P. seems to be fond of giving popular etymologies. The etymologies of Triguṇa, Caturvyūha, Ātmā, Ṛṣi, Viṣṇu, Nārāyaṇa etc. are interesting. Some of these are however grammatically correct e.g., Viṣṇu —viś—'to pervade', ṛṣi—ṛ 'to go'.

30. He is selfborn and receding (?), he is Kāla and the foremost among all the castes. It is not possible to specify him exclusively in the course of hundreds of Manu's years.*

31. The Parārdha of Brahmā is remembered as being reckoned is so many Kalpas. He has another period of the same duration and he wakes up at the end of that period.

32. Thousands and crores of years that had been the abode of Kalpas have passed by. As many are yet to come.

33-34. The Kalpa that is current now, is Vārāha, know ye all. It is the first Kalpa and it is the present Kalpa. The Kings should govern till thousand Yugas are completed.

CHAPTER FIVE

The Creation of the Universe

[The Boar incarnation of Viṣṇu—Primary and secondary creation—creation of gods, sages and their dissolution].

Śrī Sūta said :

1. At the beginning, the waters were present everywhere, on the surface of the earth. When this (visible world) had been annihilated and when the winds had become quiet, nothing could be known.

2. In that vast ocean-like expanse of water,[1] when the whole world consisting of mobile and immobile beings had

---

* For *Varṇāgratas*, Vā.P.5.46b reads *Varṣāgrajas*. If this is accepted as emendation, the verse would mean: "It is not possible to calculate even with hundreds of Manvantaras as a unit of the time etc.

1. *Ekārṇava*—Also called *Mahārṇava, agādha stabdha salila*, or *Salila* only, *Yugānta-toya* in Mt. P., HV., Bh.P. VP. and other Purāṇas. This primeval watery flood expresses the infinite unmanifest cause—the *Kāraṇa Brahman* as explained by Nīlakaṇṭha (on HV.P. 3.9.1-4) 1/2 from which all life

perished, the only entity present there was that lord Brahmā with thousand eyes and thousand legs.[1]

3. At that time Brahmā named Nārāyaṇa lay asleep in the waters. He had a thousand heads. He was the Puruṣa with golden colour and was beyond the ken of the sense-organs.

4. Prohibited* (?) on account of the excess of Sattva, he saw the empty world. In this context, as regards Nārāyaṇa they cite this *śloka* (verse).

5. Waters are called *Nāras* (because) the waters are indeed the children of (*Nara*) (Man) ; the waters are his place of resort. Hence, he is remembered as Nārāyaṇa.[2]

6. (Defective text). He remains meditating for a period equal to a thousand Yugas. He performs meditation on a (lotus) with golden petals in order to reach the ideal state of Brahman.**

7. Like a glow-worm at night during the rainy season, Brahmā moves about here and there in the water, stooping down with his face turned downwards.

8-9. After knowing that the great (universe) had gone deep into that vast expanse of water, he thought of uplifting the earth with steadiness of composure. Then he thought of the other eightfold cosmic body (as evolved by) Oṁkāra, in the beginnings of Kalpas as before. Then the great soul thought of his divine form.

10. On seeing that the earth had sunk into the water he thought—"what form shall I assume and uplift the earth ?"

---

comes into being. VP.I.2.22 states that this Ekārṇava doctrine is very ancient and *Brahma-vādins* have elaborated it to explain the process of creation and dissolution. Mt.P. 182 identifies Nārāyaṇa with Mahārṇava.

1. Cf. Puruṣa-sūkta (ṚV.X.90.1).

* *niṣiddha* in the text is illogical. Vā.P.6.4 (an identical verse) reads: *Prabuddha* 'awakened' by the dominance of Sattva.

2. The usual derivation of Nārāyaṇa found in other Purāṇas also but for a different derivation vide *supra* 4.28.

** Vā.P.6. reads : *naiśaṁ kālam upāsya saḥ* /
Śarvaryante prakurute Brahmatvaṁ sarge-kāraṇāt //

'Having passed the night-time in sleep, at the end of the night, creates god Brahmā for the creation of the universe'.

11. He remembered the form of a Boar[1] that is suitable for the aquatic sports. It was invisible* unto all living beings. It is of the nature of speech termed Brahman.

12. Its girth was ten Yojanas (1 Yojana = 12 Km) and the length was a hundred Yojanas. It resembled the dark cloud, in complexion. It had a rumbling sound like that of the clouds.

13. It had a huge body like a great mountain. It had curved fangs, white, sharp and terrible. It bore resemblance (in lustre to) lightning and fire. Its brilliance was like that of the sun.

14. It had thick long and round shoulders. It used to walk with the (steady) steps of Viṣṇu. The region of its hips was raised up (well-developed) and stout. It was honoured with the characteristic features of a bull.

15. Assuming this inimitable form of a boar, Hari entered the nether worlds for uplifting the earth.

16-22. (The description of *Yajña-vārāha*).[2] The conclusion on the *Dikṣā* (initiation) and *Iṣṭi* (sacrifice) were his curved fangs, the *Kratu* (sacrifice) was his tooth.[3] The *Juhū* (the crescent-shaped wooden ladle) was his mouth; the fire was his

---

1. VV.8-11 remind of Tait.Brāhmaṇa 1.2.1.3 which states

āpo vā idamagre salilam āsīt |
tasmin prajāpatir vāyur bhūtvā
acarat | sa imām apaśyat | tāṁ
varāho bhūtva'harat ||

Purāṇas elaborated this statement in the full-fledged description of the Boar-incarnation of Viṣṇu. *Vide* Bh. P. III.13 17-33, Mt.P.Chs. 246-248; VP.I.4. 1-52, Mbh. Sabhā 37.29 ff. and Bd. P. *infra* Ch. 8. 1-10.

* *adhṛṣyam* 'unassailable' in Vā.P.6.11.

2. This poetic description of the Divine Boar in Yajña terminology is so beautiful that not only Purāṇa-writers but writers on Smṛti works, Tantra works and even Śaṅkara adopted it. For example, vide Vā.P.Ch.6 (a number of verses identical with Bd.P.), Bm P. 213.33-42; Bh.P. III.13 34-39, Viṣṇu Smṛti 1.3-12; Śaṅkara on Viṣṇu-sahasra-nāma verse 118 on *Yajñāṅga.*

Though it is a self-explanatory translation some expressions are explained briefly.

3. Mt.P. 247.68 reads differently.

Veda-pādo Yūpa-daṁṣṭraḥ Kratu-dantas Citī-mukhaḥ

tongue;[1] the Darbha grasses were his hairs,[2] the Brahmā (one of the four Ṛtviks employed at a Soma sacrifice or vedic knowledge of great penance was his head.[3] The Vedas were his shoulders; he had the fragrance of the *Havis*. The *Havya, Kavya* etc. were his velocity;[4] *Prāgvaṁśa* (the sacrificial room facing the east) was his body;[5] he was brilliant; he was equipped with different kinds of *Dikṣās* (initiations); he was the master of Yoga with Dakṣiṇā for his heart; he was the lord full of *Śraddhā* (faith) and Sattva (good quality);[6] he had *Upākarma* (extra study of the Vedas by way of expiation) for his *Ruci*[7] (lustre or taste); he had *Pravargya* (the ceremony preliminary to Soma sacrifice) as his *Āvartabhūṣaṇa*[8] (ornamental whorls of hair on his chest), the way of the different *Cchandas* (Metres) was his pathway; the *Upaniṣads* with their esoteric doctrines constituted his seat. He was assisted by Māyā in the capacity of his spouse; he had the height of the peak of a mountain; he had the day and the night as his eyes;[9] he had the ancillary subjects

1. A Vedic concept. *Agni* (fire) is the tongue of gods with which they eat the food (offered in sacrifices), cf. ṚV.IV.57.1.

2. *darbha-romā*. The *darbha*-grass spread on the altar is compared to the shaggy hair on the body of the boar.

3. *Brahma-śirṣaḥ—Brahma* means also the Vedic knowledge and naturally its position is the highest viz. the head.

4. It is difficult to understand why the velocity of the Divine Boar is compared to the *Havya* and *Kavya* rites meant for gods and Pitṛs. Probably *Agnihotra* and *Śrāddha* and their association with the sacrifice may be the reason.

5. *Prāgvaṁśa-kāya—Prāgvaṁśa* also means 'a room in which the family and friends performing the sacrifice assemble.' This body (*Kāya*) of the *Yajña-Varāha* is so much spacious as to accommodate many people.

6. Vā.P.6.21. gives a better reading viz. *mahā-sattra-mayo* : *Mahā-sattra* is a long (and great) Soma-sacrifice continuing for 13 to 100 days. Varāha has assumed the form of a great Soma sacrifice.

7. The Mt.P. and Śaṅkara read *upākarmoṣṭharucakaḥ* : Whose pendant lower-life was *upākarma* (recitation of the Vedas). Can we take *ruci* for *rucaka*?

8. The whorls of hair on the front of horse's chest is regarded as ornamental. The same on the chest of the boar would be beutifying.

The *Pravargya* ceremony is introductory to the Soma sacrifice. In this, fresh milk is poured into a heated vessels called *Mahāvīra* or *Gharma*, or into boiling ghee (MW.P.693.ii). The vapour-fumes coiling up from the *gharma* is imagined as circular whorls of the Boar's hair.

9. Day and night represent the Sun and the Moon. They are the two eyes of this Divine Boar.

of the Vedas as the ornament unto his ears. He had the odour of the *Ājya* (ghee-offering; in the sacrifice) ; the *Sruvā* (the sacrificial ladle) was his snout; he had the loud pitch in chanting of the *Sāman* hymns as his voice; he was glorious, an embodiment of truth and virtue; he was honoured by the exploits of his actions; expiation was his claw; he was terrible; he had the knee joints of the animals; he was the great sacrifice incarnate; *Udgātā* was his entrail;[1] the Homa was his *Liṅga* (symbol) ; he had fruits and seeds as great medicinal herbs[2](?) *Vādyantara*[3] (Another disputant) was his own *Śastra* (sacrifice) (?). Absence of egotim as well as Soma juice was his blood.

23. [The text in Bd.P. is corrupt. The corresponding verse in Vā. P. 6.23 is as follows :]

> bhūtvā Yajña-varāho vai antaḥ sa prāviśat prabhuḥ/
> adbhiḥ sañchāditām ūrvīṁ sa tām aśnan prajāpatiḥ
> upagamyojjahārāśu apas tāś ca sa vinyasan //

'It is reported that he verily became Yajña-varāha and the Lord entered the waters. That Prajāpati found that earth which was covered over with waters. Removing (displacing) those waters, he seized and quickly lifted it up.'

24. He allocated the waters of the ocean in the oceans and those of the rivers in the rivers. After making them separate and equal, he gathered the mountains on the earth for its stability.

25. These mountains had been burnt in the previous Sarga (period of creation) by the *Saṁvartaka* fire (i.e. fire of destruction at the time of universal annihilation). Along with that fire these mountains had got merged in the earth completely.

---

1. It is the length of the Sāma song sung by the Udgātṛ which resembles the long entrail of the animal.

2. *Phala-bīja-mahauṣadhīḥ*. This reading though accepted in the translation is obscure. Mt.P.,Bm.P., Viṣṇu Smr. read *Bījauṣadhi-mahāphalaḥ*. *Mahāphala* is the scrotum. The idea seems to be that the herbs and plants which produce the seed are comparable functionally to the testicle of the Boar.

3. This is obscure. The reading in Viṣṇu Smṛ.(I.6) is *Vedyantarātmā*. It means the *Vedi*, the altar of the sacrifice was the heart of the Boar.

26. (Defective text). In that vast expanse of water [due to cold (*śaityāt*—Vā. P.)], they became stored up by the wind. Wherever this (water solution with burnt mountains) was sprinkled, a mountain cropped up in each of those places.

27. After they had been scattered, Viśvakarman divided the worlds, oceans and mountains. He divides like this again and again at the beginning of every Kalpa.[1]

28. He created again and again this earth consisting of seven continents along with the oceans and the mountains. He (also) created again the four worlds beginning with *Bhū* (earth).

29-31. After creating the worlds, Brahmā, the self-born lord began the creation of Prajās (subjects). Desirous of creating different subjects (creatures), he created them in the same form as had been created before. As he meditated and pondered about (the forthcoming) creation preceded by (cosmic) intellect, Avidyā unfolded itself into five forms simultaneous with *Pradhāna*[2] (?). These five forms were Tāmasika. They were darkness, delusion, great-delusion, pitch darkness and blind darkness.

32. Thus Avidyā had five joints (*Parvan*).[3] It manifested itself from the great-soul. Thus the creation remained five-fold even as he was meditating over it and identifying himself with it.

---

1. The Puranic belief about the new creation of the universe at the beginning of a new Kalpa is that, despite the annihilation of the universe at the end of every Kalpa, god Brahmā re-creates the universe on the same model of the former universe. It is succinctly stated as

Dhātā yathāpūrvam akalpayat |

2. This is the translation of *Pradhāna-samakāle* in the Text. The unfoldment of the five *Parvans* of Avidyā simultaneously with the Sāṅkhya principle called *Pradhāna* is confusing. Vā.P.6.36 gives a better reading viz. *Pradhyāna-sama-kālam* "simultaneously with i.e. while he was meditating, there manifested Avidyā of five knots or *Parvans*".

3. The five joints (*Parvans*) of Avidyā are enumerated in 31b viz. *Tamas*, *Moha*, *Mahā-moha*, *Tāmisra* and *Andha*-tāmisra. These are rendered as ignorance, delusion, desire of enjoyment, anger and fear of death. *vide* Com. on VP.I.5.5). The concept called *Avidyā* is very complex. With Yoga, it means "undifferentiated consciousness" (J.H. Woods); Vedānta equates it with Māyā. Here the cosmic aspect of *Avidyā* is implied.

33. It is surrounded everywhere by Tamas like the seed and the creeper within a pot.* Within and without, it is devoid of lustre as well as devoid of consciousness.

34. Since they have (well) made intellect, miseries and sense-organs, the *Nāgas* (i.e. trees, creepers, plants) are glorified as *Mukhya* (Principal) creations.[1] Their selves have been covered up.

35 Brahmā, the self-born lord, was not fully satisfied in his mind even after seeing the evolution of *Mukhyasarga* (principal creation). He thought of creating (a fresh type of creation) then.

36. Even as he was pondering over it, another creation, the *Tiryaksrotas*[2] (oblique-currented creation, i.e. the animal world) took its origin. It is remembered as *Tiryaksrotas*, because it functioned in oblique (in non-straight) ways.

37. On account of the excess of the *Tamas* quality, they are remembered as *Ajñānabahula* (abounding in ignorance). They are *Utpādyagrāhiṇaḥ*** (comprehending what should be produced). They fancy themselves wise, despite their ignorance,

38. They possess egotism. They are proud of themselves. They are of twentyeight types.[3] The sense-organs are of eleven varieties. The soul etc. are of nine varieties.

---

* For Bd.P.—*bīja-kumbha-latā-vṛtaḥ*
(translated here) Vā.P.6.37b reads:
dīpaḥ kumbhavad āvṛtaḥ

'just as a lamp lighted in a pitcher cannot emit light outside due to the opaque wall-like cover of the pitcher. This simile in Vā.P. is the traditional and more appropriate one here. For more discussion vide note 2 on P.57 of the translation of KP (MLBD.)

1. This 'meditated' (*Vaikṛta*) creation by Avidyā was characterised by ignorance as it included immobiles (*Nāga*)-like mountains, trees. Hence it is also called *Mukhya*. As verse 55 below explains *Mukhya* means *Sthāvara* (immobile).

2. VV. 36-40 describe the second type and stage of "meditated" creation viz. *Tiryak-srotas*. It is not that the creatures in this creation always move in oblique direction. But, as verse 56 below and VP. I.5.9-11 and 22a explain, it includes birds and beasts which are by nature mostly ignorant and hence taking to wrong-ways and egotistic. This is the second stage in volution after the immobile one.

** Vā.P.6.43a reads: *utpatha-grāhiṇaḥ* 'taking to wrong ways'—a better reading.

3. The text reads *aṣṭāviṁśad-vidhātmikāḥ and* the reading is supported by Vā.P.6.44. But VP.I.5.11a reads: *aṣṭāviṁśad-vadhātmikāḥ*.

39. The Tārakas and others are of eight types, their destruction of power is remembered (?). They have inner light and all of them are again externally enveloped.

40. They are called *Tiryaksrotas.* They have their selves under control. They have three appellations.

41. After creating the second universal creation; the *Tiryaksrotas* and having observed that type of creation, the (following) idea occurred in him :

42. Even as he was pondering, the final creation of the Sāttvika type was evolved. This third creation is *Ūrdhvasrotas* upwards currented.[1] It is based upwards.

43. Since they returned upwards they are called *Ūrdhvasrotas.* They are of a pleasant nature with much of gaiety. They are not enveloped within or without.

44-46a. They are brilliant within and without. The subjects of *Ūrdhvasrotas* are remembered as nine. They are Dhātā (? creator) and others. They are remembered as wise ones of contented mind. This third creation, the *Ūrdhvasrotas,* is remembered as *Daivīka* (Divine) i.e. pertaining to gods).

When the divine creations of the *Ūrdhvasrotas* type had been created, lord Brahmā became pleased. Thereafter, he did not ponder over anything else.

46b-47. (Later on) the lord was desirous of creating another set of created beings that would be Sādhaka (aspirant after spiritual achievement).

Even as he was pondering over creation and since he was of truthful (effective) conception, the *Bhautasarga* (creation of *Bhūtas,* i.e. living beings) manifested itself. It was down-

---

The reading is worth noting as the verses concerning the creation in VP.I.5, Vā.P.6 and Bd.P. text under translation are common and the word *Vadha* in *aṣṭāviṁśad-vadhātmakaḥ* in VP. is a technical term in Sāṅkhya. It means 'weakness.' Īśvara Kṛṣṇa's *Sāṅkhya-Kārikā* enumerates them as follows:

ekādaśendriya-vadhāḥ saha buddhi-vadhair aśaktir uddiṣṭā /
sapta-daśa-vadhā buddher viparyayāt tuṣṭi-siddhīnām //49//

1. VV.42-46a describe the third Vaikṛta Creation called *Urdhvasrotas* or *Deva-sarga,* creation of heavenly beings.

ward—currented (*arvāk-srotas*)[1] as well as competent to achieve the goals of his life.

48. Since they function downwards (i.e. on the earth, below heaven) they are (called *Arvāksrotas*. They abound in brilliance but were contaminated by *tamas* and dominated with *rajas*.

49. Hence they have excess of misery. They make repeated attempts. They are enlightened within and without. They are the mortal beings capable of achieving their goal.

50. They are arranged into eight classes with hellish characteristics (i.e. such characteristic features as are conducive to hell). Those men with souls of spiritual achievement are similar in characteristic features to the Gandharvas.

51-52. The fifth creation, the *Anugraha Sarga* (creation of blessings) is arranged into four classes, viz. i) *Viparyaya* (Loss of consciousness), ii) *Śakti* (Efficiency), iii) *Siddha* (of achievement) and iv) *Mukhya* (Principal).

They are born again and again, they recede and they (come back) to be present. The sixth creation is said to be of *Bhūtādi* (elements or creatures) etc.

53-55A. Those creatures should be known as characterised by tendency to eat and obtain or grab.

The first creation of Brahmā should be known as that of Mahat (the great principle). The second creation is that of *Tanmātras*. It is called *Bhūtasarga*.[2]

55B. The third Vaikārika creation is called *Aindriya Sarga* (creation pertaining to the sense organs). These are the *Prākṛta* (of Prakṛti) creations that are evolved with consciousness and foreknowledge.

1. VV.46b-50 describe the fourth creation called *arvāk-srotas*—down-currented i.e. who function on the earth below the heavenly region. It is called *Manuṣyasarga* in verse 49 and in VP.I.5.23.

2. There seems to be confusion in the present text. Here *Bhūtādi* or *Bhūta-sarga* is called the sixth *Vaikṛta* Creation. But in the recapitulatory verses below (VV.52b-58) *Bhūta-sarga* is given as the *Second Prākṛta Creation* (V.54a) and *Vaikṛta* sargas are stated to be five in number

Pañcaite vaikṛtāḥ sargāḥ—

The fourth creation is *Mukhyasarga*. The immobile creations are remembered as *Mukhyas*.

56-57. The fifth one is *Tiryaksrotasa* creation. The *Tiryagyonis* (i.e. the lower creatures and animals) constitute it.

The sixth creation of *Ūrdhvasrotas* is called Daivata (pertaining to divine beings).

Thereafter, is the seventh creation, that of the *Arvāksrotas*, the human beings. The eighth creation is *Anugrahasarga*. It is Sāttvika as well as Tāmasa.

58. These (latter) five creations are the *Vaikṛta* (Meditated) creation. The first three are remembered as *Prākṛta* (pertaining to Prakṛti) creations. The ninth creation called the Kaumāra (brought about by Kumāra i.e. Sanatkumāra etc.) sarga. (The eight creations mentioned before are) *Prākṛta* and *Vaikṛta*.

59. (*Defective text*)* The three Prākṛta creations are *Buddhipūrvas* (created with consciousness and foreknowledge). The *Vikṛta* creations function *Buddhi-Apūrvas* (without consciousness and foreknowledge). Their classes pertain to the Brahman (?)

60-62. Understand all of it even as it is being recounted in detail. He abides fourfold (in four groups) in all the living beings, viz by (1) *Viparyaya*, (2) *Śakti*, (3) *Buddhi* (intellect and (4) *Siddhi* (see verse 51 above). He is stationed among immobile beings by means of *Viparyāsa* (i.e. *Viparyaya*—contrariety or loss of consciousness); in the lower creatures by means of *Śakti* (physical power); the human beings are with souls of spiritual achievement; there is *Puṣṭi*** (? nourishment) wholly among the Devas.

---

* The text is defective and hence the translation is confused. The corresponding verse in Vā.P.6.

Prākṛtās tu trayaḥ sargāḥ kṛtās te'buddhi-pūrvakāḥ |
Buddhi-pūrvam pravartante ṣaṭ-sargā Brahmaṇas tu te ||

'The three Prākṛta creations were brought about without planning or pre-meditation (*abuddhi-pūrvakāḥ*). But the six creations of god Brahmā came out pre-planned (with previous meditation).

** *tuṣṭi* 'contentment' in Vā.P.6.69.

Thereafter, Brahmā created mental sons on a par with himself.

63-65. Those (sons) of great splendour and strength became *Nivṛttas* (i.e. renounced the world) on account of their knowledge pertaining to *Vivarta* (unreal appearance caused by Avidyā e.g. the world instead of Brahman). All the three of them (?) addressed the name (? of the world and ceased (their activity) without creating the (primary) creation of the subjects or the secondary one. When they were found *Viraktas* (Devoid of passionate attachment) Brahmā wishing to create other Sādhakas created those Devas who took pride in their positions and identified themselves with the same. Then there is the command of Brahmā once again. Understand from me those *Sthānins* (deities in different positions) who were in the condition of non-creation (*Abhūtasṛṣṭi*).

66-68. They are the waters, the fire, the earth, the wind, the intermediate region between the heaven and the earth, the ether, the heaven, the quarters, the oceans, the rivers, the vegetable kingdom, the souls of medicinal herbs, the souls of trees and creepers, the winding plants, the units of time such as Kāṣṭhās, Kalās, Muhūrtas etc., the twilights, the nights, the days, the half-years, the months, the *Ayanas* (the period of the transits of the sun from north to south and *vice versa*), the years and yugas.

They take pride and identify themselves with their positions and currents. They are remembered as having the names of their respective positions.

69. After creating the souls of different *Sthānas* (positions), he created other beings, the Devas and the *Pitṛs* by whom these subjects flourished.

70. He created nine mental sons, viz., Bhṛgu, Aṅgiras, Marīci, Pulastya, Pulaha, Kratu, Dakṣa, Atri and Vasiṣṭha.

71. These are decisively termed nine Brahmās in the Purāṇa because they were just like Brahmā (in regard to the creation) of all Brahma Yogins their sons.

72. Thereafter Brahmā created Rudra form out of his

anger. He then created the *Saṁkalpa** (conception) and Dharma (virtue) of all in all directions.

73. Then Brahmā created *Vyavasāya* (Energetic effort) the creature of the nature of pleasure. From the Saṁkalpa of the creator whose source of origin was the unmanifest one Saṁkalpa was born.

74. From the Prāṇa Dakṣa was created and he (Brahmā) created Marīci from the speech and the eyes. Sage Bhṛgu was born of the heart of Brahmā whose source of origin was water.

75. Aṅgiras was born of the head and Atri from the ears. Pulastya was born of the life-breath called Udāna and Pulaha from the Vyāna.

76. Vasiṣṭha was born of life-breath *Samāna*. He created Kratu from the Apāna. These are remembered as the twelve** excellent sons of Brahmā.

77. Dharma and others should be known and they are remembered as the first born sons of Brahmā, Bhṛgu and others who were created (later), were not expounders of Brahman.

78. These twelve sons of Brahmā are to be known as the ancient householders. O Brāhmaṇa, these are born along with Rudra.

79. Kratu and Sanatkumāra, these two lived in perpetual celibacy. In the previous birth*** they are elder to all.

80. In the seventh Kalpa, these ancient *Sādhakas* of the world had already passed away. They shine (refulgently) in this world by means of the splendour of their own souls.

81. Both of them were Yogins by nature. Those two, of great power, carried out the duties of subjects and love by superimposing the soul (on the supreme soul) by means of the soul.

82. He continues to be in the same state as he was in, when he was born. So he is called Kumāra. Thereupon, his name Sanatkumāra became well established.

---

* Saṁkalpa and Dharma born before all.

** Dharma, Saṁkalpa, Rudra and nine sages=12.

*** If the reading is *pūrvotpannau* 'They were born before'.

83. Their twelve races are divine and are endowed with the groups of Devas; they performed holy rites; they had progeny and they had great sages ornamenting the race.

84. After seeing those twelve *Sāttvika* beings born of his vital airs, the lord created the Asuras, the *Pitṛs*, the Devas and the human beings.

85. He created the Devas from his mouth; the Pitṛs from his chest; the human beings from his organ of generation and he created the Asuras from his buttocks.

86. Carrying on his creative activities during the night, the lord of the Devas created souls of human beings from the moonlight. He created the Pitṛs from the nectar.

87. After creating the *Mukhya* (prominent) and *Amukhya* (non-prominent) Devas and Asuras, he created from his mind the human beings and the great Pitṛs who were like their own fathers.

88. He created the lightning, the thunder and the clouds, the red coloured rainbows, the Ṛks, the Yajus Mantras and the Sāman songs for the fulfilment of the Yajñas.

89. The living beings, high and low, were born of his splendour. The creation of subjects by Brahmā comprises of the Devas, the sages the Pitṛs and the human beings.

90. Again he creates living beings, the mobile and the immobile ones, the Yakṣas, the Piśācas, the Gandharvas and all the Apsaras, all round.

91. He created men, Kinnaras, Rākṣasas, the birds, the animals, the deer and the serpents. He created the two types, the mobile and the immobile, as well as the *Vyaya* (perishable) and the *Avyaya* (Imperishable).

92-94. They attain those activities created formerly by the self-born lord. Though created again and again, they betake themselves to those alone (Viz. their own previous characteristics) such as violence and nonviolence, softness and cruelty, virtue and evil as well as what is done and what is not done.[1] They know the three (entities) are not separate, though born of them alone as separate (?). This is thus, and not thus; this is neither the pair (thus and non-thus) nor the

1. This is the inexorable Law of Karman. Even after Kalpānta, the Karma follows its doer immediately after the new creation of the world.

non-pair (of thus and non-thus).[1] People who cling to Sattva-guṇa and who view with equanimity say that Karman has itself as the object.

95-97. That great lord created these five by means of the word *Diva* (*Div*—to shine, the heaven that sparkles). He caused the extension of the created five elements by way of names (?).

The lord gave them names pertaining to the sages. He gave names to those creations among the Devas that are not born during the night. Thus for the reasons cited above, the creation of the worlds by the self-born lord was effected. The evolutes of the Prakṛti beginning with *Mahat* and ending with *Viśeṣa* (particularised creations) were thus evolved.

98-99. The cosmos has the lustre of the moon and the sun; it is embellished by planets and stars; it is equipped with thousands of rivers, seas and mountains. It consists of different kinds of beautiful cities and flourishing principalities and territories. In this forest of Brahmā, the unmanifest one, the omniscient Brahmā wanders.

100-103[2]. This grove of trees of Brahmā is born of the seed viz Avyakta or Prakṛti (the unmanifest one). It is stationed

---

1. This reminds us of the stance of Sañjaya-Belaṭṭhi-putta in *Sāmañña-phala-sutta* (para 32) of *Dīgha Nikāya* (p. 51 of the Nalanda Edt.)

2. VV.100-103 give an allegorical description of the universe or Saṁsāra as the forest tree of god Brahmā. The comparison with the tree and the universe is as follows.

The Tree	*The creation or Saṁsāra*
The Seed	*Avyakta* (*Prakṛti*)
Stem	*Buddhi* (Intellect)
Inner hollow	Sense-organs
Branches (*śākhā*) in the Bd.P. (but *aṅkura* or sprouts in Vā. P.) [*Prakāśa* in Bd.P. is probably a misprint for *Praśākha* in Vā.P.]	The Mahābhūtas (elements)
Leaves (*patra*)	*Viśeṣa* (sense objects or particular categories)
Flowers	Virtue (*dharma*) Evil (*a-dharma*)
Fruits	Pleasure and pain

under its blessing. It is full of stems and branches in the form of the intellect. The sense-organs are the inner hollows; the great Bhūtas (elements) are its luminaries;* it possesses leaves, in the form of the *Viśeṣas* (particularised categories) or the objects of senses), Virtue and Evil are its beautiful flowers; pleasure and misery are the fruits (of this tree); this eternal tree of Brahmā is the sustenance of all living beings. This forest of Brahmā is constituted by and belongs to the trees of Brahmā. The eternal, *Avyakta* (unmanifest one) of the nature of *Sat* and *Asat* is the cause thereof. Persons who think of the *Tattvas* (categories) call it Pradhāna, Prakṛti and Māyā.

104. Such is the Anugraha[1] creation. It is remembered as one with Brahmā as the cause. The three creations pertaining to Prakṛti are the creations of Brahmā without the background of consciousness or meditation.

105-106. The six creations beginning with Mukhya are the *Vaikṛtas* (pre-meditated ones) and they have been created with the background of consciousness.

They function by way of *Vaikalpa* (i.e. through excitement). They are identified with the Brahman (?)

Thus nine creations[2] are remembered including the *Prākṛtas* and *Vaikṛtas*. These are the creations originating through mutual contact. The reason thereof has been remembered by the wise or learned.

107. It is that *Acintyātman* (incomprehensible soul) who is the maker of all living beings. They (the learned) say that the Vedas are his head (?); the firmament is his navel; the sun and the moon are his eyes; the quarters are his ears, know that the earth constitutes his feet.

---

* The word *Prakāśa* is inapplicable to Bhūtas. The reading: *mahābhūta-praśākha* 'The tree has big branches in the form of Mahābhūtas' in the Vā.P. is better.

1. This is called *Anugraha* creation as it is caused or created through the favour of *Avyakta* or *Prakṛti* as noted in V.100 above (*tasya=avyaktasya anugrahe sthitaḥ*)

2. As noted above three are *Prākṛta* sargas and six are *Vaikṛta ones*. This makes the total of nine creations.

108. It is from his mouth (face) that the Brāhmaṇas were born. From the front part of his chest the Kṣatriyas were born. It is from his thighs that the Vaiśyas were born and the Śūdras from his feet. All the castes were born of his limbs.[1]

109. Nārāyaṇa is greater than and beyond the *Avyakta* (the unmanifest one); the cosmic egg is termed *Avyakta*, god Brahmā himself is born of the cosmic egg; the worlds have been created by him.

110. *After staying there for ten Kalpas they go again to the (world of) Satya. (Those who reach) the world of Brahmā attain the goal from which they never return.

111. With the exception of overlordship, they are on a par with him in regard to *Aiśvarya* (prosperity, power to control etc.) They become equal to Brahmā as far as form and object are concerned.

112. There they stay endowed with pleasure and accompanied by themselves (and their possessions). On account of the inevitability of the matter, it (he) expands the Prākṛta (creation) himself.

113-114. Then, purified on that occasion, they are to be directly connected with the diversity. Just as, while one is asleep the faculty of understanding functions without intellectual consciousness. So also their knowledge functions when purified on that occasion, through the withholding of differences, but not so in the case of Śuṣmins (?) (lustrous or powerful ones).

115-116. The causal relations between cause and effects function alongwith them in regard to the residents of the world of Brahmā, who see the diversity; whose aberrations had receded and who stand by their own duties. They are Siddhas of similar (equal) characteristics, of splendid souls and are free from sullied state.

117-118. As an effect of Prakṛti, they possess sense-organs and organs of action. They are well arranged in their own souls. After establishing the soul, the Prakṛti, that appears

1. An echo from the Puruṣa Sūkta (ṚV.X.90)

* Obviously some lines are missing from the text.

in multifarious forms, and that seems to be different from Puruṣa, does not function. Thereupon begins to function the creation of those things of the nature of existing cause.

119. The contact of the *Yuktas* (sages of Yogic practice), the seers of reality should be known as *Prakṛti*. It is the cause of their Apavarga (salvation) of those persons who go on a never to return journey of those who are not reborn.

120-122. Due to *Abhāva* (Absence of rebirth) they go once again to Satya-Loka as though the flames have subsided. Thereupon, when those persons of joyous souls have gone above the three worlds, they by whom the Mahar-Loka was not reached, go along with them. When the *Kalpadāha* (the burning of the universe at the end of the Kalpa) is imminent their disciples stay here.

They are the Gandharvas and others, the Piśācas, the human beings, the Brāhmaṇas and others, the animals and the birds and the immobile beings alongwith the reptiles.

123. While on that occasion the residents of the surface of the earth are staying there,[1] the thousand rays of the sun perish (?). They become seven rays and each one of these rays becomes a sun. Gradually they assume a hundred times increased magnitude and burn the three worlds.

124-125. They burn the mobile and the immobile beings, the rivers and all the mountains : they had already been dry due to drought and absence of rain. Now they are heated by those rays. Then they are completely burnt by the sun's rays and they become helpless. These mobile and immobile beings, as well as Dharma and Adharma etc. become completely burnt by the sun's rays.

126-129a. With their bodies burnt and with their sins completely washed off at the end of the Yuga, they become well known (?). They are freed of their distress. (They are blessed) by the auspicious (stage of boundlessness). Then, after the night of Brahmā, born of the unmanifest one, has dawned, those people become joined with the people of similar forms

1. Description of the end of a Kalpa.

and in the subsequent creation they become the mental progeny of Brahmā.

129b-132. Thereafter, when the people living in the three worlds have become merged with the people, when all the worlds have been completely burned by the seven suns, when the earth is flooded by the rain, both in the secluded places and in the seas, the oceans, the clouds, the waters of the earth proceed ahead flowing fast like arrows. They are as though mountains called by the name *Salila* (water); when much water came on like this and covered this earth it became what is called *Arṇava* (sea).

133-135. (Defective text). (Water is called *Ambhas*, why is it so ?) Since it shines (*Ābhāti*) it is called *Ambhas*. The word *Bhā* is used in the sense of lustre and illumination.[1] The expanse of water has spread over everything and got into touch with all. It is known by its own lustre.

Since it stuffs the entire earth all round within itself and makes it extend, it is called *Apatanu*.[2] The root Tanoti means to extend. The waters are therefore called *Apatanu*.

The word *Śāra* indicates that which is *Śīrṇa* (shattered). It is a root having various meanings. In that vast expanse of water, the waters are not shattered. Hence they are called *Nāras*.[3]

136-138. In the waters, at the end of a thousand Yugas, when the day of Brahmā comes to a close, when it is his night of the same duration within the waters, when within the waters the earth has lost all its fires; when it is darkness all round with not even a glimmer of light, when the wind has, subsided—the lord Brahmā by whom the portion of the world is presided over desired once again to make the division of this world.

139-141. In that vast expanse of water, where the mobile and the immobile beings had perished, Brahmā lay down, Brahmā of thousand eyes, thousand legs and thousand

---

1. Bd.P. interestingly traces *ambhas* 'water' to *bhā*—'to shine.' It is merely a popular etymology.
2. MW. does not give a word like *Apatanu* or *Upatanu*.
3. *Nara na+śīrṇa*=waters, is beyond linguistics.

heads, the Puruṣa of golden colour, Brahmā named Nārāyaṇa who was beyond the ken of the sense organs lay asleep.

He became awakened due to the emergence of Sattva. He woke up and surveyed the cosmos that was a void. With the narration of this, the first Pāda (section) of the Purāṇa has been related.

SECTION TWO
ANUṢAṄGA-PĀDA

CHAPTER SIX

The Kalpas and Manvantaras[1]
Their Duration

Sūta said :

1. On hearing the first Pāda (section) the main theme of which is the Prakṛti, thus recounted, Kāpeya (Kāśyapeya in Vā.P.) who was delighted had some doubts.

2-3. After propitiating the Sūta by means of words (and desirous of hearing) another story for that purpose, (he said) — "Hereafter O Sage conversant with the Kalpa, recount Pratisandhi to me. I wish to know this, viz. : the interim period between the two Kalpas i.e. the Kalpa that has passed and the Kalpa that is current. I wish to know the Pratisandhi (the period of transit) between these two. Indeed, you are sufficiently well-versed."

4. On being thus requested by Kāpeya, Sūta, the most excellent among eloquent men, began to narrate the origin of the three worlds entirely.

Sūta said :

5. Now I shall describe factually, O men of holy vows, the Kalpa of the past and the Kalpa of the future and the period of transit that is between these two.

6. (I shall also describe) O men of holy rites, the different Manvantaras in the Kalpas. The Kalpa that is current now is Varāha—an auspicious Kalpa.

1. Description of Manvantaras is one of the main characteristics of a Purāṇa. We have a description of these Manvantaras in Bh.P. VIII.1.1-29. KP.I.51, NP.I.40-17-37, VP.III. 1.1 9 and others. But this chapter like Vā.P. 7 describes the Kalpas and the interim period joining the Kalpas. A number of verses are common to Vā.P.7 and this chapter.

7. Understand the intervening transitional stage between this Kalpa and the old (ancient) Kalpa that preceded this and passed away.

8. When the previous Kalpa recedes without a *Prati-sandhi* (intermediate period), another Kalpa begins again with Janaloka and others.

9. Two (consecutive) Kalpas have a transitional stage separating them mutually. All beings are completely annihilated at the end of a Kalpa.

10a. The Period intervening between the end of that Kalpa is called* *Pratisandhi.*[1]

10b-11. In a Manvantara, the junctions of those periods of time called Yugas are unbroken. The Manvantaras function with interconnections of the Yugas. The previous Kalpas have been recounted briefly (?) in the Prakriyā-pāda.

12-14. Each Kalpa has a *Pūrva-Ardha* (former half) and *Para-Ardha* (latter half). Therefore, when a Kalpa passes by, its latter half is followed by the former half of the next Kalpa. The other Kalpas also will follow suit with their latter halves increased(?). O Brāhmaṇas, the Kalpa that is present now is the first among them. It has a *Pūrva-Ardha* and a *Para-Ardha.* The second one is called Para. This is the period of sustenance. It is remembered that the period of dissolution is thereafter.

15. Prior to this Kalpa was the ancient Kalpa that had passed by at the end of a thousand sets of four Yugas along-with the Manvantaras.

16-18. When the Kalpa comes to a close and the time of universal burning arrives (?), the Devas moving about in the aerial chariots, the stars, planets and the constellations, the moon, the sun etc.—all these meritorious souls were twenty-eight crores in number. Their number in all the fourteen

* The reading: *na vidyate* 'The *Pratisandhi* does not exist between the past and the present Kalpa' is obviously wrong. Hence the reading of Vā.P. 7.9 (=this verse in Bd.P.) is accepted.

1. This is the definition of *Prati-sandhi.* In Manvantaras, the yuga period connecting two manvantaras is unbroken but at the end of the Kalpa, the universe gets destroyed as described in VV.16 ff below.

Manvantaras is the same. Therefore their total number in all the Manvantaras together was (14 × 28 =) 392 crores.

19. Further, in everyone of the Kalpas, the Devas moving about in aerial chariots are remembered to be seventy thousand more.

20. In the fourteen Manvantaras there were the Devas, the Pitṛs and the sages imbibing nectar (Amṛtapās) in the firmament and heaven.

21. They had their servants (followers), wives and sons. At that time, the Devas in the firmament were beyond the discipline of the *Varṇas* (castes) and the *Āśramas* (stages in life).

22. Thereafter, when the annihilation of all living beings along with objects approached, all of them became persons of equal position and condition with those that had attained *Sāyujya* (the salvation of merging with the divinity).

23-25. Thereafter, due to the inevitability of the recurrence of the intellect* of the soul (?) the Devas, the residents of the three worlds, become persons identifying with and taking pride in the different positions here.

When the time of sustenance was complete, when the *Paścimottara* (the latter and later period) was imminent, when the annihilation arrived, the enthusiasic Devas in the last days of the Kalpa, partially abandoned their abodes.[1] Thereafter, they became excited and directed their minds towards the Maharloka.

26. (Defective text). They practise Yoga and make use of the great (thing) in the body** (?) All of them abound in purity. They have achieved the mental Siddhi (achievement).

27. The Mahar-loka was attained by Brāhmaṇas, Kṣattriyas, Vaiśyas and other people born of them, alongwith those residents of Kalpa.

---

* Vā.P.8.23 (=Bd.P. present verse) reads *buddhvā* 'Having understood the inevitability.'

1. VV.24-31 describe the progress of gods upto Satya-loka, the region of god Brahmā.

** The first line in the corresponding Vā.P. verse (8.26) reads: *te yuktā upapadyante mahasi-sthaiḥ Śarīrikaiḥ'* /

with their bodies stationed in *mahas* (*Maharloka*) they practise etc.

28. After going to Maharloka, the fourteen groups of the Devas become agitated. Thereafter, they directed their mind towards Janaloka.

29. In this order the residents of the Kalpa mutually(?) proceeded for thousands of Yugas according to the reckoning of the Devas.

30. All of them abounded in purity. They have achieved the mental Siddhi (achievement of spiritual powers), the Jana (Loka) was attained by those residents of Kalpa together.

31. After staying there for ten Kalpas, they go to the Satya (Loka) once again. After going to the world of Brahmā, they attain a goal from where there is no return.

32. Except the overlordship, they become equal to Brahmā.[1] They are equal to Brahmā in regard to features and object (of the sense organs) (i.e. Viṣaya).

33. There they stay with pleasure in the Saṁyamas* (? worlds of that name). After attaining bliss from Brahman, they become liberated along with Brahmā.

34. In view of the inevitability of affairs concerning (the course of) Prakṛti, they remain (bound along) with honour, worship etc. as is produced at the same time.**

35. Just as in the case of a sleeping person the faculty of knowledge functions without (clearcut) perceptions (*Abuddhi-pūrvam*), so also when they are purified and rendered service, the bliss begins to function.

36. (The bliss begins to function) by the withholdings of differences. These are different in regard to lustrous ones. Along with them their effects and instruments (sense organs) also develop.

37-38. Of those residents of Brahmā's region who observe multiplicity (and separateness) and whose authority has been

---

1. Cf. *Brahma-sūtra* IV.4.17-18 where the released soul is stated to have all the Lordly powers except the power of creation of the universe. The powers of the released soul are not unlimited.

* Vā.P.8.33b reads: *Prasaṁgamāt*—'due to their close contact (with Brahmā)'.

** They remain (bound) in their separateness produced (retained) at that time.

withdrawn and who abide by their righteous duties. Those Siddhis have similar characteristics. They are of pure souls and are unsullied. In their Prākṛta form they are equipped with sense organs but they are stabilised in their own souls.

39. After proclaiming itself (or the soul), the Prakṛti is factually observed as different from Puruṣa and as multifarious and as such it functions.

40. Again when the creation begins to function, Prakṛti should be known in its connection with the liberated (?) souls who perceive reality and who are identical with the existent causes.

41. There, those persons attaining salvation do not return by the same path (of Saṁsāra). There non-existence had been caused once again like that of the blazing flames that had been extinguished.[1]

42. While those noble souls had gone far above the three worlds along with these, the Maharloka is not occupied by them.

43. When the burning of Kalpa is imminent, the Gandharvas and others, the Piśācas (vampires), the Brāhmaṇas and other human beings become their disciples.*

44-45. (So also) the animals and birds, the immobile beings and the reptiles. While those residents of the surface of the earth stand there at that time, the thousand rays that manifest themselves become (combined and concentrated into) seven rays and each one of the rays becomes a Sun.[2]

46-48. Rising up gradually, they burn the three worlds. The mobile and the immobile beings, the rivers and all the mountains that had already been dried up due to absence of rain are inflamed and afflicted by the suns. Completely

1. Cf. the concept of *Brahma-nirvāṇa* in the BG. VV.24-26.

* *Śiṣyāḥ* in Bd.P. is probably a misprint for *Śiṣṭāḥ* 'remaining ones' (found in Vā.P. in corres. verse 8.43b).As this is description of the Kalpānta, *Śiṣṭa* is a better reading.

2. VV. 43-60. This description of the Kalpa-dāha and the end of the universe is a verbatim repetition of VV.121-138 of the last chapter. The popular etymologies of *ambhas, salila, Nara* or *Nāra* all meaning 'water' and the derivation of Nārāyaṇa have been noted there.

burnt by the rays of the suns, they become helpless. The mobile and the immobile beings of the nature of virtue as well as evil get their bodies burned. In the interval between the two Yugas, they get rid of their sins.

49. They are well known* and freed from the sunshine by the auspicious (rain) that has great continuity showering incessantly. Thereafter, those people are joined with other people of similar forms and features.

50. After staying there during the night of Brahmā born of the unmanifest one, they become the mental sons of Brahmā at the time of subsequent creation.

51-56. Then, when the residents of the three worlds had become proper**(?) (or equipped) with people, when the worlds had been completely burned down by the seven suns, when the earth had been flooded with rain, when the seas had become desolate, all the waters of the oceans, clouds and the earth move ahead scattered (like arrows). They have the name *Salila*. They followed (one after the other). That flood of water gathered together in abundance. When that vast sheet of water covered the earth, it became known by the name *Arṇava* (sea). This water is called *Ambhas* because it shone and spread. The water reached everywhere. The root √*Bhā* has the sense of *Vyāpti* (spreading) and *Dīpti* (shining).

Since it spread over the entire earth all round within itself, water is remembered as *Tanus*. The root √*Tan* is used in the sense of extension. The root √*Śar* i.e. *Śṛ* has different meanings. It means "to become shattered or scattered".

57-62. In the vast sheet of water, the waters are not quick in motion (*śīghrāḥ*) therefore, they are called *Nāras*. At the end of the thousand Yugas, when the day of Brahmā had come to a close, when the night of so much (=the same) duration had been present within the watery expanse, when the

---

* *Yonyā tayā hyanirmuktāḥ* 'freed from that species' in Vā.P.7.49 is a better reading.

** *apravṛtteṣu* (Vā.P.7.52a) 'when all the people, residents of the three worlds are extinct'. This reading is more suitable in the context than *upapanneṣu* of the Bd.P. here.

surface of the earth had become lost within that water, when all fires were extinguished, when the wind had become totally calm and motionless, when there had been darkness all round without any light, this (universe) had been presided over by this person. He is Brahmā, the lord. He wished again to divide this world. In that vast sheet of water where the mobile and the immobile beings have perished, Brahmā becomes a person with thousand (i.e. innumerable) eyes, thousand feet, thousand heads one who has conquered all the sense-organs and one with golden complexion.

They cite this verse regarding Nārāyaṇa in this connection.

"The waters are Nāras. We have heard that they constitute his bodies. They are being filled in. Since he stays therein, he is remembered as Nārāyaṇa.

63. The first Prajāpati (lord of subjects) is a person of good mind.[1] He has a thousand heads, a thousand feet, a thousand eyes, a thousand faces (mouths) and a thousand arms. He performs a thousand acts. He is explained as a person identical with the three Vedas.

64. He has the lustre and colour of the sun. He is the protector of the universe. He is single. He is the first *Virāṭ* (cosmic personage). He is Hiraṇyagarbha of noble soul. He is beyond the Ken of mind.

65. In the beginning of the Kalpa, the Lord abounds in *Rajas* quality and after becoming Brahmā, he brought about the creation of the world. In the end of the Kalpa, he abounds in Tamas, and after becoming Kāla, he devoured it again.

66. It is reported that in the cosmic ocean, Nārāyaṇa with the preponderance of *Sattva guṇa* divides himself threefold and abides in the three worlds.

67-68. By means of the three (qualities or forms), he creates, devours and sees or protects (the world). In the vast

1. Cf. Puruṣa Sūkta (ṚV.X.90). The Vedic concept regarding *Virāj*, *Hiraṇya-garbha* here identified with Brahmā or Puruṣa of the Puruṣa-sūkta are the different stages in the evolution. That *Puruṣa* is credited with three *guṇas* for the creation, sustenance and destruction of the universe.

sheet of water, when the mobile and the immobile beings have perished, at the end of a thousand sets of four Yugas, when (the earth) is covered on all sides with water, Brahmā named Nārāyaṇa shines himself in the universe.

69. All the subjects of the four types (i.e. *Svedaja*, *Aṇḍaja*, *Udbhijja* and *Jarāyuja*) are covered with Tamas, due to the *Śakti* of Brahmā. In the Maharloka, the great sages see Kāla (God of death) sleeping.

70. At that time the great sages referred to above are Bhṛgu and others.[1] The great sages, when the Kalpa comes to a close, are the eight sages, Satya and others. The great thing that is surrounded by them when they revolve is the *Mahat** (?)

71. The root $\sqrt{}$*Rṣ* has the sense of *Gati* (movement). The above name (i.e. Ṛṣi) is derived from that root.[2] Since they move about with their Sattva and since they are great, they are called *Maharṣis* (Great sages).

72. The sleeping Kāla was then seen by those seven great sages, viz. Sattva (? Satya) and others who are stationed in the Maharloka in the previous Kalpa.

73. Thus Brahmā (continues to function) in thousands of nights. The great sages who were brought by him then saw the sleeping Kāla.

74. Since, in the beginning of the Kalpa, Brahmā evolved fourteen assemblages (worlds) (?) of diverse forms, it is defined as Kalpa.[3]

75. He is the creator of all living beings again and again, in the beginnings of the Kalpas. The great lord is both *Vyakta* (manifest) and *Avyakta* (unmanifest). This entire universe is evolved by him.

---

1. The concept of *Saptarṣis* (seven sages) *ursa major* is astronomical in the Vedic period. Varāhamihira in *Bṛhat-saṁhitā* also treats them from astronomical point. In the Mbh. and the Purāṇas, their status as "mind-born sons" of Brahmā becomes prominent. But their survival after deluges as stated here, hints at their original astronomical aspect.

2. A correct etymology.

3. Definition of Kalpa; cf. Vā.p.7.77.

* This verse is obscure. The correspondence V. in Vā.P.8.83 reads:

76. Thus the inter-relation between two Kalpas has been recounted. The present has become the antecedent state in between the two.

77. Everything has been recounted briefly in the previous Kalpa in the manner as it was factually. Now I shall recount the current Kalpa. Understand the same.

CHAPTER SEVEN

Knowledge About the World

(Geographical divisions of the earth—Four Yugas and their duration—Geography of continents—continents, towns and villages—Flora and fauna—people—castes and stages in Life).

Sūta said :

1. He passed a period of time equal to a thousand Yugas as his night. At the end of the night, Brahmā creates the universe through the cause (potentiality) of creation.

2. At that time, in that vast expanse of water, Brahmā became wind and moved about (in that ocean) enveloped in darkness when the mobile and the immobile beings had (already) perished (and became non-existent).

3-4a. He flooded the surface of the earth all round with water. When the elements had been stationed in Satya* (truth) along with their divisions, he moved about like the glowworm during the nights in the rainy season.

4b-5a. He was moving about quickly as he pleased. thinking by means of his intellect, about the means of stabilization.

---

* Vā.P.8.3 *samantāt*—all round.

5b-8a. He was searching for the earth. He realized that the earth was within the water. After knowing that one of them was blind (?) the lord who was capable of lifting up the earth assumed the truthful form of a boar as remembered in the beginnings of the previous Kalpas. Then he entered the water. That lord of subjects wished to contact the earth covered with waters. He lifted up the earth and placed it again along with its child* (Reference to Naraka ?).

8b-9a. He deposited the waters of the oceans in the oceans and the waters of the rivers in the rivers separately. After levelling the earth he picked up and gathered the mountains.

9b-11. As the previous creation was being burned formerly by the Saṁvartaka fire, the mountains of that period had been melted by that fire. They were then scattered by the wind. Due to chillness, they became solidified. Wherever the (molten rocks) were spilt there arose a mountain. They are called *Acalas*[1] (not-moving or immobile) because their ridges were immovable. They are remembered as *Parvatas* because they had *Parvans* (or joints).

12-14. They are (called) *Giris* because they had been swallowed. They are *Śiloccaya* because they had moved about (*Ayana*).

Then, after lifting up the earth from within the waters, the lord created seven times seven subcontinents in its seven continents. After levelling the uneven grounds he created mountains all round by means of rocks.

There are only fortynine sub-continents in those continents.[2] As many mountains (i.e. 49) are situated at the borders of the sub-continents.

---

* Vā.P.8a reads: *apas tāsu tu vinyasan* 'He deposited the waters (over the surface of the earth'.

1. These verses give 'etymology' of the synonyms for a mountain. This Purāṇa is full of semantic etymologies i.e. etymologies based on the meaning of the word and not its form. Sometimes, they are grammatically (even as phonetic derivation) correct, but that is none of the concern of the Purāṇa-writer. Thus *acala* 'a mountain', *giri-gṛī*—is understandable but *ayanāt tu śiloccayaḥ* 'the mountains are called *śiloccaya* because of their movements' is phonetically not defensible.

2. Every continent has seven sub-continents. Thus the number of sub-continents becomes 7 x 7=49. Their list is described later in chs. 18 and 19.

15-20. In heaven* etc. they are enveloped in splendour naturally and not otherwise. The seven continents and oceans encircle one another. They are situated after surrounding one another naturally.

The four worlds are the *Bhū* and others. As before, Brahmā created the moon and the sun along with the planets as well as the immobile beings all round, as Brahmā created the Devas of this Kalpa, who were *Sthānins* (persons occupying the abodes). He created the following things as well):— the waters, the fire, the earth, the wind, the firmament, the heaven, the Dyaus (the ethereal world), the quarters, the oceans, the rivers, the mountains, the souls of medicinal herbs, the souls of trees and creepers, the units of time such as *Lavas, Kāṣṭhās, Kalās* and *Muhūrtas*, the twilight, the nights, the days; the halfmonths, the months, the *Ayanas* (transits, one in the six months), the years and the Yugas. He created the abodes and (the dwellers therein) who take pride in the abodes separately by laying claims to them.

21. After creating the souls for the abodes, he created the period of Yugas namely Kṛta, Tretā, Dvāpara and Tiṣya (i.e. Kali).

22. At the beginning of the Kalpa, he created the subjects at the outset. Those subjects of the previous Kalpa have been recounted to you by me.

23-24. In that Kalpa that was being dissolved (i.e. terminated), the subjects were burnt by the fire. Those that had not reached Tapo-loka and those that remained on the earth, return at the time of the subsequent creation for the sake of being visible.[1] Those subjects who stay there for being visible, do so for the sake of subsequent creation.

---

* Vā.P.8.15 reads—*sargādau sanniviṣṭās te* 'They (mountains) were assembled there at the beginning of creation'. This reading is better than that in the Bd.P. here as *Svarga* (Heaven) is not relevant in the context.

1. VV.23 ff. This is the inexorable law of Karma. There may be the dissolution of the universe at the end of a Kalpa, but the beings whose Karmas have not been exhausted (i.e. who have not attained Mokṣa) are reborn in the subsequent Kalpa. This idea has been emphatically repeated in this Purāṇa.

25. Being created, they exist for the sake of their progeny. They are regarded as having achieved the four Puruṣārthas viz. : Dharma, Artha, Kāma and Mokṣa.

26. The Devas, the Pitṛs and the human beings (are created) in order; thereafter, they equipped themselves with penance; they filled the abodes at the outset.

27. Indeed, those human beings become Brāhmaṇas and souls of spiritual achievement. Due to their Karman contaminated by the faults of hatred and too much of attachment* they went to heaven (?)

28. While returning in an embodied state, they are born in every Yuga. With the remnants of the fruits of their Karman, (they are born again and again) ; they are well known as *Tadātmakas* (? Identified with them).

29-30. The people bound by the advent of (a new) Kalpa are born from the Janaloka. That which is their cause in the waters is indicated by means of the Karman**(?). From the Janaloka, they are born through auspicious and inauspicious Karmans. They assume physical bodies of diverse forms, in the different species.

31. The subjects beginning with the Devas and ending with the immobile beings are born (influencing) themselves mutually. Their pure (or sanctified) Karmans usually predominated.

32. Therefore, they attained only those names and features (which they had before). Again and again they are born with names and forms in the (different) Kalpas.

33-34. Thereafter, is the creation of Brahmā who is desirous of creating the *Upasṛṣṭi* (subsidiary creation). Even as he was meditating on those subjects, since he was of truthful meditation, a thousand couples came out of his mouth. It is but natural that they were people of great brilliance with the Sattva quality predominant.

---

* For *āsaṅga-dveṣa-yuktena*, Vā.P.8 reads: *saṅgādveṣa-yuktena* '(acts) motivated by non-hatred.'

** For *apsu yaḥ kāraṇaṁ teṣām bodhayan karmaṇā tu saḥ* / Vā.P.8.30a reads:

āśayaḥ kāraṇaṁ tatra boddhavyaṁ karmaṇāṁ tu saḥ /

'Place of residence should be known as its cause' etc.

35. He created another thousand couples through his eyes. All of them had the Rajas quality predominant. They were *Śuṣmins* (lustrous ones) and Amarṣins (intolerant).

36. He created a thousand (couples) of *Asats* (not good ones) from his arms. Dominated as they were from Rajas and Tamas, they are remembered as *gṛha-śīla** (attached to houses).

37-38. The couples alone gave birth frequently till the end of their lives. *Kūṭakas* (? deceitful ones) and *Akūṭakas* (non-deceitful) are born (of those couples) who are mortals (about to die). Since after generating the family, they abandoned their bodies. Even since then there is the occurrence of copulation in this Kalpa.

39. In the Kṛta age,[1] it is by mental meditation that pure objects of senses such as *Śabda* (sound and others) each of which is of five characteristics (became available).

40. Thus with mental emotions, those subjects without progeny stay dear** (?) So also the families were born with which this universe was filled up.

41. They resort to rivers, lakes and oceans as well as to mountains. Then those subjects have very little pleasure in that war (?) but they move in it.***

42. They say that the earth with *Rasa* (juice, water,) is their food. Desirous of mental siddhis those subjects move about as they please.

43. In the Kṛtayuga, the subjects (human beings etc.) had equal length of life, happiness and beauty. In the first Yuga, at the beginning of the Kalpa, there was no Dharma and Adharma.

---

* *īhā-śīla* (indulging in desires) in Vā.P.7.39.

1. VV.39-57 give a rosy picture of the Kṛta Yuga.

** The corresponding verse viz. Vā.P.8.46a reads:

ityevaṁ mānasī pūrvam prāk-sṛṣṭir yā prajāpateḥ |

'in this way formerly the preliminary creation was mental (after that it was born of copulation. The whole world is filled with that).

*** *Yuddhe* in the text is strange; it should be *Yuge*. The corresponding verse in Vā.P. (8.47b) reads:

tadā nātyambu-śītoṣṇā yuge etc.

'They wandered (lived) in that Yuga when there was no excess of heat, cold or rain'.

44-45a. In every Yuga, they were born with their respective rights and authority. They say that the Kṛta yuga at the beginning, had four thousand years in accordance with the reckoning of the gods. The two periods of junction consisted of four hundred years.

45b-46a. There were thousands of subjects of great repute. They had no hindrance anywhere. There were no mutually clashing opposites. There was no *Krama* (one gradually succeeding another).

46b-47. Those subjeets had no regular abodes and resorts. They were residents of mountains and seas. They were immune from sorrow. (The quality called) *Sattva* was predominant in them. The subjects were exclusively happy. They always moved about as they pleased. They were always delighted in their minds.

48. There were neither animals nor birds. There were no reptiles then. There were no plants etc. There were no drunkards, mad and furious persons. This is the manner of Dharma.

49. For their sustenance, there were flowers and fruits alongwith bulbous roots. The time was entirely and exclusively pleasant; it was neither too hot nor too chill.

50. Whatever they desire is achieved everywhere and for ever. By their meditations, everything grows up from the nether worlds through the earth.

51. (The vegetation) caused strength and fineness of complexion unto them. It destroyed their sickness and old age, Those subjects had stable (everlasting) youth with their bodies not requiring purificatory rites.

52. In their case, even without copulation subjects (progeny) are born through mere mental conception. The birth and features are the same (in regard to everyone). They are on a par (with one another) and they are pleased and happy.

53. At that time, there is truthfulness, absence of greed, satisfaction, happiness and self-control. In regard to beauty, longevity, aesthetic accomplishments and other activities, all of them are devoid of any mutual difference.

54. The sustenance of the subjects was (*abuddhipūrvika*) without any conscious intellectual effort. Since the door is open* (i.e. there are facilities to auspicious and evil activities) there is lack of conscious effort.

55. At that time there was no systematic classification of castes and stages of life. There were no thieves. They used to deal with one another without any intimate desire or hatred.

56. In the Kṛta yuga, all the subjects are born with equal beauty, features and span of life. They are devoid of inferiority and superiority. Usually they are happy, they are free from sorrow.

57-58. They have neither gain nor loss; neither friends nor enemies; no likes or dislikes. Since they are devoid of desire, their sense-object functions mentally. They do not violently injure mutually nor do they favour one another then.

59. In the Kṛtayuga, knowledge is the greatest thing.[1] In the Tretā, it is said to be the institution of Yajña (sacrifice) (as the greatest thing). In the Dvāpara, war began to function; and in the Kaliyuga, it is stealth alone.

60. The Kṛta Yuga is characterised by Sattva quality; the Tretā Yuga by Rajas quality, the Dvāpara by (a mixture of) Rajas and Tamas qualities, while the Kali, (only) by Tamas quality. Thus the situation of the *Guṇas* in the Yugas should be known.

61-64a.[2] This is the time in the Kṛta Yuga. Understand (the period of) its junction. Four thousand (divine) years constitute the Kṛta Yuga. The parts of its junction are eight hundred years, according to divine reckoning. It comprises of four thousand human years. (?) Then, among them there are

---

* Vā.P.8.61a (a corresponding verse) reads:

....*kṛtayuge karmaṇoḥ* for *Kṛta-dvāre karmaṇaḥ* in the Bd.P. which is obscure: The verse means : "In the Kṛta Age, there was no inclination both to pious and impious deeds".

1. VV.59-60 give a comparative statement of the special features of four Yugas.

2. VV.61-71 describe the state in the period intervening between Kṛta and Tretā.

neither sudden clamour and outcry, nor contrarities (?). Then, when that Kṛta yuga along with the part of the junction has passed, the entire Yugadharma (Duty etc. characteristics of the Yuga) becomes reduced to a quarter.

64b-65. That is the time of junction of the Yuga, the *Sandhyā* (transitional period) of what has passed off. Thus when the *Sandhyādharma*(Duty characteristics of the transitional stage from Kṛta yuga) is reduced to a quarter (?) it vanishes within the Kṛtayuga without any vestige*.

66. When the junction has passed away, there was mental progeny. The achievement of spirituality was in another Yuga called Tretā, next to Kṛta.

67. The eight mental Siddhis that had been recounted (as existent) by me in the beginning of the creation, become reduced gradually.

68. In the beginning of the Kalpa, there is one single mental Siddhi, in the Kṛta Yuga, in all the Manvantaras in accordance with the division of the four Yugas.

69. The origin of *Karmasiddhi* (achievement of Karman) in Kṛta is brought about by the conduct of the people of different castes and stages of life (?). The *Sandhyā* (junction) of the Kṛta is reduced by a quarter (?)

70. These parts of the junctions of Kṛta take up the three (? other parts) and those *Yuga Dharmas* as well as penance, learning, strength and longevity decrease and decline.

71. When the Kṛta yuga and its transitional part have passed, O excellent sages, it is the beginning of Tretā yuga along with its parts.

72-73. When the part of Kṛta yuga has passed off and those seven (? siddhis) remained lingering at the beginning of the Tretā yuga that had begun to function in the early part of the Kalpa, the (one remaining) Siddhi perishes due to efflux of time and not otherwise; when that Siddhi disappeared another Siddhi was born.

---

* The corresponding verse Vā.P.70b-71a:

"When at the end of the yuga, when even the transitional period also expires, the quarter of the *dharma* characteristic of this transitional period of the yuga, remains."

74. (Defective) Parts of waters returned (to the firmament) in the form of clouds. From the thundering clouds the showering of rain began to function.

75. When the surface of the earth had been perfected (watered) by that rain occurring only once the subjects came into being. Thereupon, the trees became designated as their abodes.

76. All kinds of worldly enjoyment of those subjects emanated from them (the trees). In the beginning of the Tretā yuga, the subjects maintained themselves with them.

77. (Defective) then, after the lapse of a great deal of time, due to their own change, they had a sudden emotion in the form of a great desire for close contact.

78. In the case of women (of the modern days) menstruation occurs till the end of their life (?) But then (i.e. in the Tretā yuga), that did not take place on account of the power of the Yuga.

79. But in the case of those women (of later days), the menstrual flow began to function month by month. As a consequence thereof, sexual intercourse also takes place then.

80-81. They had the physical contact every month because of their emotional feelings at that time. When there is no menstrual flow at the proper time, the conception took place. On account of their contrary nature (?), all those trees designated as their abodes and evolved at that time, perish thereafter.

82. When they had perished, the subjects became bewildered and agitated in all their sense-organs. They began to meditate on their Siddhi. They were truthful in their meditation then.

83-84. Those trees designated as their abodes appeared in front of them. They yielded clothes, fruits and ornaments. Similarly, honey of great potency of metaphysical* significance was produced in every leafy cup. It was accompanied by the juice of the Gandharvas(?).** [*Gandharvāṇām rasānvitam* in Bd.P. It should be *Gandha-varṇa-rasānvitam.*]

---

* *ānvikṣikam* in Bd.P. should be *amākṣikam* ('with no flies in it).

** The verse contains misprints. The original verse seems to be as in Vā.P.8.90:

85. Those subjects maintained themselves with that at the beginning of Tretā yuga. With that Siddhi they became hale, hearty and well-nourished. They were free from feverish ailments.

86. Thereafter, on other occasions also, the subjects became overwhelmed by greed thus, once again. They seized the trees and took by force the nectar and honey.

87. On account of this misdemeanour on their part brought about by their covetousness, the Kalpa trees (wish-yielding trees) perished here and there along with the Lord *(?)

88. When that achievement (*Siddhi*) was reduced to a very little quantity with the passage of time, they maintained themselves with this. Their Dvandvas (rivalries or mutual opposites) rose up tremendously.

89. The chillness, the wind and the sunshine were severe. Therefore they were much tormented. Being afflicted by the mutually opposed pairs of feelings and reactions, they bewailed their wounds** (?)

90-93. (Defective) they had been vexed in their minds when formerly they had no abodes. They were wandering about as they pleased. After building houses to remedy the (evil effects of) *Dvandvas* (like heat and cold), they stayed in the abodes as they pleased as they could secure. (When they had no abodes) they resorted to difficult passages in mountains and on rivers(?) dripping with honey***, in plains and even in (hilly) regions where water was available. They lived as they pleased and as much as they could enjoy. They began to build those abodes in order to ward off cold (blizzards) and hot (winds). Thereafter, they built hamlets and cities.

Teṣveva jāyate tāsāṁ gandha-varṇa-rasānvitam /
amākṣikam mahāvīryam puṭake puṭake madhu //

The honey was endowed with good flavour, colour and taste and had no flies in it.

* Vā.P. 8.93b *madhunā* 'along with the honey'.

** Vā.P.8.95 *cakrur āvaraṇāni ca* 'created shelters and covers.'

*** *madhu-dhunvatsu* in the text is absurd in the context. Vā.P.8.97 (a corresponding verse) appropriately reads: *marudhanvasu*—'in sandy deserts and wildernesses'.

94-95. They built villages and cities with their due shares, extent and dimensions and built other settlements as well, in accordance with their knowledge. After measuring with their own fingers (in the beginning), they made thereafter other units also for the sake of measurement.[1]

96-100. (Defective) with *Aṅgulas* (finger-width) as the basis they made the units, *Pradeśa*, *Hasta*, *Kiṣku* and *Dhanus*. Ten joints of the fingers (Aṅgulas) constitute what is called *Pradeśa*. The space delimited by the tips of the extended thumb and index finger is called *Pradeśa*. The same with (the tip of the extended) middle finger is remembered as *Tāla*. The same with (the tip of the extended) ring finger is *Gokarṇa*. The same with (the tip of the extended) small finger is called *Vitasti*. It has twelve *Aṅgulas*.

Twentyone *Aṅgulas* make the unit *Ratni*. Twentyfour *Aṅgulas* make one *Hasta*. Two *Ratnis* or fortytwo *Aṅgulas* make a *Kiṣku*. Four *Hastas* make one *Dhanus* or (?) *Daṇḍa*. The same is a pair of arrows (Nālikās). Two thousand *Dhanus* make one *Gavyūti*. This had been made by them then.

101. Eight thousand *Dhanus* make one *Yojana* as determined by them. With this *Yojana* (as the unit of measurement) settlements (i.e. colonies) were made thereafter.

102. Among the four (types of) fortresses, three are natural and the fourth (type of) fort is artificial. I shall mention its decisive features.

103. It has a thick elevated rampart (esp. a surrounding wall elevated on a mound of earth) with cavities (or openings).

---

1. VV. 96-101 give the units of measurements of distance as follows. Aṅgula = Finger-breadth.

10 Aṅgula	=	Pradeśa
12 Aṅgulas	=	Vitasti
21 Aṅgulas	=	Ratni
24 Aṅgulas	=	Hasta
2 Ratnis or		
42 Aṅgulas	=	Kikṣu
4 Hastas	=	Dhanus or Daṇḍa (?)
2000 Dhanus	=	Gavyūti
7000 Dhanus	=	Yojana

It is surrounded with a moat on all sides. It has a beautiful front-door and a gynaeceum in which girls are kept.

104. (Defective text)* The moats two Hastas in breadth are excellent in the case of the Kumārīpura. The total breadth of the current of water in (the moat) may be eight, nine or ten (?).

105-106. (I shall mention)[1] the girth and length of hamlets, cities, and villages entirely as well as those of the three types of (natural) forts viz. mountains, waters (i.e. rivers) and waste-lands such as deserts etc., and the artificial forts as well. The diameter shall be half a Yojana. Its length shall be one and one eighth Yojanas.

107. The extent of a Pura (city) shall be half of the maximum length (?). There must be a river(?) flowing to its east or north. It should be divided into a hypotenum and segments. It must be laid out in the shape of a spread fan.

108. A city that is long, diamond-shaped or circular is not praiseworthy. A city endowed with the symmetrical parts and quadrangles and heaven-like, commendable was made by them.

109. The *Vāstu* (site of a building; dwelling place) that is not more than twenty four *Hastas* is short; that of one hundred and eight (*Hastas*) is great. In this matter they praise the middle one and the short one which has no (wooden structure).

110. The chief settlement should be eight hundred *Kiṣkus*. The hamlet should be of half the diameter of the city. The Pāna** (? Drinking place) shall be above it(?).

111. The hamlet shall be a Yojana (about 12 km) from the city and the village shall be half a Yojana from the hamlet. The outermost boundary shall be two Krośas (1 Krośa = 3 kms). The boundary of a field is four *Dhanus*.

---

* The corresponding verse in Vā.P.8.110 runs as follows:

srotasī saṁhata-dvāraṁ nikhātam punar eva ca |
hastāṣṭau ca daśa śreṣṭhā navāṣṭau vā'pare matāḥ ||

Different opinions about the breadth of the moat in front of Kumāripura are given here as 2, 8, 9, 10 *hastas*, the last being the best.

1. VV.105-116 delineate the ancient ideas of town (and village) planning.

** Vā.P.7.116b (in the corresponding verse) reads : *grāmaṁ* for *Pānaṁ* of the Bd.P. It means: a *grāma* should be beyond that'.

112. The pathway along the quarters (i.e. East-west and North-south) was made twenty *Dhanus* wide by them. The road in the village was also twenty *Dhanus* (wide). The path in the boundary was only ten *Dhanus* (wide).

113. The glorious royal road was made ten *Dhanus* wide. The movement of (traffic of) men, horses, chariots and elephants (shall be) without any hindrance.

114. The branch-streets were measured by them (and made) four Dhanus (wide). The roads joining the high-ways shall be three Dhanus (wide) and their branches two Dhanus wide.

115. (Defective text) The *Jaṅghāpatha** (? the thigh-road) has four Pādas width; the passage between rows of houses is three quarters (wide). *Dhṛtimārga*** (? path of courage) if more than one sixth. The *Padika* (Foot-Path ?) is remembered thus in due order.

116. The enclosure for excrement is a quarter all round. After those places have been made, the houses and dwellings (should be constructed).

117. They thought over it again and again about the trees designated as their houses as to how they were before, and began to build like them.[1]

118. The branches of trees have gone down. Others have gone this way. Still others have gone up. In the same way, some have gone obliquely.

119. With their intellect, they have observed carefully how the branches have gone. Apartments were constructed by them in the same way. Hence they (the apartments) are remembered as *Śālās*.

120. Thus *Śālās* (apartments, dwellings) became well-known from the branches. So also the abodes. Therefore they are remembered as *Śālās*. That is remembered as their *Śālātva*[2] (state of being a Śālā).

******jaṅghā-patha*** is probably a 'misprint' for "ghaṇṭā-patha" 'a bell-road' i.e. the chief road through a village or a highway. *Pada*=15 fingers' breadth.**

**** *Vṛtti-mārga* in Vā.P.8.121.**

1. VV.117-121 refer to construction of buildings. It is interesting to note that the *Śāla* tree played an important part in ancient ideas of housing.

2. Popular but important etymology of *Śālā* 'an apartment or dwelling'.

121. Since people are delighted therein (*Prasidanti*), they are designated as *Prāsādas* (palaces). Therefore, the abodes, apartments and palaces are designated as Prāsādas.[1]

122. When the wish-yielding Kalpa trees perished along with the honey, (the subjects) attached by the *Dvandvas* (mutual opposed pairs of feelings etc.) began to think about the means of agriculture and other occupations for livelihood.

123. The subjects created were seen agitated due to exhaustion and sorrow. Thereafter, the Siddhi appeared in front of them in the Tretā yuga.

124. Another (type of) rain became the means of achieving all objects for them. The waters of the rain were sweet and were as much as they wished for.

125-126. Thus a (new) way of life and conduct began to function during the creation of the second type of rain. Due to the contact of the earth with the small collections of water that gathered together on the surface of the earth, the medicinal herbs began to grow. Those medicinal herbs began to put forth blossoms, roots and fruits.

127. The fourteen (types of lands in) villages and forests (began to flourish) without being ploughed and without the seeds being sown. The trees and the bushes put forth flowers and fruits at the proper seasons.

128. In the Tretā yuga, medicinal herbs and plants began to appear themselves on the earth. In the beginning of the Tretā yuga, the subjects sustained themselves with those plants and herbs.[2]

129. Thereafter, due to the inevitability of affairs and due to the Tretā yuga those subjects began to have passion and covetousness for ever.

130. Then, they forcibly seized rivers, fields, mountains, trees, bushes and medicinal herbs as much as they could (in accordance with their strength).

---

1. Etymology of *Prāsāda* 'a palace'.

2. VV 128ff show the prevalence of food-gathering economy in the Tretā yuga. The evolution of four Varṇas is another sociological feature of this Yuga.

131-132. Previously I have already explained to you about the spiritually enlightened souls in the Kṛtayuga. They were born as mental sons of Brahmā and they had come here (to the earth) from the Janaloka. They were quiescent lustrous *Karmins* (devoted to the pursuit of holy rites) and (unhappy and dejected). Returning from there (i.e. Janaloka), they were born again in the Tretā yuga.

133. In the previous births, due to the glory of their auspiciousness (i.e. meritorious acts) as well as sins they were conceived as Brāhmaṇas, Kṣatriyas, Vaiśyas, Śūdras and malicious people.

134-135. Then (among them some became) powerful, truthful in conduct, non-violent, devoid of greed and persons who had conquered their selves. They used to abide by those that were remembered* (? Smṛti texts ?). They never accepted charity. Their tasks were carried out by those who were weaker than they. They (these weaker people) approached them speaking to them (?)

136-137. Those others who were less brilliant than they, remained serving them. Thus when they were mutually related and also resorted to each other, due to that fault the medicinal herbs diminished much then. Like sands they perished on being held in the fists.

138-139. Then due to the power of the Yuga, the fourteen (types of people, animals etc.) villages and forests began to pluck (and destroy) the flowers, fruits and roots (of those trees). Then, when they perished the subjects became perplexed. All of them were overwhelmed with hunger; then they went to the self-born (deity i.e. Brahmā).

140-141. In the beginning of Tretā yuga, those subjects desired for some means of livelihood. The self-born lord Brahmā knew their desire. He pondered over this (situation) by means of his vision that can see everything directly. He understood, that the medicinal herbs have been devoured (i.e. drawn within) by the earth. He made them grow once again.

---

* Vā.P.8.141 reads: *sma teṣu vai* for Bd.P. text here: *smṛteṣu vai*. As the question of memory or *smṛti* text does not arise here Vā.P. reading is better,

142. After making the Sumeru mountain (as) the calf, he milked this earth in the form of a cow that yielded seeds on the surface of the earth in the form of the milk.[1]

143. The lord made those seeds grow as the medicinal herbs (and other plants) that ended when the fruits became ripe. (That is, the plants yielded fruits but once and then they perished) they are the group of seventeen.

144-145. The following types of seventeen grains and pulses constitute the group of seventeen, viz., Rice, barley, wheat, Bengal-gram, gingelly *Priyaṅgu* (Long pepper), *Udāra* (?), *Koraduṣṭa* (a kind of grain eaten by the poor people i.e. *Kodrava*), *Vāmaka* (?), the black gram, the green gram, the *Masūra* (*dāl*), *Nīvāra* (rice), the horse-gram. the Harika* (?) and the Caraka*(?).

146a. Thus these were remembered as the species of rural medicinal herbs (*Grāmya-Oṣadhi*).

146b-147. *Śyāmāka* (a variety of rice), *Nīvāra* (another variety of rice), *Jartila* (wild sesamum), *Gavedhuka* (?) *Kuruvinda* (a king of barley), *Veṇuyava* (*Bamboo seeds*, Tāmātīrkāṭaka(?) ** etc. are remembered as the fourteen types of medicinal herbs of the villages and forests.

148. All these fourteen varieties (of medicinal herbs and plants) peculiar to villages and forests grew at the beginning of the first Tretā yuga. They are not grown by ploughing.

149. The trees, hedges, creepers, winding plants, spreading creepers and (various) species of grasses yielded roots, fruits,*** shoots etc. unto them. They plucked their fruits.

---

1. This is the Puranic presentation of the ancient Vedic concept of milking the Virāj cow recorded in AV.VIII. Sūkta 10. Purāṇa-writers used this motif later with god Brahmā, king Pṛthu etc. as the milker. Funnily enough Mt.P. 10.25 makes Vararuci as the milker and the science of Dramaturgy (Nāṭya-Veda) as the milk.

Here god Brahmā milked seeds of medicinal herbs and plants. Men gathered food from them for their livelihood.

* Vā.P.8.152a reads :

'āḍhakyaś caṇakaś caiva' which means:

'The pulse *cajanus Indicus spreng* as well as chick Peas.

** a misprint for tathā markaṭāś ca ye). Cf. Vā.P.8.154 as MW. gives no word like tāmātirkāṭaka. *markaṭaka* is a species of grain.

*** Vā.P.8.149 reads: *puṣpaiḥ* for *puṣṭāḥ*.

150. Those seeds which were milked out of the earth formerly by the self-born lord, began to grow as medicinal herbs putting forth flowers and fruits at the proper seasons.

151. When the medicinal herbs created before did not grow and flourish again, he made means of livelihood for them by means of agricultural occupations.[1]

152. The self-born lord (blessed them) with the power of working with their own hands and achieving great results. Thenceforth, the medicinal herbs became *Kṛṣṭapacyas* (ploughed and grown).

153. After achieving his purpose in the matter of agricultural occupation, the Prajāpati (lord of the subjects i.e. god Brahmā established the bounds of decency by means of which they protected one another.

154. Among them some were very powerful and they seized the realm. He established them as Kṣatriyas and it was their duty to protect others.

155. (Defective).[2] All those subjects who had been created will be worshipping you. 'Tell the truth in accordance with the fact'. Those (subjects) who said this were the Brāhmaṇas.

156-158. Some stood by in the activity of protecting others who were weak. They destroyed Kīṭas (worms). They were established on the earth. The people call them Vaiśyas and cultivators of soil. They were the achievers of livelihood. Those who were engaged in the service (of others), those who ran errands and served others, were devoid of brilliance and deficient in virility. (Since they were deficient they served others). He called them Śūdras. Lord Brahmā ordained and prescribed their respective duties and holy rites.

---

1. VV.151ff described the transition from food-gathering economy to the food-growing one by the introduction of Agriculture. This stage crystalized the four-fold classification of the society with their specific duties (*vide* VV 161-165 below).

2. Vā.P.8.162a gives a better reading:

upatiṣṭhanti ye tān vai yāvanto nirbhayās tathā./

'So long all those who worship or respect and obey those Kṣattriyas, they are free from fear'.

159. Although the establishment of the classification into the four castes had been made by him (Lord Brahmā), the subjects, out of delusion, did not conform to those rules.

160. The subjects who lived in accordance with the duties of the (different) castes became antagonistic to one another. Lord Brahmā understood everything factually.

161-162. He ordained that meeting out punishments, maintenance of armies and waging wars should be the means of sustenance for the Kṣatriyas. Performance of Yajñas, teaching of the Vedas and acceptance of charitable and monetary gifts—lord Brahmā prescribed these as the holy duties and rites for those Brāhmaṇas. Breeding of cattle, carrying on trading activities and cultivation of the soil—he granted these to the Vaiśyas.

163-165. Again he ordained that arts and crafts should be the means of livelihood for the Śūdras.

To the Brāhmaṇas, Kṣatriyas and Vaiśyas he prescribed the common duty of performing Yajña and studying the Vedas as well as giving charitable gifts. To the others the common duty ordained was performance of their duties for livelihood. After prescribing these duties and holy rites, the lord ordained their abodes in the other worlds above :

The *Prājāpatya* (that belonging to Prajāpati or Brahmā) world is remembered as the abode of the Brāhmaṇas who performed their holy rites and duties.

166. The world belonging to Indra is the abode of Kṣatriyas who never flee from the battlefield. The abode of the Vaiśyas who sustain themselves by their respective duties is the Māruta world (i.e. the world belonging to the wind god).

167. The abode of the Śūdras who abide by their duty of rendering service is the world belonging to the Gandharvas. These are the abodes (after death) of the people of the different castes who remain good and maintain the conduct of life befitting their respective station in life.

168. When this mode of disciplined life of the four castes had been well-established, the people of the different castes strictly adhered to the duties of their respective castes because they were afraid of punishment otherwise. Then, after the castes had been established, he stabilised the stages of life.

169. The Lord established as before the following four *Āśramas*[1] (stages in life) viz. the householder, the celibate religious student, the forest hermit and the ascetic.

170. (Defective text) the people of the four castes performed the duties of the respective castes. After doing their duties they erected their residences and maintained their stages of life and then enjoyed themselves.

171. Brahmā established those *Āśramas*. He directed and guided those who swerved from these and recounted righteous virtues to them.

172-173. He instructed them in the methods of self-restraint, observances, and controls of sense-organs etc.

Among the four castes, the stage of the life of a householder stood at the outset because it was the source of origin for the sustenance of the other three *Āśramas*[2] (stages of life). I shall mention (the duties) in due order along with the holy vows and observances.

174. The following are the duties of the householder in brief : Marriage, maintenance of sacrificial fire, hospitability to guests, performance of Yajñas and continuation of his race (procreation).

175. The duties of the religious student are as follows : He must wear the girdle (of the *muñja* grass) and hold the staff. He must wear the skin of an antelope. He must sleep on the ground. He must serve his preceptor. He must beg for alms. He must be eager to acquire learning.

176. These are the duties of the forest hermits; wearing barks and leaves or skins of antelope (for clothes), maintaining themselves by means of roots, fruits and medicinal herbs found in the forests, bathing both at dawn and dusk and performance of *Homa*.

177-178. The duties of the mendicant (recluse) are as follows : He must beg for alms when the noise of pestles has died down. He must not steal. He must maintain cleanliness.

---

1. VV.169-189 describe the duties of the four Āśramas or stages in life.
2. Cf. *teṣāṁ gṛhastho yonir aprajanatvād itareṣām—Gaut.Dh.S.*III.3.

He must not err or be elated. He must refrain from sexual intercourse. He must have mercy on all living beings. He must have forbearance. He must listen to the instructions of the preceptor. He must serve the preceptor. He must be truthful. This righteous conduct of ten items (as enumerated above) was laid down by the self-born lord as the duty of a recluse.

179. Five of them pertain to *Bhikṣus* viz. : begging, knowledge (of vedas) and religious vows.*

He mentioned their abodes after death as well as Aśuṣmi (absence of lustre) (?)

180. There are eightyeight thousand sages who live in perpetual celibacy. The place remembered as their is alone the abode of those who live with their preceptor (i.e. (*Brahmacārins*).

181. The place remembered as the abode of the seven sages (the great Bear) is (assigned as) that of the forest-dwellers. The world of Prajāpati is the abode of house-holders and Brahmā's abode is that of the ascetics.

182.** (Defective text)The abode of the Yogins has not been created (?) without conquering them, it does not exist (?) Those abodes of the persons of different stages of life are indeed in the abode of Brahmā.

183. Only four paths have been created as Devayānas (paths of the Devas). Only four paths are remembered as Pitṛyānas (paths of the manes).

184. Formerly, in the first Manvantara (these had been created) by Brahmā who administered the worlds. *Ravi* (the sun) is remembered as the entrance to those paths that (are known as) Devayānas. The moon (*Candramas*) is mentioned as the entrance of Pitṛyānas.

185-186. Thus even though the castes and stages of life had been clearly defined, the subjects adhering to the duties of the different castes did not flourish. Then, in the middle of

---

* Probably a misprint for *amuṣmin*.

** Vā.P.8.196 (corresponding verse) reads as follows:

yogināṁ amṛtaṁ sthānaṁ nānādhīnāṁ na vidyate /

"Immortal (*amṛtam*) is the abode of Yogins which is not meant for non-Yogins.

Tretā yuga he evolved another mental creation from the bodies of his own self and similar to himself.

187. In that first Tretā yuga, when it gradually reached its middle period he began to create mental progeny other than (what was before).

188. Then the same lord created the subjects with predominating Sattva and Rajas qualities. They had the pursuit of virtue (Dharma), wealth, love and liberation and they accomplished their professions for livelihood.

189. They were the Devas, the Pitṛs, the sages and the Manus (i.e. human beings ?) In regard to their characteristics they were in accordance with the respective Yugas. By these, the subjects (in the universe) flourished.

190-195. (Defective) Formerly, I had mentioned to you about those people who in the previous Kalpa resorted to Janaloka. As when he meditated upon them, all these created beings, approached him for the purpose of being born (again). In the course of Manvantaras, they were first junior-most* (?) They were well-renowned by the people of their race (?). They had all the faculties of cleverness or otherwise, unimpaired. They had minor calamities due to the defect of the fruits of their own activities. Those who were present consisted of Devas, Asuras, Pitṛs Yakṣas, Gandharvas, human beings, Rākṣasas, Piśācas, animals, birds, reptiles, trees, worms of hells etc. For the sake of food of the subjects, he created Vidātmans* (knowing souls) (?)

---

* Vā.P.8.209 reads: *ādhīnārtham prajānāṁ ca ātmano vai vinirmame*, 'for the control of the subjects, it is reported that he created himself'.

CHAPTER EIGHT

God Brahmā's Mental Creation : Gods, sages, manes, and human beings created

Sūta said :

1. Even as he was meditating, the mental progeny were born along with those causes and effects arising out of his body.

2-4. There cropped up *Kṣetrajñas* (Individual souls) of the *Kṣetra* (Cosmic body) of this intelligent person i.e. Brahmā). Thereafter, he was desirous of creating thousands and thousands of the four groups of living entities viz. the Devas, the Asuras, the Pitṛs and the human beings. Prajāpati engaged himself therein and meditated upon the creation. While meditating thus, an effort arising out of his Tamas constituent was involved. So, at the outset the Asuras were born as his sons from Prajāpati's loins.

5. *Asu* is considered by scholars as the vital breath. Therefore, those who were born of it were Asuras.[1] He discarded that physical body whereby the Asuras had been created.

6-7a. That physical body discarded by him immediately became Night. Since that physical body had the Tamas element predominant, the night too consisting of three *Yāmas* (watches of night of the duration of three hours each) became *Tamobahulā* (one in which darkness prevails).

Therefore at night the subjects (people) are themselves enveloped by darkness.

7b-9. After creating the Asuras, he adopted another body that was unmanifest, with the Sattva element predominant within it. Then he engaged himself with it. As the lord joined himself to it, he felt very happy. Thereafter from his shining face the Devatās (gods and goddesses) were born. Since they were born of the refulgent face (*Divyataḥ*) they are glorified as Devas.

(1) A noteworthy derivation of *asura* as contrasted with the usual *a* + *sura*.

10. The root √"*Div*" is used in the sense of "to play".[1] Therefore, the Devas were born of his divine (lit. "shining") body (and called *Devatās*).

11. After creating the Devas, he discarded that divine body. That physical body discarded by him became "day".

12. Therefore, people worship the Devas with holy rites performed during the daytime. After creating the Devas, he adopted another body.

13-14. He adopted another body that was solely constituted by the Sattva element and engaged himself therein. The lord meditated upon those sons considering them like father (of fatherly nature). The *Pitṛs* were born of that body in the juncture of night and day; therefore those Pitṛs are Devas. That state of being *Pitṛs* is declared about them.

15. He discarded that body whereby the *Pitṛs* were created. The body that had been discarded by him forthwith became the twilight.

16. Hence, the daytime is considered as belonging to the Devas and the night is remembered as belonging to the Asuras. The body that belongs to the *Pitṛs* and that is in between those two is the most important.

17. Hence the Devas, the Asuras, the sages and the human beings, while practising Yoga, worship that body which is in between dawn and morning (day-break).

18. Hence, Brāhmaṇas perform *sandhyā* at the junction of the night and day. Thereafter, Brahmā engaged himself in another body of his.

19. That body which the lord created mentally was solely constituted by the Rajas element. They (the progeny so created) are his sons through the mind. Since they were begotten (*Prajananāt*), they became *Prajās* (subjects).

20. Since, he meditated (before creation) (*Mananāt*), they are called *Manuṣyas* (Men); they became wellknown as *Prajās* because they were procreated. After creating the subjects again, he discarded his own body.

---

1. Correct etymology —*div*—means both 'to play' and 'to shine'.

21. That body discarded by him became the moonlight immediately. Hence, the subjects become delighted when the moonlight comes out.

22. Thus these physical bodies discarded by that noble-souled person immediately became night, day, twilight and moonlight.[1]

23. The moonlight, the twilight, and the day these three are constituted solely of the Sattva element. The night is constituted of Tamas only. Hence that is *Niyāmika** (that which checks, restrains and restricts).

24. So, the Devas were created by means of the shining divine body with pleasure and sportiveness through the face (mouth). Since their birth was during the day time, they are powerful during the day time.

25. Since the lord created the Asuras at night from his loins through the vital breaths, and as they were born during the night, they are invincible during the night.

26-28a. These following, viz.: the moonlight, the night, the day and the twilight—these alone become the causes (of origin) of all future Devas, Manes, human beings along with the Asuras in all the Manvantaras that had passed by and that have not yet come. Since these four spread and shine there, the water is called *Ambhas*. The root √bhā is used in the sense of spreading and shining.[2]

---

1. VV. 22-27 summarise the four main creations from god Brahmā's body and their other features as follows:

* He emended as *triyāmikā* 'consisting of three Yāmas' as in verse 6 above, Vā.P.9.22 (an identical verse) also reads *triyāmikā*.

	Creation	*Born from Brahmā's part of the body*	*When discarded His Body transformed into*	*Prevailing guṇas.*
i.	Asuras	Loins & vital breath	Night	Tamas
ii.	Devas	Shining face	Day	Predominant Sattva.
iii.	Pitṛs.	Mind	juncture of day and night	Pure Sattva.
iv.	Human beings.	mind	moonlight (but dawn in other Purāṇas)	Rajas.

2. Popular derivation of *ambhas*.

28b-29a. After creating the waters, the lord created the Devas, the Dānavas, the human beings, the *Pitṛs* and various kinds of other subjects.

29b-30. The lord discarded (that body) the moonlight and attained another physical body predominently constituted of Rajas and Tamas. Thereafter, he engaged himself therein (he united himself to it.). Therefore, he created in darkness those who were overwhelmed by hunger.

31-34. Those created beings, overwhelmed by hunger, attempted to seize the waters. Those among them who said—"we shall protect these waters", are remembered as Rākṣasas. Those night-walkers (demons) who felt hunger within themselves and who said "Let us destroy the waters, let us be delighted in our mutual company", became Yakṣas and Guhyakas of ruthless action due to that work. The root √*rakṣ*- is considered to have the meaning "to protect." The root √"*kṣi*" has the meaning "to destroy". Since they protected (*Rakṣaṇāt*) they were called Rākṣasas. Since they destroyed(*Kṣapaṇāt*), they are called Yakṣas.[1]

35-36. On seeing them (the ruthless Yakṣas), the intelligent self-possessed lord became displeased. Due to this displeasure, his hairs became shivered. Those shivered hairs moved up and ascended again and again. Those hairs that dropped off from the head moved and crawled up. They are considered *Vyāla,* because they were (originally) *Bālas* or *Vālas* (hairs). Since they drooped off (*Hīnatvāt*) they are remembered *Ahis* serpents).[2]

37. They are Pannagas[3] because they moved and wriggled. The state of being *Sarpas* is due to the fact that they crawled. Their abode of repose is in the earth under the sun, the moon and the clouds*.

---

1. Puranic etymology of *rākṣasa* and *Yakṣa.*

2. Another derivation of *Vyāla—vāla* and *ahi—hi*—generally *ahi* is derived as follows : *a—han—in sa ca ḍit āṅo hrasvaśca*—Apte Sk. Hindi Koṣa P.134.

3. VV. 37-41 describe the creation of various tribes of demi-gods and gives popular etymologies of *Piśāca* and *Gandharva.*

* The text *sūryācandramasau ghanāḥ* is obscure. Vā.P. (in an identical verse reads. .*sūryācandramasoradhaḥ* 'below the Sun and the moon !'

38. The terrible fiery foetus born of his (Brahmā's) anger entered in the form of poison in those serpents who were born along with them.

39. After creating the serpents out of his anger a set of terrible beings whose diet was flesh and who were furious by nature were created. They had the tawny colour.

40. Since they had been born (*Bhūtatvāt*), they are remembered as *Bhūtas*; and as they ate flesh (*Piśitāśanāt*), they were called *Piśācas*. Even as he (Brahmā) was singing words, the Gandharvas were born as his sons.

41. The root *Dhay* is recited by poets in the sense of 'drinking'. Since they were born drinking the (musical) words, they are remembered as Gandharvas.

42. After creating these eight divine beings, he created the *Cchandas* (Prosody, Vedas) as he pleased (*Cchandataḥ*). He created the birds through his age (? *Vayasā*).

43. After creating the birds, he created the groups of animals. He created goats out of his mouth and the sheep out of his chest.

44-45. Brahmā created the cows from his belly and the horses, donkeys, *Gavayas* (a species of ox), deer, camels, boars and dogs along with the elephants from his sides as well as feet. Other species of animals too were created. The medicinal herbs (and plants and creepers) with fruits and roots were born out of his hairs.

46. Formerly, at the beginning of this Kalpa, at the advent of the Tretā yuga, he created the five types of medicinal herbs and then engaged himself in the sacrifices.

47-48. The cow, the goat, the man,[1] the sheep, the horse, the mule and the donkey—these are remembered as seven rural (*Grāmya*) domesticated animals. There are other seven forest animals, the beasts of prey, the tigers. the elephants, the monkey, the birds as the fifth of the set, the aquatic animals as the sixth ones and the reptiles as the seventh ones.

49. The buffaloes, the Gavaya oxen, and the camels, the cloven-footed animals, the *Śarabha* (the eight-footed fabulous

---

1. Strangely enough the Purāṇa includes the human species among domesticated animals.

animal), the elephant, with monkey as the seventh of this set, are the forest animals.

50. Through his first face (mouth), he created the following,[1] viz : the Gāyatrī, the Ṛk, the *Trivṛtstoma*[2] and *Rathantara*[3] and Agniṣṭoma among the Yajñas.

51. Through his right-hand (southern) face (mouth), he created the Yajurveda hymns, the Traiṣṭubha metre, the fifteenth Stoma (hymn) and the *Bṛhatsāman* hymn.

52. Through his backward (western) face (mouth), he created the Sāman hymns, the Jagatī metre, the seventeenth *Stoma* (hymn), the Vairūpya and Atirātra (part of Jyotiṣṭoma) sacrifices.

53. Through his fourth face (mouth), he created the twentyfirst (*stoma* i.e. hymn). The Atharva-Veda, the *Āptor-yāma*[4] and the Anuṣṭubh metre along with Vairāja.

54. It is wellknown that after creating the great cloud wellknown as *Parjanya,* the holy lord created lightning, thunder-clouds and the red-coloured rainbows.

55. He created the Ṛk, Yajus and Sāman Mantras for the accomplishment of Yajñas. The living beings both high and low were born of the limbs of Brahmā.

56-58. The Prajāpati (Lord of the subjects) who was creating at the outset the fourfold set viz.: the Devas, the sages, the Pitṛs and the human beings, created the living beings both mobile and immobile. After creating Yakṣas, the Piśācas, the Gandharvas, the Apsaras, the human beings, the Kinnaras, the Rākṣasas, the birds, the animals, the deer and the serpents, he created the *Avyayas* (changeless ones) and Vyayas

---

1. VV. 50-53 give the creation of Vedic literature, Vedic metres and special sacrifices from the mouths or faces of Brahmā.

2. *Trivṛtstoma*—A three-fold *stoma* (in which at first, the three 1st verses of each Tṛcā of Ṛv.IX.11 are sung together, then the 2nd verses and lastly the 3rd verses).

3. *Rathantara*: the verses to be sung according to Sāma-music are ṚV.VII.32.22-23 *abhi tvā Śūra* etc.=S.V. II.1.1.11.

4. *Āptoryāma* is a Soma sacrifice—an amplification of *Atirātra* sacrifice. According to Tāṇḍya Br.XX 3.4-5, it is so called as its performance secures whatever one desires.

(the changeables) as well as the mobile and the immobile beings.

59-60. Even when created again and again, these beings adopted only the Karmans that had been committed before.[1] The previous natures and features such as violence and non-violence, softness of heart and ruthlessness, virtue and evil as well as truth and falsehood—all these were adopted by them (in their later creations). Hence, they are liked by them.

61. It was Brahmā, the creator himself, who ordained the diversity in the great elements and their allotment to different physical bodies afflicted by the sense-organs (*Indriyārteṣu*) *.

62. Some men say that the manly endeavour (is the sole cause of achievement). Some men say that it is the *Karman* (previous actions). Other Brāhmaṇas say that it is the destiny. The *Bhūtacintakas* (those who think about the elements—perhaps the Cārvākas) say that it is nature and latent instinct.

63. (But real thinkers) know that there is no difference or superiority among the manly endeavour, previous action and the destiny. The same is understood through the nature of the outcome of fruits (of actions etc.)

64. (Some say)[2] this is thus and not thus—this is both nor is it both. But persons abiding by Sattva and having impartial vision say (that the Universe) is the object of its own activity.

65. It is only through the words of the Vedas that the great lord created at the outset, the different forms and features of the living beings and the development of the created ones.

---

1. As noted above this Purāṇa emphasizes the law of Karman. The end of a Kalpa does not destroy the Karma of an individual.

* If the reading *Indriyārtheṣu* is adopted the meaning is "and their allotment to different physical bodies and the objects of the various sense organs."

2. Apparently the view (*aniścitatāvāda*) of Sañjaya Belaṭṭhi Putta in *Sāmañña-phala-sutta—Dīgha Nikāya* p. 51 (Nalanda Ed.): when asked about the existence of the other world he states:

evaṁ ti pi me no, tathā ti pi me no, aññathā ti pi me no, no ti pi me no, no no ti pi me no.

But I think the Purāṇa probably voices the view of Syādvāda.

66. The names pertaining to the sages and the visions belonging to the Devas—these, the unborn lord assigns to those who are born at the end of the night.

CHAPTER NINE

The Progeny of Rudra : Birth of Bhṛgu and others

Sūta said :

1. By means of his mind, the lord then created five *Kartṛs* (doers or agents of creation). viz.: Rudra. Dharma, Manas (mind), Ruci and Ākṛti.

2. All these are mighty-armed and they are the causes of the sustenance of the subjects. When the medicinal herbs decline again and again, it is Rudra who sustains them and revives them.

3-4. By those who seek benefits, the Lord was well worshipped with whatever fruits and medicinal herbs were available (to them). He (that God) is called Tryambaka[1] as in times of (impending?) extinction of medicinal herbs etc., sacrifice is offered to him by sages with three Kāpālas (plates or potsherds containing) of cakes sacred to him (Rudra).

5-6. It has already been mentioned by me that the three Vedic metres, Gāyatrī, Triṣṭup and Jagatī are the sources of origin of the *Ambakas* (i.e. *Kapālas*) along with the *Vanaspati* (i.e. the medicinal herbs). These three metres join together and assume unity (i.e. when they are used in Mantras at the time of the consecration of the *Puroḍāśa* offerings). That *Purodāśa* is infused with the virility of each of these mantras. Hence the *Puroḍāśa* is remembered as *Trikapāla* (having three vessels to hold it). Therefore the *Puroḍāśa* is *Tryambaka* as well. Hence

1. Tryambaka means 'one having three eyes' and is an epithet of Śiva. Here it is identified with *Puroḍāśa*.

the lord (to whom this *Puroḍāśa* is offered) is remembered as Tryambaka.

7. Dharma sustains all the subjects. *Manas* is remembered as that which caused knowledge. *Ākṛti* is the form of splendid beauty. Ruci is remembered as one who inculcates *Śraddhā* (faith).

8-9. Thus these protectors of the subjects are the causes of the sustenance of the subjects.

Even as he continued the creative activity for the sake of the multiplication of the subjects, those created subjects did not increase at all by any means. Therefore, he racked his intellect that should arrive at a decisive conclusion.

10. Then he saw the Tamas element moving within himself. Thanks to its own action, it had abandoned Rajas and Sattva and was existing by itself.

11. Thereupon, due to that sorrow, the lord of the universe felt grieved. He pushed out the Tamas element and afterwards covered it with Rajas.

12. That Tamas pushed out by him gave birth to a pair. On account of his unrighteous conduct, *Hiṁsā* (Violence) and *Śoka* (grief) were born.

13. When that pair in the form of *Varaṇa* (covering up), was born, the lord became delighted. He resorted to this.

14. From a half of the body of the lord who was delighted within himself thus, a woman conducive to great welfare, and charming and fascinating to all living beings, came out.[1]

15. That beautiful looking lady was indeed created from Prakṛti by him (as he was) desirous (of progeny) and was called Śatarūpā. And she was again and again called so.

16. It was then that the subjects were born of that noble-souled being in the middle of Tretā yuga as has already been mentioned by me to you in section-I *Prakriyāpāda*.

17. When those subjects created by that intelligent self-possessed being did not increase in number, he created other mental sons similar to himself.

1. Cf. Manu I.32.

18-19. He created these nine mental sons[1] viz. : Bhṛgu, Aṅgiras, Marīci, Pulastya, Pulaha, Kratu, Dakṣa, Atri and Vasiṣṭha. In the Purāṇa, these are decisively called the "nine Brahmās" (because they were like) Brahmā (the creator) unto all beings of controlled souls, having the Ātman as their source of origin.

20. Then Brahmā created again Dharma who was delightful and pleasant unto all living beings; as well as the Prajāpati Ruci. These two were the eldest of all ancient ones.

21. He created from his intellect, Dharma who was delightful and pleasant unto all living beings. He who is named Ruci was born of the mind of (the lord of) unmanifest birth.

22-24. Sage Bhṛgu was born of the heart of the lord whose source of origin was water. Brahmā created Dakṣa from his vital breath and Marīci from his eyes. He created Rudra (also known as) Nīlalohita in the form of *Abhimāna* (prestige, honour). He created aṅgiras from his head and Atri from the ears. From his *Udāna* (?) vital breath (*prāṇa*) he created Pulastya and Pulaha from *Vyāna*. Vasiṣṭha was born of *Samāna* and he created Kratu from *Apāna*.

25. Thus these twelve are remembered as the sons of Brahmā at the beginning (of creation) of subjects. Dharma was the first-born among those Devatās.

26. Bhṛgu and others who had been created are remembered as Brahmarṣis (Brahminical sages). They are the ancient house-holders and Dharma (virtue) was initially established by them.

27-28a. In the Kalpa, these twelve give birth to subjects again and again. Their twelve races are divine and equipped with Divine qualities. They perform holy rites and have (i.e. procreate) progeny. They are adorned (honoured) by great sages.

28b-29. When the progeny created by Dharma and other great sages (who themselves) had been created (by him) did not multiply, the intelligent and self-possessed lord became slightly enveloped by Tamas and afflicted by grief.

---

1. Cf. Manu I.35 also VP.I.8.4-6.

30. Just as Brahmā was enveloped by Tamas elements, so also in the case of his sons too another Tamas element issued forth.

31-32. Adharma is in the nature of return flow (?) and Hiṁsā (Violence) is inauspicious by nature. Then when he was obstructed and the nature of the covering was manifest, Brahmā discarded his own shining physical body. After dividing his own body into two, he became a man by one half.

33. By (another) half he became a woman and she was Śatarūpā. She was the Prakṛti,[1] the mother of all living beings (and manifested thus) because the lord was creating out of desire.

34-36. With her grandeur, she pervaded the firmament and the earth and remained steady. That was the former body of Brahmā who stayed enveloping the firmament. The half that was created as a woman became Śatarūpā. That divine lady performed a very difficult penance for a hundred thousand years and obtained Puruṣa of brilliant fame as her husband. Indeed, he is called Manu, the Puruṣa, the earlier son of the self-born lord.

37-38a. Seventyone sets of four Yugas constitute what is called his Manvantara (reign of a Manu). After obtaining as his wife, Śatarūpā who was not born of any womb, the Puruṣa sported with her. Hence it is called *Rati* (sexual dalliance).

38b-40. The first union took place in the beginning of the Kalpa. Brahmā created Virāṭ (the immense Being). That Virāṭ became the Puruṣa. He, accompanied by Śatarūpā, is remembered as Vairāja, Manu and Samrāṭ (Emperor). That Puruṣa, Manu, the Vairāja created subjects (begot progeny). From Vairāja, the Puruṣa, Śatarūpā gave birth to two heroic sons.

41. They were Priyavrata and Uttānapāda. These two sons were the most excellent sons that persons possessing sons could expect. (She gave birth to) two daughters also of great fortune. From them these subjects were born.

---

1. The Sāṅkhya pair of Prakṛti and Puruṣa are represented here as Śatarūpā and Manu. The terms Vairāja, Puruṣa, Manu (and Samrāṭ) are used as synonyms.

42. They were the divine lady named Ākūti and auspicious lady Prasūti. Both of them were auspicious. The lordly son of the self-born lord gave Prasūti to Dakṣa.

43. He gave Ākūti to Ruci, the Prajāpati. An auspicious pair was born of Ākūti as the progeny of Ruci, the mental son (of Brahmā).

44. They were the twins Yajña and Dakṣiṇā. Twelve sons were born to Yajña and Dakṣiṇā.

45. They were the Devas named Yāmas in the Svāyambhuva Manvantara. They were the sons of twins, viz : Yajña and Dakṣiṇā. Hence they are remembered as Yāmas.[1]

46. (?) Two groups of Brahmā are remembered viz : Ajitas and Śukras. The Yāmas who have the appellation *Divaukas* (heaven-dwellers) circumambulated the former.

47. Lord Dakṣa begot of Prasūti, the daughter of Svāyambhuva Manu, twenty-four daughters who became mothers of the world.

48-49a. All of them were highly fortunate. All of them were lotus-eyed. All of them were wives of Yogins and all of them were Yogic mothers. All of them were expounders of Brahman and all of them were the mothers of the universe.

49b-50. Lord Dharma accepted (the following) thirteen daughters of Dakṣa as his wives, viz : Śraddhā, Lakṣmī, Dhṛti, Tuṣṭi, Puṣṭi, Medhā, Kriyā, Buddhi, Lajjā, Vasu, Śānti, Siddhi, and Kīrti as the thirteenth.

51-52. These door-ways of his (creative activity) were ordained by the self-born lord. The others that remained were the eleven younger daughters of beautiful eyes. viz : Satī, Khyāti, Sambhūti, Smṛti, Prīti, Kṣamā, Sannati, Anasūyā, Ūrjā, Svāhā and Svadhā.

53-54. Other great sages accepted them (as wives). They were Rudra, Bhṛgu, Marīci, Aṅgiras, Pulaha, Kratu, Pulastya, Atri, Vasiṣṭha, Agni and Pitṛs. He gave (in marriage) Satī to Bhava and Khyāti to Bhṛgu.

55. To Marīci, he gave Sambhūti, and Smṛti to Aṅgiras. To Pulastya he gave Prīti and Kṣamā to Pulaha.

1. Derivation of Yāma, the gods of the Svāyambhuva Manvantara.

56. To Kratu, he gave Sannati and the (daughter) named Anasūyā to Atri. He gave Ūrjā to Vasiṣṭha and Svāhā to Agni (the fire-god).

57-58. He gave Svadhā to the Pitṛs. Listen from me their children. All these were highly fortunate ladies; their subjects (children) obediently followed them in all Manvantaras till the time of ultimate annihilation (of the world). Śraddhā gave birth to Kāma and Darpa (arrogance) is remembered as the son of Lakṣmī.[1]

59. Niyama (Restraint) was the son of Dhṛti (Courage). Santoṣa (Contentment) is mentioned as the son of Tuṣṭi (Satisfaction). Lābha (gain) was the son of Puṣṭi (Nourishment) and Śruta (Learning) was the son of Medhā (Intellect).

60. Dama (Restraint of sense-organs) and Śama (Restraint of the mind) are mentioned as the sons of Kriyā (Activity). Bodha (Understanding) and Apramāda (Absence of Errors) were the sons of Buddhi (Intellect).

61. Vinaya (Modesty) was the son of Lajjā (Bashfulness). Vyavasāya (Enterprise) was the son of Vasu. Kṣema (Welfare) was the son of Śānti (Tranquility). Sukha (Happiness) was born of Siddhi (Achievement).

62. Yaśas (Fame) was the son of Kīrti (Renown)—These were the sons of Dharma. Kāma's (Love's) son Harṣa (Delight) was born of the noble lady Siddhi (Achievement).

63. Through Adharma (Evil), Hiṁsā (Violence) gave birth to the two children *Nikṛti* (Dishonesty, Wickedness) and *Anṛta* (Falsehood).

64. Two twins were born of Nikṛti and Anṛta viz Bhaya (Fear), Naraka (Hell), Māyā (Illusion) and Vedanā (Pain).

65. Through Maya, Māyā gave birth to Mṛtyu (Death) that takes away all living beings. Then Duḥkha (Misery) was born of Vedanā through Raurava (Hell).

66. Vyādhi (Sickness) gave birth to Jarā (Old age), Śoka (Grief), Krodha (Anger) and Asūyā (Jealousy) through Mṛtyu. All these are remembered as characteristics of Adharma (Evil) with misery as the ultimate end.

1. VV. 58-67 personify virtues and vices and state their parentage. Out of these VV.63-68 describe the Tāmasa creation.

67. Their wife, son,—everyone is remembered as deathless.

Thus this Tāmasa creation took birth with Adharma as the controlling one.

68. Nīlalohita was commanded by Brahmā, "Beget progeny". He contemplated on his wife Satī and created sons.[1]

69. They were neither superior to him nor inferior. They were his mental sons on a par with himself. He created thousands and thousands of such childern wearing elephant hides.

70-80. All of them had these characteristics and features: All of them were on a par with himself in form, brilliance, strength and learning. They were tawny-coloured. They had quivers and matted hair. They were dark blue-red in complexion. They were devoid of tufts. They had no hairs. They were killers with eyes (by casting a look). They had Kapālas (skills) with them. They had huge beautiful forms and hideous cosmic forms. Some occupied chariots and wore coats of mail. They were defenders wearing armours. They had hundreds and thousands of arms. They were able to go through the firmament, earth and heaven; they had big heads, eight fangs, two tongues and three eyes. (Some were) eaters of rice, (some) eaters of flesh, (some) drinkers of ghee and (some of) Soma juice. (Some) had penises of great size; fierce bodies and blue necks. Some had fierce fury. They had quivers and armours, bows, swords and leather shields. Some were seated; some were running. Some yawning and some occupying (seats). Some were reciting (the Vedas), some performing Japas, Yogic practices and meditations. Some were blazing. Some were showering, some shining and some smoking. Some were enlightened. Some were wakeful, alert and enlightened. Some had the property of Brahmā (?). Some had the vision of Brahman. They had blue necks and thousand eyes. All of them were walking over the earth. They were invisible to all living beings. They had great Yogic power, virility and splendour. They were shouting and running. On seeing Rudra creating

1. VV. 68-80 describe the Raudrī Sṛṣṭi (creation by Rudra) and he was asked by Brahmā to stop creation as he was procreating immortal progeny and Rudra complied.

these excellent Devas with these qualities and features, in thousands even before the expiry of the period of a Yāma, Brahmā told him—"Do not create subjects like these. The subjects should not be created on a par with oneself or superior to oneself; welfare unto you. Create other subjects vulnerable to death. Subjects devoid of death do not begin to perform holy rites".

81. Thus addressed, he (Rudra) said to him (Brahmā): "I will not create progeny subject to death and old age. Prosperity unto you. I am standing by (i.e. cease to procreate); you please create, O lord.

82. These hideous and bluish-red coloured subjects who had been created by me in thousands and thousands, have come out of my own self.

83. These Devas will be known by the name of Rudras. They are highly powerful. Those Rudrāṇīs are well-known over the earth and firmament.

84. Enumerated in the (Vedic text) *Śatarudra*, they will become worthy of Yajñas. All of them will partake of the Yajñas along with the groups of Devas.

85. Till the end of the Yuga, they will remain, on being worshipped along with those Devas born of *Cchandas* (Vedas or—born as they are pleased) in the Manvantaras.

86. On being told thus by Mahādeva, that lord Brahmā, the delighted lord of subjects replied to the terrible Rudra.

87. "O lord welfare unto you. Let it be as spoken by you."

When it was permitted by Brahmā, everything happened that way.

88. Thenceforth, the lord Sthāṇu did not beget subjects. He remained celibate till the ultimate annihilation.

89-91a. He is remembered by learned man as Sthāṇu[1] because it was said by him thus—"I am standing by". All these qualities are present in Śaṅkara—viz: knowledge, penance, truthfulness, glorious prosperity, virtue, detachment and comprehension of the self. He excels all the Devas and sages along

1. Derivation of *Sthāṇu*.

with the Asuras, by means of his splendour. Hence the lord is remembered as Mahādeva[1] (Great god).

91b-92. He excels the Devas through his glorious prosperity, the great Asuras through his power, all the sages through his knowledge and all the living beings through Yoga. It is thus that Mahādeva is bowed to by all the Devas. After creating the subjects devoid of enterprise, he refrained from creation.

CHAPTER TEN

*Magnificence of God Śiva : Birth of Nīlalohita : His eight Names and Forms**

The Sage said :

1. The manifestation in this Kalpa of the noble-souled great lord Rudra along with the *Sādhaka* (spiritual aspirants) has not been narrated by you.

Sūta replied :

2. The origin of the primordial creation has been succinctly mentioned by me. I shall now narrate in detail the names along with the physical bodies.

3. Mahādeva begot of his wives many sons in the other Kalpas that have passed by. Listen to those (procreated) in this Kalpa.

4. In the beginning of the Kalpa, the lord contemplated on a son on a par with himself. Thereafter, the child Nīlalohita appeared on his lap.

---

1. Derivation of *Mahādeva*.

*This chapter deals with the eight forms of god Śiva—a popular conception in Purāṇas and classical literature. It is an amplification of a similar concept in *Śatapatha Brāhmaṇa* as noted below. This chapter is textually very close to Vā.p.Ch.27.

5-6. He cried loudly in a terrible manner (voice). He appeared as though he would burn by means of his brillance. On seeing the child Nīlalohita[1] crying suddenly, Brahmā spoke to him—"Why do you cry, O child ?" He replied— "Give me at the outset a name, O Grandfather."[2]

7. "O lord, you are named Rudra". On being told thus he cried again. "Why do you cry, O child?" asked Brahmā to him.

8. "Give me a second name", said he to the self-born Lord. "You are Bhava by name, O Lord". On being told thus he cried again.

9. "Why do you cry?", enquired Brahmā of the crying child. "Give me a third name". On being told thus, he said again.

10. "O lord, you are Śarva by name." On being told thus he cried again, "Why do you cry ?", asked Brahmā again to the crying child.

11. "Give me a fourth name." On being told thus, he said again, "O lord, you are Īśāna by name". On being told thus he cried again.

12. "Why do you cry", said Brahmā to that crying child again. He replied to the self-born lord—"Give me a fifth name."

13. "You are the lord and master of all *Paśus* (Animals, living beings)". On being told thus, he cried again. "Why do you cry?" said Brahmā to that crying child, once again.

14. "Indeed, give me the sixth name". On being told thus he replied to him—"O lord, you are Bhīma by name". On being told thus he cried again.

15. "Why do you cry ?", asked Brahmā again to that crying child. "Give me the seventh name". On being told thus he replied :

---

1. This name signifies identification of Rudra and Fire.

2. VV. 5 ff. This episode of crying for a name and god Brahmā's assigning eight names is a reproduction of the same in Śatapatha Brāhmaṇa (ŚB. 6.1.3.1-18). It is from this concept in ŚB that Bd.P. (and other Purāṇas such as Vā.P., LP) developed the *Aṣṭa-mūrti* conception of Rudra. See the next note.

16. "O lord, you are Ugra by name". On being told thus, he cried again. To that crying child he said— "Do not cry".

17. He said—"Give me, O lord, the eighth name". "You are Mahādeva by name". On being told thus, he stopped crying.

18. After securing these names, Nīlalohita requested Brahmā—"Indicate the abodes of these names".[1]

19-20. Then the bodies were allotted by the self-born lord unto these names (abodes). They were—the sun, the water, the earth, the wind, the fire, the Ether, the initiated Brāhmaṇa and the Moon. Thus the bodies were of eight varieties. The lord is to be worshipped, saluted and bowed to in those bodies.

21-23. Brahmā said again to the child Nīlalohita—"O lord, at the outset, your name has been mentioned by me as Rudra. The sun shall be the first body unto thy first name".

---

1. The abodes of the names of Nīlalohita are the eight forms (*aṣṭa-mūrtis*) of Śiva and they symbolize the five *Mahā-bhūtas* (gross elements), the two principle vital airs Prāṇa and Apāna and the principle of the Mind. The following tabular statement of the eight forms of Rudra, their abodes, names of their consorts and children will clarify this chapter.

	Name or Form of Śiva	Abode or bodies alloted	Designation of that body	Name of the consort	No of the sons
1.	Rudra	the sun (i.e. Prāṇa or Heat)	Raudrī	Suvarcalā	the saturn (Śani)
2.	Bhava	the water	Āpaḥ	Dhātrī	The Venus (Śukra)
3.	Śarva	the earth	Bhūmī	Vikeśi	The Mars (Aṅgāraka)
4.	Īśāna	the wind	Vāta	Śivā	i) Manojava ii) Avijñāta-gati
5.	Paśupati	the Fire	Agni	Svāhā	Skanda
6.	Bhīma	the Ether	Ākāśa	Quarters	Svarga
7.	Ugra	Initiated Brāhmaṇa	Dīkṣita Brāhmaṇa	Dīkṣā	Santāna
8.	Mahādeva	The Moon (Apāna) or cold	Candramas	Rohiṇī	Budha

When this was uttered his splendour became an eye, which illuminates, then it entered the sun. Hence he (the sun) is remembered as Rudra. One shall avoid seeing the sun while rising or while setting.

24. Since the sun comes into view frequently and since it vanishes frequently, one, who desires for longevity, should not directly see the sun. One should always be pure.

25-26. Worshipping during the two periods of junctions (the dawn and the dusk), and repeating the Sāman, Ṛk and Yajus hymns, the Brāhmaṇas propitiate and strengthen Rudra of the past and the future. At the time of rising, the sun stands on the Ṛks, at midday he stands on the Yajus and in the late afternoon, Rudra lies down and takes rest gradually. Hence, in fact, the sun never rises nor does he set.[1]

27. One shall never pass urine in the direction of Rudra (i.e. the sun) in whatever condition he may be.

28. Lord Rudra does not oppress the Brāhmaṇa who strictly adheres to these principles. Then Brahmā said again to that lord Nīlalohita.

29. Your second name has been mentioned by me as Bhava. Let the waters be the second physical body of this name of yours.

30. On this being mentioned, the element of the nature of *Rasa* (Juice)(i.e. water) became stationed in his body. Since he entered it, the water is remembered as Bhava.

31. Since the living beings are born (bhavanāt) of him, and since he evolves (bhāvanāt) the living beings through them (i.e. the waters) he is called Bhava[2] (due to his creation and evolution of beings).

32. Hence, one shall never urinate or pass faeces into the waters. One should not spit into water, nor plunge into the water in the nude nor should anyone have sexual intercourse within the waters.

The Soma-yājī Brāhmaṇa Yajamāna is regarded as the principle of the mind. Cf. *mano vai Yajamānasya rūpam—Śat.* Br.1.2.8.84.

1. This Puranic speculation turned out to be a scientific truth.
2. This etymology of 'Bhava' is confirmed in Vā.P.

33. Nor should one enumerate (?) these whether flowing or still. These bodies of the waters are declared by the sages as *Medhya* (Pure) and *Amedhya* (Impure).

34. Waters devoid of taste, waters of bad odour and colour and water in very little quantity should be avoided on all occasions. The sea is the source of origin of waters. Hence waters desire it.

35. After reaching the sea, the waters become sacred and *Amṛta* (nectarine). Hence one should not obstruct the waters since they love the sea.

36a. Lord Bhava does not oppress or injure him who treats water thus.

36b. Then Brahmā said again to child Nīlalohita :

37. "O lord, the third name of yours that had been mentioned by me is Śarva. Let this earth be the physical body of that third name.

38. On this being mentioned, the hard and firm (part) in his body, namely bones entered the earth. Therefore, it is called Śarva.

39. Hence, one should not evacuate the bowels or urinate in the ploughed land. One should not urinate in the shade of trees, or in the pathway or in one's own shadow.

40. After covering the ground with grass and covering one's head, one should evacute the bowels. Śarva does not oppress or injure him who behaves like this towards the earth.

41-43. Then Brahmā said again to child Nīlalohita. "Your fourth name that had been declared by me is Īśāna. Vāyu (Wind) should be the fourth physical body of your fourth name. As soon as this was spoken that (vital breath) which was stationed in him in five groups and is termed *Prāṇa* (Vital breath) entered Vāyu. Hence wind is Īśāna. Hence one should not censure or revile at Vāyu the lord himself as it blows violently.

44. Lord Maheśāna does not oppress or injure him who properly behaves towards the wind and those who honour the wind by means of Yajñas and those who serve it.

45-49. Then Brahmā said again to that lord Dhūmra (smoke-coloured) Īśvara. "The fifth name of yours that had been mentioned by me is *Paśupati*. Let this Agni (Fire) be the fifth body of your fifth name". On this being mentioned, the fiery brilliance that had been stationed in his body and is termed *Uṣṇa* (Hot) entered the fire. Hence it (fire) is Paśupati. Since Agni is Paśu (Animal) and since he protects animals, the physical body of Paśupati is designated (defined) as Agni. Hence, one should not burn impure ordure nor should one warm one's feet. One should not place it beneath nor should one trespass it. Lord Paśupati does not oppress or injure him who behaves properly like this.

50-54. Then Brahmā said once again to that lord *Śvetapiṅgala* (White-and-tawny-coloured). "O lord, the sixth name of yours that had been mentioned by me is Bhīma. Let *Ākāśa* (Ether) be the sixth body of that name". On this being uttered, the cavity that had been in his body entered the ether. Hence, it is the body of Bhīma. Since the lord is remembered as existing in the ether. One should not evacuate the bowels, urinate, take food, drink water, have sexual intercourse or throw up leavings of food consumed without having a cover on. The lord does not oppress or injure him who behaves towards Bhīma thus. Then Brahmā said once again to that lord, who is mighty.

55. O lord, your seventh name that had been mentioned by me was Ugra. The initiated Brāhmaṇa becomes the body of that name of yours.

56. On this being uttered, the *Caitanya* (consciousness, alertness) that was in his body entered the initiated Brāhmaṇa who performs the Soma sacrifice.

57. For that duration, the initiated Brāhmaṇa becomes lord Ugra. Hence, no one shall abuse or revile at him nor shall anyone speak vulgar word s about him.

58. Those who censure him take away his sins. Lord Ugra does not oppress or injure those Brāhmaṇas who behave properly thus.

59-61. Then Brahmā once again said to that lord with the lustre of the sun, "Your eight name that had been mentioned by me is Mahādeva. Let the moon be the physical body of that eighth name of yours". On this being mentioned, the mind of the lord that had been conceiving and contemplating entered the *Candramasa* (Moon). Therefore, the moon is Mahādeva. Hence, this great lord is considered to be the Moon.

62. On the new moon day a Brāhmaṇa should not cut trees, bushes or medicinal herbs. *Soma* (Moon) is remembered as Mahādeva and his Ātman (soul) is the group of medicinal herbs.

63-65. Mahādeva does not slay him who always remains thus on the Parvan days (new moon, full moon etc.) and who understands that lord thus.

The sun protects the subjects by the day and the moon, at the night. On the night (i.e. on the new moon) the sun and the moon join together. On that Amāvāsyā (New Moon) night one shall always be *Yukta* (properly performing Yogic exercise). All this visible universe has been pervaded by Rudra, through his bodies and names.

66. This sun that wanders alone is called Rudra. It is due to the light of the sun that the subjects see with their eyes.

67-69. Rudra remains a liberated soul and drinks water through his rays. Food is eaten and water is drunk with a desire for food, water etc. The body arising out of water develops and nourishes the bodies.

That earthen body of the lord is good as it sustains the subjects. It is through this that the lord upholds all the subjects by means of a steady splendour.

70-75. The gaseous body of *Iśāna* is the vital breath of all living beings. It is stationed in the bodies of all living beings along with the functions of the vital breath.

The body of Paśupati cooks and digests the food consumed and the beverages drunk, in the bellies of the living beings. That which cooks is called Agni (fire i.e. Gastric fire).

The cavities that are within the bodies for the purpose of the free movement of the air constitute the body (of the lord) called Bhīma.

The existence of expounders of Brahman is, due to Caitanya (consciousness) of the initiated ones. That body is of the form of Ugra. Therefore, the initiated one is remembered as Ugra.

The part of the body that conceives and contemplates and which is stationed in the subjects is the mental body, the moon—it is stationed in the living beings. Being born again and again he becomes fresh and fresh. It is being drunk at the proper time by the Devas along with the *Pitṛs*. The moon of aquatic nature with nectar within him is remembered as Mahādeva.

76. His first body has been glorified by the name Raudrī. Its wife is Suvarcalā and her son is Śanaiścara (the Saturn).

77. The second body of Bhava is remembered by the name of Āpaḥ. Its wife is remembered as Dhātrī and the son is remembered as Uśanas (the Venus).

78. The body of the third name of Śarva is Bhūmi (the earth). Its wife is Vikeśī and the son is remembered as Aṅgāraka (the Mars).

79-84. Vāta (wind) is the body of the fourth name of Īśāna. Its wife is Śivā by name. Anila (Wind) has two sons, viz. : Manojava (Having the speed of the mind) and Avijñātagati (One of inscrutable movement).

Agni (Fire) is remembered by Brāhmaṇas, as the body of Paśupati. Svāhā is remembered as its wife. Skanda is remembered as its son.

The Ether (Ākāśa) is called the body Bhīma, his sixth name. The quarters are remembered as its wives and Svarga (heaven) is remembered as its son.

The seventh body Ugra is remembered as the initiated Brāhmaṇa. Dīkṣā is remembered as its wife and Santāna is called the son.

The body *Mahat* of the eighth name is remembered as *Candramas* (Moon). Its wife is Rohiṇī. Her son is remembered as Budha.

Thus these bodies of his have been recounted along with the names.

85-87. The lord is to be saluted and bowed to in those bodies with the respective names for each body. He should be saluted by devotees in the sun, the waters, the Earth, the wind, the fire, the Ether, the initiated one as well as the moon. He should be honoured with great devotion along with the names. He who knows that lord thus with the bodies and names acquires progeny and attains the *Sāyujya* (Identity) of Lord Bhava. Thus the esoteric fame of Bhīma has been recounted to you.

88. O Brāhmaṇas, let there be welfare unto the bipeds. Let there be welfare unto the quadrupeds. Now the names and bodies of Mahādeva have been recounted. Listen to the progeny of Bhṛgu.

CHAPTER ELEVEN

*The Creation of Sages**

Sūta said :

1-3. Khyāti gave birth to a daugher and two sons. The sons were masters of happiness and misery. They grant auspicious and inauspicious results unto all living beings. They were the gods Dhātṛ (supporter) and Vidhātṛ (Dispenser of destiny). They used (to live and) walk about throughout the Manvantara. Their elder sister, goddess Śrī, purified the worlds. The splendid lady attained lord Nārāyaṇa as her husband. Bala (strength) and Unmāda (lunacy) were born of her as the sons of Nārāyaṇa.

4-5a. Tejas (fiery brilliance) was the son of Bala and

*This chapter deals with the progeny of the famous seven sages such as Bhṛgu, Aṅgiras, Atri, Pulaha and others. After mentioning their important descendants we are told that all these races passed away in the Svāyambhuva Manvantara.

This chapter corresponds to Vā.P.ch.28.

Saṁśaya (Doubt) was the son of Unmāda. Other mental sons too were born of him. They move about in the firmament. They drive and carry the aerial chariots of the Devas and persons of auspicious rites.

5b-6. Āyati (future) and Niyati (Restraint), the daughters of Meru* are remembered as the wives of Vidhātṛ and Dhātṛ. Prāṇa and Mṛkaṇḍa of firm holy vows were their sons. They are eternal and *Brahmakośas* (the treasury of Brahman or Vedas).

7. Mārkaṇḍeya was born of Manasvinī (as the son) of Mṛkaṇḍa. His son Vedaśiras was born of Dhūmrapatnī.

8. Sons of Vedaśiras in (through) Pīvarī are remembered as Propagators of the race. These sages who are well-known as Mārkaṇḍeyas (Descendants of Mṛkaṇḍa) were masters of the Vedas.

9-10. Dyutimān was born of Puṇḍarīkā, as the son of Prāṇa. Dyutimān had two sons, viz.: Unnata and Svanavāta. These two sons had sons and grandsons through mutual alliances among the descendants of Bhṛgu. They passed away during the Svāyambhuva Manvantara.

Listen to the progeny of Marīci.

11. Understand that, Sambhūti, the wife of Marīci the Prajāpati, gave birth to the son Pūrṇamāsa and the following daughters :

12. Kṛṣi, Vṛṣṭi, Tviṣā and the splendid Upaciti. Pūrṇamāsa begot of Sarasvatī two sons:

13. The two were Viraja who was righteous and Paravaśa. Viraja's son was a scholar, well known by the name Sudhāman.

14. Sudhāman, the son of Viraja and Gaurī, resorted to the Eastern quarter. He was a valorous and noble-souled guardian of the quarter, (ruler of the world).

15-16. Parvaśa, of great fame, entered (the task of)

* Vā.P.8.4 reads: *dve tu kanye* for *meru kalpa* hereof. It means according to Vā.P. Meru was not the father of Āyati and Niyati. May we take Meru as a Kalpa?

counting holy occasions (*Parva-gaṇana* ?). Parvaśa* begot of Parvaśā two sons, viz. : Yajurdhāman the intelligent and Stambhakāśyapa. Their two sons Sanyāsa and Niścita stabilised their line.

17-18. Smṛti, the wife of Aṅgiras, gave birth to these children—four daughters and two sons. The four daughters who were holy and well-reputed in the worlds, were viz. Sinīvālī, Kuhū, Rākā and Anumati. The two sons were Bharatāgni and Kīrtimān.

19. Sadvatī gave birth to Parjanya the son of Agni (i.e. Bharatāgni). (Another) Parjanya (otherwise called) Hiraṇyaroman was born of Marīci.

20-21. He is remembered as a Lokapāla (ruler of the world, guardian of the quarter) staying till the ultimate deluge.

Dhenuka gave birth to Cariṣṇu and Dhṛtimān, the two sinless sons of Kīrtimān. Both of them were the most excellent among the descendants of Aṅgiras. Their sons and grandsons ran to thousands. They have all passed away.

22-24. Anasūyā gave birth to five Ātreyas (i.e. sons of Atri) who were free from sins. She gave birth to a daughter also named Śruti who was the mother of Śaṅkhapāda. She was the wife of Kardama, the Prajāpati (Lord of subjects) and son of Pulaha. The five Ātreyas were Satya-Netra, Havya, Āpomūrti, Śanaiścara and Soma the fifth one among them. They passed away along with the Yāmadevas in the Svāyambhuva Manvantara.

25. The sons and grandsons of those noble-souled Ātreyas were hundreds and thousands. They all passed away in the Svāyambhuva Manvantara.

26. Dānāgni was the son of Prīti, the wife of Pulastya. He is remembered as Agastya in his previous birth in the Svāyambhuva Manvantara.

27-28a. The middle one was Devabāhu and the third son was Atri by name (thus Pulastya had) three sons. Their younger sister named Sadvatī was well-known. She is remem-

* The corresponding verse in Vā.P.28 reads: *Sarvagaṇānām*. It means 'Parvaśa entered into all the gaṇas (?)

bered as the splendid and pure wife of Agni (i.e. Bharatāgni) and mother of Parjanya.

28b-29. Sujaṅghī, the wife of Dānāgni, the intelligent son of the Brahmanical sage Pulastya and Prīti, gave birth to many sons. They are well known as Paulastyas. They are remembered (to have lived) in Svāyambhuva Manvantara.

30. Kṣamā gave birth to the sons of Pulaha*, the Prajāpati. All of them had the brilliance of the three sacrificial fires. Their fame is well-established.

31. They were three viz. Kardama, Urvarivān and Sahiṣṇu. Sage Kanakapīṭha (also was his son). There was a beautiful daughter named Pīvarī.

32. Kardama's wife Śruti who was the daughter of Atri gave birth to a son named Śaṅkhapāda and a daughter named Kāmyā.

33. It is reported that this Śaṅkhapāda was prosperous ruler of the world and lord of the subjects. He was devoted to the southern quarter.

Kāmyā was given in marriage to Priyavrata.

34. Kāmyā bore to Priyavrata ten sons on a par with the Svāyambhuva Manu and two daughters. It is through these that the Kṣatriya race spread.

35. Yaśodharā, the lady of beautiful waist, gave birth to Sahiṣṇu, the son of Kanakapīṭha. (She gave birth) to Kāmadeva (also).

36. Sannati bore auspicious sons to Kratu. They were equal to Kratu. They had neither wives nor sons. All of them were celibate.

37. They were well known as Vālakhilyas and are sixty thousand in number. They surround the sun and go ahead in front of Aruṇa.

38-39a. All of them are (perpetual) associates of the Sun till the time of ultimate annihilation (of the universe). They had two younger sisters, Puṇyā and Satyavatī. They were the daughters-in-law of Parvaśa, the son of Pūrṇamāsa.

---

*Corrected from Vā.P.28. 25a. as Pulastya in this text is an obvious misprint.

39b-40. The seven (Vasiṣṭhas) were born of Ūrjā as the sons of Vasiṣṭha. Their elder sister was a daughter of beautiful waist named Puṇḍarīkā. She was the mother of Dyutimān and the beloved wife of Prāṇa.

41-42a. Her younger brothers, the seven sons of Vasiṣṭha are well known. They are—Rakṣa, Garta, Ūrdhvabāhu, Savana, Pavana, Sutapas and Śaṅku. All of them are remembered as seven sages.

42b-45. The famous daughter of Mārkaṇḍeya, the noble lady of excellent limbs, gave birth to Ratna, the king of western quarter. (He was also known as) Ketumān and he was a Prajāpati. The races of the noble-souled sons of Vasiṣṭha passed away in the Svāyambhuva Manvantara.

Listen to the progeny of Agni.

Thus the creation of sages has been recounted along with their attendants. Henceforth, I shall recount the family of Agni in detail and in the proper order.

CHAPTER TWELVE

*The Race of Agni**

Sūta said :

1-2a. A mental son of Brahmā is remembered as the deity identifying itself with fire in the Svāyambhuva Manvan-

*This chapter presents the forty-nine ritualistic functions of the Fire as so many different Agni gods and gives their arrangement or correlations in a genealogical form. As a matter of fact, it is a Vedic concept as can be seen from the notes. This section concerning *Agnivaṁśa* must have been possibly a part of the original (Ur-) purāṇa as many verses hereof are textually identical with those in Vā.P. 29, Mt.P.51. The *Mbh. Vana* Chs. 217-22 (Āṅgirasa upākhyāna) give a detailed description of the ritualistic functions of fire.

tara. Svāhā bore to him three sons,[1] viz. : Pavamāna and Śuci who is remembered as Agni also.

2b-3. The Pavamāna fire is that which is obtained by churning (the *Araṇi*), Pāvaka is the fire originating from lightning. Śuci should be known as the solar fire. These are the three sons of Svāhā. [(Repetition)* the Pavamāna fire is that which is obtained by churning (the Araṇi), and Śuci is remembered as solar fire.]

4-6. The Pāvaka fire has water as the source of origin and it originates from the lightning. They are their respective abodes (viz. : Araṇi, the sun and the lightning). Kavyavāhana is said to be the son of Pavamāna. Saharakṣa was the son of Pāvaka and Havyavāha was the son of Śuci.

Havyavāha is the fire of the Devas; Kavyavāhana is the fire of the Pitṛs; Saharakṣa is the fire of the Asuras. There are (thus) three fires pertaining to the three (i.e. the Devas, the *Pitṛs* and the Asuras). The sons and grandsons of these are fortynine in number.

7. I shall mention their divisions separately along with their names. The secular fire is well known as the first son of Brahmā.

8. The good son of Brahmadattāgni[2] (the fire handed over by Brahmā) is well known by the name Bharata. Vaiśvānara was his son, and he carried Havya for a hundred years.

---

* The text repeats this, hence included here.

1. *VV*.1-6 : The following genealogical tree will clarify the relation of these fires:

Agni=*Śvāhā*

Pavamāna (=Gārhapatya) | Pāvaka (=Dakṣiṇāgni) | Śuci (=Āhavanīya)

born of or source: Araṇi (cf. Rv. III.29.2) | Water or Lightening | The Sun

Functions: *kavya-vāhana* (pertains to Pitṛs) | (*Vaidyuta*) *Saharakṣa* (belongs to Asuras) | *Havya-vāhana* pertains to Devas

2. Vā.P. 29-7 reads *Brahmaudanāgni* instead of *Brahmadattāgni* of BD. P. That reading is supported by Mt.P. The genealogy is: Brahmadatta or Brahma-

9-10. Formerly the fire Edhiti was gathered by Atharvan in the ocean Puṣkara.[1] Hence that secular fire is Ātharvaṇa. Darpahā is remembered as the son of Atharvan. Bhṛgu was born as Atharvan and Fire is remembered as Ātharvaṇa (son of Atharvan). Hence the secular fire is considered Dadhyaṅ,[2] the son of Atharvaṇa.

11. Pavamāna, the son of Atharvan, is remembered by the wise as one that should be generated by churning. It should be known as Gārhapatya fire. His two sons are remembered as follows :

12. (They are Śaṁsya and Śuka* (śukra in Vā. P. 9-11) Śaṁsya is Āhavanīya fire who is remembered as Havyavāhana. The second son is Śuka (śukra in Vā. P.) and he is said to be the fire that is gathered and carried.

13. Savya and Apasavya** were the two sons of Śaṁsya. Śaṁsya, the Havyavāhana, loved sixteen rivers.

14-18. The fire Śaṃsya who is remembered as Āhavanīya fire as well as one who is identified with fire (*Abhimānin*, one

---

udana Bharata Vaiśvānara who carried *Havya* to gods. ŚBr. (Śatapatha Brāhmaṇa) I.4.2.2 explains that Agni is called *Bharata* as he supplies *Havya* to gods:

eṣa agnir hi devebhyo bharati tasmād
bharatognir ityāhuḥ |

In other words this genealogy becomes an equation thus:

Brahmadatta = Bharata = Vaiśvānara, the carrier of food to gods.

1. This has a reference to Ṛv.VI.16.13 where Agni is said to have been churned out of Puṣkara. According to ŚBr. VI.4.2.2, *Puṣkara* = Waters (*Āpo vai Puṣkaram*). ŚBr.VII.4.1.13 explains that when Indra got frightened after slaying Vṛtra, he resorted to waters which created a city (*Pur*) for him and henc came to be known as Puṣkara (*asmai puram akurvaṁs tasmāt puṣkaram ha vai tat puṣkaram ācakṣate parokṣam*).

2. It is probably the same as Dakṣiṇāgni.

* *kṛtttike cāriṇī dhiṣṇī*—the fireplace movable in a carriage (Kṛttikā). The idea is obscure. The Vā.P. 29.16a. reads differently as follows:

dhiṣṇyād avyabhicāriṇyas tāsūtpannās tu dhiṣṇayaḥ ||

** This is a wrong reading as '*savya*' and '*apasavya*' are no fires at all. '*Sabhya*' and 'āvasathya' are the names of the fire. Vā.P.29.12 correctly reads:

tathā sabhyāvasathyau vai Śaṁsasyāgneḥ sutāvubhau.

who takes pride) by the Brāhmaṇas loved these sixteen rivers :[1] viz. : Kāverī, Kṛṣṇaveṇā, Narmadā, Yamunā, Godāvarī, Vitastā, Candrabhāgā, Irāvatī, Vipāśā, Kauśikī, Śatadru, Sarayū, Sītā, Sarasvatī, Hrādinī and Pāvanī. He divided himself into sixteen *Dhāmans* (abodes) and in those abodes he deposited himself. The *Dhiṣṇis* (abodes i.e. fire-places) were caused to move by vehicles (Kṛttikas) (?) and the sons were born in those Dhiṣṇīs. Hence those sons are called "Dhiṣṇis". Thus these sons of the rivers were born in the Dhiṣṇis and they are glorified as Dhiṣṇis.

19. Some of these fires are *Viharaṇīyas*, (portable, those that should be carried or removed), and others are *Upastheyas*[2] (those that should be made to sit, deposited (?). They shall be briefly but factually recounted.

20. The following are the sons of Śaṁsya. All of them are remembered by Brāhmaṇas as *Upastheyas*. Vibhu, Pravahaṇa and Āgnīdhra and others, Dhiṣṇis (already deposited fires)

1. This is a poetic way of describing the spread of the Vedic Yajña-cult. This portable fire was carried from the Sītā (The Oxus—V.S. Agrawala; the Jaxartes—N. L. De) in the Central Asia down to the Kāverī in the South India. Modern political maps of India blind us to the vast geographical area which was India to the Purāṇa-writers. It was on the Sītā that Nārada met his brothers Sanatkumāra etc. and where probably the N.P. was presumed to have been narrated.

For the ancient names of the rivers hereof modern names are given in brackets : Vitastā (The Jhelum), Candrabhāgā (The Chinab), Irāvatī (The Ravi), Vipāśā (The Bias), Kauśikī (The Kosī), Śatadru (The Sutlej), Sītā (the Oxus or the Jaxartes or the Tarim—Yarkand), Hrādinī or Hlādinī (The Brahmaputra?), Pāvanī (The Ghaggar ?).

The list of rivers shows that the spread of the Yajña-cult covered parts of Central Asia, the Panjab and Kashmir, the Uttar Pradesh (and probably Bihar), the Madhya Pradesh, Maharashtra and part of Southern Karnatak.

'The sons of the rivers' is obviously the riperian population which followed the Yajña cult.

2. The Purāṇa classifies *Dhiṣṇya* fires into *Viharaṇīyas* and *Upastheyas*. The translation gives only the literal interpretations of the terms. The *Dhiṣṇya* was a side-altar of a heap of earth covered with sand. On that altar fire was placed.. In the Soma-sacrifice, these fires were placed between the altar (Vedī) of the Śrauta Yajña and the Uttara Vedi meant for the Soma sacrifice. The designation *Upastheya* is given to those fires as they were to be approached at their fixed place in the Uttara-Vedī. The *Viharaṇīya* fires are so called as they could be taken to any spot considered necessary on the day of the Yajña.

are serially laid down in their proper places in a *Savana* (Soma sacrifice) on the day when the Soma-juice is extracted.

21-22. Listen to the due order of the fires that are to be laid down Anuddeśya* (without being given any particular direction). Brāhmaṇas** worship the eight fires beginning with Samrāḍagni. They are Samrāḍagni etc. The second one is Kṛśānu and it is inside the Altar. The third one is Pariṣat-pavamāna. It is laid down as directed (*anudiśyate*).***

23. Another fire is *Pratalka*, (otherwise) named Nabhas. It is manifested in the *Catvara* (levelled spot of ground specially prepared for the sacrifice). *Havya* that is not besmeared (with ghee) is deposited in the fire in the *Śāmitra* vessel (particular vessel used in the sacrifice).

24. (Thereafter is the fire) Ṛtudhāman that is glorified as Sujyoti and Audumbarya Viśvavyacas is the ocean fire† ? and is glorified in the abode of Brahmā.

25-26. (The fire) Vasurdhāman that is Brahmajyoti is mentioned in the abode of Brahmā. Ajaikapāt that is an *Upastheya* is also Śālāsukhīyaka. Ahirbudhnya is an Anuddeśya fire. That fire is remembered as Gṛhapati.

27-28. Thereafter, I shall enumerate his eight sons who are called Viharaṇīyas.[1] [Here there is a repetition of verse No. 20]. The fire Havyavāhana is declared as Hotrīya fire (i.e. fire used by the Hotṛ).

29-30. The second fire here is named Pracetas that is a subdued fire. Thereafter is the fire Vaiśvadeva. It is called Śaṁsi‡ by the Brāhmaṇas. The fire Uśik that is Kavi is conceived as *Pota* fire. It is also conceived as Āvāri fire, Vābhāri and Vaiṣṭhīya.

---

* For *anuddeśya nivāsyānām* here cf. Vā.P.29.19a. *anirdeśyānyavācyānām*, 'undefinable or indescribable'.

** The printed text shows some confusion, verse 21A should be followed by 22a after which 21b should be taken. The translation is of the rearranged lines.

*** Vā.P.29.20 *atra dṛśyate*, 'is seen here'.

† In Vā.P.29.22 *viśvasyāyasamudra* seems to be the name of the fire.

1. It is not known why there should be a different list of such fires as this list differs from that in Mt.P.

‡ Vā.P.28a—*brahma-sthāne sa ucyate*.
'is spoken of as being in the abode of Brahmā.

31. The fire Avasphūrja is also called Vivasvān and Āsthān. The eighth one which is fire Sudhyu is also called Mārjālīya.

32. Those *Dhiṣṇyas*, the Viharaṇīyas, are being worshipped on the Sautya day (that is the day on which Soma juice is extracted) by the Brāhmaṇas. It (i.e. Sudhyu) is remembered as the source of origin of the waters. Indeed it is conceived in waters.

33. The fire by name Pāvaka that is born of waters and that is called *Abgarbha* (Having the waters as the womb) should be known as the fire at the Avabhṛtha (the holy ablution at the end of a sacrifice). It is worshipped along with Varuṇa.

34. Hṛcchaya (Abiding within the heart) is the fire that is his (Pāvaka's) son.[1] It is the fire that digests (food-stuffs) in the stomach of men. Mṛtyumān is remembered as the scholarly son of the Jaṭhara-fire (Gastric fire).

35-36. That fire born mutually may burn all the living beings here. The terrible Saṁvartaka fire is remembered as the son of the fire Manyumān (? Mṛtyumān). It drinks water and lives in the ocean and has the face of a mare. Saharakṣa is conceived as the son of Samudravāsin (residing within the ocean).

37. Kṣāma, the son of Saharakṣa, burns the houses of men. His son is the fire Kravyād and it consumes dead persons.

38. Thus the sons of Pāvaka fire have been described here. Thereafter is the solar fire Śuci.[2] It is called Āyus by the Gandharvas.

39. This fire generates other fires on being churned in the Araṇi; this fire is taken from one place to another; this lord is known by the name Āyus.

---

1. VV.34-38 give the list of Pāvaka's sons. But actually they are given here in the genealogical order as follows:

Pāvaka—Hṛcchaya—Mṛtyumān (Manyumān)—Saṁvartaka (Vaḍavānala)—Saharakṣa—kṣāma—Kravyādagni.

2. The fires under group of Śuci are given in a genealogical order as follows:

Śuci or Āyus, Mahiṣa, Sahasa, Adbhuta, Vividhi, Arka—nine sons of Arka as enumerated in V.43.

40. Mahiṣa was the son of Āyus. His son is named Sahasa. That fire Sahasa is remembered as the *Abhimānin* (Identifying itself with it) in the Yajñas of *Pāka* (cooking).

41. The son of the fire Sahasa was Adbhuta of great fame. Vividhi is remembered as the great son of the fire Adbhuta.

42. (This fire) is one that identifies itself with expiatory rites. It always consumes the Havis-offering that is consigned into the fire. Arkka was the son of Vividhi. The following were the sons of that fire (Arkka).

43. They are—Anīkavān, Vājasṛk, Rakṣohā, Yaṣṭikṛt, Surabhi, Vasu, Annāda, Apraviṣṭa and Rukmarāṭ.

44. These fourteen fires are the Progeny of the fire Śuci. These fires are said to be those that are consecrated in the sacrifices.

45. In the Manvantara of Svāyambhuva in the first Sarga (creation), these fires that are *Abhimānins* (those that identify themselves) had passed away along with the Yāmas, the excellent Devas.

46. Formerly in the world, these Havyavāhanas (fires) were those that identified themselves with the abodes called Viharaṇīyas, both sentient and insentient.

47. These fires were stationed in the holy rites and Yajñas. They were (both) *Kāmyas* (those with the fruit desired) and *Naimittikas* occasional ones or that are utilised when cause arises). They had passed away in the previous Manvantara along with those Śukras and Yāgas (?)

48. In the Manvantara of the first Manu, they had passed away along with the holy noble-souled Devas. Thus the abodes of these *Sthānins* (those that identify themselves with the abodes) have been enumerated by me.

49. The characteristics of Jātavedas (fires) in the Manvantaras of the past and future are enumerated through them.

50. All of them are remembered as ascetics and Brahmabhṛts (those that sustain the knowledge of Brahman). All of them were lords of subjects. They are remembered as Luminous.

51. These are to be known (as present) in all the seven Manvantaras beginning with Svārociṣa and ending with the Sāvarṇya Manvantara in regard to their names, forms and purposes.

52. The present fires exist along with the current Yāma Devas. The future fires (lit. those that have not yet come) shall exist along with the future Devas.

53. Thus the group of fires has been duly described in the proper order.

Now henceforth the race of the Pitṛs will be narrated in detail and in the due order.

CHAPTER THIRTEEN

The Real Nature of Kāla—Time : Seasons (Ṛtus) as Pitṛs (Manes)

Sūta said :

1. Even as Brahmā was creating sons formerly in the Svāyambhuva Manvantara, the human beings, the Asuras and the Devas were born out of his limbs.

2. The Pitṛs also were born, considering him as their father (?). The mode of their creation has been described before. Let it be heard briefly once again.

3. After creating the Devas, Asuras and the human beings, Brahmā took pride in them. (He conceived of a further creation also). (The Pitṛs) who were being considered like fathers, were born of his flanks.

4. The six seasons beginning with Madhu (Spring) (were born of his flanks). They call them Pitṛs. The vedic text says,—"The seasons are the Pitṛs and Devas."

5. In all the Manvantaras, past and future (the same is repeated). Formerly, these were born in the auspicious Manvantara of Svāyambhuva.

6-7a. They are remembered by the name *Agniṣvāttas* and *Barhiṣads*. Those of them who were householders, who did not perform Yajñas are remembered as the Pitṛs of the group *Agniṣvāttas*. They were not *Āhitāgnis* (those who regularly maintained sacrificial fires).

7b-9. Those of them who performed Yajñas are the Pitṛs (known as) *Somapīṭhins*. Those who performed *Agnihotras* are remembered as the Pitṛs called *Barhiṣads*. In this sacred lore, it has been decisively mentioned that the Ṛtus (seasons) are the Pitṛs and the Devas. The months of Madhu and Mādhava (i.e. Caitra and Vaiśākha) should be known as *Rasas*; the month of Śuci and Śukra (i.e. Jyeṣṭha and Āṣāḍha) are *Suṣmins* (Lustrous ones). The months of Nabhas and Ṅabhsys (i.e. Śrāvaṇa and Bhādrapada)—these two are cited as *Jivas*.

10. The months of Iṣa and Ūrja (i.e. Āśvina and Kārttika) are cited as *Svadhāvats*. The months of Saha and Sahasya (i.e. Mārgaśīrṣa and Pauṣa) are cited as Ghoras.

11. The months of Tapas and Tapasya (i.e. the months of Māgha and Phālguna) pertain to the winter, they are *Manyumats*. The units of time called *Māsas* (months) are included in the six periods of time (seasons).

12. These are called *Ṛtus*. The *Ṛtus* are the sons of Brahmā. They should be known as those identifying themselves with both sentient and non-sentient (objects).

13. In the abodes of *Māsa* (month) and *Ardhamāsa* (fortnight), the *Ṛtus* (seasons) are considered the *Sthānins* (the abiders). By means of the change of abodes, the *Sthānābhimānins* (those who identify themselves with the abodes) should be understood.

14. The days, the nights, the months, the seasons, the *Ayanas* (tropical transits of the sun) and the years are the abodes; the names of *Abhimānins* (deities identifying themselves) are in the same order.

15. The *Sthānins* (those who identify themselves with the abodes) who are established in these, are the states of time. They are having those as their own selves, since they are of the same essence as they. Understand as I shall mention them.

16.[1] The various units (or states) of time are the *Tithis* of *Parvans* (dates of lunar fortnights), the junctions, the fortnights that are on a par with halves of months, the moments, the Kalās, Kāṣṭhās, Muhūrtas, days and nights.

17-18. Two half-months make one *Māsa* (month). Two months make what is called *Ṛtu*. Three *Ṛtus* make one *Ayana* and the two *Ayanas*, (viz.: the southern and the northern) together constitute a year. These are the abodes for the *Sthānins*. The *Ṛtus* are the sons of Nimi. Similarly, they should be known as six in number.

19-20. The five types of subjects (i.e. human beings, quadrupeds, birds, reptiles and trees) are remembered as the sons of *Ṛtu*. They are characterised by their seasonal change. Since the mobile and the immobile beings are born through the *Ārtavas* (seasonal changes, menstruation etc.) the *Ārtavas* are fathers and the *Ṛtus* are grandfathers. When they come together, the subjects of the Prajāpati are born.

21. Hence the *Vatsara* (year) is considered the great grand-father of the subjects. These *Sthānins* of the nature of the abodes in their respective abodes have been recounted.

22. They are declared as those who have the same names, the same essence and the same nature as they (i.e. units of time). It is *Saṁvatsara* (the year) that is considered and remembered as Prajāpati.

23. Agni, the son of Saṁvatsara, is called *ṛta* by scholars. Since they are born of Ṛta, they are called Ṛtus.

24-25. Years should be known as having six seasons. To the five types of subjects, viz.: bipeds, quadrupeds, birds, reptiles and the stationary beings, there are five *Ārtavas* (seasonal changes). The flower is remembered as Kālārtava (seasonal change indicating particular period of time of trees. The state of being *Ṛtu* and *Ārtava* is recounted as Pitṛtva (the state of being Pitṛs).

26. Thus the *Ṛtus* and the *Ārtavas* should be known as

1. VV. 16-18 detail the units of time.

Pitṛs because all the living beings are born of them through the *Ṛtukāla* (the time of *Ṛtu*—period favourable for conception).[1]

27. Hence these *Ārtavas* are indeed the *Pitṛs*—so we have heard. These have stayed throughout the Manvantaras as *Kālābhimānins* (identifying themselves with the *Kāla* or time).

28-30. They are endowed with causes and effects; they have pervaded everything through their supremacy and indeed these identify themselves with the abodes and they stand here in consequence of that special contact (?).

The *Pitṛs* are of various kinds viz.: *Agniṣvāttas* and *Barhiṣads*. Two daughters well known in the worlds were born of Svadhā and the Pitṛs. They were Menā and Dhāraṇī by whom the entire universe is sustained. These two were expounders of Brahman. These two were Yoginīs also.

31-34. Menā was the mental daughter of those Pitṛs who are mentioned as *Agniṣvāttas*. They are remembered as *Upahūtas* too.

Dhāraṇī is remembered as the mental daughter of *Barhiṣads*. These Pitṛs, the *Barhiṣads* are remembered as *Somapāyins* too.[2]

These two Pitṛs gave their splendid daughters in marriage for the sake of righteousness.

The *Agniṣvāttas* gave Menā as the wife unto the Himavān, The Barhiṣads gave the splendid daughter Dhāraṇī as wife unto Meru. Understand their grandsons.

Menā the wife of Himavān gave birth to Maināka.

35. She gave birth to Gaṅgā also, the most excellent river who became the wife of the salt sea. Krauñca is the son of Maināka. It is due to him that the continent Krauñca has been so named.

36. Dhāraṇī, the wife of Meru, gave birth to the son Mandara endowed with divine medicinal herbs as well as three well reputed daughters.

---

1. This explains why *Ṛtus* (Seasons) are regarded as *Pitṛs* (manes).

2. There is a difference of opinion among the Purāṇas about the names of the daughters of these Pitṛs. Such differences are reconciled by presuming that the events in Purāṇas refer to different Kalpas or Manvantaras.

37. They were Velā, Niyati and the third (daughter) Āyati. Āyati is remembered as the wife of Dhātṛ and Niyati that of Vidhātṛ.

38. The progeny of these two, formerly in the Svāyambhuva Manvantara have already been recounted. Velā (seashore) gave birth to a praiseworthy (lit. uncensured) daughter of Sāgara (the ocean).

39. The daughter of the ocean named Savarṇā became the wife of Prācīnabarhiṣ. Ten sons were born to Savarṇā of Prācīnabarhiṣ.

40. All of them were called Pracetasas and were masters of the science. Lord Dakṣa, the son of the self-born lord, assumed the status of their son.

41. It was on account of the curse of the three-eyed lord (and it took place) in the Cākṣuṣa Manvantara.

On hearing this, Śāṁśapāyani asked Sūta.

42. "How was it that Dakṣa was born formerly in the Cākṣuṣa Manvantara, due to the curse of Bhava ? Even as we ask, narrate that to us."

43. On being told thus, Sūta addressed Śāṁśapāyani and told the story connected with Dakṣa (along with) the cause of the curse of Tryambaka.

Sūta said :

44. "Dakṣa had eight daughters who have already been mentioned by me. The father brought them from their (husbands') houses to his own house and honoured them.

45-46. Then, honoured very well thus, all of them stayed in their father's house.

The eldest among them was named Satī who was the wife of Tryambaka (Three-eyed god Śiva)

Dakṣa who hated Śiva did not invite that daughter. Maheśvara never bowed down to Dakṣa.

47-48. The son-in-law who was stationed in his own brilliance did not bow down to his father-in-law.

On knowing that all her sisters had arrived at her father's house, Satī, too went to her father's house although she had not been invited. The father accorded to her an honour inferior to that accorded to other daughters and which was disagreeable to her as well.

49-50. That goddess who had been infuriated and annoyed spoke to her father :—"O Lord, by according to me a welcome and honour inferior to that of my younger sisters, O father, by dishonouring me thus, you have done a despicable thing. I am the eldest and the most excellent. It behoves you to honour me."

51. On being told thus, Dakṣa spoke to her with his eyes turned red :— "These girls, my daughters, are more worthy of respect and more excellent than you.

52. O Satī, their husbands also are highly respected by me. They are highly proficient in the Vedas, endowed with good power of penance; possessing great Yogic power and very pious.

53-54a. O Satī, all of them are superior to Tryambaka, on account of their good qualities and are more praiseworthy. They are my excellent sons-in-law, viz. : Vasiṣṭha, Atri, Pulastya, Aṅgiras, Pulaha, Kratu, Bhṛgu and Marīci.

54b-56. Since Śarva always defies and disregards me, I do not honour and welcome you. Indeed Bhava is antagonistic to me." Thus spoke Dakṣa then, on account of his deluded mind, the consequence of which was a curse unto himself and to the great sages who were mentioned by him.

On being told thus the infuriated goddess said to her father thus—

57. "Since you insult me although I am devoid of defects verbally, mentally and physically, O father, I am abandoning this body born of you".

58. Then, being infuriated and aggrieved on account of that dishonour, goddess Satī bowed down to the self-born lord and spoke these words.

59-60a. "Wherever I am born again with a brilliant body whether I am not born (of a womb) or whether I am born of a righteous person, I should necessarily attain the status of the virtuous wife of the self-possessed three-eyed lord alone."

60b-61. Seated there itself she entered the Yogic trance. She united her soul (to the supreme lord). With her mind she retained the *Āgneyī Dhāraṇā*. Then the fire born of her soul rose up from all her limbs. Kindled by the wind it reduced her body to ashes.

62. The trident-bearing lord heard about that death of Satī. Śaṅkara came to know about their conversation factually. Hence, the lord became angry with Dakṣa and the sages.

Rudra said :

63. "Bhūrloka is spoken of as the first one among all the worlds. At the behest of Parameṣṭhin (supreme lord), I shall sustain it always.

64. All the lustrous worlds stand by on being held on to this earth. At his behest, I shall hold them here always.

65. There is the fourfold classification of the Devas. Still they partake of food at one place. I will not partake of food along with them. Therefore, they will offer it separately unto me.

66-68. O Dakṣa, since, on account of me sinless Sati had been insulted, and all other daughters were praised along with their husbands, hence when the Vaivasvata Manvantara begins, these great sages who are not born of a womb will be born again during my second Yajña". After announcing this to all of them, he cursed Dakṣa once again, "In the Cākṣuṣa Manvantara when Śukra's *Homa* is performed by *Brahmā* (?), you will become a human king in the family of Cākṣuṣa.

69-71. You will be born as the grandson of Prācīnabarhiṣ and the son of Pracetas. You will be born by the name of Dakṣa itself, as the son of Māriṣā, the daughter of *Śākhins* (trees).

When the Vaivasvata Manvantara arrives, there also, O evil-minded one, I will cause obstacles in a holy rite endowed with virtue though it may be difficult of access".

Sūta said :

72. On hearing that, Dakṣa cursed Rudra once again :— "Since, on account of me you rendered evil to the sages, the Brāhmaṇas will not worship you along with the Devas in the course of a Yajña.

73. O ruthless one, after offering the Āhuti unto you in the course of their holy rites, they will touch the holy water again. At the close of the Yuga, they will abandon heaven and will stay here alone".

74-75. Thereafter, he (Rudra) is not worshipped along with the Devas. He is worshipped separately.

Thereupon, Dakṣa who was thus addressed by Rudra of unmeasured. splendour and cursed abandoned his body originating from the self-born lord, and was born among human beings.

76. After realising the lord and deity of Yajñas, Dakṣa, the householder, worshipped him with the entire Yajña along with the other deities.

77. After the advent of the Vaivasvata Manvantara, the lord of mountains begot of Menā the goddess Umā who had been the noble lady Satī previously.

78. She who had been the noble lady Satī previously became Umā afterwards. She is the wife of Bhava always. Bhava is never abandoned by her.

79-80. Just as the noble lady Aditi follows for ever Kaśyapa, the son of Marīci; just as goddess Śrī follows Nārāyaṇa, just as Śacī follows Maghavan (i.e. Indra), (so also satī follows Bhava.)

These following noble ladies never leave off their husbands, viz. : Lakṣmī does not leave off Viṣṇu, Uṣā does not leave off Sūrya (the Sun) nor does Arundhatī leave of Vasiṣṭha.

81. They return and are born again and again in the Kalpas along with them.

Thus Dakṣa was born as the son of Pracetas in the Cākṣuṣa Manvantara.

82. This has been heard by us that on account of the curse he was born second time as king, as the son of Māriṣā and the ten Pracetas.

83-86. The seven great sages, Bhṛgu and others were born formerly in the first Tretā yuga of the Vaivasvata Manvantara. They assumed body from Varuṇa, at that sacrifice of the great lord.

Between Dakṣa, the Prajāpati, and Triyambaka, the intelligent self-possessed Lord, there was intense enmity continued from their previous birth. Hence intense enmity should never be pursued at the time of personal antagonism.

Due to merits and demerits, the living being does not leave off the awareness of what is intensely conceived in the mind, though it may pertain to the previous birth. That should not be pursued by a learned person.

87. Thus began the story that rids one of sins and that pertains to Dakṣa.[1] It has been formerly urged for narration by you.

88. This story had been recounted in the context of narration of the line of the Pitṛs.[2] Henceforth, I shall recount the Devas in the same order as that of the Pitṛs.

89. Formerly, in the beginning of the Tretā yuga in the Svāyambhuva Manvantara, there were the Devas well-known as Yāmas and they were the sons of Yajña.[3]

90. They were the well-reputed sons of Brahmā. Since they were *Ajas* (unborn), they are *Ajitas* (unconquered). These are the mental sons of Svāyambhuva. They are named Śakta.

91. Therefore, these are remembered as the three groups of Devas (? Yāma, Ajita and Śakta). The Cchandajas* were thirty-three in the creation of Svāyambhuva.

92-94. The twelve Yāmas are recounted as follows: Yadu, Yayāti, Vīvadha, Trāsata, Mati, Vibhāsa, Kratu, Prayāti, Viśruta, Dyuti, Vāyavya and Saṁyama. Yadu and Yayāti were two Devas (?)

The twelve Ajitas are as follows: Asama, Ugradṛṣṭi, Sunaya, Śuciśravas, Kevala, Viśvarūpa, Sudakṣa, Madhupa, Turīya, Indrayuk, Yukta and Ugra.

---

1. This and a number of verses from this chapter are found in Vā.P.Ch.31

2. Dakṣa, in the 2nd incarnation, was a descendant of Pitṛ-gods (vide V.40 above). Hence the story of Dakṣa and the destruction of his sacrifice by Śiva is inserted here.

3. From this verse, the section of the race of gods (*Deva-vaṁśa*) begins.

* Vā.P.31.5 reads *chandogāḥ* 'Chanters of the Sāma-veda'.

95-96. The twelve Śaktas are recounted as follows :

Janiman, Viśvadeva, Javiṣṭha, Mitavān, Jara, Vibhu, Vibhāva, Ṛcika, Durdiha, Śruti, Gṛṇāna and Bṛhat.

These were *Somapāyins* in the Svāyambhuva Manvantara.

97. These *Gaṇas* were lustrous, valorous and very powerful at the outset; lord Viśvabhuk was their Indra.

98-100. The Asuras who lived then were their cousins and kinsmen.

The Suparṇas, Yakṣas, Gandharvas, Piśācas, Uragas and Rākṣasas—these along with the Pitṛs (and the Devas) constituted the eight Devayonis (divine groups), they passed away in the Svāyambhuva Manvantara. They have thousands of subjects (progeny). They were richly endowed with majestic lustre, beauty, longevity and physical strength. They are not mentioned in detail here, lest there should be irrelevancy of context.

101-102. The Svāyambhuva creation should be understood by means of the current one.[1] The past creation is observed through the present one which is Vaivasvata in regard to the subjects, deities, sages and Pitṛs. Understand the seven sages who had been existing before.

103. Bhṛgu, Aṅgiras, Marīci, Pulastya, Pulaha, Kratu, Atri and Vasiṣṭha, these seven (?) were in the Svāyambhuva Manvantara.

104-105. Āgnīdhra, Agnibāhu, Medhā, Medhātithi, Vasu, Jyotiṣmān, Dyutimān, Havya, Savana and Sattra—these were the ten sons of Svāyambhuva Manu. They were extremely mighty with the velocity of the wind. They were kings of great magnificence in the first Manvantara.

106-107. That race along with the Asuras, the excellent Gandharvas, the Yakṣas, the Uragas, the Rākṣasas, the Piśācas, the human beings, the Suparṇas and the groups of Apsaras cannot be recounted in due order even in the

1. The author regards the first Manu (Svāyambhuva) and the present Manu (Vaivasvata) as more important and gives so to say a comparative statement between the events etc. in these two Manvantaras.

course of hundreds of years. Since their names are many where is the limit to their number in that family.

108. Those subjects who were in the Svāyambhuva Manvantara with the names of the *Yugas* (?) passed away due to the great efflux of time in the order of Ayanas, years and Yugas.

The sages asked :[1]

109. Who is this lordly Kāla (Time) ? Who is this annihilator of all living beings? Of what is he the source of origin? What is his beginning, what is the intrinsic essence, his soul ?

110. What is his eye? What is the form? What are remembered as his limbs? What is his name ? What is his self? Mention these factually.

Sūta said :

111. Let the real nature of Kāla (Time) be listened to.[2] After listening, let it be retained in the mind. The sun is his source and the period of the twinkling of the eye is his beginning. He is called *Saṅkhyācakṣus* (Having the number for his eyes).

112. The day and night together constitute its form. The *Nimeṣas*(moments)are his limbs. The year (*Saṁvatsara*) is his essence. His name is *Kalātmaka* (one whose soul is the digit).

113-115. That lord of subjects is of the nature of the present, future and past times. Understand the condition of the Kāla divided into five, by means of the day, the fortnight, the month, the reasons and the *Ayanas*. The first (year) is *Saṁvatsara*; the second one is *Parivatsara*; the third one is *Iḍvatsara* ; the fourth is *Anuvatsara*; and the fifth among them is *Vatsara*. That period of time is termed *Yuga*.[3]

---

1. This is a new section dealing with the nature of Kāla (Time). Cf. Vā.P.31.22 ff.

2. VV.111-112 describe the person of Kāla, while V.113 gives the five divisions of Kāla (time) viz. the day, the fortnight, the month, the season and the *Ayana*.

3. Kāla is now identified with Yuga. It is comprised of five years which are named as (1) Saṁvatsara, (2) Parivatsara, (3) Iḍvatsara, (4) Anuvatsara

116. I shall explain their principle (*Tattva*). Even as it is being recounted, understand it that which is mentioned as *Kratu* and *Agni* is considered *Saṁvatsara*.

117-120. This sun, the son of Aditi, and the fire of time is *Parivatsara*.

Soma (the moon) which is of the nature of the essence of waters, which has two movements, the bright and the dark ones (i.e. the bright half and the dark half of the month) is *Iḍvatsara* and has been decisively determined so in the *Purāṇas*. He who purifies the worlds with his seven times seven bodies (i.e. 49 Maruts); he who blows favourable to the world—that wind is *Anuvatsara*.

He who was born of the *Ahaṁkāra* (ego) of Brahmā as *Udagrudra**—that blue-red (complexioned) Rudra should be known as their *Vatsara*.

I shall explain his *Satattva* (essential nature); understand it even as it is being recounted.

121. Due to the contact of limbs and minor limbs, the Kālātman (the soul of time) is the great-grandfather. He is the lord and source of origin of Ṛk, Yajus and Sāman; he is the master of the five (i.e. day, fortnight etc.).

122-126. He is Agni, Yama, Kāla, Sambhūti and Prajāpati. He is source of origin of the sun. He is mentioned as *Saṁvatsara* by learned men.

The sun should be known as *Parivatsara*. He is the source of origin of the divisions of Kāla (Time), of the months, seasons and the two *Ayanas*; of the planets, stars, chillness, heat, rain, span of life and holy rites; the Bhāskara (sun) is the source of origin of the smaller divisions and the days; he is *Vaikārika* (an evolute ?), of kindly disposition, the son of Brahmā and the Lord protector of subjects. He is one. He is (in a way) not one. He is day, month, season and grandfather. He is Āditya, Savitṛ,

---

and (5) Vatsara. The following verses describe the "principle" as to how and why (1) Kratu-Agni, (2) The Sun-god, (3) Soma or the Moon-god with Pitṛs, (4) The Wind-god and (5) Rudra should be associated with these five years.

*Udagrudra=Udagra Rudra. Or we may adopt the reading of Vā.P.31.32a. *ahaṅkārād rudan rudraḥ* /

'Rudra who roared out of haughtiness and conceit'.

Bhānu, Jīvana (Enlivener) and honoured by Brahmā. He is the *Prabhava* (source of birth) and *Apyaya* (end or that in which they merge themselves at death) of all living beings. Therefore, Bhāskara the presiding deity of the Tārās (constellations), should be known as the second *Parivatsara.*

127-129. Since Soma (the moon god) is the lord of all medicinal herbs, since he is the grandfather, since he is the enlivener of all living beings, since he is the lord, causing *Yoga* (acquisition of what is not attained) and *Kṣema* (preservation of what is acquired); since he always looks after and upholds the universe by means of his rays; since he is the source of origin of the *Tithis* (days of the lunar fortnight), junctions of *Parvans*, full moon and the New moon; since he causes the night; since he is the Prajāpati with nectarine soul—for all these reasons Soma (Moon) with the Pitṛs is remembered as *Iḍvatsara.*

For the following reasons Vāyu (the Wind god) is *Anuvatsara :*

130. In the world he is the propeller of all activities of the living beings through the five types of vital winds viz. : Prāṇa, Apāna, Samāna, Vyāna, and Udāna.

131. He causes the unified and simultaneous activities of the five units of the physical body. viz. : the sense organs, the mind, the intellect, the memory and the strength.

132. He is the soul of all; he is the lord of all worlds through the (spatial winds) Āvaha, Pravaha etc. He exists through his seven times seven bodies (known as Maruts) that render help to others.

133-134. He is the maker of the destiny of all living beings; he is the *Prabhañjana* (violent gust of wind also); he perpetually causes the well-being of all living beings; he is the source of origin of fire, waters, earth, the sun and the moon; the wind is Prajāpati : he is the soul of all the worlds; he is the great grandfather and he causes days and nights. Hence, it is that Vāyu (wind god) is *Anuvatsara.*

135. All these four (i.e. Kāla, the sun, the Moon and the wind god) are lords of subjects; they are born of the flanks (of Brahmā); they are the fathers of all the worlds. They have been glorified as the souls of the worlds.

136-137. Bhava came out crying, through the mouth of Brahmā who was meditating. The great lord is mentioned (in the Vedas) of *Ṛṣi* (sage), *Vipra* (Brāhmaṇa), the soul of the living beings, the great grandfather, the lord of all living beings and the *Praṇava* (Om). It is through the penetration of the *Ātman* (soul) that the limbs and minor limbs of the living beings take shape.

138-139. Rudra who causes *Unmāda* (Madness) and (at the same time) blesses, is called *Vatsara*. Thus the sun, the moon, the fire, the wind and Rudra are all identifiers with *Yuga* (?). Lord Rudra who is the soul of Kāla is always the cause of annihilation. Lord Rudra entered this universe by means of his own brilliance.

140-141. Due to the contact with the soul that is the support, by means of the bodies and the appellations (he enters the universe). Therefore, through his own vitality he has the status of Deva, Pitṛ and Kāla and this status blesses the worlds. It is the greatest. So Rudra is always worshipped by those who are the knowers of that (Rudra ?)

142-144. Since the lord is the master of the lords of subjects, since he is Prajāpati, since he is the conceiver of all living beings, since Nīlalohita is the soul of all, since Rudra resuscitates the fading and declining medicinal herbs again and again; since at the time when medicinal herbs decline, the lord is worshipped by the Devas, the leader of whom is Prajāpati and who seek fruits eagerly desired by them—(He is worshipped by offering Puroḍāśa in three Kapālas) otherwise called Three Ambakas—So the lord is called *Tryambaka*.[1]

145. The three Vedic metres viz. : Gāyatrī, Triṣṭubh and Jagatī are remembered by the name Tryambakas. Out of love they are the sources of origin of the vegitable kingdom.

146. The Puroḍāśa offering consecrated by the repetition of those three metrical verses united into one is called *Trikapāla* because it has three means and it is instilled with their virility in three ways.

---

1. This is a repetition of the explanation of the identification of Tryambaka and the three Kapālas (pot-sherds) on which Puroḍāśa is offered.

147. Hence that Puroḍāśa is *Tryambaka*. Therefore, he (the lord Rudra) is also declared as *Tryambaka*.

Thus the Yuga is mentioned by learned men as one that consists of five years.

148. The *Saṁvatsara* that has been mentioned by Brāhmaṇas as one having five selves became a unit of six selves[1] with the names of *Madhu* (spring) and other seasons.

149-151. The five *Ārtavas* are the sons of the *Ṛtus*. Thus the creation is recounted briefly.

Thus the unattached Kāla with many measures and units removes the lives of living beings and runs like the rapidly speeding current of water.

The progeny of these, cannot be enumerated authoritatively, because they are innumerable. The group of sons and grandsons is endless.

Glorifying this family of great lords of subjects of holy rites and meritorious fame, one shall achieve great *Siddhi* (spiritual attachment).

CHAPTER FOURTEEN

The race of Priyavrata

Description of Continents and their Sub-Divisions

Sūta said :

1. In all the Manvantaras of the past and the future, all the subjects are born with similar identification in regard to names and forms.[2]

---

1. The year, said to be of five souls (vide V.113), is again divided into six divisions according to season (*ṛtus*).

2. This is the main thesis of the Purāṇa. This chapter deals with Puranic cosmography. It associates the names of continents (*dvīpas*) with the descendants of Svāyambhuva Manu. For similar description vide A.P.107, KP.I.40 Bh. P.V 16.1-26, Mt.P.112, 121, 122.

2. The Devas who are of eight types are the overlords in that Manvantara. The sages and the Manus—all of them serve the same purpose.

3. The creation of the great sages was already recounted. Now understand the race of Svāyambhuva Manu, that is being recounted in detail and in due order.

4-5. Svāyambhuva Manu had ten grandsons who were similar to him. The entire earth consisting of seven continents was colonised by them along with its towns, oceans and mines in every sub-continent in the first Tretā yuga of the Svāyambhuva Manvantara.

6. This (Earth) was colonised by those sons of Priyavrata, the grandson of Svāyambhuva (Manu) who were endowed with progeny, strength and penance.

7. Kāmyā that extremely fortunate daughter of Kardama the Prajāpati, bore unto Priyavrata heroic sons endowed with their own progeny.[1]

8-9. She gave birth to two daughters, viz. : Samrāṭ and Kukṣi. Both of them were splendid. She gave birth to ten sons also. The brothers of those two daughters were ten in number, valorous and similar to the Prajāpatis. They were Āgnīdhra, Agnibāhu, Medhas, Medhātithi, Vasu (later mentioned as Vapuṣmān), Jyotiṣmān, Dyutimān, Havya, Savana and Sattra.

1. The race of Priyavrata :

Names of Priyavrata's Sons	Names of the Dvīpa assigned as kingdom
1. Āgnīdhra	Jambū
2. Agnibāhu	—
3. Medhas	—
4. Medhātithi	Plakṣa
5. Vasu (Vapuṣmān)	Śālmala
6. Jyotiṣmān	Kuśa
7. Dyutimān	Krauñca
8. Havya	Śāka
9. Savana	Puskara
10. Sattra	—

10. Priyavrata crowned seven of them in seven-continents as kings with due religious rites. Understand them as well as those continents.

11. He made the excessively powerful Āgnīdhra, the lord of Jambūdvīpa. Medhātithi was made by him the lord of Plakṣadvīpa.

12. He crowned Vapuṣmān (Earlier mentioned as Vasu) as king in the Śālmala dvīpa. The lord made Jyotiṣmān, the king in Kuśa dvīpa.

13. He coronated Dyutimān as the king in Krauñca dvīpa; Priyavrata made Havya the lord of Śāka dvīpa.

14-17. The lord made Savana the overlord of Puṣkara. In Puṣkara dvīpa, Savana had two sons, viz. : Mahāvīta and Dhātaki. These two sons were the most excellent ones that parents could desire. In accordance with the name of that noble soul, his sub-continent is remembered as Mahāvīta varṣa. In accordance with the name of Dhātaki, his sub-continent is called Dhātakīkhaṇḍa.

Havya (the lord of Śākadvīpa) begot seven sons, rulers of Śākadvīpa. They were, viz. : Jalada, Kumāra, Sukumāra, Maṇīvaka, Kusumottara, Modāka and the seventh one Mahādruma.

18-21.[1] The first sub-continent of Jalada is called Jalada. The second sub-continent of Kumāra is glorified as Kaumāra.

The third one Sukumāra is remembered as the sub-continent of Sukumāra. The fourth one is called Maṇīvaka, the sub-continent of Maṇīva.

The fifth sub-continent Kusumottara is that of Kusumottara. Modāka the sixth sub-continent is glorified as that of Modāka.

The seventh sub-continent is Mahādruma in accordance with the name of Mahādruma.

All those seven sub-continents there are called after their names.

22-23. There were seven sons born of Dyutimān, the

1. VV.18-22. The seven sub-divisions of Śākadvīpa are named after the seven sons of Havya.

lord of Krauñcadvīpa[1] viz. : Kuśala, Manonuga, Uṣṇa, Pāvana, Andhakāraka, Muni and Dundubhi. These were the sons of Dyutimān. They have after their own names, the splendid sub-continents situated in the Krauñcadvīpa.

24-26. The land of Kuśala named Kauśala was very famous. Manonuga is remembered as the land of Manonuga.

Uṣṇa is remembered as the land of Uṣṇa and Pāvana that of Pāvana. That land of Andhakāra is glorified as Andhakāra.

Maunideśa was the land of Muni and Dundubhi is remembered as the land of Dundubhi.

These seven lands in the Krauñcadvīpa were radiant ones.

27-30. Jyotiṣmān too in the Kuśadvīpa had seven very powerful sons[2] viz. : Udbhijja, Venumān, Vairatha, Lavaṇa, Dhṛti, the sixth one Prabhākara and the seventh one remembered as Kapila.

The first sub-continent is called Udbhijja; the second sub-continent was Veṇumaṇḍala; the third sub-continent was Vairathākāra; the fourth sub-continent is remembered as Lavaṇa; the fifth sub-continent was Dhṛtimat; the sixth sub-continent was Prabhākara; the seventh sub-continent named Kapila was glorified as that of Kapila. Their lands in the Kuśadvīpa have the same names as they.

31. The Lords of Śālmala were (as if) embellished with subjects endowed with the disciplined conduct of life pertaining to the various Āśramas (stages of life).

They were the seven sons of Vapuṣmān.[3]

32. They were :—Śveta, Harita, Jīmūta Rohita, Vaidyuta, Mānasa and Suprabha, the seventh one.

33-34. Śveta was the land of Śveta; Suharita was that of Harita ; Jīmūta was the land of Jīmūta and Rohita that of Rohita. Vaidyuta was the land of Vaidyuta and Mānasa that

1. VV.22-26 enumerate seven sub-divisions of Krauñcadvipa which are named after the seven sons of Dyutimān.

2. VV.27-30. The seven sub divisions of Kuśadvīpa are named after the seven sons of Jyotiṣmān, king of Kuśadvīpa.

3. The seven sons of Vapuṣmān mentioned in the next verse have given their names to the *Varṣas* or sub-continents they headed.

of Mānasa. Suprabha was the land of Suprabha. All these seven were the protectors of the lands.

35. I shall recount Plakṣadvīpa after the Jambūdvīpa. The seven sons of Medhātithi were the kings ruling over Plakṣadvīpa.

36-37[1]. These were the sons of Medhātithi who are mentioned (as follows :) The eldest was named Śāntabhaya; the second is remembered as Śiśira: Sukhodaya was the third; the fourth is called Nanda; Śiva was the fifth among them; Kṣemaka is called sixth, and Dhruva should be known as the seventh.

38-43. Those seven Varṣas (sub-continents) are known after the names of those seven (sons). Therefore the following (are well known), viz. : Śāntabhaya, Śiśira, Sukhodaya, Ānanda, Śiva, Kṣemaka and Dhruva. Those Varṣas were all equal (to one another). They were colonized in the different parts formerly in the Svāyaṁbhuva Manvantara by those sons of Medhātithi who were kings and rulers of Plakṣadvīpa. The subjects in the Plakṣadvīpa were made to closely adhere to the disciplined conduct of life of the various castes and stages of life.

It is the Dharma[2] (piety, virtue) that is the criterion for the classification of the Varṇas and Āśramas in the five continents beginning with Plakṣadvīpa and ending with Śākadvīpa (i.e. Plakṣa, Śālmala, Kuśa, Krauñca and Śāka). Happiness, span of life, beauty, strength and Dharma (Virtue) are remembered to be common to all perpetually, in these five Dvīpas. Plakṣadvīpa has been described. Understand the Jambūdvīpa.

44. Priyavrata installed Āgnīdhra, the extremely powerful son of Kāmyā and his eldest successor as the king and overlord of Jambūdvīpa.

---

1. VV.36-40 enumerate seven sons of king Medhātithi, who became kings of seven Varṣas—sub-continents—which were named after their founder-kings.

2. VV.41-43 describe the common features of the five continents from Plakṣa to Śākadvīpa.

45-47. Nine sons were born to him.[1] They were on a par with the Prajāpatis.

The eldest was well known as Nābhi. Kimpuruṣa was his younger brother. Harivarṣa was the third and the fourth was Ilāvṛta. Ramya was the fifth son, Hiraṇvān is mentioned as his sixth son. Kuru was the seventh among them. Bhadrāśva is remembered as the eighth and the ninth was Ketumāla.

Understand their realms.

48-52 The father gave Nābhi the southern Varṣa named Hima; he gave Kimpuruṣa that Varṣa, called Hemakūṭa. He gave Harivarṣa that sub-continent which is remembered as Naiṣadha. He gave Ilāvṛta the sub-continent that was in the middle of Sumeru. The father gave Ramya, the sub-continent that is remembered as Nīla. The sub-continent Śveta that was situated to the north of it was given by the father to Hiraṇvān. He gave to Kuru the sub-continent that was to the north of Śṛṅgavān. Similarly, he allotted to Bhadrāśva the sub-continent Mālyavat. He assigned the sub-continent Gandhamādana to Ketumāla. Thus these nine sub-continents have been narrated by me, part by part.

53. Āgnīdhra crowned those sons in due order in those sub-continents. Thereafter, that pious-souled one became engaged in penance.

54. Thus the entire earth consisting of the seven continents was colonized by the seven sons of Priyavrata, who were the grandsons of Svāyambhuva Manu.

55. Thus, when annihilation takes place, these seven settlements (continents) are created again and again by the kings in all the seven sub-continents.

56-58. This is the nature of colonization of the continents and the Kalpas.

With regard to the eight sub-continents beginning with that of Kimpuruṣa (the following things should be noted). Their attainment is natural. Without effort they are generally happy. There s no annihilation or calamity in them. There is

1. VV.45-52 enumerate the sub-continents in Jambūdvipa. For the identification of mountains vide Ch. 1 Footnotes on pp. 11, 12.

no fear from old age and death. There is neither Dharma (Virtue) nor Adharma (evil) among them. There is no classification of people as the excellent, the middling and the base. In all those eight Kṣetras (i.e. Varṣas, sub-continents) there is no *Yugāvasthā* (the state of Yugas).

59-61. I shall recount the procreation by Nābhi in the sub-continent called Hima. Understand it. Nābhi begot a highly lustrous son, of Meru-Devī. He was Ṛṣabha,[1] the most excellent of all kings. He was the eldest of all Kṣatriyas. Heroic Bharata was born of Ṛṣabha. He was the eldest of hundred sons. Ṛṣabha crowned his son and engaged himself in Mahāpravrajyā (the great migration of renunciation i.e. journey or pilgrimage till death). He allotted the southern sub-continent named Hima to Bharata.

62-63. Hence learned men know this sub-continent as Bhāratavarṣa[2] after his name. Bharata's son was a virtuous scholar named Sumati. Bharata crowned him in that realm. After transferring the royal glory to his son the king entered the forest.

64. His son Tejasa was a lord of the subjects and conqueror of enemies. The great scholar, Indradyumna is remembered as Tejasa's son.

65-66. Parameṣṭhin, his son, was born after his death and his son was Pratīhāra and the family came to be known after his name. In his family a son well known as Pratihartṛ was born. To that intelligent Pratihartṛ, son Unnetṛ was born. Bhūman is remembered as his son.

67. His son was Udgītha. Prastāvi was his son. Vibhu was the son Prastāvi and Pṛthu was his son.

68. Pṛthu's son was Nakta. Gaya was Nakta's son. Nara was born as the son of Gaya and Virāṭ was the son of Nara.

69. Mahāvīrya was the son of Virāṭ. His son was Dhīman. Mahān was the son of Dhīman and Bhauvana was the son of Mahān.

---

1. He is regarded as the first Tīrthaṅkara by Jains. He is mentioned in the Bh.P. V.Chs. 4, 5 and in VP. II.1-28.

2. Jaina tradition supports this theory regardin the name of Bhāratavarṣa.

70. Tvaṣṭṛ was the son of Bhauvana. His son was Virajas. Rajas was the son of Nirajas and Śatajit was the son of Rajas.

71. He had hundred sons. All of them were kings. The important one among them was Viśvajyotis. It is through them, that these subjects flourished.

72. This Bhārata sub continent was marked by them as one with seven islands. Formerly, this Bhāratī land was enjoyed by those born of their family.

73-75. Each set of Yugas consists of Kṛta, Tretā etc. (The Manvantara consists of) such seventy-one sets of Yugas. People belonging to their family had been kings throughout the past Yugas in the Svāyambhuva Manvantara. They were hundreds and thousands.

Thus is the creation (race) of Svāymbhuva by which this universe is filled with sages, deities, Pitṛs, Gandharvas, Rākṣasas, Yakṣas, Bhūtas, Piśācas, human beings, animals and birds. This is said to be their creation. It undergoes change along with the Yugas.

CHAPTER FIFTEEN

The length and extent of the Earth : Description of Jambūdvipa.

Sūta said :

1-3. On hearing about the settlement of the subjects thus, Śāṁśapāyani asked Sūta about the length and extent of the Earth* as it had been determined—"How many continents are there ? How many oceans ? How many mountains are proclaimed ? How many are the *Varṣas* (sub-continents) ? What are the

---

* Vā.P.34.1b reads : *Pṛthivyāyāma-vistarau.* It is better than Bd.P.'s *Pṛthivyodadhivistaram.* Hence Vā.P. reading accepted.

rivers declared therein ? Mention all these things to us in detail and factually such as the magnitude of the great elements, the Lokāloka mountain, the transits, the extent and the movements of the moon as well as the sun.

Sūta said :

4-6. O ! I shall recount to you the length and extent of the earth, the number of the oceans and the number and extent of the islands. There are thousands of different islands that are included in the seven continents. They cannot be recounted in due order, because this world is studded and constantly (surrounded by them). I shall recount the seven continents along with the moon, the sun and the planets.

7-8a. Men mention their magnitudes by means of guess alone. One cannot arrive by means of guess alone, at those beings (or things) which cannot be even pondered upon. That which is beyond nature is called *Acintya* (that which cannot be even pondered upon).

8b-10. I shall recount the Jambūdvīpa as exists actually, consisting of nine Varṣas. Understand it through its extent and girth in terms of Yojanas. It is more than a hundred thousand Yojanas all round. It is full of different rural countries and different kinds of splendid cities. It is filled with Siddhas and Cāraṇas and is embellished with mountains.

11. (It is full of mountains) endowed with all kinds of minerals originating from clusters of rocks. It is full of rivers flowing from mountains.

12. Jambūdvīpa is immense and glorious with huge zones all round. It is encircled by nine worlds that evolve a number of living beings.

13. It is surrounded on all sides by the briny sea the extent of which is equal to that of Jambūdvīpa itself.

14.* The following are the six *Varṣaparvatas*[1] (Mountains

---

* After verse 14 there read verse No.28 which tells: the six mountains are Nīla, Niṣadha, Śveta, Hemakūṭa, Himavān and Śṛṅgavān.

1. The Varṣa-parvatas are the mountains (mountain-chains) which divide one Varṣa (sub-continent) from another. Thus they may be regarded as boundary mountains. The names and other characteristics are described in the following verses. Their geographical location is given in *supra* Ch.1 Footnotes on pp. 11, 12.

dividing the sub-continents). They have good ridges. On either side they merge into the Eastern and Western oceans.

15. Himavān is practically covered with snow. Hemakūṭa is full of *Heman* (gold). The great mountain Niṣadha is equally pleasant in all the seasons.

16. Meru is remembered as the most beautiful.[1] It has four colours (like four castes—*Varṇas*). It is golden. On its top its extent is thirtytwo thousand Yojanas.

17. It is circular in shape. It is symmetrical and very lofty. It is endowed with the qualities of Prajāpati. It has different colours at its sides.

18. It is originated from the umbilical cord of Brahmā born of the unmanifest one. In the east it is white in colour. Hence, it is on a par with the Brāhmaṇas.

19. Its northern side has a natural red colour. Hence, the Kṣatriya-hood of Meru on account of various reasons and purposes. (?)

20-21. In the southern side it is yellow. So its *Vaiśyatva* (state of being a Vaiśya) is evident. In the West it is like the *Bhṛṅgapatra* (A kind of leaf black in colour) all round. Hence it has the state of Śūdra. Thus the colours are recounted (as well as the castes). Its nature through colour and magnitude has been explained.

22. The Nīla mountain is full of sapphires (has that colour). The Śveta is white and full of gold. Śṛṅgavān has the colour of the peacock's tail and it is full of gold.

23. All these lordly mountains are frequented by the Siddhas and Cāraṇas. Their internal diameter is said to be nine thousand Yojanas.

24. The sub-continent of Ilāvṛta is in the middle of Mahāmeru. Its extent all around is thus nine thousand Yojanas.

---

1. There is a consensus among Purāṇas like KP., Mt.P., Mk.P., Vā.P., and Bd.P. about the shape and size of Meru. M. Ali points out that ancient Persians, Greeks, Chinese, Jews, and Arabs repeat the traditional nodality of Meru. After discussing the problem, he comes to the conclusion that Mt. Meru is identical with the Pāmirs, in central Asia.

His diagrammatic representation of the Jambūdvīpa and its cross-section (Fig.4) on p.65 of *Geog. of the Purāṇas* is interesting.

25. In its middle is the Mahāmeru like a smokeless fire. The southern side of Meru is like the middle of the altar. Its upper half is its upper surface.

26. The Varṣa-Parvatas which belong to the six Varṣas are two thousand Yojanas in extent and in height.

27-31a. Their length is said to be in accordance with the extent of Jambūdvīpa. The two mountains, (Nīla and Niṣadha) are hundred thousand Yojanas long. The other four mountains are shorter than these. The mountains Śveta and Hemakūṭa are each ninety thousand Yojanas long. The mountains Himavāṇ and Śṛṅgavān are each eighty thousand Yojanas long. There are Janapadas (territories or counties) in between them. The Varṣas are seven in number. They are encircled by mountains that are difficult to cross on account of steep precipices. They are criss-crossed with different kinds of rivers. It was impossible to travel from one Varṣa to another (lit. they were mutually unapproachable).

31b. Animals of different kinds live in them. This Haimavata sub-continent is well known by the name Bhārata.

32-34. Hemakūṭa is beyond this. It is remembered by the name Kimpuruṣa. Naiṣadha sub-continent is beyond Hemakūṭa and it is called Harivarṣa. Ilāvṛta is beyond Harivarṣa (and in the middle) of Meru. Nīla is beyond Ilāvṛta and it wellknown by the name Ramyaka. Śveta is beyond Ramyaka and it is wellknown as Hiraṇmaya. The sub-continent Śṛṅgavat is beyond Hiraṇmaya and it is remembered as Kuru.

35. The two sub-continents in the south and the north should be known as situated in the form of a bow. Four others are stationed lengthwise and the middle one is Ilāvṛta.[1]

36. Vedyardha which is on the hitherside of Niṣadha,

---

1. This Purāṇa supports the *Sapta-dvīpī* (seven-continent) theory about the earth. The distribution of the continents may be represented as under.

is known as the southern Vedyardha and that which beyond the Nīlavān is the northern Vedyardha.[1]

37. In the southern side of Vedyardha, there are three Varṣas and on the northern side of Vedyardha also there are three Varṣas. Meru should be known as existing in between them and Ilāvṛta is in the middle of Meru.

38. To the south of the Nīla and to the north of Niṣadha, there is a great mountain stretching to the north named Mālyavān.[2]

39. It stretches a thousand Yojanas from Nīla to Niṣadha. It is glorified as one, thirtyfour thousand Yojanas in extension.

40. The mountain Gandhamādana should be known as situated to its west. In length and extent it is reputed to be like Mālyavān.

41. Meru, the golden mountain, is in the middle of two circles. That golden mountain has four colours. It is symmetrical and very lofty.

North: (Uttara) Kuru Varṣa
Śṛṅgavān Mt.
Hiraṇmaya Varṣa
Śveta Mt.
Ramyaka Varṣa
Nīla Mt.

Ilāvṛta Varṣa
Meru Mt.
Ilāvṛta Varṣa

Niṣadha Mt.
Hari Varṣa
Hemakūṭa Mt.
Kimpuruṣa Varṣa
Himavān (Himālaya) Mt.
South Bhārata or Haimavata Varṣa

Does the bowlike formation of these Varṣas suggest the spherical shape of the earth?

1. Called Veyaḍḍha in Jain (Ardha Māgadhī) canon.

2. Purāṇas give different locations of Gandhamādana and Mālyavān. So do modern scholars, as the names of extra-Indian mountains were adopted by the Indo-Aryans as they penetrated deep in the Indian Peninsula. Thus Mālyavān due to its association with Gandhamādana and Meru should be identified with the Sarikol range, as Gandhamādana was the northern ridge of the great Hindukush arch with its northern extension, the Khwaja Mahammad. The southern ridge of Hindukush is Niṣadha which merged into Northern Karakorum and Kunlun (M. Ali.—*Geog. of Purāṇas*, pp. 58-59).

42. The brilliant Sumeru shines, established like a king. It has the colour and brilliance of the midday sun. It is refulgent like the smokeless fire.

43. It is eightyfour thousand Yojanas high. It has entered (down the ground level) sixteen thousand Yojanas. Its width is also sixteen thousand Yojanas.

44. Since it is stationed like a platter its width on the top is thirtytwo thousand Yojanas. Its girth all round is three times its width.

45-47. When the mass is circular the reckoning is triangular (?) (According to the triangular reckoning) its girth all round is fortyeight thousand Yojanas. Now the magnitude is recounted in the triangular reckoning. According to the quadrangular reckoning (?) the girth all round is laid down as sixtyfour thousand Yojanas. That mountain is highly divine and equipped with divine medicinal herbs.

48-49. The entire mountain is surrounded by worlds splendid and golden. All the groups of the Devas, the Gandharvas the serpents, and the Rākṣasas are seen on that king of mountains, as well as the splendid groups of Apsaras. That mountain Meru is encircled by worlds causing welfare of living beings.

50-53. Four lands (Realms) are established on the four sides. They are Bhadrāśvas (with east), Bhāratas (south), Ketumālas in the west and the Kurus in the North[1] which are the resorts of meritorious persons.

At the side of the Gandhamādana, there is this another great Gaṇḍikā (hill?). It is charming and fascinating in all the seasons. It is auspicious and pleasant. East to West it extends to thirtytwo thousand Yojanas. The (gross) length is

1. This appears to be the four-continent (*Catur-dvīpī*) theory about the earth where the distribution of Varṣas is as follows:

North
(Uttara)—Kuru
West. Ketumāla (Mt. Meru) Bhadrāśva. *East*
|
Bhārata
South

thirtyfour thousand Yojanas. The people Ketumālas of auspicious holy rites are established there.

54. All the men there are black and very strong. They have great inherent vitality. The women have the colour and lustre of the petals of lilies. All of them are pleasing to behold.

55. There is a great divine jack-tree there. It has all the six tastes. It is Īśvara (masterly and powerful). It is the son of Brahmā. It is as swift as mind and wanders wherever it pleases.

56. They drink the juice of its fruits and live for ten thousand years.

At the side of the Mālyavān, in the east there is a wonderful Gaṇḍikā Hill ?

57. It has the same length and extent as the western Gaṇḍikā. Bhadrāśvas[1] should be known (as the people) there. They are always delighted in their minds.

58. There is a forest of Bhadraśālas (excellent silk cotton trees). The great tree is the Black Mango tree. The men there are white-complexioned, highly enthusiastic and endowed with strength.

59. The women have the colour and lustre of the water-lilies. They are beautiful and pleasing to behold. They have the lunar brilliance and hue. Their faces resemble the moon.

60. Their limbs are cool of touch like the moon. They have the odour of lilies. Their span of life is ten thousand years and is free from ailments.

61-63. By drinking the juice of the black mango all of them have perpetual youth.

To the south of the Śveta and to the north of the Nīla, there is the Varṣa (sub-continent) Ramaṇaka.[2] Human beings are born there. They are free from impurities. They give importance to amorous dalliance. They are devoid of old age and bad odour. They are white-complexioned and richly endowed with nobility of birth. All of them are pleasing to

1. This seems to be modern China.

2. Identified with ancient Sogdiana as the description tallies with the land, plant-life and people of those times, M.Ali—*Ibid.* pp. 83-84.

behold. There also is a great Nyagrodha tree (holy fig tree) red (in colour).

64-66. They maintain themselves by drinking the juice of its fruits. Those highly fortunate ones live for eleven thousand five hundred years. They are excellent men and are always full of delight.

To the south of the Śṛṅgavān and to the north of the Śveta there is the Varṣa named Hairaṇvata.[1] There is a river here, the Hairaṇvatī. Men of great strength and good brilliance are born there.

67-69. They are heroic Yakṣas of great inherent vitality. They are rich and pleasing to behold. They have great vigour and they live for eleven thousand five hundred years.

In that Varṣa, there is a great *Lakuca* (bread fruit) tree of six tastes. By drinking the juice of its fruits, they live without ailments.

The Śṛṅgavān has three great and lofty peaks.

70. One of them (peaks) is full of *Maṇis* (jewels). One is golden and (the third) one all sorts of *Ratnas* (precious stones); it is embellished with houses.

71. To the north of Śṛṅgavān and to the south of the sea are the Kurus.[2] That Varṣa (sub-continent) is sacred and frequented by the Siddhas.

72. The trees there have *Madhu* (honey, wine) for its fruit. They put forth perpetual flowers, fruits and sprouts. They yield garments and ornaments by way of fruits.

73. Some of the trees are very delightfully charming and they bestow all desires. They exude excellent honey full of sweet smell, colour and taste.

---

1. Hairaṇvata Varṣa is closely associated with the river Hairaṇvatī (mod. Zarafshan) both forms of the name of the river mean 'The scatterer of gold'. In that case it must be presumed to be adjacent to Sogdiana—M.Ali, *ibid.* pp. 84,85.

2. Kuru or Uttarakuru: This region as described here and in other Purāṇas includes the basin of rivers—The Irtysh, the Ob, the Tobol, in other words "Western Siberian Regions' M.Ali—*Op. Cit.* pp. 84,85.

As M.Ali points out the main tree which is supposed to feed the population indicates the peculiar climate prevailing there.

74. Other trees are kṣīrins (Milky ones) by name. They are very delightful and they always exude milk comparable to nectar having six tastes.

75. The entire ground is full of jewels with fine golden particles for sand. It richly accords happiness in all seasons. It is devoid of mud and dust. It is splendid.

76. Splendid human beings displaced and dropping down from the world of the Devas are born there. They are white-complexioned and richly endowed with nobility of birth. All have steady perpetual youth.

77-80. Women on a par with the celestial damsels give birth to twins. They drink the milk of the *Kṣirin* trees comparable to nectar. The twins are born in a trice and they grow together. Their conduct of life, habits, forms and features and lovable qualities are all equal. They love one another and have the same activities and practices as the Cakravāka birds (Ruddy geese). They are always free from ailments and devoid of sorrows. They resort to perpetual pleasure. They are of great vigour and vitality. They live for fourteen thousand five hundred years. They never carnally approach another men's wives.

CHAPTER SIXTEEN

The Description of Bhārata

Sūta said :

1. "The (mode of) creation of the sub-continents in the auspicious Bhārata had been viewed thus alone, by those who were conversant with the greatest principles. What shall I describe once again unto you?"

The sage said :

2-3. "We wish to know (more about) this sub-continent Bhārata[1] where these fourteen Manus, Svāyambhuva and others were born in the course of the creation of the subjects.

1. This topic is discussed in details in other Purāṇas also e.g. AP.118, VP.II.3, Vā.P. 45.68-137.

O excellent one, recount that to us." On hearing these words of theirs

Romaharṣaṇa said :

4. "I shall recount to you all the subjects here in the Bhārata Varṣa.

This is a mysterious sub-continent in the middle (of the universe) where the fruits (of Karmas) are enjoyed whether auspicious or inauspicious.

5. The sub-continent that is to the north of the ocean as well as to the south of the Himavān, is called the sub-continent of Bhārata where the subjects are Bhāratī (pertaining to Bhārata).

6. Manu is called Bharata because of his (efficiency in the) maintenance and nourishment of the subjects. That sub-continent is thus remembered as Bhārata in view of the expression defined thus.[1]

7. It is from here that heaven and salvation are attained and people go to the middle (?) and ultimate end.[2] Nowhere else on the Earth has the holy rite been enjoined on the human beings.

8. Understand that there are nine different divisions or zones of Bhārata Varṣa.[3] It should be known that they are separated by oceans and it is impossible to traverse from one to the other.

---

1. This is a new definition of Bhārata attributing the credit to Manu who is called Bharata, as he maintained the subjects. This supersedes the old tradition which attributed this name to Bharata the son of Nābhi. Cf. Mt.P.114.5-6.

2. This is claimed as the special feature of India. Due to this special importance, Bhārata is called Karmabhūmi, cf. Bm.P.27.2, Mk.P.55.21-22, Mt.P.114.6-7 also Siddhānta Śiromaṇi III.4.

3. Cf. MK.P. 57.5, Mt.P.113.7-9. This is a new definition which includes what is known as 'greater Bhārata' today. It indicates the period when Hindu culture was assimilated by countries in the south and south-east Asia. V.S. Agrawala identifies some of the divisions of Bhārata as follows:

Indra-dvīpa=Indradyumna or Andamans
Nāgadvīpa=Nicobars (Nakkavara in Cola inscriptions)
Tāmraparṇī=Ceylon
Varuṇa-dvīpa=Borneo
Kaseruman=Malaya-dvīpa.

9-11. The nine divisions are—1) Indradvīpa, 2) Kaśerūmān, 3) Tāmravarṇa, 4) Gabhastimān, 5) Nāgadvīpa, 6) Saumya, 7) Gandharva, 8) Varuṇa and this 9) is the island surrounded by the sea. This sub-continent (of Bhārata) extends north-south, from the source of the river Gaṅgā to Cape Comorin, a thousand Yojanas (1 Yojana = 12 Km). The extent obliquely(i.e. the breadth)on the northern part is nine thousand Yojanas.

12. All round in the bordering regions the sub-continent is colonized by Mlecchas (barbarous tribes). The Kirātas live in the Eastern border lands and the Yavanas in the Western border lands.

13. The Brāhmaṇas, the Kṣatriyas and the Vaiśyas live in the central areas and the Śūdras (are scattered) in different parts. They are well settled maintaining themselves by means of performance of sacrifices, wielding of weapons and carrying on trading activities.

14-16. The mutual inter-dealings among those different castes continue (indefinitely), based on virtue, wealth and love, in regard to their holy rites. The conception of the different stages of life as well as of the Pañcamas (outcastes?) is duly maintained here among these people who have the tendency and endeavour to attain heaven and Mokṣa (Liberation).

The ninth division which is an island is said to extend obliquely. He who conquers it completely is called Samrāṭ (Emperor).

It is suggested that *Gabhastimān* and *Saumya* may be identified with Java and Sumatra (*Mt.P.—a study*, pp.191-193). For the different opinions of scholars on the above identifications *vide* M. Ali: Geog. of *Purāṇas*, pp. 126-127. M. Ali contradicts the claim of Agrawala, Majumdar and others regarding the inclusion of countries in south East Asia in Bhāratavarṣa (*Ibid.* pp. 128-130). M. Ali identifies them as follows:

Tāmravarṇa=Indian peninsula south of the Kāveri.

Kaserumat=The coastal plain between the deltas of Godāvari and Mahānadī.

Gabhastimān=The hilly belt between the Narmadā and Godāvari

Saumya=The coastal belt west of the Indus.

Gandharva=The trans-Indus region.

Varuṇa=The Western coast of India.

But these are mere speculations of scholars.

17. Indeed this world is Samrāṭ. The firmament is remembered as Virāṭ. That (other) world is remembered as Svarāṭ. I shall mention in detail once again (later on).

18-19. There are seven mountains of excellent knots and ridges wellknown as *Kulaparvatas*.[1] They are Mahendra, Malaya, Sahya, Śuktimān, the Ṛkṣa mountain, the Vindhya and the Pāriyātra. These seven are *Kulaparvatas*. There are thousands of other mountains near these mountains.

20-23. They are not well known (i.e. well explored). They possess good and essential things. They are vast (in expanse). Their ridges and peaks are of various shapes and sizes. They are[2] Mandara, the excellent mountain, Vaihāra,

---

1. Out of the seven mountain ranges mentioned here the Mahendra, Malaya, Sahya ranges are well-known. The Vindhya of the Purāṇas included the Satpurā range south of the Narmadā, the Mahādeo Hills, the Hazaribagh Range and the Rājamahal Hills. *Śuktimān*, according to De (p. 196) is the portion of the Vindhya-range joining Pāriyātra and Ṛkṣa mountains including the hills of Gondwana and Chhota Nagpur. But M. Ali. in the topographical Map of Bhārata, shows it as a ring of ranges encircling the Mahānadī basin, very nearly coinciding the present Mahākosala (Purāṇic Dakṣiṇa Kosala) region.

The Pāriyātra mountain is the ring of ranges north of the Narmadā, nearly encircling the catchment areas of the Chambal and the Betwā and thus corresponds with the Aravallis and (modern) Western Vindhya.

The Ṛkṣa mountain represents the modern Vindhya from the source of the Sonar to the eastern ranges marking the catchment area of the river Son. (M. Ali. *Op. Cit.*, pp. 112-113.)

2. Some of these mountains are identified as follows:

Mandara—A portion of the Himalayas to the east of Sumeru in Garhwal. The hill in the Banka sub-division of Bihar is, however, popularly believed as Mandara (De, pp. 124-125).

Vaihāra (?)

Dardura =The Nilgiri hills (De, p. 53)

Kolāhala =The Brahma-yoni hill in Gayā (De, p. 101)

Maināka =The Sewalik range from the Gaṅgā to the Bias (De, p. 121)

Vaidyuta =The Gurla range, south of lake Manasasarovar; the Śarayū is said to rise in this mountain (De, p. 16)

Vātandhama (?)

Kṛṣṇagiri =The Karakorum mountain, Mus-tagh (De, p.104)

Godhana =Garatha Hills in Bāṇa's *Harṣa-carita* VI (De, p. 70)

Puṣpagiri =The part of the Malaya range, the source of the Kṛtamālā or Vaiga (De, p.164).

Ujjayanta=Mt. Girnar (De, p. 211)

Dardura, Kolāhala, along with Surasa, Maināka, Vaidyuta, Vātandhama, Nāgagiri, the mountain Pāṇḍura (Pale-white in colour), Tuṅgaprastha, Kṛṣṇagiri, the mountain Godhana, the Puṣpagiri, Ujjayanta, the mountain Raivataka, Śrīparvata, Citrakūṭa and the mountain Kūṭaśaila. There are many mountains other than these. They are smaller than these, less well known and lesser number of living beings dependent on them.

24. The regions interspersed with these mountains are partially inhabited by Āryas and partially by the Mlecchas (tribal-barbarous-people). The following rivers (beginning with) the Gaṅgā, the Sindhu and the Sarasvatī are utilised by them for drinking purposes.

25-27a. The foregoing three and the following rivers originate from the foot of the Himalayas,[1] viz. : the Śatadru, the Candrabhāgā, the Yamunā, the Sarayū, the Irāvatī, the Vitastā, the Vipāśā, the Devikā, the Kuhū, the Gomatī, the Dhūtapāpā, the Budbudā, the Dṛṣadvatī, the Kauśikī, the Tridivā. the Niṣṭhīvī, the Gaṇḍakī and the Cakṣurlohitā.

27b.29a. The following rivers are remembered as dependent on (i.e. originating from) the Pāriyātra mountain :[2] The

---

Raivataka=Mt. Girnar near Junagarh in Gujarat.
Śrīparvata=The famous hill in Eastern ghat in Kurnool Dist. Andhra Pradesh.
Citrakūṭa—Kāmptānāth giri in Bundelkhand, Madhya Pradesh (De, p.50)

1. The ranges of mountains described in note 1 p. 152 above are watersheds which bound wholly or partly the catchment areas of important rivers in India. Here is a list of rivers rising from the Himalayas. The modern names of the rivers are given in brackets:

The Śatadru (Sutlej), the Candrabhāgā (Chenab), the Irāvatī (Ravi), the Vitastā (Jhelum), the Vipāśā (Beas), the Devika (Deeg-a tributary of the Ravi), the Kuhu (Kabul), The Dhūtapāpā (Śāradā, with its head streams), the Budbudā (misprint for Bāhudā-Rapti), the Dṛṣadvatī (Chitang, a tributary of the Ghaggar), the Kauśikī (Kosi) with its three headwaters.

The Tridiva (?), the Niṣṭhīvi (?)

The Cakṣurlohitā (Brahmaputra?)—M. Ali. *Op. Cit.* pp.114-115.

2. The modern names of the rivers are bracketed:

The Vedasmṛti (Banās), Vedavatī (Berach), Vṛtraghnī (Banganga-Utangan). These were the big, perennial rivers of ancient Matsya-desha (now a part of M. P.) The Varṇāśā is W. Banas which flows west of Aravallis

Vedasmṛti, the Vedavatī, river Vṛtraghnī, the Varṇāśā, the Nandanā, the Sadānīrā, the Mahānadī, the Pāśā, the Carmaṇvatī, the Nūpā, the Vidiśā, the Vetravatī, the Kṣiprā and the Anantī (Avantī?).

29b-32a. These rivers originate from the Ṛkṣavān.[1] They are sacred and their waters are crystal-like. They are: The Śoṇa, the Mahānada, the Narmadā, the Surasā, the Kriyā, the Mandākinī, the Daśārṇā, the Citrakūṭā, the Tamasā, the Pippalā, the Śyenā, the Karamodā, the Piśācikā, the Citropalā, the Viśālā, the Vañjulā, the Vāstuvāhinī, the (Sa) Nerujā, the Śuktimatī, Maṅkutī, the Tridivā and the Kratu.

32b-33. The following auspicious rivers of holy waters have originated from the foot-hills of the Vindhya ranges.[2]

---

the Nandanā (Sābarmatī), the Sadānīrā (Sarasvatī), the Mahānadī, the Pāśā (If Pārā = Pārbatī), the Carmaṇvatī (Chambal), the Nūpā, (Gambhira), the Vidiśā (Bes), the Vetravatī (Betwā), the Kṣiprā (Śiprā); the Anantī (should be Avantī. It rises near Mhow) M. Ali. *Op. Cit.* pp. 116-117)

1. The Purānic mountain ranges are so much mixed up in our times that some rivers are attributed to either of them:

The Śoṇa)(These do not rise in the Puranic
The Mahānada (mahānadī))(Ṛkṣa Parvata.
The Narmadā)(
The Surasā (?))(
The Kriyā (?))(
The Mandākinī)(
The Daśārṇā (Dhasan))(
The Citrakūṭā)(These are rivers
The Tamasā (Tons))(from Bundel-
The Pippalā)(Seems to be one river called)(khand (M.P.)
The Śyenā)(*Pippaliśyenī* as in Mt.P., (mod.)(
)(name : Paisunī))(
The Karamodā (Karam-nāśā))(
The Piśācikā)(
The Citropalā)(
The Viśālā (Bewas near Sagar in M.P.)
The Vañjulā (As in Vā.P. it should be Jambūlā mod. Jammi.
The Vastuvāhinī (Baghain, a tributary of the Yamunā)
The (Sa)Nerujā (rather Sumerujā as in Vā.P. (Sonar-Bearma)
The Śuktimatī (Ken)—M. Ali *Op. Cit.* pp. 118-119.

2. As noted above Puranic writers include even Satpurā hills in the Vindhya ranges. The modern names of the rivers are given in Brackets:

The Tāpī (The Taptī and Tāpī also)
The Payoṣṇī (Pain-ganga—De, p. 150)

viz. : The Tāpī, the Payoṣṇī, the Nirvindhyā, the Sṛpā ; the river Niṣadhā, the Veṇī, the Vaitaraṇī, the Kṣiprā, the Vālā, the Kumudvatī, the Toyā, the Mahāgaurī, the Durgā, and the Annaśilā. [Probably *durgā* (difficult to cross) and *anna—rather anta—śilā* (rocky within) are adjectives of Mahāgaurī.]

34-35. The Godāvarī, the Bhīmarathī, the Kṛṣṇaveṇā, the Vañjulā, the Tuṅgabhadrā, the Suprayogā, the Bāhyā and the Kāverī are the rivers originating form the foot-hills of the Sahya range.[1] They flow to the south.

36. The following rivers have originated from the mountain Malaya.[2] All of them are auspicious and they have cool waters. They are : the Kṛtamālā, the Tāmraparṇī, the Puṣpajātī and the Utpalāvatī.

37. The following rivers remembered as daughters of the mount Mahendra :[3] The Trisamā, Ṛṣikulyā, The Vaṁjulā, the Tridivā, the (A) balā, the Lāṅgūlinī and the Vaṁśadharā.

The Nirvindhyā (Newuj) R. mentioned in *Meghadūta*
The Sṛpā or Śiprā
The Niṣadhā (Sind, on this Narwar, the capital of Niṣadhas was located)
The Veṇī (Wainganga)
The Vaitaraṇī (Baitarani)
The Kṣiprā (Probably. the same as *śiprā*)
The Vālā (?)
The Kumudvatī (Suvarṇa-rekhā)
The Toyā (Brāhmaṇī)
The Mahāgaurī (Damodar)
The following : *Durgā* (difficult to cross) and *anna* (*anta-*) *Śilā* (full of rocks) are probably the adjectives of the Mahāgaurī.—M. Ali—*Op. Cit.* pp. 120-121.

1. Most of these rivers continue the same old names though some of them are modified e.g. The Bhīmarathī (Bhīmā), Kṛṣṇaveṇā (Kṛṣṇā), the Vañjulā (Mañjirā), the Suprayogā (Vedavatī. Its original name signifies easiness to bathe), the Bāhyā (Varadā, The AP. correctly reads it as *Varadā*).

2. Modern names of these rivers are bracketed: the Kṛtamālā (Vaigai), the Tāmraparṇī, the Puṣpajāti (or Puṣpajā=Pambiar), the Utpalavatī (Periyar). —M. Ali—*Op. Cit.* pp. 122-23.

3. The modern names of these rivers are given in brackets:
The Trisamā (Ghoda-hada, Bhagava, Patama—these three headwaters of the Ṛṣīkulya have this collective name)
Ṛṣikulyā (repeated under rivers from Śuktimān), the Vañjulā (?), the Tridivā (collective name for Vegavatī, Nāgavatī and Suvarṇamukhī—the three headwaters of the Lāṅgūlinī).
The Langulini (Lānguliā) —M. Ali—*Op. Cit.* p. 24.

38. The following rivers are remembered as originating from Śuktimān:[1] The Ṛṣikulyā, the Kumārī, the Mandagā, the Mandagāminī, the Kṛpā and the Palāśinī.

39. All these rivers are identical with the Sarasvatī and the Gaṅgā. They flow into the sea. All of them are remembered as the mothers of the universe and dispellers of the sins of the worlds.

40-42. They have hundreds and thousands of ancillary tributaries. The following territories and realms have been founded on (the banks of) these rivers:[2] the Kurus, the Pāñcālas, the Śālvas, the Mādreyas. the Jāṅgalas, the Śūrasenas, the Bhadrakāras, the Bodhas, the Paṭaccaras, the Matsyas, the Kuśalyas, the Sauśalyas, the Kuntalas, the Kāśis, the Kosalas, the Godhas, the Bhadras, the Kaliṅgas, the Magadhas and the Utkalas. These are the realms in the middle of the country[2] and most of them have been recounted.

---

1. The modern names are given in brackets:

The Ṛṣikulyā (the same as mentioned above).

The Kumārī (Suktel, joins the Mahānadī near Sonpur, Orissa), The Mandagā (Mand), The Mandagāminī (Mahānadī—proper), The Kṛpā (Arpā), Palāśinī (Jonk in Raipur Dist.. M.P.)—M. Ali—*Op. Cit.* p. 125.

2. The author of this Purāṇa includes the following parts of India in "Madhyadeśa". These are originally names of tribes applied to the land where they settled:

Kurus : Between the Ghaggar in the West and the Gaṅgā on the east and with forest belt on the north and the south.

Pañcālas :—coterminus with modern Rohilkhand with the central portion of the Ganga-Yamuna doab added to it.

Śālvas: Near Kurukṣetra to the west of the Matsyadeśa. De thinks it comprised of some portion of former Jodhpur, Jaipur and Alwar states (De, p. 175).

Mādreya or *Madra* : The region between the Rāvi and the Chinab in the Punjab (De, p. 116).

Jāñgala:—generally associated with Kurus and called Kuru-Jāñjgala. Probably it occupied the wooded north eastern part of Kurus (M. Ali.—*Op. Cit.* p.135).

Bhadrakaras and *Bodhas* (along with Śālvas) occupied the border land of the Middle country (Madhya-desha of Purāṇas).

Paṭaccaras on the south bank of the Yamunā are located in Banda district (M. Ali. *Op. Cit.* p. 171).

The *Matsyas*:—consisted of the territory of the former Alwar state and some adjoining areas from former Jaipur and Bharatpur (De, p. 128).

43. The land towards the northern extremity of the Sahya mountain where the river Godāvarī flows, is the most fascinating realm on the whole of the earth.

44-45. A city named Govardhana[1] was built there by Rāma. Heavenly trees and divine medicinal herbs liked by Rāma were planted there by sage Bharadvāja to please Rāma. Hence the region of that excellent city became charming.

46-51a. The following ones are the realms in the northern parts.[2] The Bāhlikas, the Vātadhānas, the Ābhīras, the

---

1. Now a village in Nasik District of Maharashtra. Formerly it was an important centre of learning and Brāhmaṇas coming from that area are known as Govardhana Brāhmaṇas. It is mentioned several times in the famous Nasik Inscription of uṣasadāta (100 B.C.)—E.I.VIII p. 78. (Epigraphia Indica).

2. Generally realms or countries are named after the names of the tribes or peoples settled there. The identifications of the realms on northern part are based on M. Ali's discussion in his *Geog. of the Purāṇas*, pp. 137-146. D. C. Sircar's GAMI is also referred to and only the page no. is mentioned.

The Bāhlikas or Vāhlikas=People of Balistan-region covered by the Bolon, Nari and Gokh rivers. It coincides with former British Baluchistan. But Balkh (N. Afghanistan) according to D. C. Sircar, p. 32.

The Vātadhanas=probably Waziristan. But Panjab-Rajasthan region.—Sircar p. 32.

The Ābhīras=South of Sauvīra but east of the Indus-Western Part of Hyderabad, District Sind.

The Kālatoyakas=Residents of Kalat region in Baluchistan.

The Aparantas=This is the North-Western region called Aparita in Vā.P.

The Suhmas (?)=This is in eastern India.

The Pāñcālas=Rohilkhand (?)

The Carma-maṇḍalas or Carma-khaṇḍa at the mouth of the river Hab and the Churma island.

The Gandharas=Kandahar—lower Kabul valley.

The Yavanas=Ionians, Greeks.

The Sindhu-Sauvīra-Maṇḍals=Sindhu and Sauvīra are different regions. Sauvīra coincides with Rohri-Khairpur region of Sind and the remaining portion is Sind.

The Tuṣāras=Tokharians in north Afghanistan, but people on the Tochi according to M. Ali p. 142.

The Pallavas or Pahlavas=Region adjoining the Hingol Valley on the Parikan river.

The Śaka=Scythians.

The Kulinda=The Same as Pulinda in Mt. P. Kunets of Kulu. But formerly they extended to Saharanpur and Ambala—Sircar p. 33.

Kālatoyakas, the Aparāntas (? Westerners), the Suhmas, the Pāñcālas, the Carmamaṇḍalas, the Gāndhāras, the Yavanas, the Sindhusauvīramaṇḍalas, the Cīnas, the Tuṣāras, the Pallavas, the Girigahvaras (dwellers of mountain caves), the Śakas, the Bhadras, the Kulindas, the Pāradas, the Vindhyacūlikas, the Abiṣāhas, the Ulūtas, the Kekayas, the Daśamālikas the Brāhmaṇas, the Kṣatriyas, the Vaiśyas and the families of the Śūdras, the Kāmbojas, the Daradas, the Barbaras, the Aṅgalauhikas, the Atris, along with the Bharadvājas, the Prasthalas, the Daśerakas, the Lamakas, the Tālaśālas, the Bhūṣikas and the Ījikas. Now understand the realms of the eastern parts.[1]

The Pārada=The same as Parita in Vā.P.=Mithankot region of Dera Gazi Khan District Pakistan. But Parthians of Khorasan according to D.C. Sircar p. 33.

The Kekayas=People of the country between the Beas and the Sutlej (De, p. 97).

The Kāmbojas=People from Kafiṙstan who colonised the Kunar basin.

The Daradas=The same ancient tribe living in the valley of the Kisenganga in Kashmir.

The Barbaras=People migrated from Barbary or North Africa.

The Prasthalas=The district between Ferozepur, Patiala and Sirsa (De, 159).

The Daśerakas=Malwa? But Marwar region of Rajasthan—Sircar, p.35.

The Lamakas=Probably the same as Lampāka or Lamghan of today—associated with upper Kabul

1. The ancient tribes and their locations from Eastern India are identified as follows:

The Aṅgas=The country about Bhagalpur including Monghyr (De, 7).

The Colabhadras=The Coromandal Coast (?)

The Kirātas=Tipara and Morung west of Sikkim. They lived from Nepal to extreme east. (De, p. 100).

The Tomaras=The Garo hills of south west Assam (De, p. 205).

The Tanganas=Country from the Rāmgaṅgā river to the upper Sarayū (De p. 204).

The Hūṇadarvas=Country round Manasa-Sarovar? (De, p. 78).

The Mudgarakas=Monghyr and country around (?) (De, p. 132).

The Antargiris=Rajmahal hills in Santal Pargana Bengal (De, P. 8). But Sircar locates Antārgiri and Bahirgiri towards the north of Assam (p. 36).

The Maladas=A part of the district of Shahabad—The site of Viśvāmitra's Āśrama near Buxar (De, p. 100) Malda District of Bengal and Rajashahi and West Dinajpur of Bengal (M. Ali p. 151).

51b-55a. The Aṅgas, the Vaṅgas, the Colabhadras, the Kirāta tribes, the Tomaras, the Haṁsabhaṅgas, the Kāśmīras, the Taṅgaṇas, the Jhillikas, the Āhukas, the Hūṇadarvas, the Andhravākas, the Mudgarakas, the Antargiris, the Bahirgiris, the Plavaṅgus, the Maladas, the Malavartikas, the Samantaras, the Prāvṛṣeyas, the Bhārgavas, the Gopapārthivas (cowherd kings), the Prāgjyotiṣas, the Puṇḍras, the Videhas, the Tāmraliptakas, the Mallas, the Magadhagonardas. These are remembered as the realms in the East.

55b-59. Then, there are the other realms of the dwellers of the southern territories.[1] They are the Pāṇḍyas, the Keralas,

---

The Prāgjyotiṣas=Kāmarūpa District in Assam.

The Puṇḍras=Between Aṅga and Vaṅga and on the north side of the Gaṅgā (De, p. 155) (M. Ali, p. 151).

The Videhas=Tirhut country between the Kosi and the Gaṇḍak to the north of the Gaṅgā (De, p. 35).

The Tāmraliptakas=Tamluk in Midnapur District including Kontai (De, p. 203), (M. Ali, p. 152).

The Mallas=Country round the Paraśnath hills (parts of Hazaribagh and Manbhum Districts), but at Buddha's time they were at Pāvā and Kusinagar (De, p. 123).

The Magadha-Gonardas=Magadha is South Bihar. De identifies Gonarda with Gonda in Oudh (p. 71), but no such combined name is found in De and Sircar.

*The Bhargava-*Aṅgaya was the Yamuna-Meghna Doab (M.Ali, *Op. Cit.* p. 152), but he does not mention merely Bhārgava as in this text.

1. The following identifications are based on De.

The Colas=The Coromandal Coast to the South of the Pennar including Tanjore (p. 51).

The Mūṣikas=Travancore on the Malabar coast (p.134). But Sircar suggests that they were probably people living on the Muri river (p. 36).

The Mahiṣikas=Southern Mysore (p. 120). also Sircar p. 39.

Setukas—People of Setubandha, Rāmeśvara.—Sircar p. 38.

The Kaliṅgas=South Orissa. (Puri and Ganjam Districts)—Sircar p. 39.

The Ābhīras=South-eastern portion of Gujarat about the mouth of the Narmadā (Sircar p.1.).

The Vaidarbhas=Vidarbha, a part of Maharashtra.

The Daṇḍakas=Daṇḍakāraṇya (Maharashtra) (p.52).

The Maulika=If 'Mūlaka', a part of Maharashtra near Aśmaka (p. 133). Mod. Aurangabad District (—Sircar p. 39).

The Aśmakas=Aurangabad district and Bodhan country round about in Nizamabad District—(Sircar p. 40.

the Colas, the Kulyas, the Setukas, the Mūṣikas, the forest dwelling Kṣapaṇas, the Mahārāṣṭras, the Mahiṣikas, the entire realm of the Kaliṅgas, the Ābhīras, the Aiṣīkas, the Āṭavyas (Forest-dwellers), the Sāravas, the Pulindas, the Vindhyamaulīyas, the Vaidarbhas, the Daṇḍakas, the Paurikas, the Maulikas, the Aśmakas, the Bhogavardhanas (those who increase sensual pleasures), the Koṅkaṇas, the Kantalas, the Āndhras, the Kulindas, the Aṅgāras and the Māriṣas. These are the lands of the south; understand the western regions.

60-63a. (Now) know the realms in the western regions.[1] They are the Sūryārakas, the Kalivanas, the Durgālas, the Kuntalas, the Pauleyas, the Kirātas, the Rūpakas, the Tāpakas, Karīṭis, the whole of Karamdharas, the Nāsikas, the others who are in the valleys of the Narmadā, the (Saha) Kacchas, the (Sa) māheyas, the Sārasvatas, the Kacchipas, the Surāṣṭras, the Ānartas and the Arbudas. The above realms are the western ones. Now listen to those who reside on the Vindhyas :[2]

The Bhogavardhanas=(Mod. Bhokardan Taluqa of Aurangabad District (Sircar, p. 40).

The Ka(Ku)ntalas=Southern Maharashtra and Northern Canara District —now a part of Karnataka.

The Kulindas=Garhwala (p.106). But it is surprising that it is mentioned as a state in the South.

1. Some of these can be identified as follows:
The Kirātas=Possibly a reference to Kirāta settlement in the West.
The Nāsikas=Nasik, now in Maharashtra.
The Kacchas=Cutch, now in Gujarat State.
The Ānarta=Gujarat and a part of Malwa (De, p. 8).
The Arbuda=Country around mt. Abu (De, p. 16).

2. The following can be identified as per De and M. Ali.
The Karūṣas=The country around Rewa (De, p. 95).
The Mekalas=Country round Amarkaṇṭaka, the source of the Narmadā (De, p. 130).

The Utkalas=Orissa.

The Daśārṇa=Modern Eastern Malwā—(Sircar, p. 43).

The Bhojas=Country around Bhilwara in the Chambal basin (M.Ali p. 159). Sircar identifies them with the people of Vidarbha who founded a Kingdom in Goa (p. 43).

The Kiṣkindhakas=Kikarava in other Purāṇas. Sircar identifies this Kiṣkandhā with mod. Kalyanpur, South of Udaipur Division (p. 43).

63b-66. The Maladas, the Karūṣas, the Mekalas, the Utkalas, the Daśārṇas, among the excellent ones the Bhojas, the Kiṣkindhakas, the Tośalas, the Kośalas, the Traipuras, the Vaidiśa, the Tuhuṇḍas, the Barbaras, the Ṣaṭpuras, the Naiṣadhas, the Anūpas, the Tuṇḍikeras, the Vītihotras and the Avantis. All these realms are founded on the ridges of the Vindhya.

Hereafter, I shall recount the realms founded on the mountains (Hill-tribes).

67-68a.[1] They are the Nihīras, the Haṁsamārgas, the Kupathas, the Taṅgaṇas, the Śakas, the Apaprāvaraṇas, the Ūrṇas, the Darvas, the Hūhukas, the Trigartas, the Maṇḍalas, the Kirātas and the Tāmaras.

68b-69. Sages have said that there are four Yugas, in the Bhārata sub-continent, viz. Kṛta, Tretā, Dvāpara and Tiṣya (Kali). I shall mention their detailed divisions wholly later on.

Continued

The Tośalas=It is the Southern part of Kosala or Gondwan District round Tosali (Mod. Dhanti) in Puri District (De, p. 43).

The Kosalas=Sircar identifies with Dakṣiṇa (Southern) Kosala—Mod. Raipur, Sitapur, Santalpur Districts.

The Vaidiśa=Eastern Malwa with Vidiśā or Bhilasa as the capital.

The Tripura=The region round Tewar—This covers upper Narmadā valley (present Jabalpur and parts of Mandla and Narasimhapur Districts.)

The Naiṣadhas=Marwar with Narwar as the Capital (De, p.141).

The Anūpas=South Malwa. Country on the Narmadā about Nimar (De, p. 8).

The Vītihotras=The country is founded in the South by the Narmadā and North East, West by the Vindhya. The centre was Satwas 30 miles North West of Harda.

The Āvantis=Country around Ujjain.

The Tuṇḍikera=M. Ali locates it within the Narmada basin around the town Sainkheda (p.161).

The Nihāras=Location uncertain, D. C. Sircar GAMI, p. 45.

The Haṁsa-mārgas=People of Humza in North West Kashmir. This tribe had a location there—D. C. Sircar *Ibid.* p. 30 and 43.

The Kupathas=Hill tribes in the North West of India.

1. The Mountain-system described in this with Mt. Meru as the centre is substantiated by the geographer M. Ali. in *Geog. of the Purāṇas,* pp. 47-59. For the modern names of the Puranic mountains *vide Supra* Ch. 1. p.11 FN.1.

CHAPTER SEVENTEEN

*Varṣas of Jambūdvīpa, Kimpuruṣa, Hari and Ilāvṛta**

The sages said :

1. Recount to us the sub-continents of Kimpuruṣa and Harivarṣa as actually they are really. The sub-continent of Bhārata has already been recounted by you.

Sūta said :

2. Listen attentively, O Brāhmaṇas, to what you are desirous of hearing. There is a very large grove of Plakṣa trees in the sub-continent Kimpuruṣa. It can be compared with the (heavenly) Nandana park.

3. It is remembered that the span of life in Kimpuruṣa is for ten thousand years. The men have golden complexion and the women are comparable to celestial damsels.

4. All people there, are free from ailments and sorrows. They are perpetually joyous in their minds. They have the lustre of hot glowing gold.

5. In the holy sub-continent of Kimpuruṣa, there is an auspicious tree oozing out (exuding) honey. All the Kimpuruṣas drink its excellent juice.

6. They say that the sub-continent Harivarṣa is beyond Kimpuruṣa. The people there are born resembling gold in the colour of their complexion.

7. All the people in the sub-continent of Harivarṣa are those who have been dropped down from the Devaloka (Region of the Devas). All of them have the characteristics and racial features of the Devas. They drink the auspicious sugarcane juice.

8. In the sub-continent Harivarṣa, all the people live for eleven thousand years without any ailment. All of them are joyous in their minds.

9-10. Old age does not affect them nor do they die prematurely.

The middle land which had already been described by me, is known by the name Ilāvṛta. The sun does not blaze very hot there. The men do not become aged. In Ilāvṛta, the moon and the sun as well as the stars are not very bright.

11. Men are born there with the lustre of the lotus. They have the colour of their complexion resembling that of the lotus. They have eyes like lotus and fragrance like that of the lotus petals.

12. Their diet consists of the fruit and juice of the rose-apple. They do not have sweat trickling down from their bodies. They are sweet-smelling. They are intelligent. They enjoy all sensual pleasures, and the fruits of their meritorious actions.

13-14a. They are fallen down from the world of the Devas. They have golden garments. The excellent men who live in the sub-continent Ilāvṛta have a span of life extending to thirteen thousand years.

14b-15. It (Ilāvṛta) extends to nine thousand (Yojanas) in every direction from the Meru.

Its overall area is thirtysix thousand Yojanas square. It is situated like a platter.

16-17. The Gandhamādana mountain is nine thousand Yojanas away from the Meru on the western side. It extends to thirtyfour thousand Yojanas from north to south. It extends as far as the Nīla and Niṣadha mountains. Its height above the ground level is fortythousand Yojanas.

18. It goes down a thousand Yojanas deep into the earth. Its girth also is the same. The mountain Mālyavān is to its (i.e. Meru's) east and its dimensions have been already recounted (as the same).

19. The Nīla mountain is in the south and the Niṣadha is in the north. The Mahāmeru is well established in their midst with its dimensions.

20. In the case of all these mountains, the girth is the same as the extent to which they go deep down into the earth. It is remembered that their total length is a hundred thousand Yojanas.

21*. (?) Their outward appearance is circular (spherical) like the earthern sphere (within the enveloping) ocean. The lengths dwindle down and they are then remembered (more or less) equal to a square.

22. There is a river composed of the juice of the rose apple. It flows through the middle of the oblong-shaped Ilāvṛta dividing it (into two). It has the colour of the fresh collyrium.

23. On the southern side of the Meru and to the north of the Niṣadha, there is an ancient eternal Rose-apple tree named Sudarśana.

24. It is perpetually laden with blossoms and fruits. It is resorted to by Siddhas and Cāraṇas. The whole continent is called Jambūdvīpa after the name of that tree.

25. The height of that noble-souled lordly tree is one thousand and one hundred Yojanas. Everywhere it touches the firmament on all sides.

26. The thickness (diameter) of its fruit is calculated by the sages with visions of principles (of reality) as eight hundred and sixty one *Aratnis* (I *Aratni* = 18-20 Cms.)

27. As they fall on the ground, these fruits make a loud sound. The juice of the fruits of that Jambū (Rose apple) tree flows as a river.

28. This river circumambulates the Meru and penetrates into the ground deep down at the root of the Jambū tree. The delighted (inhabitants) of Ilāvṛta always drink the juice of the Jambū.

29. When the juice of the Jambū is drunk neither old age nor hunger, neither weariness nor death nor languor oppresses them.

30. A type of gold named Jāmbūnada is produced there. It is a glowing ornament of the gods. It has the resemblance of Indra so far in lustre.

31. The auspicious juice of the fruits of the respective representative trees of all the sub-continents is hailed by all.

---

* Vā.P.46.21b and 22a is found combined here as Bd.P.I. 2.18.21. This being the translation of Bd.P., the text of the Bd.P. (though slightly confusing) is followed.

When it (the juice) becomes scattered over it (the alluvial remains of it) become shining gold, an ornament fit for gods.

32. It is due to the grace of god that their (= of the inhabitants) urine and faeces scattered over all directions as well as bodies of the dead are swallowed up by (absorbed in) the earth.

33. It is declared that the Rākṣasas, Piśācas and the Yakṣas—are all the residents of the Himavat. It should be known that the Gandharvas live on the Hemakūṭa along with the groups of the Apsaras.

34. Śeṣa, Vāsuki, Takṣaka—(yes) all the serpents (live) on the Niṣadha. The thirtythree (groups of) Devas (gods) authorised to partake of the shares in the Yajña, sport about on the Mahāmeru.

35. The Siddhas and the Brahmanical sages devoid of impurities live on the Nīla full of Vaiḍurya (Lapis Lazuli). It is mentioned that the mountain Śveta belongs to the Daityas and the Dānavas.

36-37. The excellent mountain Śṛṅga-vān is the place where the Pitṛs frequently move about. Living beings—both the mobile and the immobile—are settled in these nine sub-continents with their different divisions duly situated.

Their prosperous growth, both divine and human, is seen in diverse ways. It cannot be adequately enumerated. It should be believed by those who wish to be* (?)

CHAPTER EIGHTEEN

The Description of the Jambūdvīpa The Bindu Lake—source of the Gaṅgā : Its four streams

Sūta said :

1. In the midst of the Himalayan ridges, there is a

* Vā.P.46.38b—*anububhūṣata*—(be believed) by one desirous to comprehend.

mountain named Kailāsa.[1] The glorious and prosperous Kubera lives there along with the Rākṣasas.

2-3. The king, the overlord of Alakā, rejoices (there) with the celestial damsels attending on him. The sacred splendid and chill water originating from the foot of the Kailāsa mountain has formed a lake named Mada[2] (Manda, in Vā.P. 47.2). It abounds in white lilies and it resembles a sea. The auspicious river Mandākinī[3] (the Gaṅgā) rises from that divine (lake).

4-5. On its banks there is the great divine park called Nandanavana. To the North-east of the Kailāsa, in front of that divine mountain of all medicinal herbs, the mountain full of jewels and minerals, the powerful mountain of wonderful mysteries, there is a mountain named Candraprabha.[4] It is perfectly white and it resembles splendid jewels.

6. At its foot there is a great divine lake named Svacchoda. From that divine lake rises a river named Svacchodā.

7-8a. There is a great splendid divine park on its banks called Çaitraratha. On that mountain lives Maṇibhadra along with his followers. He is the ruthless lord of the armies of Yakṣas. He is surrounded by the Guhyakas.

---

1. The description of mount Kailāsa, though a poetic one, shows that the Purāṇa writer was conversant with the topographical features of the Mānasa-sarovara basin.—vide M. Ali. *op.cit.*, pp. 55-58.

2. For understanding the Purāṇic presentation of the ancient river-system, the following points are to be noted:

(1) According to Purāṇas, a river normally originates from a lake either over-ground or under-ground and is associated with a mountain.

(2) They believed that rivers can penetrate through subterranean channels, mountain-ranges and can flow in more than one current, if intervened by ridges.

(3) A river with all its tributaries is sometimes treated as one river.

3. Unless mentioned otherwise all the references are to M. Ali's *Geog. of Purāṇas*.

Probably this is the river Umā and the Zhong Chhu which flows through Gaurī Kuṇḍa on the eastern flank of Kailāsa into the Rākṣasa Tāl (the twin-lake of Mānasa Sarovara)—M. Ali, p. 65.

4. This is probably the Surange La, the north-east range of Kailāsa from which water flows into Lake Kongys Tso or Lake Gounche—M. Ali. p.65.

8b-9a. The holy rivers the Mandākinī and the Svacchodakā enter the great ocean through the middle of the sphere of the earth.

9b-10. To the south-east of the Kailāsa, in front of the mountain abounding in medicinal herbs and auspicious animals, the divine mountain of diversified and wonderful components, the mountain full of red arsenic, there is the great mountain Sūryaprabha (having the lustre like that of the sun). It is red in colour and it has golden peaks.[1]

11. At its foot there is a great divine lake named Lohita. The great holy river named Lauhitya rises from that (lake).

12-13a. On its bank is the great park named Devāraṇya which is devoid of sorrow. On that mountain lives Maṇidhara, the Yakṣa of good self-control. He is surrounded by the Guhyakas who are gentle and highly virtuous.

13b-14. To the southern side of the Kailāsa is the mountain abounding in medicinal herbs and cruel, wild animals. In front of the three peaked Añjana that originated from the body of Vṛtra, there is that very great mountain Vaidyuta[2] possessing all sorts of minerals.

15. At its foot is the holy lake Mānasa, frequented by the Siddhas. From it rises the holy river Sarayū that is well known in all the worlds.

16-17. On its banks is the well-reputed divine forest named Vaibhrāja. There lives the son of Praheti, who is a Rākṣasa of self-control, a follower of Kubera, and of unlimited exploits (but) who is Brahmāpeta (far removed from the Vedas). He is surrounded by hundreds of Yātudhānas (demons) who are very terrible and who can traverse the skies.

18. To the west of the Kailāsa is the mountain abounding in medicinal herbs and auspicious animals, Aruṇa[3] (Pink

---

1. This red-coloured mountain is Kanglung Kangri (a south-east range of Kailāsa) and the river Lauhitya is the Brahmaputra. From a small lake at the foot of the mountain, the Brahmaputra enters Tamchok Khambah, the headwater of the Brahmaputra. —M. Ali.—p.66.

2. This is the peak Gurla Māndhātā, since Lake Mānasa Sarovara lies below its northern face and the river Karnāli (Map Chhu of Tibetans)—a major tributary of the Sarayū rises here—M. Ali.—p. 66.

3. This is the Ladakh or Leh range—(*Ibid*).

in colour) the splendid and excellent mountain full of gold and minerals.

19. This glorious mountain is a favourite resort of Bhava. It resembles clouds (in colour). It is covered with splendid clusters of cliffs of gold.

20. The mountain Muñjavān is highly divine. It appears to scrape the heaven by means of its hundreds of golden peaks. It is very difficult to climb or pass through as it is enveloped by show.

21-22. There stands Girīśa (King of mountains), called Dhūmra-locana[1] (of smoke-coloured eyes). The Lake named Śailoda[2] is at its foot.

It enters the briny sea in between the (rivers) Cakṣus and Sītā.

23-24. On its banks is the well known divine forest 'Surabhi'.

To the left and to the north of the Kailāsa is the auspicious mountain abounding in medicinal herbs and animals. In front of the excellent mountain named Gaura, full of Haritāla (yellow orpiment) there is the mountain Hiraṇmaya.[3] This mountain is divine, very great and full of precious gems and jewels.

25-26a. At its foot is the highly divine, splendid and charming lake named Bindusara.[4] It has golden sandy bed.

---

1. This is Nanga Parbat. (For details *vide* M. Ali.—*Op. cit.* p. 66-67.
2. The lake Śailoda seems to be the Wular lake which once covered the whole of Kashmir valley. The river Śiloda is the Jhelum which still flows through it and runs towards the west between the Indus and the Sutlej (the Cakṣu and Sītā in the Purāṇa)—M. Ali. p. 67.
3. Gaura, Hiraṇmaya and Soma (mentioned later in v.27 and in Vā.P.) are the Tibetan ranges north of Kailāsa and are called now Tanglha, Aling Kangri and Nychenthangla—M. Ali. (p.68).
4. Bindusara can be explained in two ways:
   (1) a collection of drops of water: The basin between Mt. Aling Kangri and Kailāsa Tanglha is dotted with innumerable small and large lakes.
   (2) a lake of frozen particles of snow. In the past, the basin Aling-Kangri and Kailāsa—Tanglha was an extensive snow-field. The Purāṇa writer must have known it through hearsay etc. According to De (p.38) it is on the Rudra Himalaya, two miles south of Gangotri.

For the sake of getting the Gaṅgā, king Bhagīratha, the saintly king spent many years near it.

26b. He thought "My ancestors will go to heaven on being bathed in the waters of the Gaṅgā." After determining thus, he performed penance with the concentration of his mind in Śiva.

27. The divine river Tripathagā (the Gaṅgā) (lit. the river with three courses) was at the outset established there as the deity. That river originating from the foot-hills of Soma flows in seven channels.

28. Golden sacrificial posts studded with jewels have been scattered there. Śakra performed a sacrifice there along with all the Devas and attained Siddhi (spiritual enlightenment).

29. The luminous Milky way that is seen at night in the firmament near clusters of stars is the divine goddess, the Tripathagā[1] (the Gaṅgā).

30. Sanctifying the heaven and the firmament, the celestial river fell on the head of Bhava (god Śiva) and got blocked up by means of his Yogic Māyā.

31. The lake Bindusaras was formed by those few drops of water that fell from the infuriated Gaṅgā. Therefore it is remembered as Bindusaras.

32. Being impeded smilingly by Bhava (Śiva), the river goddess mentally thought of hurling down Śaṅkara.

33-34. "I shall pierce (the earth)", she thought (to herself), "and enter the netherworlds taking Śaṅkara too along with my current". He understood what she was desirous of

---

1. Are the three ways of Gaṅgā its three stages ?

(1) Milky way in the sky, (2) Snowy or glacial Gaṅgā. (3) Fluvial Gaṅgā.

These are the three stages of the formation of that river which are symbolised in the legend of the descent of Gaṅgā (*Gaṅgāvataraṇa*). The heavenly Ganges (Ākāśa Gaṅgā) is a poetic name for the galaxy in the north. But the blocking up of the Gaṅgā in the tresses of Śiva (mentioned in V.30 and 35) is the Snowy or glacial stage and the melting of the snow-fields and glaciers is the release of the Gaṅgā. The legendary part played by king Bhagīratha in bringing the Gaṅgā to the scorched plains of northern Bhārata is still shrouded in mystery.

doing and having realized her cruel intention, he intended to conceal (absorb) the river within his limbs.

35-38. He blocked the river on his head as it fell on the ground with great force and velocity.

In the meantime he saw the king (i.e. Bhagīratha) in front of him, weary with protruding network of veins and with all his sense-organs overtaken by hunger. Then he remembered the boon granted to him. He thought—"I have been propitiated by this king earlier for the sake of the river (Gaṅgā)". Then he recollected the words of Brahmā that he had heard—"Hold the celestial river"; thereupon he controlled his anger. On being propitiated by means of severe penance, he set river free for the sake of Bhagīratha. He released the river that had been blocked by his own prowess.

39-41. On being released, the river began to flow in seven channels.[1] Three of them flowed towards the east and three to the west. The river Gaṅgā flows through seven channels. The Nalinī, Hrādinī and Pāvanī are those which flow towards the east. The Sītā, the Cakṣus and the Sindhu flow towards the west. The seventh among them followed Bhagiratha towards the south.

42. Hence that river is Bhāgīrathī. It joined the salt sea. All these seven (channels, rivers) sanctify the sub-continent named Hima.

43-45. Originating from the lake Bindusaras, those seven splendid rivers flow over different climes almost all of them being the lands of the Mlecchas (Barbarous tribes) and reach the place where Vāsava (Indra) showers, namely the lands of Śilīndhras, Kuntalas, Cīnas, Barbaras, Yavanas. Andhakas, Puṣkaras, Kulindas and Añcoladvicaras* (?). After dividing

1. M. Ali. (p. 69) identifies Nalinī, Hrādinī and Pāvanī—the east-flowing rivers—with the Yangtse, Mekong and Salween, the rivers flowing to the west, viz. the Sītā, the Cakṣus and the Sindhu with the Yarkand, the Shyok and the Indus, while the southern river Bhāgīrathī is the Gaṅgā. De however identifies Sītā with the Jazartes (p. 181) and the Cakṣus with the Oxus or Amudaria (p. 43).

* *Aṅga-loka-varāś ca ye,* in Vā.P.48, 43a.

the land of simhavān in three parts, the river Sītā flowed into the western ocean.

46-47a. The river Cakṣus flows over the following climes viz. Cīnamarus, the Tālas, the Camasamūlikas, the Bhadras, the Tuṣāras, the Lāmyākas, the Bāhlavas, the Pāraṭas and the Khaśas. Then it falls into the sea.

47b-49a. The Sindhu flows over the following territories, viz. the Daradas, along with the Kaśmīras, the Gandhāras, the Raurasas, the Kuhas, the Śivaśailas, the Indrapadas, the Vasati, (?) the Visarjamas* (?), the Saindhavas, the Randhrakarakas, the Śamathas, the Ābhīras, the Rohakas, the Śunāmukhas and the Ūrddhvamarus.

49b-52. The Gaṅgā sanctifies the following praiseworthy countries (climes) viz. the lands of the Gandharvas, Kinnaras, Yakṣas, Rākṣasas, Vidyādharas and the Nāgas, the residents of Kalāpagrāma, the Pāradas, the Tadgaṇas (their cousin tribes), the Khaśas, the Kirātas, the Pulindas, the Kurus, the Bharatas, the Pāñcālas, the Kāśis, the Matsyas, the Magadhas, the Aṅgas, the Suhmottaras, the Vaṅgas and the Tāmraliptas. Thereafter, obstructed by the Vindhya (?) it falls into the briny sea.

53-55. Then the sacred Hrādinī flows towards the east flooding the banks on either side, the territories of the Naiṣadhas, the Trigartakas, the Dhīvaras(fishermen), the Ṛṣīkas, the Nīlamukhas (bluefaced) the Kekaras, the Auṣṭrakarṇas, the Kirātas, the Kālodaras, the Vivarṇas (outcastes), the Kumāras and the Svarṇabhūmikas** (the golden grounds) that had been covered up to the extent as far as the sea shore on the east.

56-57. Then, the river Pāvanī too flows towards the east flooding the Supathas, the Indradyumna lake, the Kharapathas and the Vetraśaṅkupathas. Through the middle of Jānakī*** it flows over the Kuthaprāvaraṇas. It enters the ocean of Indradvīpa, the briny sea.

---

* Vā.P.48.45 reads: *vadātīṁśca visarjayan* /

** Vā.P.48.52: *Svarṇabhūṣitān*, 'who are beautified with gold ornaments.

*** Vā.P.48.55a. *Madhyenodyāna-makarān*

58-61a. Then the river Nalinī flows rapidly towards the east sanctifying the countries of the Tomaras, the Haṁsamārgas and the Haihayas; piercing through the mountains in various places it flows over various eastern territories. After reaching the Karṇaprāvaraṇas, it flows over the Śvamukhas because they are contiguous. After flowing over desert regions abounding in sand dunes, it flows over the Vidyādhara lands. It enters the briny sea after flowing through the mountainous territories.

61b-62. These rivers have hundreds and thousands of tributaries. All of them flow there where Vāsava showers. There is a well-known fragrant (Surabhi) forest on the banks of the Vasvaukasā (?)

63. The scholarly Kauberaka (son of Kubera) of great self-control stays on Hiraṇyaśṛṅga (Golden Peak). He practises the performance of Yajñas. He is very great and valorous and his strength and splendour cannot be measured.

64. He is surrounded by those scholarly Brahma-Rākṣasas who stay there. It is declared that these four followers of Kubera are on a par with one another.

65. The prosperity of the residents of the mountain should also be known in the same manner. In regard to virtue, love and wealth each is double than the former (?)

66-67a. On the top of the Hemakūṭa there is a lake named Varcovān.[1] Two rivers viz. the Manasvinī and the Jyotiṣmatī rise from it and they flow on either side falling into the eastern and the western seas.

67b-68a. There is a lake named Viṣṇupada[2] on the excellent mountain Niṣadha.

Two rivers rise from it. They are the Gāndharvī and the Nākulī.

68b-69a. There is a great deep lake at the side of the Meru called Candra-Prabha.

---

1. Noted as Lake Śayanā or Nāga in other Purāṇas is the Lake 'Nāk Tso' which with Pangong Tso forms an extensive water-sheet—M.Ali.p.71.

2. Modern Lake Chakmaktin, the source of the Wakhan river which flows west in the land of Gandharvas. It is in the Wakhan region that Meru and Niṣadha come closest to each other. —M. Ali. (p. 71).

The sacred river Jambū rises from it. It is remembered that Jāmbūnada (gold) is obtained from it. (The gold obtained from it is called Jāmbūnada).

69b-70a. The lake Payoda[1] is on the mountain Nīla. It is very clear and it abounds in lotuses. Two rivers rise from it, viz. the Puṇḍarīkā and the Payodā.

70b-71a. The sacred Sarayū flows from the mountain Śveta.

It is indeed from the Mānasa lake that the two rivers Jyotsnā and Mṛgakāmā have originated.

71b-73. In the Kurus is the lake well known as Rudrakānta.[2] It abounds in lotuses, fishes and (aquatic) birds—It is created by Bhava. There are twelve other deep lakes here. They are well known by the name Jaya. They abound in lotuses, fishes and (aquatic) birds and they are like seas.

From them two rivers, the Śāntā and the Mādhvī have originated.

74. In the sub-continents Kimpuruṣa etc., the lord does not shower rains. Excellent rivers flow here with waters that pierce through the ground.

75. The following three mountains of great knotty ridges extend towards the east. They are immersed under the briny sea. They are the Ṛṣabha, the Dundubhi and the great mountain Dhūmra.

76. The mountains of great lofty cliffs—the Candra, the Kāka and the Droṇa extend towards the north. In the northern end they are immersed under the salt sea.

77. The mountains Somaka, Varāha and the Nārada extend towards the west where they have entered the briny sea.

---

1. M.Ali. (p.71) identifies it with the Kara Kul of northern Pamirs. It is a twin-lake mentioned as Payoda and Puṇḍarīka (like lakes Mānasasarovara and Rākṣasa Tāl in the Kailāsa region).

2. These are lakes in Siberia. It shows that the Puranic authors had some idea that there were big lakes in that region. I doubt Ali's identification of the Balkash and the Baikal with the Jaya lake.

78. These great mountains—the Cakra, the Balāhaka and the Maināka, extend towards the southern sea.

79-81. In between the Cakra and the Maināka in the south-east quarter, there is the fire named Saṁvartaka. It drinks the water. This sub-marine fire is known by the name *Aurva*. It has the face of a mare. These twelve mountains had entered the briny sea formerly because of the fear of getting their wings chopped. They were terrified by Mahendra. This is seen in the white (i.e. circular moon on the full Moon night) moon in the shape of a black rabbit (or deer and a rabbit).

82-84. The different divisions of Bhārata have been recounted. They are nine. What has been narrated here is seen elsewhere too. The sub-continents vie with one another in regard to good qualities, health, span of life, piety, love and wealth. The living beings are endowed with merits. In the different sub continents different classes of people live in the different parts. Thus this earth sustains the cosmos stationed in the universe (i.e. the whole of this universe).

CHAPTER NINETEEN

The Description of Plakṣa and other Continents

Sūta said :

1. I shall succinctly recount (information about) the continent of Plakṣa[1] in the manner it really is. Listen to this, O excellent Brāhmaṇa even as I speak about it factually.

2. Its width is twice the width of Jambūdvīpa. Its round girth (perimeter) is twice its width.

---

1. This *dvīpa* is next to Jambūdvīpa. Its name Plakṣa (a fig tree) indicates a land of warm temperate climate. M.Ali, 'without hesitations', identifies this with the basin of the Mediterranean (*Geog. of Purāṇas*, p. 41). The name Plakṣa still persists as Placia, a town in Myria.

3. The salty sea is encompassed by that continent. There the Janapadas (the countries or rural regions) are all sacred. People do not die for a long time.

4. Whence is the fear of famine there ? (i.e. there is no fear of famine there). Whence is the fear of old age and sickness ? There too, there are seven holy mountains bedecked in jewels.

5-6. They are the receptacle of precious gems. There are rivers also. I shall mention their names. In those five continents. viz. : Plakṣadvīpa and others, there are seven long and straight Varṣaparvatas (mountains belonging to the sub-continents) stationed in every quarter. I shall mention the seven extremely powerful (sub) continents in the Plakṣadvīpa.

7. Here the first mountain is Gomedaka. It is like the clouds. It is on account of its name that the sub-continent is also named Gomeda.

8. The second mountain is the Candra, which is endowed with all types of medicinal herbs. It is from here that medicinal herbs were collected by the brothers (Aśvins) for the sake of Amṛta (Nectar).

9. The third mountain is high and unscalable. It is named Nārada. It was on this mountain that Nārada and Parvata were born formerly.

10-11a. (Text partially defective) The fourth mountain there is named Dundubhi. It was on this mountain that the Asura Dundubhi, who had the boon of having death as he pleased, was formerly overpowered by the Devas. This demon had a great desire for swinging in a rope-swing on a Śālmali (silk cotton) tree and this brought about his death.

11b-12a. The fifth mountain is named Somaka, where nectar was formerly collected by the Devas. It was also brought by Garutman (Garuḍa) for the sake of his mother.

12b-13a. The sixth leading mountain is called by the name Sumanas. It was on this mountain that Hiraṇyākṣa was killed by the divine Boar.

13b-14. The seventh mountain there is Vaibhrāja. It is luminous. It is very lofty. It is crystalline. Since it shines with its rays, it is remembered as Vaibhraja.

I shall mention their sub-continents in due order and by their names.

15. The first sub-continent is Gomeda. It is remembered by the name Śāntabhaya (having all fears subdued). The sub-continent of (the mountain) Candra is named Śiśira. That of the Nārada is Sukhodaya.

16. Ānanda is the sub-continent of the Dundubhi. Śiva is remembered as the sub-continent of the Somaka. Kṣemaka is the sub-continent of the leading mountain (Sumanas) and Dhruva that of the Vaibhrāja.

17. In all these (sub-continents) the Devas, the Gandharvas and the Siddhas play and sport about along with the Cāraṇas. They are being seen along with them.

18. There are seven rivers in every one of the sub-continents. They flow into the seas. I shall mention these seven Gaṅgās by name, O ascetics.

19. The following are the seven excellent rivers, viz. the Anutaptā, the Sukhī, the Vipāśā, the Tridivā, the Kramu, the Amṛtā and the Sukṛtā.

20. Those rivers grow towards those places where Vāsava (i.e. Indra) showers (rains). They have plenty of water and (swift) currents. Thousands of other rivers flow into them.

21-22. The delighted people of these territories always drink (the waters of) these rivers. Those people, viz. the splendid Śāntabhayas, the joyous auspicious Śaiśiras, the Śivas, the Ānandas, the Sukhas and the Kṣemakas along with the Dhruvas. The subjects who have settled in them are endowed with the disciplined conduct and behaviour of the Varṇas (castes) and Āśramas (stages in life).

23. All the subjects were strong and free from ailments. They are devoid of sickness. Among them none deteriorates and no one goes high up in arrogance (*or* there is no evolutionary and involutionary eras.[1]

1. The terms *Utsarpiṇī* and *Avasarpiṇī* are the Jain terms to indicate timecycles. *Utsarpiṇī* is the ascending cycle and *Avasarpiṇī* is the descending cycle. They are divided into six stages each viz. good-good, good, good-bad, bad-good, bad, bad-bad (MW p. 105). The use of Jaina terms like those of the Buddhists in a Brahmanical work is not impossible. The next verse explains this by assuming the existence of a perpetual Tretā yuga.

24. There is no peculiar state of affairs as pertaining to the Yugas, conditioned by the four Yugas. A period like Tretā yuga is perpetually present there.

25. These are the things to be understood in the five continents, Plakṣadvīpa etc. The assignment of period is in conformity with the conditions of the region.

26-27. It should be known that the people in these continents beginning with Plakṣadvīpa and ending with Śākadvīpa, are handsome, well-dressed, strong and free from sickness. They possess adequately happiness, long span of life, strength, handsome features, health and virtuousness. Men live upto five thousand years.

28-30. The continent of Plakṣadvīpa is prosperous and vast. All round, it abounds in wealth and food-grains. It abounds in divine medicinal herbs and fruits. It possesses all types of medicinal plants and herbs. Thousands of rural and wild animals of all varieties surround the regions. O excellent Brāhmaṇas, in its middle there is a great tree named Plakṣa. It has been reckoned on a par with the Jambū tree (in the continent Jambūdvīpa). The continent is named after that tree. In a place in the middle of the inhabited country, it is worshipped by all the people.

31-32. That continent of Plakṣadvīpa is surrounded by a sea of sugarcane juice.[1] This sea is equal to Plakṣadvīpa in length and extent.

Thus the position of Plakṣadvīpa has been recounted to you all succ nctly and in the proper order. Now understand the continent Śālmala.

33-34. Thereafter, I shall (now) recount the third excellent continent Śālmala.[2]

The ocean of sugarcane juice is encompassed by the continent Śālmala that is twice as much as Plakṣadvīpa in extent.

It should be known that there too are seven mountains that are the sources of precious stones.

---

1. The Ikṣu is the river Oxus. The river is taken as a sea (De, p.179). Can it be regarded as a boundary surrounding Plakṣadvīpa ?

2. Puranic description of Śālmala dvipa leads, M. Ali to identify it with tropical Africa bordering on the Indian ocean, including Madagasgar.

35. In those seven sub continents even the rivers are sources of precious gems.

The first mountain is named Kumuda. It resembles the sun in brilliance.

36-37a. It stands with lofty peaks full of all minerals and rugged with clusters of cliffs.

The second mountain here is well known by the name Uttama. It encircles the firmament with its peaks full of *Haritāla* (yellow orpiment).

37b-38a. The third mountain there is well reputed as Balāhaka. It encircles the firmament with its peaks full of natural collyrium.

38b-39a. The fourth mountain is Droṇa and it is here that the great medicinal herbs *Viśalyakaraṇī and Mṛtasañjīvinī* (are found).

39b-40a. Kaṅka is the fifth mountain there. It rises up magnificently.

It is perpetually endowed with flowers and fruits. It is surrounded by tree and creepers.

40b-41a. The sixth mountain there is Mahiṣa. It is like a cloud. On it the water-originating fire named Mahiṣa lives.

41b-42. The seventh mountain there is called by the name Kakudmān. It is there that Vāsava saves duly from the subjects many precious gems and keeps them to himself and approaches Prajāpati with them.

43. Thus, these are the seven mountains in the Śālmala continent. They are bedecked in jewels. I shall mention their splendid sub-continents. They are only seven (in number).

44-48. The sub-continent of the mountain Kumuda is remembered as Śveta; that of Uttama is Lohita; that of Balāhaka is Jīmūta; Hārīta is remembered as (the sub-continent) of Droṇa. The sub-continent of Kaṅka is named Vaidyuta and that of Mahiṣa is Mānasa. The sub-continent of the Kakudmān is Suprada by name. These are the seven sub-continents and (the connected) mountains. Understand the rivers in them.

They are the Jyoti, Śānti, Tuṣṭā, Candrā, Śukrā, Vimocanī and Nivṛtti the seventh among them. They are remembered as the rivers in the different sub-continents. There are hundreds and thousands of other rivers flowing near them. No man is capable of counting their number.

Thus the situation of the continent Śālmala has been recounted to you.

49. In its middle there is a great Śālmali (silk cotton) tree reckoned on a par with the Plakṣa tree. It has large branches. The continent is named after the tree.

50. The Śālmala continent is surrounded on all sides by the sea of liquor that is equal to Śālmala in extent.

51. Listen to the subjects in the northern continents, O sages conversant with piety. Understand them even as I recount properly in the manner I have heard.

52-53. I shall recount the fourth continent Kuśadvīpa[1] succinctly. The sea of liquor is surrounded on all sides by Kuśadvīpa that is twice as much as Śālmala in extent. Understand the seven mountains there as they are being described.

54. It should be known that the mountain Vidruma is the first mountain in the Kuśadvīpa; the second one is the mountain Hema.

55. The name of the third mountain is Dyutimān. It is a mountain resembling clouds. The fourth mountain is named Puṣpavān and the fifth one is Kuśeśaya.

56. The sixth one is Harigiri by name and the seventh is remembered as Mandara. The word (*Manda* means 'waters' and the mountain is called Mandara because it pierces or splits water.

57. Their internal diameter is twice as much as the cross-section (*Pravibhāga*).

The first sub-continent is Udbhida and the second one is Veṇumaṇḍala.

1. After detailing the main features of Kuśa dvipa M. Ali concludes that it is identifiable with the tropical grass-lands viz. Iran, Irac and the fringing lands of hot desert, op. cit. (pp. 40-41).

58. The third sub-continent is Rathākāra and the fourth one is remembered as Lavaṇa. The fifth one is Dhṛtimad Varṣa and the sixth Varṣa is Prabhākara.

59. The seventh one is named Kapila. In all those (sub-continents) the Devas and the Gandharvas are the sanctifiers of the Varṣas and the subjects* are the lords of the universe (?)

60. They play and sport about everywhere in great delight. There are neither robbers nor Mleccha (barbarous) tribes in them.

61-62. The people are mostly white-complexioned and they pass away in the due order (i.e. the younger ones only after the older ones).

There too the rivers are seven. They are—Dhūtapādā, Śivā, Pavitrā, Santati, Vidyut, Dambhā and Mahī. There are hundreds and thousands of rivers other than these. They are not well known.

63-64. All those flow to that place where Vāsava showers: Externally the Kuśadvīpa is incircled by the sea of ghee (clarified butter). It should be known that the sea of ghee is equal to Kuśadvīpa in extent.

Thus the situation and position of Kuśadvīpa has been recounted to you all.

65. Hereafter, I shall recount the extent of Krauñca dvīpa.[1] It is remembered to be twice as much as Kuśadvīpa in extent.

66-69. The sea with ghee as its liquid content is in contact with Krauñcadvīpa.

In that continent, the excellent mountain Krauñca is the first mountain. Beyond the Krauñca is the Vāmana and beyond Vāmana is the Andhakāra. Beyond Andhakāra is the mountain named *Divāvṛt*. The excellent mountain Dvivida is

---

* Vā.P.49.54a. reads *prabhāsu* (they are like the lords of the universe) in brilliance. A better reading.

1. M. Ali examines the description of this *Dvīpa* from different sources and concludes that 'the Krauñca dvipa of the Purāṇas is represented by the basin of the Black Sea. (op. cit. pp. 45-46)

beyond Divāvṛt. The great mountain Puṇḍarīka is beyond Dvivida. The Dundubhisvana is mentioned as the mountain beyond Puṇḍarīka.

These are the seven mountains of the continent Krauñcadvīpa. They are full of precious gems.

70. They are covered with different kinds of trees and creepers endowed with plenty of flowers and fruits. They are twice as much as each other in extent. They increase the delight of residents.

71-74. I shall recount the sub-continents thereof by name. Understand them.

The land (i.e. Varṣa) pertaining (adjacent) to Krauñca is Kuśala; that of Vāmana is Manonuga; Uṣṇa is mentioned as the third Varṣa and it is beyond Manonuga. Pīvaraka is beyond Uṣṇa and Andhakāra is beyond Pīvara. Munideśa (land of the sages) is remembered by the learned men as the land beyond Andhakāra. Dundubhisvana is mentioned as the land beyond Munideśa. The land is populated by Siddhas and Cāraṇas. The people are remembered as mostly white complexioned. There too the rivers are remembered as seven in number in every sub-continent. They are splendid.

75. The seven rivers Gaurī, Kumudvatī, Sandhyā, Rātri, Manojavā, Khyāti and Puṇḍarīkā are remembered as Gaṅgā.

76. There are thousands of other rivers flowing near them and approaching them (i.e. flowing into them like tributaries). They are large with plenty of water.

77. The glorious Krauñca Dvīpa is surrounded on all sides by the sea with curds and whey as its liquid content. This sea is equal to the Krauñca Dvīpa in extent.

78-79. The Plakṣadvīpa and other continents have been succinctly recounted. It is impossible to describe in due order the natural features of all these continents in detail even in the course of hundreds of years according to divine reckoning. It is difficult to describe in detail the creation and annihilation of the subjects therein.

80. I shall recount Śākadvīpa[1] definitely as it exists. Listen even as I recount factually and realistically.

81. Its extent is twice as much as that of Krauñca Dvīpa. It stands encircling the sea with curds and whey as its liquid content.

82. There the territories of the general public are very sacred. The people die after a long life. Whence is there famine among them ? (i.e. they do not experience famine). Whence is the fear from old age and sickness ?

83. There too there are only seven splendid mountains bedecked in jewels. The seven rivers are sources of origin of precious gems. Listen to their names from me.

84. The first mountain Meru is said to possess (i.e. to be inhabited by) the Devas, the sages and the Gandharvas. The mountain named Udaya is golden and it extends towards the east.

85-86. The clouds take their origin there or go there for the sake of rain. To the west of it is the extremely great high mountain Jaladhara from which Vāsava perpetually receives a large supply of water. Therefore, it pours showers among the subjects during the rainy season.

87. To the north of it is the Raivataka, where the constellation Revatī is perpetually established in the firmament as ordained by Lord Brahmā.

88. To the west of it is the extremely great mountain named Śyāma. Due to it, it is said, that the subjects here attained darkness of complexion formerly.

89. To the west of it, it is remembered, is the great silvery mountain Aṣṭagiri. To the west thereof is the "impossable mountain" (*Durgaśaila*), the great mountain belonging to Ambikā (*Ambikeya*) (but Āmbikeya in Vā.p. 49.83)

90. To the west of Āmbikeya is the beautiful mountain Kesarin equipped with all medicinal herbs. It is from this that Vāyu, the Prajāpati, became possessed of Kesara* ?

---

1. Strangely enough, two scholars come to different conclusions about the location of Śākadvīpa. M. Ali identifies it with the Monsoon lands of Asia where teak abounds viz. Malaya, Siam, Indo-China and southern China, while De identifies it with Tartary including Turkestan in central Asia (pp. 172-173).

*Vā.P.49.74 reads : *sa caiva Keśarītyukto yato Vāyuḥ pravāyati.* 'That moun-

91. The first Varṣa (sub-continent) is (away) from the mountain Udaya. That great Varṣa is remembered as 'Jalada'. The second (Varṣa) of Jaladhara is remembered as Sukumāra.

92. The (Varṣa) of Raivata is Kaumāra; that of Śyāma is Maṇīvaka. The splendid sub-continent of the Asta mountain should be known as Kusumottara.

93-95. The sub-continent of the mountain Āmbikeya is Modaka and that of Kesara is Mahādruma. The dimensions of the continent such as narrowness, length etc. is to be reckoned in accordance with the Krauñca Dvīpa. The great tree, the emblem of that continent is Śāka by name and it has great height. It has great following (?) It deserves worship*. The territories of the rural folk are holy. They are endowed with the system of *Cāturvarṇya* (having the four castes). The rivers too are extremely sacred (like) Gaṅgā. They are of seven varieties (i.e. they are seven in number).

96. They are :—Sukumārī, Kumārī, Nalinī, Veṇukā, Ikṣu, Veṇukā** (?) and the seventh one Gabhasti.

97. There are other rivers too, thousands of them with sacred waters and cool currents. They are splendid rivers flowing in the places where Vāsava showers.

98. Neither their names nor their magnitude can be adequately understood or fully enumerated. Those excellent rivers are very holy.

99. The delighted folks of the clime, O Śaṁśapāyana, drink the (waters of those) rivers. This continent is vast and is situated in the form of a wheel.

100. It is covered with the waters of the rivers and mountains that resemble clouds, that are wonderful and variegated by means of all sorts of minerals and that are embellished with jewels and corals.

---

tain is designated as Keśarin, whence the wind blows (all over the world).

* Vā.P.49.77b reads : *Tasya pūjām prayunjate* for Bd.P.'s *tasya pūjyā mahānugāḥ*.

** Though the list of the seven rivers of this continent is somewhat different in Vā.P. 49.91-94., the reading *Dhenukā* from that list may be accepted here to avoid repetition of *Veṇukā* in the list of seven rivers in this text.

101. It is endowed with different kinds of cities and flourishing rural territories. The trees therein are laden with flowers and fruits all round (the year) and the continent abounds in wealth and food grains.

102. It is surrounded on all sides by the sea with milk for its liquid content. The sea is equal to Śākadvīpa in its extent.

103. Therein, the rural regions, the mountains, and the rivers are splendid and sacred. The lands (sub-continents) are fully inhabited by persons following the discipline of the four castes and the stages of life. They (the sub-continents), are seven in number.

104. In those sub-continents there is no clash of castes or mixed castes. Since Dharma is practised unswervingly, the subjects enjoy exclusive happiness.

105. There is no greediness amongst them nor the eagerness for deception as a result of rivalry and jealousy. There is no adversity among them. Everything is extremely natural and timely.

106. In them there is no acquisition (imposition) of taxes. There is neither punishment nor persons worthy of being punished. They are conversant with virtue and piety. They protect one another by means of their adherence to their own respective duties.

107. Only this much can be described in regard to that continent. Only this much need be heard in regard to the residents of Śākadvīpa.

108-111. I shall describe Puṣkara[1] the seventh continent. Understand it. The ocean with milk as its liquid content is externally surrounded on all sides by the continent Puṣkara[1] which is twice as much as the Śākadvīpa in extent. There is only one glorious mountain with huge rocky cliffs. It possesses peaks, clusters of cliffs of various (sizes and shapes), full of precious jewels. It is extremely lofty and it has variegated

1. Puṣkara is identified by M. Ali with Japan, Manchuria and the South-eastern Siberia op. cit. (pp. 42-44), while De identifies it with a portion of central Asia from the north of the Oxus including Western Tartary. Puṣkara is a Sanskritisation of Bhushkara or Bokhara, op. cit. (p. 163).

ridges. This great mountain has diversified ridges in the eastern half of the continent. It is very extensive—of twentyfive thousand (Yojanas)—with a number of ridges. It rises up from the ground level upto thirtyfour thousand (Yojanas).

112. The mountain range Mānasottara covers half of the continent. It is situated near the sea-shore just like the rising moon.

113. It rises upto a height of fifty thousand Yojanas. Its circular extent all round is also the same (number of Yojanas.)

114. The same mountain is known as Mānasa in the western half of the continent. There is only one great mountain of inherent strength situated in two parts.

115. The continent is surrounded on all sides by the sea with sweet water as its liquid content. This sea is as extensive on all sides as the continent of Puṣkaradvīpa.

116-117. It is remembered that there are two splendid and sacred countries on that continent. They are opposite to the two ranges of the mountain Mānasa. The sub-continent Mahāvīta is outside the Mānasa mountain range. It is said that Dhātakīkhaṇḍa is on its inner side.

118. The men there live for ten thousand years. They are free from sickness. They have plenty of pleasurable experiences. They have attained mental powers (to a great extent).

119. The span of life and the handsome features of all the people in both the Varṣas are declared to be the same. There is no distinction among them as superior or inferior. They are equal in features and conduct.

120. There is neither a robber nor an oppressor. There is no jealousy nor the fear of malicious envy. There is neither seizure nor the meting out of punishment. There is neither covetousness nor (secret) acceptance (of gifts).

121. There is no (such distinction as) truth and falsehood or virtue and evil (i.e. all are truthful and virtuous). There is no agricultural activity or breeding of cattle or trade routes.

122. The three Vedas, the (fourteen) Vidyās, the system of civil and criminal administration, the desire to serve and arts and crafts—all these are not present in either of the two sub-continents of Puṣkara.

123. There is neither rain nor (the flow of) rivers. There is neither chillness nor hot atmosphere. There are no water fountains breaking through (the ground) here. There are no mountain cascades or springs.

124. The season there is just the same as in the northern Kurus. The people are well pleased and contented in all the seasons. They are devoid of the onslaught of old age.

125. Thus the entire mode of activity and life in the Dhātakīkhaṇḍa and Mahāvīta in the continent of Puṣkara has been recounted in the due order.

126. The continent Puṣkara is surrounded by the sea with sweet water for its liquid content. This sea is equal to Puṣkara in extent and circumference.

127. Thus, the seven continents are surrounded by the seven seas. The sea that is immediately after a continent is equal to that continent.

128. Thus, the mutual increase in size, of the continents and the seas should be understood. The sea is called *Samudra* on account of the *Samudreka*[1] (the state of being plentiful) of the waters.

129. The sub-continent is called *Varṣa*[2] because the four types of subjects enter (*Viśanti*) or live (*Nivasanti*) in it and also because it accords pleasure unto the subjects.

130. The root √ṛṣ means "to sport about" and the root √vṛṣ means "to strengthen." Since the sub-continent enables the people to sport about and to stengthen their power for sexual dalliance, it is called *Varṣa*.

131. The sea is always filled (is in flow-tide) in the bright half along with the increase in the size of the moon. When the moon wanes and decreases in size in the dark half, the sea also subsides.

132. It is natural that the sea gets filled when it fills itself. When it becomes reduced it gets reduced (withdrawn) in itself.

---

1. A popular etymology of *Samudra* 'a sea'.
2. *Varṣa* 'a sub-continent' is traced to —*viś*—'to enter', *ni—vas*, 'to live', —ṛṣ—'to sport' and —vṛṣ—'to strengthen'.

133. Just as the water in the boiler appears to increase due to its contact with fire, so also the water in the great ocean becomes increased by itself naturally.

134. During the bright and dark fortnights when the moon rises and sets, the waters in the sea increase and decrease in a quantity that is neither more nor less than usual.

135. The increase and decrease in the quantity of water of the sea in accordance with the increase and decrease in the size of the moon is five hundred and ten Aṅgulas.

136. During the *Parvan* days the increase and decrease of the waters of the ocean can be seen. The continents surrounded everywhere by water are remembered as Dvīpas because of *Dvirāpkatva* (i.e. the state of having water on either side.

137. The sea is called *udadhi*[1] because it is the ultimate rest (*Ayana*) of water (*Udaka*).[1] Mountains without knotty ridges are remembered as *Giris* and those with them are *Parvatas*.

138. The mountain Gomeda in the Plakṣadvīpa is therefore called *Parvata*. The Śālmali (Silk-cotton tree) is worshipped by persons of great holy rites in the continent Śālmaladvīpa.[2]

139. In the Kuśadvīpa, the stump of Kuśa grass is (worshipped) and it is called after its name. In the Krauñcadvīpa there is the mountain Krauñca in the middle of the clime.

140. The main tree in the Śāka Dvīpa is *Śāka* and it is called after its name. In the Puṣkaradvīpa, the *Nyagrodha* (holy fig tree) is bowed to by the inhabitants therein.

141. The great lord Brahmā, the overlord of the three worlds is worshipped there. Brahmā, the Prajāpati, lives in that (sub-continent) along with the Sādhyas.

142. There, the thirtythree Devas perform the worship along with the great sages. That lord, the most excellent of all the Devas is worshipped there by the Devas.

243-144. Different kinds of jewels and precious gems originate (are quarried) in Jambūdvīpa.

---

1. Etymology of *udadhi* 'a sea'.

2. VV 138-140 explain why particular continents are named Śālmala, Krauñca, etc.

In all these continents, the size of the subjects is respectively twice those of the earlier ones on account of the span of life and state of health, their adherence to celibacy, truthfulness and control of the sense-organs.

145. The self-born lord protects the subjects both the sluggish as well as scholarly in the two sub-continents that had been mentioned in the Puṣkaradvīpa.

146. Raising up his rod of chastisement, lord Brahmā, the overlord of the three worlds, protects the subjects. That lord is the Minister of Viṣṇu. He is the father and grandfather.

147. The subjects always take in the meal that approaches them(automatically) by itself. The meal has great nutritive value and it consists of all the six tests.

148. The great sea with sweet water as its liquid content envelops the halves of Puṣkara. The sea encircles it all round.

149. Beyond it, appears the existence of a great world. It is golden. The entire ground is like a single rocky slab. It is twice as large as the sea.

150. Beyond that world is a mountain that is circular at the terminals. It is partially visible and partially invisible. It is called Lokāloka.

151. On this side of that Mountain is all brightness and beyond it is all darkness. Its height is remembered as ten thousand Yojanas.

152. Its extent is also that much. It can go over the earth as he pleases. The *Āloka* (brightness) is in the midst of worldly activities and the absence of brightness (i.e. darkness) is beyond the mundane.

153. All the worlds are included in the half that is bright and the dark regions are external ones. The (region having the absence of brilliance outside extends all round to the extent of the worlds within.

154. It is circumscribed all round. It is encircled by water. (That portion) beyond the brilliant region stands encircling the cosmic egg.

155-156. These worlds and the earth consisting of the seven continents are within the cosmic egg. The worlds are Bhūrloka, Bhuvarloka, Svarloka, Mahas, Jana, Tapas and Satya lokas. This much constitutes the group of worlds. This much alone need be known about the ultimate end of the worlds and the great expanse beyond.

157. In the beginning of the bright half of the lunar month the moon appears as though it rests on a pot (i.e. is crescent-shaped) in the western quarter. The body of the cosmic egg too is like that.

158. It should be known that there are thousands and crores of cosmic eggs like this, above, below and sideways. The cause of origin thereof is the unchanging Ātman.

159. Each of these is encircled by seven *Dharaṇas**[1] (? *Varaṇas*—coverings) evolved of the Prakṛti. In groups of ten or more (?), they sustain one another.

160. All of them are encircled mutually and are evolved mutually. All round this *Aṇḍa* (Cosmic egg) is situated the *Ghanodadhi*—sea of solidified waters.

161-163. It stands, on being held all round by *Vanoda* (? Mistake for *Ghanada*), solidified water.

The circular zone of the solidified water stands on being held by *Tejas* (fiery matter) all round, sidways and above. This fiery matter is like a ball of iron. It has a circular shape.

It stands on being held all round by solidified air. Similarly, it is the ether that holds and sustains the solidified air.

164. The *Bhūtādi* (the cosmic Ego) holds the ether and Mahān (the great principle) sustains (supported) by the Infinite principle, the *Avyakta* (the unmanifest one).

165-168. It is endless and unmanifest. It is subtle in ten ways (?). It is boundless It is non-selfpossessed. It has neither a beginning nor an end. When compared with the supreme Being, it is non-permanent. It is *Aghora* (not terrible). It has no support. It is free from ailment. It is many thousand Yojanas away. It is non-concealed. It is darkness itself. It has no brilliance. It is unlimited. It has no space (or support). It is unknown even unto the Devas. It is devoid of all activities. It is well known as the extremity of darkness. It is non-brilliant

---

* Vā.P.49.152b reads *Kāraṇaiḥ* 'By causes'.

1. This is the Puranic concept of protective 'sheaths' round the universe (Brahmāṇḍa). The influence of Sāṅkhya categories is obvious.

at the extremity of the ether. It is within the limit. It is the great abode of the lord.

169-170. The Śruti says that that divine abode is inaccessible to the Devas. The regions well-known to the learned ones are called 'Loka's. They are situated within the jurisdiction of the great lord of the Devas. The regions which are beneath the Moon and the sun, are called the worlds of the universe, by the wise.

171. The nether-worlds beneath the Rasātala are seven in number and those above them are also seven in number. O Brāhmaṇas, there are seven Skandhas (layers) of the wind along with the *Brahmasadana* (abode of Brahmā).

172. Its movement is five-fold from the Pātāla (Netherworld) to the heaven. This is the extent of the universe. This is the ocean of worldly existence.

173. The Living beings, originating from many species go about (here and there). They are beginningless and endless. The Prakṛti stationed in (resting on) the Brahman is the cause of the universe. It is mysterious and variegated.

174. The creation of the lord is extensive. It is not comprehended even by the Siddhas, of great fortune and nobility who can understand things beyond the pale of sense-organs.

175-176. O excellent Brāhmaṇa, there is neither decline or decay nor transformation, nor end of the earth, water, fire, wind, ether, darkness, mind and the infinite body. This is endless everywhere. So it is cited in wisdom.

177-179. Previously his name has been mentioned by me while recounting the names (of deities). It is he who has been wholly glorified by the name of Padmanābha. He is omnipresent. He is worshipped in all abodes, viz. on the earth, the nether-worlds, the firmament, the wind and the fire. Undoubtedly He is worshipped in all the seas and in the heaven. This self-same Lord of great splendour is worshipped in darkness as well, it should be known.

180. Lord Janārdana is a great Yogin. His limbs are divided in many ways. This lord of the worlds is worshipped in all the worlds in diverse ways.

181. Thus the worlds born of each other are sustained mutually. These *Vikāras* (products or effects) of the *Avikārin*

(that which does not undergo change or distortion) are sustained by the relationship of the supporter and the supported.

182. The earth etc. are the *Vikāras* (effects). They are restricted by each other. They are superior to each other and they have penetrated mutually.

183. Since they have been created mutually, they have attained stability. In the beginning they were without *Viśeṣas*. They are called *Viśeṣas* because they qualify others.

184. The three (Elements) beginning with the earth and ending with *Vahni* (fire) * are limited ones. In view of the essence of the increase of qualities, they have *Pariccheda* (exact determinateness, concrete state) in particular.

185. The accurate decision or judgement about the remaining principles is not perceived, owing to their subtleness (*Śaukṣmya*). That earth is remembered as *Vyālokā* (something that has a special brilliance?) beyond all these other elements.

186-187. All the *Bhūtas* (elements) are circumscribed on all sides (and hence accommodated) in the space (or firmament) just as in a big vessel smaller vessels are accommodated and due to their mutual support become smaller (to each other). Similarly, the different elements are considered ensconsced in the lustre of the firmament.

188. The whole of these four elements are bigger and superior to one another. As long as these elements exist the period of creation lasts to that extent.

189. It is as though like an interturning of threads that the different elements are considered enmeshed into one another. There can be no generation of an effect if Bhūtas (elements) are excluded.

190. Hence, the differences which are of the nature of effects are declared to be limited. The differences such as Mahat and others are of the nature of cause.

191. Thus, O Brāhmaṇas, the real situation comprising of the seven continents, oceans etc. has been recounted by me topic by topic as it exists— (realistically).

---

* The reading in the printed text is *vādyanta* which is meaningless. It should be *vahnyanta* in view of the mention of three elements.

192. The partial transformation of the *Pradhāna* with the cosmic form has been mentioned in detail. The zones have been enumerated.

193. This entire universe is presided over by the glorious Lord. Thus the seven groups of elements have mutually penetrated.

194. Only this much of the situation (of the universe) can be recounted by me. Only this much has to be heard (i.e. listened to and understood) in regard to the situation of the earth and things connected with it.

195. These seven *Prakṛtis* sustain one another. I am not able to enumerate them with reference to their extents and dimensions.

196. The *Prakṛtis* are innumerable, above, below and at the sides. The situation of the constellations is in firmament in different zones and regions.

197. The situation of the earth is thereafter in the form of circle or globe.

Henceforth, O clever ones, I shall recount the situation of the earth.

CHAPTER TWENTY

*Tha Description of the Netherworlds**

Sūta said :

1-2a. Understand the details of the earth, the wind, the ether, the water and the fire which is the fifth one—that are being recounted later on, that had been recounted earlier along with the proofs thereof.

---

*The Cosmic Egg consists of fourteen worlds arranged vertically as follows:

These elements are proclaimed as constituted of infinite ingredients and they are all-pervading.

2b-4a The earth is the mother of all living beings. It sustains all animals and living beings. It is full of many kinds of rural regions and territories. It consists of many towns and places of shelter. It possesses many rivers, streams and mountains. It is crowded with many species of living beings.

The earth, the divine goddess, is sung about as infinite and extremely extensive.

Continued

I. *The Upper Regions* :

Satya Loka
|
Tapo-loka
|
Jana Loka
|
Mahar Loka
|
Svar Loka
|
Bhuvar Loka
|

II. The Middle Region :

The Earth
|

III. The Lower Regions or Nether-worlds:

|
Atala
|
Vitala
|
Sutala
|
Talātala
|
Rasātala
|
Mahā-tala
|
Pātāla

All these are supported by Lord Śeṣa, the Serpent-King.

These lower regions are not dark or devoid of sunlight. They are full of light and have the affluence and comforts of the world of gods. Cf. Bh. P.V.24, VP.V.2. Vā. P. 50.1-54.

Baladeva Upādhyāya makes out a plausible case for identifying the Nether-worlds with the continent of America. (vide : *Purāṇa-Vimarśa*, pp. 43-49).

4b. The waters also should be understood as infinite—the waters contained in the rivers, streams, oceans and small receptacles such as ponds and puddles, those situated on the mountains and in the firmament and those within the bowels of the earth.

5. Similarly, the element of fire pervades all the worlds. It is cited as infinite, all-pervasive and originating from everything.

6. Similarly, the Ether is remembered as unscrapable, beautiful, and accommodating all or various objects, endless and infinite.

7. The Vāyu (wind) originated from the Ether. The waters are stationed within and above the earth. The earth is established on the water.

8. The Ether or the sky is that which has nothing else greater than it. Then the earth and then the water. This is the opinion that there is no state of being endless in regard to the *Bhautika* (objects evolved of the elements) *

9-10a. Understand that the earth becomes developed due to the interaction (of. the elements), The sequence—the earth, the water and the Ether is well known. In the seventh (Netherworld) Rasātala this is the situation (?)

10b-11a. The nether-world called Rasātala has the land portion extending to ten thousand Yojanas. It has been reckoned by noble-souled persons that each of the netherlands is more extensive than the former.

11b-13a. The first one is Atala by name. Thereafter is Sutala. The next one, one should know, is Talātala. Atala (? or Vitala) is very extensive. Beneath that is the world named Tala (should be *Mahātala*?) and beyond that is Rasātala. Beneath all these, it is remembered, is the seventh world, the Pātāla.

13b-15a. The first portion of the ground is glorified as one with black soil.

The second world has pale white coloured ground. The third one has blue soil. The fourth one has yellow soil and the fifth one has a gravel-covered soil.

---

* The text is a bit obscure. Vā.P.50.9 (corresponding verse) reads: *evam anto hyanantasya bhautikasya na vidyate*. 'In this way, there is no end to the objects evolved from *bhūtas*—as they are infinite.'

The sixth world should be known as (consisting of) rocky grounds and the seventh one is remembered as one with golden ground.

15b-20a. The well-known palace of the lord of the Asuras—Namuci, the enemy of Indra is in the first nether-world. The following abodes too are in the first nether world, viz. the abode of Mahānāda, the city of Śaṅkukarṇa, the palace of Kabandha, Niṣkulāda's town fully inhabited by delighted (jolly) people, the abode of the demon Bhīma, the abode of Śūladanta, the city of Lohitākṣas and Kaliṅgas, the town of Śvāpada, the city of Dhanañjaya and of the noble-souled Nāgendra (Lord of serpents), the city of Kāliya the serpent and that of Kauśika. Thus it should be known that there are thousands of cities (and abodes) of the serpents, Dānavas and Rākṣasas in the first Nether-world with black soil.

20b-25a. In the second nether-world Sutala, O Brāhmaṇas, are the abodes of the following, viz. the city of the first lord of the Daityas and Rākṣasas i.e. of Mahājambha, the palace of Hayagrīva, Kṛṣṇa and Nikumbha, the city of the Daitya named Śaṅkha and that of Gomukha, the abode of the demons Nīla, Megha and Kathana, the abode of Kukupāda and that of Mahoṣṇīṣa, the city of Kambala the serpent and that of Aśvatara and the city of Takṣaka the noble-souled son of Kadru. Thus there are, O Brāhmaṇa, thousands of cities belonging to the serpents, Dānavas and the Rākṣasas in the second nether-world of pale white coloured soil.

25b-31. In the third nether-world is the well known city of the noble-souled Prahlāda, Anuhrāda and Agnimukha, the city of (the Daitya) named Tāraka, the city of Triśiras, the city of Śiśumāra the city of Tripura, the demon Purañjana's city full of commotion, due to the gay, well-nourished people, the palace of Cyavana the Rākṣasa, the city of Kumbhila and Khara the leading Rākṣasas, the city of the ruthless Virādha with fire-emitting mouth, the city of Hemaka the serpent as well as that of Pāṇḍuraka, the city of Maṇināga, the palace of Kapila, the palace of Nandaka the lord of the serpents, and that of Viśālākṣa. Thus there are thousands of cities of the serpents, Dānavas and Rākṣasas, O Brāhmaṇas in the third netherworld with blue soil.

32-34. In the fourth netherworld is the city of Kālanemi the lion among Daityas, that of the noble-souled Gajakarṇa, the city of Kuñjara, the vast and extensive city of Sumāli the leading Rākṣasa, the abode of Muñja, Lokanātha and Vṛkavaktra and the city of Vainateya, that extends to many Yojanas and that is crowded with many birds. All these are in the fourth netherworld.

35-38. In the fifth netherworld that is covered with sand and full of gravel is the intelligent Virocana, the lion among Daityas, the abodes of Vaidyuta, Agni-Jihva and that of Hiraṇyākṣa, the city of the intelligent Vidyujjihva, the lord of Rākṣasa, the city of Sahamegha, that of Mālin, the leading Rākṣasa, the city of the serpent Kirmīra and those of Svastika and Jaya. Thus there are thousands of cities of the serpents, Dānavas and the Rākṣasas in the fifth netherworld full of gravel. This should be known (as the situation) for ever.

39-42a. In the sixth netherworld is the excellent city of Kesari, the lord of the Daityas, the cities of Suparvan, Puloman and Mahiṣa, and the city of the noble-souled Sureṣa, the leading Rākṣasa. It is there that Śataśīrṣa the son of Suramā lives joyfully. The king of serpents named Vāsuki, the affluent and glorious friend of Mahendra (stays there). Thus there are thousands of cities of the serpents, Dānavas and the Rākṣasas in the famous sixth netherworld, Rasātala with rocky ground.

42b-46a. It should be known that the city of Bali is in the seventh and the last netherworld Pātāla. It is beyond every world. It is gay and full of men and women. It is full of Asuras, serpents and the happy and joyous enemies of the Devas. There itself is the great city of Mucukunda, the Daitya. It is teeming with innumerable great cities of Daityas full of bustle and commotion, thousands of the brilliant cities of the serpents, the great rising (flourishing) cities of the Daityas and the Dānavas and the many flourishing abodes of the Rākṣasas.

46b-47. O leading Brāhmaṇas, at the extreme end of Pātāla that extends to many Yojanas resides Śeṣa the noble-souled (king of serpents). His eyes are like the red lotus. He is devoid of death and old age. His body is as white as the inner part of well-washed Śaṅkha (conchshell). He wears blue clothes. He is very powerful.

48-49. His physical body is huge. He is lustrous and mighty. He wears garlands of variegated colours. He has a thousand faces (hoods) with mouths shining and brilliant and resembling the golden-peaked (mountain) in purity (lustre). He has single Kuṇḍala (Ear-ring). He appears splendid with his thousand faces. He is refulgent, due to a series of tongues emitting sparks of waving flames of fire.

50-54. With his two thousand eyes that have the reddish splendour of the rising sun and with his body that is white and glossy, he appears like the mountain Kailāsa surrounded by clusters of flames. He has the white complexion like the Moon as well as the Kunda flowers. Hence the cluster of his eyes shines like the cluster of midday suns on the peak of the white Mountain (Śveta Parvata).

He has a huge terrible body. With it (resting) in his reclining pose on his couch, he appears like a thousand-peaked mountain of vast dimensions (resting) over the earth.

This (enormously) huge lord of serpents, himself of great splendour, is being attended upon by extremely wise and noble-souled great serpents of huge physique. He is the king of all serpents. He is Ananta, Śeṣa, of excessive brilliance.

55. That is the commandment (or act) of Viṣṇu. That is the final established boundary (of the Nether-world). Thus the seven netherworlds that could be discussed have been recounted.

56-58. They are always inhabited by the Devas, the Asuras, the great serpents and the Rākṣasas. Beyond this is total absence of light. It cannot be traversed by the Siddhas and the Sādhus (good people). It is unknown even to the Devas. With a desire to expatiate on the general position, O excellent Brāhmaṇas, the greatness of the earth, water, fire, wind and the ether is undoubtedly narrated thus. Hereafter, I shall recount the movement of the sun and the Moon.

CHAPTER TWENTYONE[1]

The Solar System. Movements of Heavenly Luminaries: Division of Time

Sūta said :

1. As long as the Sun and the Moon revolve, they are elevated by means of their lustre and brilliance through their discus.

2-3. (?) The space covered by the brilliant refulgence of the sun and the moon is the extent of the seven seas and the continents. The light falls over half the extent of the earth and the other side remains external. The sun and the moon illuminate the area around facing them.

In extent and magnitude the heaven (i.e. the firmament) is remembered as equal to that of the Earth.

4. The root √*av* means illumination and protection. Revolving all round, the sun illuminates and protects the three worlds. Hence, on account of illumination and protection, he is remembered as 'Ravi.'[2]

5-6. Hereafter, I shall recount the magnitude of the moon and the sun.

The word *Mahi* (earth) is (arbitrarily) assigned to this sub-continent because of its state of being honoured (*Mahītatvāt*) The Solar disc is as extensive as the diameter of this sub continent of Bhārata. Understand that in Yojanas (1 Yojana = 12 km.).

7. The extent of the disc of the sun is nine thousand Yojanas. Its girth is three times the extent.

---

1. The present chapter deals with the ancient astronomical ideas in the pre-telescope age. Similar information about the stellar region regarding the size of the planets and other stars, movements of the Sun, the Moon etc. are found in other Purāṇas like the Bh.P. V Chs. 21-24, Mt. P. Chs. 124-128, V.P. II Chs. 8-12 and Vā. P. I.50. 57 to Ch. 53—the last being textually the same as the Bd. P. and was useful in correcting the misprints in the present text. The astrological aspect of these planets etc. is found in GP. 59-64 and AP. 121 etc. Some of these ideas regarding the distances, positions and dimensions of planets are outdated due to advance of modern astronomy.

2. The author of this Purāṇa is fond of giving popular etymologies. Thus *Ravi* 'the Sun' is normally traced to √*ru*—according to *Uṇādi* IV 138 Ujjvaladatta, but here the author traces it to √*av*—"to protect".

8. In diameter as well as girth (Circumference), the moon is twice as much as the sun.

Now I shall recount the extent of the earth in Yojanas.

9. The extent and girth (circumference) of the earth consisting of seven continents has been reckoned in proper measure in the Purāṇas.

10. I shall recount that, after enumerating the current *Abhimānins* (Deities etc. who preside or have the sense of possession etc.). Those *Abhimānins* who have gone by are on a par with the current ones.

11. The Devas who have gone by are on a par with the current ones in forms and names. Hence, I shall describe the surface of the earth through the current Devas.

12. (I shall recount) the situation of the heavenly world entirely through the current (Devas).

The entire Earth is remembered as fifty crores (of Yojanas) in extent.

13-16. Its situation from an upword measure (?) is as far as the Meru. Half the extent of the earth is stated in terms of Yojanas. The extent of the earth towards all the sides (quarters) from the middle of the Meru is remembered as one crore and eightynine lakhs (of Yojanas) and fifty thousand*. Hence, the extent of the circular section of the earth is roughly eleven crores and thirtyseven lakhs. This is reckoned as the extent of the surface of the Earth.

17-18. (This is reckoned as the extent of the earth) namely as much is the extent in the firmament of the fixation of constellations, so much is the situation of the revolution as far as the sphere of the earth. By the measure of the *Paryāsa* (Revolution, Rotation), it is remembered that the firmament is equal to the earth. This is recounted as the abode of the seven continents.

19. The situation of the spheres of the worlds is one over the other with the girth gradually reduced falling within the previous sphere.

---

* It is considered as the radius of the circular zone.

20. The entire situation has been laid down thus and in them the creatures stay. This magnitude of the bowl of the Cosmic Egg has been recounted.

21-22. These worlds as well as this earth with its seven continents are within this cosmic Egg. The worlds are Bhūrloka Bhuvarloka, Svarloka, Maharloka, Janaloka, Tapoloka and Satyaloka. These seven worlds have been created and they are arranged in the shape of an Umbrella.

23-24. They are held by means of their own subtle coverings individually. These sources of origin are exterior coverings and they are ten times more than (what they envelope). They are filled with special characteristics originating mutually. All round this Cosmic Egg is present (as a fixed envelop) the solidified ocean.[1]

25. The entire sphere of the Earth is held by the solidified water. The solidified ocean is held by a greater solidified fire.

26. The solidified fiery element is surrounded on all sides externally, sideways and upwards by a solidified wind element. Being held thus it rests stabilized there.

27. The solidified wind is surrounded by the firmament. The entire firmament is enveloped by the *Bhūtādi* (i.e. Ahaṃkāra —Ego). The *Bhūtādi* is enveloped by the (principle called) Mahat.

28. The *Mahat* is enveloped by the *Pradhāna* that is infinite and it is of immutable nature.

I shall mention in due order the cities of the guardians of the worlds.

29-32. (It is being mentioned) for the achievement of the proof of spreading the qualities of the luminary bodies* (?) [*Rather :* The extent of the movements of the host of luminary bodies will now be described.]

---

1. Purāṇas believe that this cosmic egg is protected by sheaths consisting of solid (*ghana*) gross elements, the earth being covered by the sheath of solidified water and the sheath of water being enveloped in the sheath of solidified fire (*ghana-teja*) and so on. These sheaths of gross elements are progressively protected by sheaths of Ahaṅkāra *Mahat* and *Pradhāna*. Sāṅkhya influence is evident on this belief.

* The text is corrupt here. The line in Vā.P.50.86b is as follows :

To the east of Meru and on the top of the Mānasa is the city of Mahendra.[1] It is the excellent abode of Vasus (of whom Indra is the head). It is decorated with gold.

To the south of the Meru and on the top of the Mānasa itself, lives Vaivasvata Yama, (Yama the son of the Sungod) in the city called Saṁyamana.

To the west of the Meru and the top of the Mānasa itself, is the beautiful city named Sukhā. It belongs to the intelligent Varuṇa. Varuṇa, the lord of the aquatic beings, lives in the city named Sukhā.

33. To the north of the Meru, on the top of the Mānasa itself, is the city of Soma, named Vibhāvarī. It is on a par with the city of Mahendra.

34. It is for the stabilization of Virtue (Dharma) and for the protection of all the worlds that the guardians of the worlds (i.e. quarters) have stationed themselves in all the four quarters on the top of the Mānasa.

35. Understand the movement of the sun during the southern transit, as he goes to that quarter. His movement is above all the guardians of the quarters.

36. During his southern transit, the sun rushes forward like an arrow that is discharged. He revolves always, taking the circle of luminaries with him.

37-38a. When the sun is in the middle (of the firmamant) at Amarāvatī (city of Indra) his rising is seen in Saṁyamana belonging to Vaivasvata (i.e. Yama). At Sukhā it shall be the middle of the night and the sun (appears to) set at Vibhā (i.e. Vibhāvarī).

38b-39a. When the sun is in the middle (of the firmament) at Saṁyamana belonging to Vaivasvata (i.e. Yama), he is seen rising at Sukhā belonging to Varuṇa. At Vibhā it shall be the middle of the night and (the sun appears to) set at Māhendrī (Amarāvatī, the city of Indra).

39b-41. When it is afternoon for the people of the southeast (or the South and the East), it is mentioned as forenoon for

---

Jyotir-gaṇa-pracārasya pramāṇam parivakṣyate. The translation is given in the bracket, in this verse above.

1. Cf V. P. II 8.9-11.

the people of the South-West (or, of those who are other than the people of the south). It is the latter part of the night for them who are in the north. It is earlier part of the night for the people of northeast. It is in this manner alone that the sun shines in the northern worlds.

42. When the sun is (in the middle of the sky) during midday at Sukhā, (the city) belonging to Varuṇa, he (the sun) (appears) to rise in Vibhā, the city of Soma.

43-44. It is midnight at Amarāvatī and it (appears to) set at Yama's city.

When the sun is (in the middle of the sky) during midday at Vibhā the city of Soma, the sun appears to rise at Amarāvatī of Mahendra. It is mid-night at Saṁyamana (Yama's city) and the sun sets at the city belonging to Varuṇa.

45. The sun revolves rapidly like the whirling firebrand. Moving about, the sun traverses the revolving constellations.

46. Thus the sun thereby moves to the south among the four quarters. The sun rises and sets again and again.

47. The sun warms two Devālayas (abodes of gods i.e. those of Indra and others) in the forenoon and two (other) Devālayas in the afternoon. During the midday also, he blazes with his own rays.

48. After rising up the sun blazes and increases in warmth by means of his own rays till the midday. Thereafter, with his rays decreasing (in warmth) the sun sets.

49-50. The two quarters of the East and West are remembered by means of sunrise and sunset. While it blazes in front, (the heat is felt) behind as well as at the sides.

Where the sun appears rising, it is remembered as sunrise to the people there-of, where the sun vanishes, it is called sunset in regard to the people there.*

51-54. The Meru is to the north of all and the Lokāloka[1] is in the south.

---

* Cf. Ait. Br. III.44 which clearly states that there is rising or setting of the Sun. Also VP.II.8.16. Contrast the Greek idea of having a new sun every day.

1. This is a mythical mountain surrounding the outermost border of the world. It is so called as it divides the visible world from the region of darkness. For its description vide VV. 104-107 below.

Due to the far distant position of the sun and due to his being covered by the line (horizon) of the earth, the rays of the sun disappear (obstructed from sight). Hence it (the sun) is not seen at night.

The setting and rising of the planets, stars and the moon should be understood through the magnitude of the altitude of the sun. So also their rising and setting.

The fire and the water have a white glimmer (?), while the earth has a dark shadow.

Since the sun is far off, it has no (fiery) rays even when it has risen. Its redness is due to the fact that it has no rays and the absence of heat is due to the redness.

55. Wherever the sun is seen occupying the line (horizon), it is seen more than a hundred thousand Yojanas above.

56. When the sun sets along with his rays, the lustre of the sun enters the fire at night. Hence it shines from a distance.

57. The heat of the fire enters the sun when it rises up. The sun blazes during the day time on being united with the fire.

58. The lustre and the heat are the brilliance of the sun and the fire. They shine and flourish day and night, due to their mutual penetration.

59. In the northern as well as southern halves of the earth, the night enters the water when the sun rises.

60-64. Hence due to the penetration of the night during the day, the waters are cool then. When the sun sets, the day penetrates the waters. Hence the waters are warm during the night due to the penetration of the day. Both in the southern half and the northern half of the earth, it is in this order that the day and night enter the waters when the sun sets or rises.

That (part of time) is called 'day' when there is sunlight and the night is called Tāmasī (full of darkness). The night is well defined due to this. The day is remembered at that (period of time) which is dependent on the sun.

Thus, when the sun traverses the middle of the sky, it passes through parts of the earth in the course of a Muhūrta as it were (?) Understand the number of Yojanas here in the course of a Muhūrta.

65-67. It is one hundred and eightyone thousand Yojanas. This is the speed of the sun in a Muhūrta.

When the sun proceeds to the southern quarter with this velocity, it covers the middle and the extremity of the quarter.

Then during the Dākṣiṇāyana, it whirls in the middle of the firmament.

68. Understand that it traverses in the southern quarter in the mountain Mānasottara. The Viṣuva (Equinox) is in the middle (?)

69. The circumference of the sun is estimated to be nine crores of Yojanas as well as fortyfive hundred thousands (i.e. 9,45,00000 Yojanas).

70-72. This is laid down as the movement (? total distance traversed) of the sun in the course of a day and a night.

When the sun, after returning from the south, remains in the equinox, it traverses the northern regions of the milk-ocean. Understand its girth in Yojanas. It is estimated that during the equinox it is three crores and eightyone hundred (3,81,00000).

73-74. When the sun is in the (constellation) Śravaṇa and Uttarāṣāḍhā it traverses the regions (quarters) to the north of the sixth (continent) Śākadvīpa. O Brāhmaṇas, the magnitude of the northern quarter and the sphere (? of the sun therein) is estimated to be a crore of Yojanas.

75-77a. The divisions of the planetary system are: Nāga-*vīthi*,[1] the northern one and Ajavīthi, the southern one. These divisions comprise three asterisms each. The constellations Mūla, Pūrvāṣāḍhā Uttarāṣāḍhā are the points of rising in the Ajavīthi while the contellations Aśvinī, Bharaṇī (lit. that of which Yama is the deity) and Kṛttikā are the

1. According to Varāhamihira's *Bṛhatasaṁhitā, Vīthi* is a particular division of the planetary sphere comprising of three asterisms. Thus the division comprising asterisms Mūla, Pūrvāṣāḍhā and Uttarāṣāḍhā constitutes the *Aja-Vīthi*, while Aśvinī, Bharaṇī and Kṛttikā form the *Nāga-vīthi.*

three points (constituting) in the Nāgavīthi. The magnitude of the northern orbit as well as the southern orbit is eighty hundred thousand and five thousand eight hundred Yojanas (?) (or 80+58=138 lakhs of Yojanas.)

77b-79a. I shall henceforth mention the distance between the quarters in Yojanas.

This distance is eight hundred thousand four hundred and thirtythree Yojanas (?)

Thus the distance between the quarters has been mentioned in Yojanas.

79b-80a. I shall mention the distance between the two quarters and Meridians, the southern as well as the northern, in Yojanas. Understand it.

80b-81. The exterior and the interior distances between the quarters and the meridians are seven million and one hundred and seventyfive thousand Yojanas.

82. During Uttarāyaṇa the sun goes round the internal zones. During the Dakṣiṇāyana it goes round the external zones always in the due order.

83. There are one hundred and eightythree zones in the north. In the south also the sun traverses that much.

84-85. Understand the magnitude of the zone in Yojanas. It is seventeen thousand two hundred and twentyone Yojanas (in magnitude).

86. This magnitude of the zone has thus been recounted in so many Yojanas.

The diameter of the zone is laid obliquely.

87-88. Everyday the sun traverses those (zones) in due order. Just as the outer rim of the potter's wheel comes back quickly (i.e. revolves), so also the sun functions quickly during his Southern transit. Hence, he traverses a major portion of the Earth in the course of a shorter period.

89-91. During Dakṣiṇāyana, on account of his rapidity, the sun covers thirteen and a half constellations in the course of a day of twelve Muhūrtas. He covers the same number of constellations during the night of eighteen Muhūrtas.

Just as the central region of the potter's wheel whirls slowly so also, during his northern transit the sun traverses with less rapidity. Hence, during his northern transit, the sun traverses with less velocity. Hence, he covers a lesser portion of the earth in the course of a greater period.

92-93. After the advent of the northern transit, the day consists of eighteen Muhūrtas, the sun of slow speed traverses thirteen and a half constellations during the day. He covers the same number of constellations during the night of twelve Muhūrtas.

94. The Potter's wheel whirls still more slowly at the Navel. In the same manner, like the lump of clay in the middle, the pole star (Dhruva) revolves.

95-96. They say that the day and the night together consist of thirty Muhūrtas. Whirling in between the two quarters, Dhruva revolves in circles.

Just as the navel of the potter's wheel remains there itself, so also, it should be known that Dhruva whirls there (without changing its place) itself.

97-99. It (pole star) whirls in circles in between the two quarters. The movement of the sun is slow by day and quick at night. Dur ng the northern transit the movement of the sun by day is slow and very quick by the night.

During the southern transit the movement of the sun by the day is quick and that by the night is slow.

100. Thus, by means of regular and irregular movements and proceeding along its orbit, the sun divides days and nights.

101. These guardians of the four quarters are stationed on the Lokāloka mountain. Agastya (the star Canopus) quickly traverses over them.

102-106. Day and night he undergoes these diverse motions to the south of the Nāgavīthī and to the north of the Lokāloka.

Outside the path of Vaiśvānara, he is the extender of the worlds.

As long as the lustre of the sun shines from behind, there is brightness in front of and at the sides of the Lokāloka.

The mountain is ten thousand Yojanas in height. It is partially lighted and partially not lighted (in darkness). It is circular all round. The stars, the moon and the sun, along with the planets and the groups of constellations shine within the boundary of the world encircled by the mountain Lokāloka.

The world is only this far. Beyond this is darkness.

107-111. This (mountain) has the illumination on the side of the world. Beyond the worlds, it is devoid of illumination. The inter-space between Uṣā (Night or Dawn) and *Vyuṣṭi* (Morning) joins the Lokāloka accepted by the sun* (?) Therefore, they call it *Sandhyā* (Twilight). Uṣā is remembered as night and *Vyuṣṭi* is remembered as the day, by the Brāhmaṇas

The demons were bent on devouring the sun and the fire at the time of dusk. A curse was cast on these wicked persons at the instance of Prajāpati.

(They had) *Akṣayatva* (the state of imperishability) of the body but they were made to die.

Three crores of demons are well known as Mandehas. Every day they seek the rising sun. These evil-minded ones wish to devour the sun that blazes.

112-113. A terrible battle ensued between the sun-god and those demons. Thereupon, the Devas, the most excellent Brāhmaṇas and god Brahmā performed the Sandhyā-prayer and poured water charged with the Mantras of Gāyatrī along with Oṁkāra (the symbol of) Brahman.

114-115. With a sudden flash of splendour then the sun shone with fierce rays. He became excessively resplendent with great strength and valour. Protected by the Brāhmaṇas, he rises a hundred thousand Yojanas upwards and proceeds ahead. Protected by the sages Vālakhilyas and his brilliance along with his rays (he is held aloft.)

116. Fifteen Nimeṣas constitute one Kāṣṭhā. Thirty Kāṣṭhās make one Kalā. Thirty Kalās make a Muhūrta and thirty such Muhūrtas make a full day consisting of day and night.

---

*Vā P. gives a better reading : *sūryaḥ parigraham* i.e. It is the sun who joins and therefore the period is called Sandhyā (the joining period).

Or : As it joins together Lokāloka which surrounds the sun, it is called Sandhyā (the connecting link between light and darkness). It is the interim period between us as (dawn) and the morning.

117-123. The shortening or the lengthening of days by means of units of time happens duly. The Sandhyā (junction) spreads over a period of a Muhūrta. It is remembered as the limit for the shortening or lengthening of the days.

Rising from the circle of the horizon, when the sun traverses for a period of three Muhūrtas, that is remembered as Forenoon.[1] It is a fifth of the daytime. The period of time of three Muhūrtas after the forenoon is called *Saṅgava*. The period of three Muhūrtas from *Saṅgava* is called *Madhyāhna* (Midday). The period of three Muhūrtas from the midday is remembered as *Aparāhṇa* (Afternoon). A period of three Muhūrtas alone is remembered by scholars as the unit of time, (A period of three Muhūrtas) after the *Aparāhṇa* is called *Sāyāhna* (Evening). There are only three (sacred ?) Muhūrtas in a day of fifteen Muhūrtas. It is remembered that an equinotical day has fifteen Muhūrtas. During the southern transit and the northern transit, the nights and days increase and decrease. The day swallows the night and the night swallows the day.

124. The equinox is expected to be in the middle of the Autumn and the Spring. The moon has equal number of Kalās in the night and day.

125. A period of fifteen days is mentioned as a Pakṣa (fortnight). Two Pakṣas make a month and two solar months make a season.

126-129. Three seasons (make one Ayana), and two Ayanas make a solar Year.

(Defective Text). Nimeṣas are *Vidyutas*[2]*. Fifteen of them make a Kāṣṭhā. Thirty Kāṣṭhās make a Kalā (?) It consists of one hundred and sixty Mātrās.

Thirty Mātras increased by two and seven consist of thirty-six of the latter (?). With sixtytwo and seventythree Mātrās constitute Kalā. It has forty thousand and eight hundred

1. These verses state the five parts of the day, each part being of three Muhūrtas in duration.

2. It appears that a new term called *Vidyut* is introduced in the units of Time here.

*Vā.P.50.179 reads : *nimeṣādī kṛtaḥ Kālaḥ* 'The time covered by twinkling of the eye 'etc'.

Vidyuts. They are seventy (?) Know for certain that they are ninety. They say that there are four hundred and two Vidyuts (?)

130. This should be considered as the excellent part. Nāḍikā Ghaṭi (24 minutes) is the cause hereof. The five (units of time beginning with Saṁvatsara are diversified, due to four measures[1] (?) (See verse 137).

131-132. The decisive basic unit of all time is called Yuga (Age).[2] The first year is Saṁvatsara. The second is Parivatsara. The third is Iḍāvatsara. The fourth is Anuvatsara. The fifth is Vatsara. Their period of time is called Yuga.

133-134. In a solar Yuga, there shall be three thousand (lit. thirty hundred) *Parvans* (junctions) and one thousand eight hundred and thirty risings of the sun (i.e. days.)

There shall be thirty Ṛtus and ten Ayanas (Defective Text). There are three hundred and sixtyfive days (5+300 +60) in a solar year.

135. Thirty units of days and nights make one solar month. Sixtyone such days make one Ṛtu.

136. The extent of a solar Ayana is one hundred and eightythree days.

137. The following are the four measures (for calculating time) viz.: *Saura* (Solar), *Saumya* (Lunar), *Nākṣatra* (sidereal) and *Sāvana* (based on Savana calculation of days from sunrise to sunset). These measures are decisively mentioned in the Purāṇas.

---

1. V. 137 gives the four measures of systems in calculating time (or year) viz. *Saura* (Solar), *Saumya* (Lunar), *Nākṣatra* (sidereal).

2. This Purāṇa records the age-old tradition that the Yuga period consisted of five years. Even in the Vedic times Yuga was of five years and the names of those five years (with a slight variations in the name *Iḍāvatsara* viz. *Iḍā-Iḍu—Vatsara*) are the same as given here (*vide* Tai.S.V.7.1-3, Vāj.S.27.45, Atharva VI 55.3). Tai. Br. I. 4. 10.1 identifies *Saṁvatsara, Parivatsara* etc. with god Agni, Āditya etc. Kauṭilya in *Arthaśāstra* II Ch. 20 in measures of time declares "A Yuga consists of five years" (*Pañca-Saṁvatsaro Yugam*). This Purāṇa records the same.

138. There is a mountain named Śṛṅgavān towards the north of the Śveta. It has three peaks which appear to touch the surface of the firmament.

139. That mountain is said to be Śṛṅgavān, due to those peaks. Its girth and sectional diameter are equally glorified (? are the same).

140. Its middle and eastern peak is golden. The southern peak has crystal-like lustre and it is made of silver.

141. The excellent northern peak is full of all kinds of jewels. Thus, due to the three peaks, the mountain is well known as Śṛṅgavān.

142. During the time in between the Autumn and the Spring, the sun proceeds with a medium speed and he resorts to its eastern peak.

143. Hence, the dispeller of darkness makes the day and night equal. Divine green-coloured horses are yoked to his great chariot. They appear as though they are smeared with the rays red as lotus.

144. To the close of *Meṣa* and *Tulā*, the duration of the day from sunrise to sunset is fifteen Muhūrtas. The night is also equally long.

145. When the sun enters the first degree or part of the constellation *Kṛttikā*, it should be known that the moon enters the fourth part of the constellation *Viśākhā*.

146. When the sun moves through the third part of the constellation Viśākhā, it should be known that the moon has occupied the top of the constellation Kṛttikā.

147-149. The great sages say that one should know that time as *Viṣuva* (Equinox). One should understand the equinox through the position of the sun and should see the time through the moon. When the day and the night are of equal duration, it shall be the *Viṣuva*. Then during the equinox, religious gifts should be offered to the manes and to the Brāhmaṇas particularly because it happens to be the face of gods.

150. (The following are to be known in connection with the various units of time) : they are *Ūnamāsa* (month of a shorter duration), *Adhimāsa* (Intercalary lunar month), Kalā, Kāṣṭhā, Muhūrtaka, Paurṇamāsī (full moon), Amāvasyā (New

moon), Sinīvālī, Kuhū (different kinds of new moon), Rākā and Anumati (kinds of full moon day).[1]

151. The months of Māgha, Phālguna, Caitra, Vaiśākha, Jyeṣṭha and Āṣāḍha constitute Uttarāyaṇa (Northern transit). The months of Śrāvaṇa, Bhādrapada, Āśvina, Kārttika, Mārgaśīrṣa and Pauṣa constitute Dakṣināyana.[2]

152-154. The five years called *Ārtavas* should be known as the sons of Brahmā.

Hence, the *Ṛtus* should be known. They are remembered as *Ārtavas* on account of the *Ṛtus*. Hence, from this Parvan, Amāvāsyā should be known as having *Ṛtus* as its face. Hence, from this Parvan, the *Viṣuva* should be known. It is always conducive to the welfare of the Devas and the Pitṛs. One should not lose sense regarding rites concerning the Pitṛs and the Devas, after knowing the Parvan.

---

1. The Amāvāsyā (the new moon day) mixed with the 14th Tithi is Sinivālī and that which merges with the 1st Tithi of the next fortnight is Kuhū. It is treated as a divinity and invoked for wealth and Sons. (*vide* Atharva VII 47.1). According to Nirukta XI 29, Paurṇamāsī (the full moon day) mixed with the 14th tithi is Anumati, while that mixed with the 1st day of the next fortnight is Rākā. In vedic times it was worshipped for a rich and famous son.

2. This verse records the ancient names of the months with which modern names Caitra, Vaiśākha came to be identified. For the convenience of readers the modern names are given in translation. The correspondence of ancient and modern names of the months is as follow:

Old Term	*New Term*
Tapas	Māgha
Tapasya	Phālguna
Madhu	Caitra
Mādhava	Vaiśākha
Śukra	Jyeṣṭha
Śuci	Aṣāḍha
Nabhas	Śrāvaṇa
Nabhasya	Bhādrapada
Iṣu	Āśvina
Ūrja	Kārttika
Sahas	Mārgaśīrṣa
Sahasya	Pauṣa

155. Hence, *Viṣuva* that is present everywhere (?) is always remembered by the subjects. The (mountain) Lokāloka is called so because the world is remembered on account of (?) its being illuminated (by the sun).

156. The guardians of the quarters are stationed in the middle of the Lokāloka. Those four (?) noble-souled guardians remain till the annihilation of all living beings.

157. They are Sudhāmā, Vairāja, Kardama, Śaṅkhapā, Hiraṇyaroman, Parjanya, Ketumān and Rājasa. (Perhaps they are in pairs and hence called four ?).

158. They are free from Dvandvas (mutually opposed pairs) and false prides. They are boundless and free from parigrahas (acceptances of gifts from others). These guardians of quarters are stationed on the Lokāloka in all the four directions.

159. To the North of the star Agastya* and to the south of Ajavīthī is the pathway called Pitṛyāṇa. It is outside the path Vaiśvānara.

160. There stay the sages who are endowed with progeny and who perform Agnihotra sacrifices. Those who stay in the path of *pitṛyāṇa* are those who continue the series of worlds (who perpetuate the lines or race of the worlds).

161. The southern path is of those who, being *Ṛtviks*, commence the work of procreation of living beings by their blessings and are desirous of the world.

162. In every Yuga, they establish Dharma that goes astray. They perform austerities. They strictly adhere to the bounds (of decency) and pursue the art of learning.

163. Here, in this world the predecessors are born in the houses of the successors (those who come after) and the successors are born on the death of the predecessors.

164. Repeatedly being born thus, they remain till the annihilation of all living beings. These sages who are householders are eightyeight thousand in number.

165-168a. They resort to the southern path of the sun as long as the moon and the stars are existent. This is the total

---

* *Yadapastasya* is wrong. Vā.P. 50.209a reads correctly *yad Agastasya* 'of the star Agastya'.

sum (i.e. 88000) of those persons who perform holy rites and who resorted to the cremation grounds. Their routine activities in the world consist of creation of living beings, activities prompted by desire or hatred, indulgence in sexual intercourse, activities induced by lust and resorting to sensual objects.

Those Siddhas (persons with spiritual attainment) who resorted to cremation grounds on these or similar grounds and those sages who seek progeny are (re-born in the Dvāpara age.

168b-169. The pathway that is towards the north of Nāgavīthī and to the south of the group of seven sages (i.e. the Great Bear) is the northern path of the sun. It is remembered as *Devayāna*. Those who stay there are Siddhas of great celibacy, free from impurities.

170-173. They contemptuously hate progeny. Hence, death is conquered by them. These sages of sublimated sexual urge are eightyeight thousand in number. They closely cling to the northern path, till the annihilation of all living beings Due to their association with the world, avoidance of sexual intercourse, abstention from desires and hatreds, eschewal of creation of living beings, non-lustful contacts and seeing defects in sound etc. (i.e. sensual objects), they have become Siddhas. And also due to various other reasons also. Hence they became immortal. Immortality is considered to be (the attainment) of those who stay till the annihilation of all living beings.

174-175a. They approach their wives once again for the sustenance of the three worlds.* Others of sublimated sexual urge are sinners as well as meritorious on account of their killing the child in the womb or performing horse sacrifices. They wither away at the end of annihilation of all living beings.

175b-76. To the north and above the worlds of the sages, where Dhruva is remembered to be present, is the divine region of Viṣṇu, the third one in the firmament. It is the shining

* This is strange of those *Ūrddhva-retas* sages. Vā.P.50. 222a reads: *Trailokya-sthiti-kālo'yam apunarmārgagāminaḥ* |

world on reaching which no one is affected by sorrow or pain. It is the greatest region of Viṣṇu where Dharma, Dhruva and other Sādhakas of the world stay.

CHAPTER TWENTYTWO*

The Description of the Divine Luminaries
Varieties of clouds: Divisions of Stratosphere:
The chariot of the Sun-God

Sūta said:

1. All the *Antaras* (i.e. Manvantaras) during the creation of Svāyambhuva have been recounted. I shall recount all the future ones in due order.

2. On hearing this, the sages asked Romaharṣaṇa about the movement of the Sun, the Moon and the planets.

The sages said:

3-4. "How do these luminaries revolve in the stratosphere without any clash or confusion or without any structural formation? Does any one make them revolve or do they revolve of their own accord? O excellent one, we wish to understand this. Narrate this unto us.

Sūta said:

5. This is something that confounds all living beings. Understand this even as I tell you. Although this is visible and directly perceptible, it perplexes the people.

6. The star that (diffuses light) in the four quarters and is established at the tail of the *Śiśumāra* (i.e. a collection of stars resembling a dolphin or a Gangetic porpoise) is Dhruva,

*This chapter corresponds to Vā.P. Ch. 51.

the son of Uttānapāda.[1] He is, as though, the main pivot to which all the stars and planets are attached.

7. It is reported that it is he who perpetually makes the moon and the sun revolve along with the planets. As it (the sun) revolves like a wheel, the stars also follow it.

8. The group of luminaries, the sun and the moon, the stars and constellations along with the planets move about, at the will of Dhruva.[2]

9-10. They are fastened to Dhruva by means of bonds in the form of rows of winds. Their junction, difference, time, movement, rising and setting, portentious phenomenon, the southern and northern transits, the equinox and the colours of the planets (?)—all these function, due to Dhruva.

11. Rain, heat, snowfall, day, night, the twilight, the welfare and woes of the subjects—all these take place due to Dhruva.

12. Presided over by Dhruva, the sun takes up water and showers it.[3] This sun whose rays are ablaze, is the fire of the destruction of the universe.

13-15. In the course of his revolution, O Brāhmaṇas, he illuminates the quarters. With the mass of his rays and accompanied by the wind all round, the sun takes away the water of the entire world, O excellent Brāhmaṇas. The moon transmits the entire water drunk by the sun. The torrential current of water (Downpour of rain) functions through *Nāḍis* (veinlike vessels) accompanied by the wind. The water that oozes out of the moon remains in the food (i.e. plants and food crops).

---

1. For a better and detailed description how all the stars and constellations are located as different parts of the body of this heavenly porpoise (*Śiśumāra*) vide Bh. P. V. 23.4-7. This system of heavenly luminaries is poetically compared to the body of a porpoise and Lord Vāsudeva is stated therein to have assumed the form of the *Śiśumāra.*

2. Bh. P. *ibid* V. 2 attributes the power of setting in motion this stellar system to the Almighty Kāla (Time) and not to Dhruva.

3. VV 12-17 describe the ancient concept of the water-cycle. Their belief in the indestructibility of water (V.17) is surprisingly modern, but the later description from 19b ff shows old climatological concepts.

16. Being obstructed by the wind, the clouds scatter water over the earth. Thus water is continuously thrown up (i.e. turned into vapour) and dropped down.

17. There is no total distruction of water. The same water gets transformed. It is for the sake of sustenance of all the worlds that this cosmic Māyā has been created (by the lord).

18-19a. The three worlds along with the mobile and immobile beings are pervaded by this Māyā. The sun is the lordly creator of the worlds. Endowed with a thousand (innumerable eyes) he is the lord of the universe. He is the mighty lord of the subjects, the creator of the entire universe.

19b-20. The water that has fallen down from the moon, from the sky, is conducive to the welfare of all the worlds. The entire universe has the moon as its support. This has been truthfully recounted. The *Uṣṇa* (hot virility) oozes out of the sun, and the *Śita* (chill virility) functions from the moon.

21. These two, viz. the moon of cool virility and the sun of hot virility, sustain the world by means of their combination.

The river Gaṅgā with the Moon as support, is holy. Its waters are free from impurities.

22. (The Gaṅgā), the great rivers beginning with Bhadrasomā and the waters (humids) that flow within the bodies of all living beings mobile and immobile, become smoke (i.e. vapour).

23. When the mobiles and immobiles get heated (and burnt) they spread everywhere as vapour.

24. Clouds are formed thereby. It is remembered that the abode (waters) is full of clouds (or, is in the form of clouds).

With his rays the sun takes up water, the very splendour, from all living beings.

25. In combination with the wind, the rays (of the sun) carry the waters from the ocean that water (then) becomes the nectar-like life-giver unto the plants.

26. Then, as the season approaches at the proper time, the sun changes (the saltish water into sweet water) and gives

water to the clouds by means of his white and non-white rays.

27. The waters stationed in the clouds fall down when they are wafted by the wind. Accompanied by the wind (they spread everywhere), for the welfare of all living beings.

28-29. Then for six months it continues to rain in order that all living beings may flourish. The thundering sound pertains to the wind and the lightning originates from fire. The *Meghatva* (the state of being a cloud) is indicated through the root √*Mih* (to pour down), since the cloud showers (rain). The wise people know the cloud as *Abhra* because the waters do not fall down (*na bhraṁśyanti*).[1]

30. The origin of the clouds is threefold.[2] They are of different kinds in view of their sources of origin. They are *Āgneya* (fiery ones), *Brahmaja* (born of *Brahmā*) and *Pakṣaja* (born of Wings).

31. The three kinds of clouds have been enumerated. I shall mention the manner of their origin.

Āgneyas are said to be originating from heat. They produce smoke (vapour).

32. Cold winds and winds on cloudy days are their characteristics. They take the shapes of buffaloes, boars and intoxicated elephants.

33. Assuming these forms, they come to the Earth, sport about and wander here and there. They are named *Jimūtas*. Living beings are born of these clouds.

34. They are devoid of lightning streaks. They hang down with torrents of water. They are silent clouds of huge bodies. They are under the control of *Āvaha* (A kind of wind).

---

1. This is a fanciful derivation of *Abhra* 'a cloud'. Normally Abhra is derived from √*abhr*— + suffix—*ac* (i.e.—*a*) or from *ap* + *bhṛ*—suffix—*a*, meaning "bearer of water.

2. VV. 30-46 give the pseudo-scientific classification of clouds as believed by the ancients. Some of the poetic flashes of imagination herein are interesting. *Āvaha, Pravaha, Vivaha, Udvaha, Saṁvaha, Parivaha* are wind-bearing clouds of different types and functions.

35. They shower rain from within one and a half to three kilometres. They shower rain on the tops and ridges of the mountains and roar out.

36. Those clouds named Brahmajas are born of the breath of god Brahmā. They cause impregnation of the white cranes and they sustain their young ones in the womb.

37. Indeed they are endued with streaks of lightning and reverberations of thundering that are pleasing. Due to their continuous rumbling sound, the earth expresses horripilation in the from of (plants and trees) sprouting from it.

38. Like a queen who has been installed (on the throne of) a kingdom, she attains the freshness of youth once again. Strongly attached to the rains, she becomes the source of the life of beings.

39. Those clouds depend on *Pravaha*, the second type of wind. These clouds (shower rain) from within twelve to eighteen kilometres.

40. Those clouds named *Puṣkarāvartakas* are born of the Wings. Its conception is threefold. The shower is glorified as continuous downpour.

41. The wings of very powerful mountains that had increased in size and who used to go wherever as they pleased, were chopped off by Indra who wished to secure the welfare of all living beings.

42. Those clouds named *Puṣkara* (were born of those wings). They increased in size competing with the waters. For the reason, they are termed *Puṣkarāvartakas* (revolving *Puṣkaras*).

43. They assume many forms. Their thundering sound is very terrible. They are the creators of the torrential rain at the end of the Kalpas. They control the Saṁvartaka fire (which burns down the universe then).

44. These (clouds) shower rain at the close of the Yugas. (Thus) those third (sets of clouds) have been recounted. They have many forms, configurations and aggregates. They fill the Earth.

45-46. They carry the wind ahead. On being resorted to, they conclude the Kalpas. *Aṇḍa-Kapālas* are the pieces of the shell of the cosmic egg (evolved out of Prakṛti) which were formed when the egg was broken and the four-faced, self-potent god Brahmā was born therein, —those very pieces of the cosmic egg are all known as clouds.

47-48. Smoke is conducive to development of all of them without any distinction. The most excellent among them is *Parjanya*. The Elephants of the quarters are four in number. (Although) these are separate, the source of origin of elephants, mountains, clouds and serpents is the same and water is remembered as that origin.

49. On being directed to make the plants and trees flourish, *Parjanya* and the *Diggajas* (Elephants of the quarters) shower snowdrops during Hemanta (early winter), born of cool virility.

50-52a. The sixth wind named *Parivaha* is their support. This powerful (wind) holds up the Gaṅgā of the firmament, the holy divine river of exquisite nectar-like water. The Gaṅgā is situated in the path of *Svāti* (i.e. firmament) in three currents. With their huge trunks, the elephants of the quarters receive the waters oozing from the Gaṅgā and scatter them in the form of water spray. That is remembered as dew-drops.

52b-53. There is the mountain remembered as Hemakūṭa in the southern region. To the north of the Himalaya mountain, there is the extensive city mentioned by the name Puṇḍra stretching from north to south.

54-56. The rain that falls over it has originated from snow-drops. Thereupon the wind named Vaha flows over the Himalaya, sprinkling the great mountain with water. It brings the mountain under its control by means of its own effort. After crossing the Himalayas it utilises the balance of rain-water for the development of the western region.

(Thus) two types of rain for the purpose of development of two types of vegetation have been recounted.

57. The clouds and their activity of causing the development (of various things)—all these have been recounted. The sun alone is mentioned as the creator of showers.

58. The rainfall has its root (source) in the sun water; proceeds from (functions on account of) the sun. It is after being presided over by Dhruva that the sun works for rain.

59-60. The wind presided over by Dhruva withdraws the shower once again.

The planet comes out of the sun, wanders throughout the entire assemblage of the stars and constellations and in the end enters the sun presided over by Dhruva.

Henceforth, understand the structure of the chariot of the sun.[1]

61-62. The sun-god proceeds by means of a golden chariot that has a single wheel with five spokes and three naves, and a single rim with six phases. Its horses are green. The whole chariot embellished with gold, shines brightly.

63. The girth and the extent of the chariot is ten thousand Yojanas (1 Yojana=12 km.) In magnitude, its pole-shaft is twice the central cockpit.

64. His chariot is divine and golden. It is yoked with horses as swift as the wind. It has no impediment anywhere. It was for a specific purpose that it was created by Brahmā.

65. The *Cchandas* (Vedic Metres) have assumed the forms of horses and are stationed in the direction of the wheel. The chariot has characteristics similar to those of the chariot of Varuṇa.

66. It is by means of this shining chariot that the sun traverses the firmament.

Now (know) that the following are the different parts of the chariot of the sun.

67-68. The parts are duly constituted by the parts of the year.

The day is remembered as the nave of the single wheel of the solar chariot. The five *Ārtavas* are the five spokes. The six seasons are remembered as constituting the rim. This is remembered as the inner seat of the chariot. The two *Ayanas* (transits) are the two poleshafts.

69. Muhūrtas and Kalās are remembered as the beautiful trappings and fittings. Kāṣṭhā is remembered as its nose and the *Kṣaṇa* (Moment) is its axle.

1. VV. 61-62 give a symbolic description of the Chariot of the Sun. The significance of each part of the chariot, the horses yoked etc. is given in VV. 67 ff below.

70. The *Nimeṣa* is its axle tree at the bottom. The *Lavas* are remembered as its shaft. The night is its wooden fender. Dharma is its flagstaff that has risen up to (a great height).

71. Artha (Wealth) and Kāma (Love) these two are remembered as the tips of the yoke and the axle.

The Vedic metres in the form of the seven horses carry the yoke by the left.

72. The seven Metres are Gāyatrī, Triṣṭup, Anuṣṭup, Jagatī, Paṅkti, Bṛhatī and Uṣṇik.

73. The wheel is fixed to the Axis and the axis is laid on Dhruva. The Axis whirls along with the wheel and Dhruva whirls (?) along with the Axis.

74. Propelled by Dhruva, the great wheel whirls along with the Axis. Thus is the structure of his chariot in view of specific purpose.

75. Similarly, by means of combination the shining chariot has been evolved. By means of that shining chariot, lord sun-god traverses the firmament.

76. There are two rein-cords fixed to the extremities of the yoke and the axis of the chariot. Those two rein-cords revolve in Dhruva (and perform the function) of a pair of wheels.

77-78. The extremities of the yoke and the axis of the chariot that move in circles in the firmament are caught hold of by Dhruva. Both the rein-cords whirl on the axis and they follow Dhruva who too revolves.

79. The extremities of the yoke and the axis of the chariot revolve all round along with the rein-cords like the rope fixed to a peg.

80. During Uttarāyaṇa the rein-cords become reduced (in length) as they move in circles. During the Dakṣiṇāyana they increase in size.

81. The two rein-cords of the chariot fixed to the extremities of the yoke and the axis are caught hold of by Dhruva and the two rein-cords lead the sun.

82. When presided over by Dhruva, those two reincords are dragged, the sun revolves in circles within (the orbit).

83-84. The intervening distance between the quarters is eight thousand circles (?) When the rein-cords are released by Dhruva, the sun once again revolves in circles outside (the orbit). It moves round in quick circles.

CHAPTER TWENTYTHREE

Information about Heavenly bodies (Stars, Planets etc.) : The movement of the Polar Star

Sūta said :

1. That chariot is occupied and presided over by the Devas, Ādityas, sages, Gandharvas, Divine damsels, *Grāmaṇīs*, Serpents and demons.[1]

2-5a. These abide in the sun for the period of two months each in due order.[2]

The following reside in the sun continuously in the months of Madhu and Mādhava (Caitra and Vaiśākha) viz. (gods) Dhātṛ and Aryaman; (sages) Pulastya, Pulaha, the Prajāpati; (serpents) Airāvata, Vāsuki, Kaṁsa, Bhīma; Ratha-kṛt, and Rathaujas—these two are cited as Yakṣas; (Gandharvas) Tumburu, Nārada; (divine damsels) Susthalā and

1. This sublime concept of the Solar chariot is based on *Yajurveda* 15.15.19. Here Devas, Sages and Gandharvas represent light and immortality-the actinic portion of the solar spectra. The serpents, Grāmaṇis and Rākṣasas signify heat or death or the Thermal field of the spectra. This Heptad of the sun signifies the mutual difference in the different "Wave lengths" of the seven colours. This may be called the Puranic VIBGYOR.

2. These verses (2-24) enumerate the names of the different devas, sages etc.—the heptad who occupy the solar chariot every month. These verses are common to the description of the Solar chariot in other Purāṇas e.g. the Mt. P. 125. 1-34, Vā. P. 52. 1-26 with slight differences in the names of the occupants of the chariot.

Puñjikasthalā, (protector-demons), Heti and Praheti these two are cited as *Yātudhānas*.

5b-8a. The following reside (in the sun), during the months of Śuci and Śukra (Jyeṣṭha and Āṣāḍha); (Gods) Mitra and Varuṇa; the sages cited being Atri and the famous Vasiṣṭha; (Apsaras) Sahajanyā, Menakā; Pauruṣeya, and Vadha who are cited as Rākṣasas, the Gandharvas Hāhā and Hūhū; Yajña (probably Yakṣa and not Yajña): Rathasvana, Rathacitra, another named Nāgasākṣaka (rather Nāga called Takṣaka) and Rambhaka.

8b-11. Other deities also reside in the sun. The following group (of Devas and others) resides in the sun during the months of Nabhas and Nabhasya (Śrāvaṇa and Bhādrapada) viz. (Gods) Indra and Vivasvān; (sages) Aṅgiras, Bhṛgu; the serpents: Elāpatra and Śaṅkhapāla; (Gandharvas) Viśvāvasu and Ugrasena, Śveta and Aruṇa; (the two Apsaras) well-known as Pramlocā and Anumlocā and the two Yātudhānas (demons) Sarpa and Vyāghra.

12-15. Other pure deities and sages reside (in the sun) during the autumn (Āśvina and Kārttika); (gods) Parjanya and Pūṣan; (sages) Bhāradvāja along with Gautama; Parāvasu and Suruci the Gandharvas; Viśvācī and Ghṛtācī the two (Apsaras) of splendid characteristics; Airāvata and Dhanañjaya the well-known serpents and Śyenajit and Suṣeṇa who are Senānīs (commanders) and *Grāmaṇīs* (or Yakṣas). Āpas and Vāta these two are cited as Rākṣasas—All these always stay in the sun during the months of Āśvina and Kārttika.

16-19. The following stay in the sun during the two months of *Hemanta* (Early Winter); they are the two (Devas) Aṁśa and Bhaga; (the two sages) Kāśyapa and Kratu; the two serpents Mahāpadma and Karkoṭaka; the two Gandharvas Citrasena and Ūrṇāyu; the two celestial damsels Urvaśī and Pūrvacittī; Tārkṣa and Ariṣṭanemi who are Senānī (commanders) as Yakṣas and Vidyutsphūrja and Śatāyu who are cited as Yātuhānas (demons)—these reside in the sun in the months of Saha and Sahasya (Mārgaśīrṣa and Pauṣa).

20-23. The following reside in the sun during the months of Śiśira (late winter). They are (gods) Tvaṣṭṛ, Viṣṇu (sages) Jāmadagnya, Viśvāmitra; the two serpents Kambala and Aśvatara who are the sons of Kadru; the two Gandharvas Dhṛtarāṣṭra and Sūryavarcas; (the two celestial damsels) Tilottamā and Rambhā; the demon Brahmāpeta and the other wellknown demon Yajñāpeta, and Ṛtajit and Satyajit who are cited as Gandharvas* (rather Yakṣas)—all these, O excellent sages, reside in the sun during the months of Tapas and Tapasya (Māgha and Phālguna.)

24. Making the Pitṛs, Devas and Human beings well nourished, O Brāhmaṇas, Savitṛ the cause of days and nights goes on revolving.

25. These Devas reside in the sun for periods of two months in due order. These twelve groups of seven (or heptads) identify themselves with their place of office and residence.

26. By means of their splendour they increase the excellent splendour of the sun. By means of words (and prayers) composed by themselves, sages eulogise the sun.

27. The Gandharvas and the Apsaras serve him by means of songs and dances. The Grāmaṇīs, Yakṣas and Bhūtas perform the worship of his rays.

28. The serpents carry the sun, the demons follow him. From sunrise to sunset, the Vālakhilyas surround the sun and lead him on.

29-31. The sun who is the lord of all these, blazes with his brilliance in accordance with the virility, austerities, virtues, contacts, realities and strength of these (Devas etc.)

Thus, these stay in the sun for periods of two months viz. the sages, the Devas, the Gandharvas, the serpents, the groups of celestial damsels, the Grāmaṇīs (or groupleaders) or the Yakṣas and especially the demons.

32-33. These blaze, shower rains, shine, blow and create. On being glorified they dispel the inauspicious demerits of all living beings.

These remove the auspicious merit of evil-minded men. In some respects they remove the sins of men of good character and conduct.

* This is wrong as the pair of Gandharvas is already cited. The reading should be *Grāmaṇyau* as in Vā.P.52.22.

34. All these followers of the day revolve along with the sun. They shower rain on the subjects, they scorch them and they delight them (too).

35-36. They protect all the living beings till the destination of the Manus. In the Manvantaras of the (Manus) of the past and future as well as those who are present, this is the abode of those who identify themselves.

Thus those fourteen sets of seven reside in the sun in the course of the fourteen Manvantaras.

37. The sun releases heat energy during the summer. He scatters rain during the rainy season and snow (during winter). He is the maker of day and night. He keeps up his movement in accordance with (the changing) seasons and gratifies the Devas, the Pitṛs and the human beings with the rays suitably adapted.

38. By means of the (ray) named Suṣumna, the sun develops the moon in the bright half day by day and makes it complete (on the full moon day). He propitiates the Devas by means of the nectar. The Devas imbibe it during the dark half.

39. When the nectar of the moon is drunk, the moon loses all his digits except one during the dark half. At the close of it, the moon does not ooze out nectar from its rays. The Devas, the pitṛs, the Saumyas and the Kāvyas imbibe that nectar.

40. Men conquer (satisfy) hunger by means of foodstuffs and beverages and medicinal herbs developed by means of rain, with waters lifted up and released by means of his rays by the sun.

41. It is during the bright half that the Devas are propitiated by means of nectar and the pitṛs (are done so) during the dark half (of the month). (The sun) perpetually sustains the human beings by means of food. He holds them well by means of his rays.

42. The sun is being led by green horses. At that time, he removes (evaporates) water by means of his green rays. At the time of discharge (of water), he releases the water. Thus the sun sustains the mobile and immobile beings.

43. The sun is being led by green horses. He drinks

water by means of thousands of green rays. Being carried by green horses, the sun releases it.[1]

44. Thus the sun traverses the quarters by means of his swift chariot with one wheel. The horses are splendid but they do not have the usual pace* (? *Akramaiḥ*).

45. In the course of a day and night, the sun traverses the earth consisting of the seven continents and oceans by means of his chariot with a single wheel.

46-48. The chariot is yoked with only seven horses. They are the Vedic Metres that have assumed the form of horses. They are stationed towards the place where the wheel is fitted. They assume the forms as they wish. They are green, imperishable; they (? are accompanied) by tawny-coloured masters expounding the Brahman. In the course of a year those horses traverse eightythree hundred circles.

It traverses the external as well as the internal circular zones, in the course of days. They have been yoked in the beginning of the Kalpa and they continue to bear till the annihilation of all living beings.

49. Surrounded by Vālakhilyas, they wander both night and day. The sun is eulogised by great sages by means of words (and prayers) of the highest order and composed by themselves.

50. He is served by Gandharvas and groups of celestial damsels by means of songs and dances. The lord of the day (i.e. the sun) thus revolves and wanders by means of horses that gallop and that are as swift as birds.

51. The chariot of Soma (the Moon) has three wheels.[2] His horses have the lustre of Kunda (white Jasmine) flowers. They are ten in number and they are yoked to the left as well as to the right. The moon traverses by means of this.

52. They traverse the stars supported by the *Vīthi* (the path of the firmament). They gain velocity by means of the

---

1. This verse practically repeats V. 42 in different words.

* The text is defective. The corresponding verse in the Vā.P. 52, 43b reads: *bhadrais tair akṣatairaśvaiḥ sarpate 'sau divi kṣaye* /' with those auspicious unbroken horses he proceeds in the region of the sky.

2. VV 51-79 describe the mythological description of the chariot of the moon. Its scientific significance is not clear.

support of Dhruva. The shrinking and lengthening of its rays are remembered as being like those of the sun.

53. It should be known that the chariot of the moon has three wheels with horses on either side. The chariot is born (i.e. evolved) out of the womb of the waters along with the horses and the charioteer.

54. It has three wheels with hundred spokes. It is yoked with ten excellent white horses. They are slim and divine. They are unimpeded and they have the swiftness of the mind.

55-57. They are yoked but once and they continue to bear it till the elapse of the Yugas. In that compact chariot, there are white serpents encircling the chariot (?) Horses of the same colour, having the lustre of conchshells carry him (the Moon). The names of the ten horses of the moon are Yajus, Caṇḍamanas, Vṛṣa, Vājin, Nara, Haya, the famous horses Gaviṣṇu, Haṁsa, Vyoma and Mṛga.

58. These (horses) carry the Moon-lord with great dedication (and respect). The moon traverses (its orbit) surrounded by the Devas and the pitṛs.

59. At the end of the dark half and at the beginning of the bright half, when the sun is steady in the opposite direction, the moon is filled up, and as days pass by (the digits are reinstilled).

60. When the (nectarine) body of the moon has been imbibed by the Devas, it becomes exhausted on the fifteenth day. Then, with a single ray the sun makes it well developed.

61. By means of the ray called Suṣumnā (the sun) fills a part (of the moon) (digit by digit) every day. On being replenished thus by the Suṣumna (ray), the white and bright digits increase.

62. During the dark half, the digits become reduced and they are developed (replenished) during the bright half. The moon is thus developed, due to the power of the sun.

63. On the full Moon day, it appears bright in a complete disc. In the bright half, the moon is thus fully replenished day by day.

64-65. From the second day of the dark half to the fourteenth day, the Devas imbibe the nectar of the moon that is of the nature of the essence of the waters and that is wholly juicy. Drinking this liquid nectar of the moon, the Devas become delighted. It is due to the splendour of the sun that, this nectarine juice has been collected together in the course of half a month.

66. The nectar of the moon is for their food (consumption). It is resorted to for a single night on the full moon day by all the Devas and Pitṛs along with the sages.

67. On being imbibed gradually by the Pitṛs and the Devas at the beginning of the dark half, the digits of the moon which face the sun become reduced gradually.

68. Thirtythree, three hundred (?) and three and three thousand and three Devas imbibe (the juice of) the moon.

69. On being sucked thus, the black digits of the moon increase. Hence, the white digits become reduced and the dark ones become increased.

70-72. Thus, the moon is sucked daily by the Devas. After imbibing it for a period of half a month, the excellent Devas go away on the New Moon day. The *Pitṛs* (thereafter) resort to the Moon on the New Moon day. Then on the fifteenth day when the digits are left over a little, the groups of Pitṛs resort to the last remanant (of the digits) in the afternoon. For a period of two *Lavas*, they imbibe the Kalās (of the moon) that are left over.

73. The nectar of Svadhā oozes from its rays on the New Moon day. After drinking that Svadhā for their own satisfaction (to the full) for the period of a month, those (Pitṛs) go away.

74. The moon is scorched by the sun (i.e. sunlight) that is present in the Suṣumna. Similarly, the nectarine moon is imbibed by the Devas in the dark half.

75. They are of three (varieties), the Saumyas, the Barhiṣads and the Agniṣvāttas. Those who are mentioned as Kāvyas are all Pitṛs.

76. The Kāvyas are Saṁvatsaras, those who are remembered by the Brāhmaṇas as *Pañcābdas* (the five years). Saumyas should be known as the Ṛtus and Barhiṣads are remembered as the *Māsas* (Months).

77-78. The Agniṣvāttas are the Ārtavas, O Brāhmaṇas, these are the creations of the Pitṛs. On being drunk by the

Pitṛs on the fifteenth day, the digit of the moon that is one fifteenth part becomes reduced on the New moon day. Then in the next fortnight it becomes replenished.

79. The increase and decrease of the moon are remembered (as occurring) on the sixteenth day at the beginning of a fortnight. It is thus that the increase and decrease in the moon occur on account of the sun.

80. Again (i.e. henceforth), I shall describe the chariots of the stars, planets and Rāhu.[1]

The chariot of the son of the Moon (Budha) is bright and full of the splendour of water.

81. The chariot of Bhārgava (the Venus) is glorious and it resembles the sun in splendour. It has the rambling sound of the cloud. It is equipped with banner, flagstaff and other paraphernalia.

82-83. It is yoked with various excellent horses of different colours born of the earth. It is fitted with the following ten horses, viz. Śveta, Piśaṅga, Sāraṅga, Nīla, Pīta, Vilohita, Kṛṣṇa, Harita, Pṛṣata and Pṛśni. They are of great grandeur. They are not lean. They have the speed of the wind.

84-86. The excellent chariot of the Mars also is glorious and golden. It has eight horses. With unimpeded red horses born of fire and capable of going everywhere, the prince (i.e., the Mars) goes about. They have straight movement as well as those curved clockwise and curved anticlockwise ones.

The Jupiter (Bṛhaspati) of the family of Aṅgiras, the scholarly preceptor of the Devas, moves about in golden chariot by means of eight grey horses born of water. They are divine horses with the speed of the wind.

Staying for a year in a constellation, he goes ahead along with Vedhas* (Brahmā) (?)

87-90a. Riding in a chariot of black steel (iron) fitted with strong horses born of the firmament, the Saturn proceeds ahead very slowly.

---

1. VV 80-92 describe the chariots of other planets such as Budha, Śukra etc.

* *Sarvagaḥ* 'one who can go everywhere and anywhere' in Vā.P.52-87.

The horses of Rāhu are eight in number, and black in colour. They have the speed of the mind. His chariot is full of darkness. The horses are yoked but once and they draw it (to the end).

Having come out of the sun, Rāhu goes to the Moon during Parvan days (the Full moon days).

90b-91. The horses of the chariot of Ketu are eight in number and they have the speed of the wind. They have the colour of the smoke of straw. They are strong. They are tawny-coloured like donkeys.

Thus these horses of the planets along with the chariots have been described.

92. All of them are fastened to Dhruva by means of gaseous rays. They are fully developed. While whirling duly they blaze as well.

93. (Repetition) They are fully developed due to invisible gaseous rays. Being bound (to Dhruva) by means of these, the moon, the sun and the planets revolve in the firmament.

94-95. Those groups of luminaries follow Dhruva that whirls. Just as the boat is carried on along with the (current of) water in the river, so also these abodes of gods (? planets etc.) are carried by the gaseous rays. The groups of gods moving about in the firmament are not seen.

96. There are as many bonds of gaseous rays as there are stars. All of them are fastened to Dhruva. They whirl themselves and they make others also revolve.

97. Just as the oil-rollers whirl and cause the wheel also to whirl so also do the luminaries fixed (to Dhruva) on all sides by means of gaseous rays.

98. Urged by the whirlwind, they move about like a firebrand. (Since the wind) carried the luminaries, (the wind is remembered as *Pravaha*.

99. Thus the group of planets attached to Dhruva, moves about. This Gangetic porpoise and Dhruva should be known as made up of constellations in the firmament.

100-107. If a sin is committed in the day, it is dispelled by seeing it (Dhruva) during the night.

He lives as many or more years as there are stars supported by the Gangetic porpoise in the firmament.

The heavenly Gangetic porpoise should be known with its parts (?).[1] (The various limbs of this porpoise are mentioned subsequently).

Auttānapāda (Dhruva the son of Uttānapāda) should be known as its upper jaw. Yajña should be known as the other (i.e. lower jaw). Dharma is based on its head, (i.e. constitutes its head).

Nārāyaṇa should be sought for in the heart and the pair of Aśvins in the forelegs. Varuṇa and Aryaman are its hind thighs.

Its penis is Saṁvatsara and Mitra clings to the *Apāna* (anus), Agni, Mahendra, Mārīca, Kaśyapa and Dhruva are in the tail.

The four stars in the milky way do not set.

The stars, the moon, the sun and the planets along with the constellations are fixed in the heaven, some with the faces up, others with faces turned away and all of them curved. They are presided over by Dhruva. They go round Dhruva who is the central pivot in the heaven and who is an excellent lord. Dhruva is remembered as the fourth and the last one after Agni, Indra and Kāśyapa.

108. On the top of the Meru Mountain, single-handed he whirls when he pulls them with face down. He observes Meru at the border and circumambulates it.

1. VV 100-104 describe the various parts of the heavenly (stellar) porpoise (Śiśumāra).

CHAPTER TWENTYFOUR

The arrangement of the Heavenly Luminaries : The sun, the source of Light to Luminaries

Sūta said :

1. On hearing this, the sages who were in doubt asked Romaharṣaṇa once again the answer (for the same).

2. What has been described in details by your honour is about the abodes. Now describe to us how may be the abodes of gods and how are the luminaries.

3-6. Mention everything decisively, the facts concerning the Luminaries.

Vāyu (The Wind god) said :

On hearing their words, Sūta of great concentration and mental purity, delivered the most excellent speech that dispelled their doubts.

Sūta said

"I shall mention to you the origin of the sun and the moon, the details as mentioned by the wise and intelligent sages of great wisdom. I shall recount how the sun, the moon and the plants came to be remembered here as Devagṛhas (Divine abodes, abodes of the Devas).

Thereafter, I shall recount the origin of the three types of Agni[1] (Fire) viz. the divine one, the terrestrial one and the one born of water (i.e. lightning).

7. When the night of Brahmā, born of the unmanifest one, dawned, this (visible comet) that had not been manifested and developed was completely enveloped by the darkness of the night.

---

1. Agni (the fire god) was regarded as a very great deity by the Vedic Aryans and different names according to its functions were given to it in the ṚV. The Purāṇas amplified the tradition. The fire is given the credit of movements of the Sun which is regarded as the source of all the planets—nay even of the three worlds. It is the fire who through the different Nāḍis or rays of the sun evaporates water and causes seasons—the summer, the rainy season and the winter. Cf. Mt.P. 128.4-23.

8-9a. When this universe remained in the form of all the original *Bhūtas* (Elements) and the specific particularities (distinctions) had been destroyed (i.e. had not been developed), the self-born lord who manages the activities of the universe, moved about like a *Khadyota* (glow-worm) i.e. he who illuminates firmament) with a desire to manifest himself.

9b-10. At the beginning of the world he saw the fire supported by the Earth and Water. The lord encased it for the purpose of light and divided it into three parts. The fire that is sanctifying in this world is called the *Pārthiva* (Terrestrial fire).

11. That which blazes in the sun is remembered as *Śuci* (pure). *Abja* (born of water) should be known as *Vaidyut* (Lightening etc.) I shall recount their characteristics.

12. The fires born of water are three, viz. : *Vaidyut* (Lightening) *Jāṭhara* (gastric) and *Saura* (Solar). It is on account of this, that the sun blazes in the heaven after drinking water by means of his rays.

13. The (fire) *Vārṣya* (originating from *Varṣā* or rain) contained in lightening, does not become cool by means of water. The fire that abides within the stomach of human beings does not become cool by means of water.

14. Hence, the solar fire, the Vaidyuta fire and the gastric fire are fires that have water for their fuel.

Some among the waters are considered *Tejas* (fiery splendour) and some are seen as having water for their fuel.

15. The *Nirmathya* fire (i.e. the fire produced by churning or friction) has wood for its fuel. That fire is brought under control by means of water.

The *Pavamāna* fire (sanctifying fire) has sparks and flames and the gastric fire is remembered as devoid of lustre.

16. (The same is the case with) the fire without heat that is in the zone (of the sun). It is white and it illuminates.

When the sun sets along with its rays (i.e. withdrawing all the rays), the solar lustre enters fire during night. Hence it glows from far off.

17-18. The heat of the fire, of the terrestrial fire, enters the sun as it rises with its rays. Hence the fire blazes. The power of illumination and heat are (respectively) the solar and fiery splendour.

19-20. By permeating each other, they make each other nourish and develop.

In the northern hemisphere as well as in the southern one, when the sun rises, the night enters waters. Hence, waters become hot during the day and cold on account of the entrance and permeation by the night.

21. When the sun sets, the day enters waters. Hence, during the night, the waters are seen white (and sparkling).

22. It is in this order that in the southern and northern hemispheres, the day and the night enter water at the times of sunrise and sunset.

23. The sun that blazes imbibing water by means of his rays, is remembered as the divine *Śuci* (pure) fire that is combined with the terrestrial fire.

24-27. This fire *Śuci* has a thousand feet (rays). It resembles one holding a pot. With a thousand *Nāḍīs* (vein-like rays) spread all round, it takes up the waters of the rivers, oceans, wells, canals etc. both blowing and stationary.

Its thousand rays exude cold showers, snowfall as well as hot ones. Among them, four hundred veins have variegated forms and they shower (rain).

These veins that cause downpour of rain are named as follows : Candanās, Sādhyās, Kūtanās, Akūtanās and Amṛtās.

28-31. There are three hundred rays other than these and they exude snow. These Veins that bring about snowfall are by name Dṛśyās (visible), Meghās, Yāmyās and Hrādinīs (Rumbling ones).

Those rays of limited lustre are called Candrās by name.

The white (pure) rays that cause heat are three hundred in number and their names are Śuklās, Kuhakās, Viśvabhṛts.

The sun brings about the satisfaction of human beings, *Pitṛs* (Manes) and Devas after distributing them impartially among them.

He gratifies human beings by means of medicinal herbs, the manes by means of Svadhā-offerings and all the Devas by means of nectar.

32-33. During *Vasanta* (spring) and *Grīṣma* (summer), the sun blazes by means of three hundred rays.

During the rainy season and autumn he showers (rain) by means of four hundred rays.

During Hemanta (early winter) and Śiśira (later winter), he scatters snow by means of three hundred rays.

(The twelve suns) are Indra Dhātṛ, Bhaga, Pūṣan, Mitra, Varuṇa, Aryaman, Aṁśu, Vivasvān, Tvaṣṭṛ, Savitṛ and Viṣṇu.

34-35. The sun during the month of Māgha is Varuṇa;[1] Pūṣan in Phālguna; lord Aṁśu in the month of Caitra and Dhātṛ in the month of Vaiśākha. Indra is the sun in the month of Jyeṣṭha and the sun in the month of Āṣāḍha is Savitṛ.

36-37a. Vivasvān is the Sun in the month of Śrāvaṇa, Bhaga is remembered as the Sun in the month of Pṛṣṭhapada (Bhādrapada). Aryaman is the Sun in the month of Āśvayuja (Āśvina) and Tvaṣṭṛ is the sun in the month of Kārttika. Mitra is the sun in the month of Mārgaśīrṣa and Viṣṇu, the eternal one, is the sun in Pauṣa.

37b-40. In the activity as the sun, Taruṇa has five thousand rays. Pūṣan blazes with six thousand rays and Lord Aṁśu blazes with seven thousand rays; Dhātṛ with eight thousand and Indra with nine thousand rays.

Savitṛ moves (about) with ten thousand rays and Bhaga with eleven thousand rays. Mitra blazes with seven thousand rays and Tvaṣṭṛ blazes with eight thousand rays.

---

1. This tabular statement shows the monthwise distribution of the sun-gods and their capacities and functions:

Month	*Name of the ruling Sun*	*Rays*
Caitra	Aṁśu	7000
Vaiśākha	Dhātṛ	8000
Jyeṣṭha	Indra	9000
Āṣāḍha	Savitṛ	10000
Śrāvaṇa	Vivasvān	9000
Bhādrapada	Bhaga	11000
Āśvina	Aryaman	10000
Kārttika	Tvaṣṭṛ	8000
Mārgaśīrṣa	Mitra	7000
Pauṣa	Viṣṇu	6000
Māgha	Varuṇa	5000
Phālguna	Pūṣan	6000

Aryaman moves about with ten thousand rays and Vivasvān (not Parjanya as in the text) blazes with nine thousand rays. Viṣṇu scorches the earth by means of six thousand rays.

41-42. During the Vasanta season, the sun is tawny-coloured;[1] during the Grīṣma season, the sun has golden lustre: during the *Varṣā* (rainy) season, he is white in colour and during autumn, he is yellowish white in colour.

During *Hemanta* (early winter) the sun is copper-coloured. During *Śiśira* (late winter) he is red in colour. Thus the colours of the sun caused by the seasons have been (traditionally) proclaimed.

43. The sun infuses strength in the medicinal herbs; he makes the *Pitṛs* (stronger) by means of Svadhā; he infuses nectar in the Devas. Thus he gives three things to the three.

44. In this manner the thousand rays of the sun achieve the requisite things of the people of the world. They differ inasmuch as they exude snow, rain or hot rays.

45. Thus, is the white resplendent sphere named sun. It is the foundation and source of origin of the stars, planets and the moon.

46. All these, viz. the moon, the stars and the planets should be known as originating from the sun. The moon is the lord of all stars and the sun is the king of planets.

47. The remaining five planets should be known as gods moving about as they please.

48. Understand the sources of origin of the remaining planets being described well. Skanda, the commander-in-chief of the army of the Devas, is cited as the planet Aṅgāraka (the Mars).

49-51. Scholars conversant with the Vedic knowledge call Nārāyaṇa by the name Budha (the Mercury).

Yama (an incarnation of) Rudra, the son of Vivasvān and the lord of the world, is the great planet Śanaiścara (the Saturn) who is the most excellent among Brāhmaṇas and who orbits very slowly.

---

1. VV.41-42 give the traditional seasonwise colours or complexions of the sun.

The two resplendent great planets are the preceptors of the Devas and Asuras.

Both of them viz. Śukra (the Venus) and Bṛhaspati (the Jupiter) are the sons of Prajāpati.

There is no doubt that the entire unit of the three worlds has the sun as its root (source).

52-54. The entire universe including the Devas, Asuras and human beings originate from the sun, O, leading Brāhmaṇas.

All the brilliance of Rudra, Upendra (Viṣṇu), Indra and Candra (the Moon), the dwellers of the heaven, the brightness of all luminaries, the entire splendour of all the worlds (is that of the sun). He is the soul of all; he is the lord of all the worlds; he is a great god; and Prajāpati the lord of the subjects). The Sun alone is the root of the three worlds. He is the highest deity. It is from him that everything is born and everything gets merged in him alone.

55. The existence and non-existence of the worlds have formerly emanated from the sun. The plant that should be understood by the whole universe, O, Brāhmaṇas, is the brilliant sun of great lustre.

56-57. (The units of time) Kṣaṇas, Muhūrtas, days, nights, fortnights, the whole months, the seasons, the years and the Yugas get merged into this and are born again and again. Hence, there is no reckoning of time without the sun.

58-60. Without the reckoning of time, there is neither (the study of) scriptures, nor (religious) initiation nor the daily routine of religious duties. If the seasons are not well defined, how can there be flowers, roots and fruits ? How can the crops or fruits of trees come out ? How can medicinal herbs and grasses grow?

Without the sun that blazes in the universe and who robs (evaporates) water, there will be complete cessation and non-existence of all sorts of human activity and the activity of other creatures both in the earth and in the heaven.

He alone is the 'Time'. He is the 'Fire'. He is the lord of the subjects. He has twelve souls (in the form of twelve Ādityas (the sun god).

61. He scorches the three worlds inclusive of the mobile and immobile beings, O excellent Brāhmaṇas.

He is the mass of splendour that dispels the darkness of the entire world.

62. After resorting to the excellent path of the wind, he gives heat to this entire universe by means of his rays, at the sides, above and below, nay, at all sides.

63-64. Just as a bright lamp suspended in the middle of a house dispels simultaneously the darkness at the sides, above and below, so also the sun who has a thousand (innumerable) rays, who is the lord of planets and the universe, illuminates by means of his rays the entire universe everywhere on all sides.

65. The most excellent among the thousand rays of the sun cited by me before, are the seven rays that are the sources of origin of the planets.[1]

66-68. They are declared as follows:— Suṣumna, Harikeśa as well as Viśvakarman; Viśvaśravas (and again another ray) Sampadvasu, Arvāvasu and Svarāṭ.

It is the solar ray Suṣumna that causes the nourishment of the Moon that wanes. This Suṣumna is glorified as one that spreads sideways and upwards.

Harikeśa, that is in front, is glorified as the source of origin of the stars.

69-72a. Viśvakarman, the ray to the south, right, nurtures Budha (Mercury). Viśvaśravas the ray to the west, behind, is remembered by learned men as the source of origin of Śukra (the Venus).

The ray Sampadvasu is the source of origin of Lohita (the Mars.)

1. This is a peculiar way of associating the particular ray of the sun as the source of origin of particular planet:

Name of the ray of the sun	*Name of the planet or star so introduced*
Suṣumnā	The moon
Harikeśa	stars in general
Viśvaśravas	Śukra (The Venus)
Sampadvasu	The Mars
Arvāvasu	The Jupiter
Svarāṭ	The Saturn
Viśvakarman	Budha (Mercury)

The sixth ray Arvāvasu is the source of origin of Bṛhaspati (the Jupiter).

The ray Svarāṭ causes the development of Śanaiścara (the Saturn).

Thus, it is due to the power of the sun that the planets, stars and constellations remain in the firmament. Nay, this entire universe is sustained.

72b-73. The stars are termed Nakṣatras because they do not become reduced (*Na*-not *Ksiyante* become reduced).[1]

These *Ksetras* (abodes) happen before on account of the rays (?) The sun, the creator of the star, takes up their abodes.

74-76. The stars are so called because they redeem (*tāraṇāt*) those persons who have crossed the planets by means of merit and who have resorted to them (once again) at the end of the merit (i.e. when merits had been enjoyed fully.)

They are *Tārakas* because they are white and sparkling.

The sun is named *Āditya* because it takes up (*ā*-√*dā*- 'to take') and dispels the splendour and darkness pertaining to the heaven, earth and night (*Ādānāt*).

The root √*Su*√*Savana* is considered in this connection in the sense of *Syandana* (flowing). The sun is considered *Savitṛ* because it causes the exudation of waters and sparkling splendours.

77. The root √*Cad* is cited so as to mean "to delight". It is considered to mean "to be white", "to be nectarine", and "to be cool".

78. The divine spheres of the sun and the moon are sparkling and white. They are of the form (or full of) of fire and water. They move about in the firmament. They resemble auspicious round pots.

---

1. VV. 72-77. Our author takes interest in popular etymologies. Here are some specimens:

(i) *Nakṣatra* 'a star' *na kṣīyante* 'Those which do not get diminished' but grammatically it is √nakṣa— +*tran*.

(ii) Āditya is normally *Aditi—ṇya=ya* (the son of Aditi) but here it is traced to ā + √dā — 'to take'.

79. The sphere of the moon is remembered to be consisting of dense water. The white and brilliantly sparkling sphere of the sun is composed of dense fiery splendour.

80-83. All the divine ones enter these abodes completely during all the Manvantaras.[1] They resort to the stars, planets and the sun.

They are the abodes of the divine ones and are called after them respectively.

The sun enters the *Saura Sthāna* (the Solar abode) and the moon the *Saumya Sthāna* (the Lunar abode).

Śukra (the Venus) enters the abode pertaining to Śukra that is very brilliant and has sixteen flames.

Bṛhaspati (the Jupiter) enters *Jaiva* (intended for Jupiter) abode and Lohita (the Mars) enters the Lauhita abode.

Lord Śanaiścara (the Saturn) enters the abode pertaining to the Saturn. Budha (the Mercury) enters the abode meant for Budha, and Svarbhānu (Rāhu) stays in the abode pertaining to Svarbhānu (Rāhu).

84. All the stars enter the *Nakṣatras* (abodes meant for constellation) and stars. All these are the luminary abodes of those who are pious-souled and meritorious.

85. These (abodes) have been created by the self-born lord (Brahmā) at the beginning of a Kalpa and they have begun to function since then. These abodes remain till the annihilation of all living beings (at the end of the world).

86-87. In all the Manvantaras, the same are the abodes of all the Devas. The *Abhimānins* (those who identify themselves) abide by these divine abodes. The past ones live along with the past ones and the future ones along with the future Devas. The present ones live along with the present *Sthānins* (those who identify themselves with the abodes) and Devas. In this Manvantara the planets are remembered as *Vaitānikas* (pertaining to Sacrifices).

---

1. VV. 80-92. The idea is that what we see as stars or planets are the abodes, the occupants of which change per Manvantara. In this Manvantara, the occupants have got their position due to performance of sacrifices and hence they are called *Vaitānikas*. The names of the present gods occupying these planets are also given e.g. Vivasvān (the present sun god), Vasu, son of Tviṣi (the present moon god).

83. Vivasvān, the son of Aditi, is the sun in the Vaivasvata Manvantara. The lord Vasu named Tviṣi, the son of Dharma, is remembered as the moon.

89. Lord Śukra, belonging to Bhṛgu clan, should be known as the performer of sacrifices on behalf of the Asuras.

The lordly son of Aṅgiras, of massive splendour is remembered as the preceptor of the Devas.

90. Budha is fascinating to the mind. He is remembered as the son of Tviṣi. Śanaiścara (the Saturn) is the ugly son of Saṁjñā and Vivasvān.

91. The youthful lord Mars was born of Vikeśī and Agni.

The stars that are named Ṛkṣas are remembered as the daughters of Dakṣa.

92. Svarbhānu (Rāhu) is the son of Siṁhikā. He is an Asura causing distress to all living beings.

Thus the *Abhimānins* (those who identify themselves) with the moon, the stars, the planets and the sun have been recounted.

93. These are mentioned as the abodes and those who occupy the abodes are deities.

The abode of Vivasvān (the Sun) of a thousand rays is *Śukla* (white and resplendent) and fiery.

94. The abode of Tviṣi of a thousand rays is white and sparkling and consists of water.

The abode of Manojña (i.e. the Mercury) of five rays, is remembered as dark in colour as well as *Āpya* (watery).

95. The abode of Śukra is a lotus among the sixteen rays. It is watery, white and sparkling.

The *Lohita* (red) abode of Bhauma (the Mars) is watery.

96. The big abode of Bṛhaspati is green and watery. It has twelve rays. The abode of Manda (the Saturn) is said to be black and watery. It has eight rays.

97-99a. The abode of Svarbhānu is *Tāmasa* (dark). It is the abode of those who cause the distress of all living beings.

All the stars should be known as watery and they have a single ray each.

They are the shelters unto those of meritorious fame. In colour they are perfectly white. They should be known as full of dense water. They have been created even at the beginning of the Kalpa. They are remembered to be intrinsically luminous due to the contact with the rays of the sun.

99b-103. The diameter of the sun is remembered as nine thousand Yojanas.[1] The extent of its sphere is three times that. The area of the moon's sphere is remembered as twice the area of the sun.

Svarbhānu is equal to them both. It moves beneath them. It has been created after taking out the shadow of the Earth and has a spherical shape.

The third large abode of Svarbhānu which is full of darkness, comes out of the sun during Parvan days (i.e. New Moon, Full Moon etc.) and goes towards the moon. During Solar Parvans it comes back to the sun from the moon.

It is called Svarbhānu because it pushes away (*Nudate*) the heaven (*Svar*) by means of its splendour (*Bhāsā*).

104. The diameter and extent of the sphere of Bhārgava (the Venus) it laid down as one-sixteenth of that of the moon.

105. Bṛhaspati (the Jupiter) should be known as one-fourth less than the Venus (i.e. three fourths of its size).

The Mars and Saturn are remembered to be three-fourths of Jupiter in extent.

106-107. In diameter and extent, Mercury is three-fourths of either of them.

The forms of the stars and constellations are similar to those of Mercury. Those that have bodies are equal in length and extent to Mercury.

A man conversant with reality should know that the stars are usually in conjunction with the moon.

108. The stars and constellations differ in extent from one another by five hundred, four hundred, three hundred and also two hundred Yojanas.

109. The spheres of the stars are lesser than the earlier ones. There is no star smaller than the ones with one and a half Yojanas.

---

1. VV. 99-126. These are the ideas of the ancient Indians about the locations, dimensions and movements of planets and the heavenly bodies in the pretelescope days. Cf Bh. P. V. 22. 8-17.

110. Three planets among them which orbit very far away and above all are the Saturn, the Jupiter and the Mars. It should be known that they orbit very slowly.

111. The great planets beneath them are the four fast moving ones, viz. the sun, the moon, the Mercury and the Venus.

112. There are as many crores of stars all round as there are constellations. The movement of these constellations has been duly regulated by god Brahmā.

113-116. The movement of the sun through them in accordance with the *Ayanas* (Solar transit) is high and low. When (the sun) is in the northern transit, the moon is seen moving fast during the Parvan days with its rays, not very clear. This is because it is very high. (?)

When the sun is in the southern path, it resorts to the lower path. It is always surrounded by the line of Earth (? horizon) during the New Moon and the Full Moon days. It is not seen at the regular time and it sets quickly.

Hence, on the new moon day, the moon stationed in the northern path is seen in the southern path; but it is not seen so regularly.

117. Hence, in view of the movements of the luminaries, the sun and the moon set and rise at the same time (every day) during the equinotical days.

118. In the northern paths, the times of rising and setting are different. During the new moon and full moon, they should be understood as following the circle of luminaries.

119. When the sun orbits through the path of the southern transit, it does so beneath all the planets.

120. Making its sphere vast and wide, the moon orbits above it. The entire galaxy of stars orbits above the moon.

121. The Mercury orbits above all the stars. The Venus orbits above the Mercury. The Mars does so above the Venus and the Jupiter above the Mars.

122. The Saturn is above it and the sphere of the seven sages (Great Bear) is above it. Dhruva (the Pole Star) is situated above the Great Bear.

123. The intervening distance between the stars and the planets high above is two hundred thousand Yojanas.

124. The planets, the moon and the sun orbit in the firmament with divine splendour. In their regular movement, they duly come into contact with the constellations.

125. The planets, the stars and the sun may be low, high or straight during their mutual contact or when separate, yet they look at the subjects simultaneously.

126. These are situated face to face. They come into contact mutually. That their mutual conjunction is without any confusion should be understood by learned men.

127-128. Thus is the regulated arrangement of the Earth, the luminaries, the continents, the oceans, the mountains, the sub-continents, the rivers and those who stay in them.

The planets have their origination in these constellations.

129. Vivasvān, the son of Aditi, the first among the planets, the sun-god, was born in the constellation Viśākhā in the Cākṣuṣa Manvantara.[1]

130. Tviṣiman, the son of Dharma, the lord moon god, the son of Vasu, the cool-rayed cause of nights was born in the constellation Kṛttikā.

131. Śukra (the Venus) who is endowed with sixteen fiery flames (rays) and who is the son of Bhṛgu and who is the most excellent among stars and planets was born in the star Tiṣya (Puṣya) after the sun.

132. The planet Bṛhaspati (the Jupiter) who has twelve fiery flames (rays), who is the son of Aṅgiras and who is the preceptor of the Universe, was born in the Pūrvāphālgunī.

---

1. VV. 129-137 give the stars (or constellations) under which these planets were 'born'.

	Name of the Planet	*The star of birth.*
(i)	The Sun god, the son of Aditi	Viśākhā
(ii)	The moon god, Tviṣiman, the son of Dharma	Kṛttikā
(iii)	Śukra (the Venus) the son of Bhṛgu	Tiṣya (Puṣya)
(iv)	Bṛhaspati (Jupiter) the son of Aṅgiras	Pūrvā-Phālgunī
(v)	Mars, son of Prajāpati	Purvāṣāḍhā
(vi)	Śanaiścara, son of the Sun god	Revatī
(vii)	Budha (Mercury) son of the moon god	Dhaniṣṭhā
(viii)	Ketu, son of Mṛtyu	Āśleṣā
(ix)	Rāhu	Bharaṇi

133. It is mentioned in the Śruti that the planet (Mars) of nine fiery flames, who has a red-complexioned body and who is the son of Prajāpati was born in the constellation Pūrvāṣāḍhā.

134. Śanaiścara (the Saturn), the son of the sun, was born in the constellation Revatī. He has seven fiery flames.

The planet Budha (Mercury), the son of the moon was born in the constellation Dhaniṣṭhā. He has five fiery flames.

135. Śikhin (i.e. Ketu) who is full of darkness, who is the sun of Mṛtyu, who causes the annihilation and decline of the subjects and who is a mighty planet that destroys everything, was born in the constellation of Āśleṣā.

136-138. The daughters of Dakṣa (i.e. the 27 stars) were born in their respective stars named after them.

Rāhu who has a naturally dark sphere, who has the virility of the *Tamas* quality and who is the planet attacking the moon and the sun, was born in the constellation Bharaṇī.

These stars and planets beginning with Bhārgava (the Venus) should be comprehended because they become devoid of goodness at the time when the constellation of nativity is being harassed. They are affected by that defect (and are redeemed), due to the devotion to the planets.

139. The first among all these planets, it is said, is Āditya (Sun).[1]

Śukra is (the first) among the stars and the planets and Ketu is the first among meteors.

140. Dhruva is the pivotal peg among the planets scattered about in all the four quarters. Śrav ṣṭhā i.e. Dhaniṣṭhā (is the first ?) among the stars and the northern transit is the first among transits.

141. The first among the five *Varṣas* (years) is remembered as *Saṁvatsara*. *Śiśira* (late Winter) is the first among seasons and Māgha is the first among the Months.

1. VV. 139-144 give what is the 'first' or the most important one among the stars, divisions of time etc. It is worth noting that Māgha is regarded as the first month of the year (probably due to Vasanta Sampāta therein) and Śiśira as the 1st Ṛtu (season) and not the spring. The second point of importance is the emphasis of the Yuga being a period of five years beginning with Dhaniṣṭhā and ending with Śravaṇa Nakṣatra.

142. Among fortnights, the bright half and among Tithis (lunar fortnightly days) *Pratipat* is the first. The day is glorified as the first among the divisions of day, night etc.

143. The first among the Muhūrtas is that which has Rudra as its deity. The unit of time *Kṣaṇa* has *nimeṣa* as its first, O excellent ones among those who know Time.

144. The Yuga (Era) consisting of five years begins with Dhaniṣṭhā and ends with Śravaṇa.

Due to the peculiar movement of the sun, this revolves like a wheel.

145. The sun is hence remembered as Kāla (Time) by those who know that (i.e. time). He is the lord. It is he who makes the four types of living beings function or desist from action.

146-147. The venerable lord Rudra himself is the cause of the functions of Time. Thus is the regulated arrangement of luminaries as conditioned by the affairs (of the world). It is evolved by the Lord (God), for the sake of regular functioning of the world.

This is compressed (?) in Dhruva by means of Uttarā-śravaṇa* (?)

148. It is extensively spread all round among them. He is situated in the form of a circle. He is made to function intelligently at the beginning of the Kalpa by the Lord.

149. He is the support. He is the *Abhimānin* (one who identifies himself) with all. He is the soul of the luminary bodies. He is the miraculous transformation of Pradhāna of the Cosmic form.

150. It is impossible for all human beings to comprehend factually the movements both inward and outward, of the luminary bodies, by means of their physical eye.

151. The learned man should comprehend and retain in belief, by means of scripture, inference, perception, and reasoning after testing intelligently and carefully.

---

* Vā.P.53.119a reads: *utpannaḥ śravaṇenāsau* : 'It started by Śravaṇa'

152. O Brāhmaṇas of the most excellent intellect these are five expedients (means) to comprehend the group of luminaries viz. : eye, scripture, water, picture and calculation.

CHAPTER TWENTYFIVE

The Origin of the Epithet Nīlakaṇṭha[1]
Śiva swallowing poison.

Sūta said :

1. After recounting this (astronomical information in the last chapter) Lord Vāyu (The Wind god) of very great intellect and who is (always) engaged in what is conducive to the welfare of the world, commenced the *Japa* (muttering in an undertone the Mantra) that was to be chanted when the sun reached the middle of the sky.

2. All those sages who had assembled there and who had perfect control over their own selves, stood up with palms joined in reverence.

3. The Wind god prayed : "O Nīlakaṇṭha, obeisance to you who ought to be worshipped at the end of religious observances, and who are the lord of all living beings, animating them all."

4-5. On hearing this, those sages of pure souls, of Praiseworthy religious observance and famous as Vā akhilyas, eightyeight thousand in number, who, of sublimated sexual impulse, walked by the side of the sun (as his associates) and subsisted on leaves (of trees), wind and water, submitted to Vāyu as follows :

1. This popular story as to how Śiva's throat became blue due to drinking the deadly poison Kālakūṭa appears in the Mbh. (Adi.18.41-43)and other Purāṇas. The text of this chapter from V. 6 onwards is the same as that of the Vā. P. 54.10 ff.

6-7. "O excellent Wind-god, O most excellent one among those conversant with meritorious things, we wish to hear (more about) what is mentioned by you as "Nīlakaṇṭha". It is the most meritorious thing among sacred ones. O excellent one, recount that unto us. O Prabhañjana (Wind-god), by your grace, we wish to hear everything.

8. What is the reason whereby the neck of the lord of Ambikā (i.e. god Śiva) had become blue ? O lord, we wish to hear this particularly from your mouth (i.e. as directly mentioned by you).

9. All verbal utterances are impelled by you, O Vāyu. The function of speech is dependent on *Varṇa* (sound of letters) and *Sthāna* (place of articulation).

10. The intelligent enthusiasm is activated by you. It is (only) when you sanctify them that the remaining *Varnas* begin to function.

11. The existenee of the *Varṇas* is only due to you, from whom the utterances recede and wherein the colours of the body are rare. O Anila (wind god), you are always omnipresent (and have access everywhere).

12. Excepting you, O Samīraṇa (wind god), there is no one who pervades everything. This living world is directly perceptible to you from all sides, O *Anila* (wind-god).

13. You know the lord of speech, Īśvara, the leader (controller) of minds. Tell us wherefore (for what) is there an aberration of the colour and feature in the region of his neck (throat)."

14. On hearing the words of those sages of sanctified souls, Vāyu who has great splendour and who is revered by the world, replied.

15. "Formerly, in Kṛtayuga, there was a Brāhmaṇa called Vasiṣṭha who was extremely interested in deciding the (meaning of) Vedas. He was a righteous soul. He was the mental son (of Brahmā). He was a Prajāpati.

16-19. He asked Kārttikeya who has a peacock as his excellent vehicle. He had stolen the collyrium from the eyes of the wives of the demon Mahiṣa (i.e. he made them widows by killing Mahiṣa). He is a noble soul (named) Mahāsena, whose voice resembles the rumbling sound of the clouds. He appeared to see the joyous ebullitions of the mind of Umā, by assuming the false form of a boy. He took away the life of Krauñca, and delighted the heart of Gaurī, (He submitted): "O excellent one, what is this radiant thing, resembling collyrium, seen in the neck (of Śiva) which is as (white and) lustrous as the Kunda flower and the Moon ? How has it happened so ? Narrate this to me, a suppliant who am brilliant, devoted and have perfect self-control.

20. O extremely fortunate one, it behoves you to detail everything without excluding anything. Narrate this auspicious and sacred story that destroys all sins. Please tell us this story for my delight."

21. On hearing those words of that noble-souled Vasiṣṭha, Skanda, the extremely resplendent destroyer of the army of the enemies of gods (i.e. Asuras), replied:

22-23. "Listen to these words repeated by me, O most excellent one among eloquent persons, (I am repeating) what has been heard by me before, as I sat on the lap of Umā. This is the conversation of the noble-souled Śarva (Śiva) with Pārvatī. I shall recount that, O great sage, for your delight.

24-40. On the beautiful peak of the Kailāsa mountain, lord Śiva the destroyer of the body of Madana (God of Love) was seated comfortably on a rocky slab covered with gold and bedecked with pure pearls, jewels, and gems.

The beautiful peak of the Kailāsa is variegated on account of different kinds of minerals. It resembled the sun at midday and had the lustre of molten gold. It had stairs built of diamonds and crystals, with steps of rocky surfaces of variegated forms. It was full of gold and was divinely variegated on account of the different kinds of minerals. It is interspersed with various kinds of trees and creepers laden with different kinds of flowers and fruits. It was filled with *Haṁsas* (swans) and Kāraṇḍavas (ducks). It was beautified by Cakravāka birds (Ruddy geese). Many bees were singing (humming) at a high pitch there. It was resonant with the continuous sound of water-falls. Its caves were resounded with the sounds of intoxicated peacocks and Krauñca birds. It was filled with bevies of celestial damsels. It was beautified by Kinnaras. The chirping sound of the different varieties of Jīvaṁjīvaka birds (a mythial bird with two heads) spread everywhere in it. In many places, the cooing sound of the cuckoo-birds was heard. It was frequented by Siddhas and Cāraṇas. It had the sound of oxen whose sound resembled the rumblings of clouds. There were other sounds as well. The elephants were agitated on account of Vināyaka and they left their caves. There were sounds of the musical instruments like Vīṇā (lute) and other (musical instruments). They were fascinating to the ears. Groups of people were swinging by means of *Dolās* (swings). It was resorted to by bevies of ladies. It was echoing with the sound of the bells fitted to the swings suspended from the flagstaff. There were many musical instruments such as the *Vallakīs* (lutes) and *Veṇus* (flutes). It was as much resounded as though there were thirty peacocks (crying). The caves were filled with the sounds of vocal music, drums, musical instruments which were played upon and which were beaten and also with (hurryings for play) and disputes (arguments). Swans, pigeons and royal cranes were happily perched there. The lord of the *Gaṇas* (i.e. Vighnarāja) was sporting about with various kinds of fixations (poses), of the body. The lord of the Bhūtas (Spirits) was surrounded by *Bhūtas* of various sorts. (For example) some had the faces of lions and tigers. Some were producing terrible cries. They had terrific speed. Others had the faces of deer, sheep, elephants and horses Others were hideous with faces of cats or form of foxes. Some were short, some were tall; some were very lean. Some had protruding bellies; some had huge bellies; some had short-shanks; some had lips hanging loose; others had huge palm-like shanks. Some had the ears of cows; some had a single ears; some had huge ears; some had no ears; some had many feet; some had huge feet; some had single foot; some had no foot; some had many eyes; some had large eyes; some had a single eye; some had no eye; some had a single curved tooth; some had huge curved teeth; some had many curved teeth; some had no curved tooth at all. Some had huge heads; some had many heads; some had no head at all. Some had a single tongue; some had huge tongues; some had many tongues; some had no tongue at all.

The daughter of the King of mountains spoke thus to lord Śiva.

41-43. "O lord, Master of the past and the future, O lord whose authority has been marked by a bullock (i.e. bull-bannered one), there is something sparkling in your neck, O great lord, resembling a cloud. O lord, O destroyer of the body of Kāma, what is this that shines in your white neck ? It is not very deep and manifest. What is the cause ? What is the reason that your neck is bluish, O lord? Narrate all these duly (as I have got curiosity and) I am eager (to hear it)."

44. On hearing the words of Pārvatī, the lover of Pārvatī, Śaṅkara, recounted the story fully endued with auspiciousness.

Maheśvara said :

45. Formerly, when the milk-ocean was being churned by the Devas and Dānavas for the sake of *Amṛta* (nectar), a terrible poison as sparkling as the dark fire cropped up.

46. On seeing, O lady of excellent face, the multitudes of Devas and Daityas became dejected. All of them approached Brahmā.

47. On seeing the frightened groups of Devas, Brahmā, of great splendour, asked : "O highly fortunate ones, why are you frightened? Why are you dejected in the mind?

48. Three-fold prosperity and power has been conferred by me on you all, O excellent Devas. By whom has your prosperity been turned off?

49. You are the lords and masters of the three worlds. All of you are free from ailments. In the creation of subjects there is no one who dares to transgress my behest.

50. All of you move about in aerial chariots. All of you go about as you please. (All of you are very competent) in regard to spiritual things, worldly beings and providential ones for ever).

51. You are competent to make all the subjects function in accordance with the consequence of their previous actions. Hence, why are you all agitated due to fear like the deer harassed by lion ?

52. What is your misery? What is your distress? Whence has fear befallen you? It behoves you to explain quickly all these things duly".

53. On hearing the words of Brahmā, the supreme soul, those Devas, leading Daityas and Dānavas accompanied by the sages said:

54-59a. "O Pitāmaha (Brahmā, the grandfather) when the ocean was being churned by the Devas and Asuras, a terrible poison had turned up. It resembled serpents and black bees. It was like the blue cloud. It had the sparkling lustre of the Saṁvarta fire (the fire that burns down the universe at the end of a Kalpa). It had cropped up like the god of death and destruction. It had the fiery splendour of the sun at the end of the Yugas. It had the brilliance of the sun capable of annihilating the three worlds. It spread all round.

Janārdana of reddish white body had been rendered black on being scorched by that poison whose lustre is on a par with the dark fire of ultimate destruction.

On seeing Janārdana of white reddish limbs being rendered black by its burning, all of us became frightened and we sought refuge in you alone".

On hearing the frightful words of the Devas and the Asuras, Brahmā of great splendour, the grandfather of the worlds replied:

59b-63. "O Devas, sages and ascetics, listen all of you. The poison that has the lustre of the dark fire of destruction and what we all know as *Kālakūṭa* has appeared while the great ocean was being churned. Immediate by its very appearance, Devas lost all lustre and they did not shine the moment it cropped up. Neither Viṣṇu, nor I nor all the leading Devas can bear the brunt of its attack excepting god Śaṅkara".

After saying this, Brahmā who had the lustre of the interior of a lotus, whose source of origin is lotus, who was not born of any womb and who was the foremost among those who were canversant with the Vedas, remembered Oṁkāra and meditated on the divine lustre (that is present all round. Thereafter god Brahmā, began to eulogise.

Eulogy of God Śiva:[1]

64. "O Virūpākṣa (Lord of uneven-three-eyes) obeisance

1. In Purāṇas it is customary to attribute the highest epithets to the deity eulogised. Sometimes it results in a string of names or adjectives. Here

unto you. Hail to you of divine eyes. Salute unto the lord with the Pināka bow in his hand. Obeisance to the god with a thunderbolt in his hand.

65. Obeisance to the lord of the three worlds. Salute to the lord of all living beings. Bow to the slayer of the enemies of the Devas. Hail to the lord with the moon, the sun and the fire for his eyes.

66. Obeisance unto thee who are Brahmā, Rudra and Viṣṇu. Bow to the Sāṁkhya; to the Yoga. Obeisance to the assemblage of all spirits (incarnate).

67. Hail to the destroyer of the body of Manmatha (God of Love). Obeisance to the lord with Time (*kāla*) for his back. Obeisance to Rudra of excellent semen. Bow to the lord of the Devas and to the Vehement one.

68. Obeisance to Kapardin (one having matted hair), to Śaṅkara the terrible one. Hail to Hara, the bearer of a skull, one of hideous features, Obeisance to Śiva the bestower of boons.

69. Obeisance to the destroyer of the three cities (of demons). Bow to the destroyer of the sacrifice (of Dakṣa). Hail to the lord of the mothers. Obeisance to the *Vṛddha* (the ancient god); Obeisance to *Śuddha* (the pure one), to the *Mukta* (Liberated one); obeisance to the mighty one.

70. Obeisance to the sole hero among the three worlds, to the moon, to Varuṇa; to *Agra* (the foremost one), to *Ugra* (the terrible one); to *Vipra* (knower of the Vedas) of many eyes.

71. Obeisance to *Rajas*, to *Sattva*; obeisance unto you of unmanifest origin. Bow to the Eternal one; to the non-eternal one; and to the eternal-cum-non-eternal one.

72. Hail to the manifest one, to the Unmanifest one, as well as to the manifest-cum-unmanifest one. Obeisance to

---

god Śiva is regarded as equivalent to the Para Brahman and in addition to his mythological exploits, epithets applicable to the Para Brahman are included in this eulogy.

We find Śiva so glorified in Tai. Saṁhitā IV.5 (Rudrādhyāya) and the *Maha Nārāyaṇīya* Upa. X 17-21. The *Sahasranāmas* (garlands of a thousand epithets) of these deities is a Purāṇic development. The Viṣṇusahasranāma in the Mbh. is perhaps the earliest example of this.

the *Cintya* (one who can be contemplated upon; obeisance to the *Acintya* (one who is beyond contemplation); Obeisance to the *Cintya-cum-Acintya* one.

73. Obeisance to the dispeller of distress of all the worlds; Bow to the lord who is fond of Nārāyaṇa; Obeisance to Śarva, the lover of Umā, Hail to the lord marked with the face of Nandin ? (*nandi-vaktrāṅkitāya*)*

74. Hail to (the lord identifying himself with) *Pakṣa* (fortnight), *Māsa* (Month) and *Ardhamāsa* (half a month); obeisance to (the Lord, the identifier with) the season and *Saṁvatsara*(year); Bow to the lord of many forms, to the lord with shaven head, to the lord bearing a staff, to the lord wearing a mailed armour.

75. Obeisance to the lord with the skull in his hand; Bow to the god having quarters for his raiment (the naked one); to one with a tufted head; Obeisance to the lord with a bow and a chariot, and to the celibate god with self control.

76-78. Obeisance to the embodiment of Ṛk, Yajus and Sāmaveda; obeisance to Puruṣa, the supreme lord. Bow unto you who are worthy of being eulogised by prayers composed like this."

After eulogising like this, O lady of excellent face, Brahmā bowed down (and praised once again).

"O lord Rudra, (even) after knowing my devotion as well as that of the Devas, you do not manifest yourself. Though you had released your (matted) hair and got it splashed with the waters of the Gaṅgā, (yet) you are too subtle, to be contemplated upon, on account of your supreme Yogic power".

Thus I was eulogised formerly by lord Brahmā, the creator of the worlds, by means of various kinds of hymns originating from the Vedas and Vedāṅgas (ancillary parts of the vedas).

Thereupon, I spoke to Pitāmaha Brahmā in important words:

79-80. "O lord of the worlds, O lord of the past, present and future, O lord of the universe, O Brahmā, what should be done by me unto you. Tell me, O lord of holy rites".

---

*Vā.P.55.76 reads : *nandī-cakrāṅkitāya* 'marked with the *cakra* of Nandi' (?)'.

On hearing these words, the lotus-eyed Brahmā replied.

81-82. "O lord of the past, present and future, let this be heard, O lord, (cause of everything), O lotus-eyed lord, when the ocean was being churned by the Devas and Asuras, a terrible poison resembling clouds appeared. O lord, It appeared like blue clouds. It had a lustre similar to that of Saṁvarta fire.

83. On seeing it, all of us were frightened and agitated in the mind. O great lord, swallow it up with a desire for the welfare of the worlds.

84. You alone are competent to swallow it. There is no one other than you O great lord, to bear the brunt of its advance".

85-87a. On hearing these words of Brahmā the Parameṣṭhin, O lady of excellent face, I accepted the proposal saying, "so be it." Then I began to drink the poison that was like the god of death. Even as I drank the extremely terrible poison that accorded great fright unto the Devas, O lady of excellent complexion, my throat turned black immediately.

87b-88. On seeing it, which had the lustre of the petals of lily, which appeared like a serpent clinging to my neck and which was like Takṣaka the king of serpents, who had risen up and begun to lick with his tongues, Brahmā of great splendour, the grandfather of the worlds spoke thus:

89-90a. "You shine splendidly O great lord of excellent holy rites, with this (such) neck".

On hearing his words, O daughter of the most excellent one among the mountains, the terrible poison was held by me in the throat itself. Therefore, I became Nīlakaṇṭha (Blue-throated god).

90b. I drank it even as the groups of Devas, Daityas, Yakṣas, Gandharvas, Bhūtas, Piśācas, serpents and Rākṣasas were looking on, O lady of excellent face.

91. That Kālakūṭa, the poison of terrible action, was retained by me in my throat. On seeing it being contained thus, the groups of Devas and Daityas became extremely surprised.

92. Thereafter, O lady of the gait of intoxicated elephant, the groups of Devas along with the Daityas, serpents and Rākṣasas said thus with palms joined in reverence.

93. "O how wonderful are your strength, virility and exploit, O lord. Your body and Yogic power are simply wonderful.

94. O lord of the Devas, your supremacy is extremely wonderful, O destroyer of the body of Manmatha.

You alone are Viṣṇu. You are the four-faced (lord Brahmā); You alone are the god of death. You alone are the bestower of boons.

95. You alone are the sun and the moon. You alone are the manifestation of this world of mobile and immobile beings.

You alone are the (element called) fire. You alone are the element wind. You alone are the (element called) earth. You alone are the water (you constitute all the elements).

96. You alone are the creator and sustainer of the entire world of mobile and immobile beings. You alone are its annihilation (i.e. annihilator)"

After saying these words, the leading Devas bowed down their heads. Taking Soma (? Nectar, Moon) with them, they went away by means of aerial chariots with a speed equal to that of Wind, till they all reached the Meru, the great mountain.

97-98. Thus the highly meritorious and extremely holy (story about the name) Nīlakaṇṭha has been recounted. It is well known in the three worlds.

This story that destroys sins has been directly recounted by the self-born lord (Brahmā) himself.

99. I shall mention the extensive benefit acquired by the person who retains in memory this splendid narrative proclaimed by Brahmā.

100. O lady of great beauty and excellent hip, all poisons whether mobile or immobile (solid or liquid?) are immediately destroyed on coming into contact with his body.

101. It subdues all terrible inauspicious features. It dispels and decreases (the effect of) evil dreams. The person

attains the state of a lover unto women and an honourable person in the council of the king.

102. He wins arguments. He becomes victorious in battle. When travelling, he does so with safety and welfare. His house is full with perpetual prosperity.

103-105. O lady of excellent face, I shall describe the mode of attainment of his body.[1] His moustache becomes reddish brown. His throat becomes blue. His hair is beautifully marked by the moon. He has three eyes and he wields a trident in his hand. His vehicle is a bullock. He holds Pināka bow in his hand. He is prosperous with the strength and exploit equal to that of Nandin. At my behest he traverses the seven worlds. His gait (movement) is unimpeded like that of the wind in the sky.

106-107. Acquiring a strength equal to that of mine, he stands steady till the annihilation of all living beings.

I shall mention the goal of those persons who devoutly listen to my story, O beautiful lady, I shall mention their destination here and hereafter.

The Brāhmaṇa acquires Vedic knowledge. The Kṣatriya conquers the earth.

108. The Vaiśya acquires profit. The Śūdra shall attain happiness. The sick man is rid of his ailments. The fettered one is released from imprisonment.

109. The pregnant woman obtains a son; the virgin gets a good husband. Every one obtains the lost wealth here and hereafter.

110. By hearing this divine story a man obtains the same benefit or merit as that obtained by duly offering as gift a hundred thousand cows to the Brāhmaṇas.

111. He who retains in memory a foot or half a foot, a quatrain or a distitch (of this story) goes to the world of Rudra for ever.

112-113. He who reads this entirely with the mind directed towards me, in the presence of deities and Brāhmaṇas

1. This is the attainment of *Sārūpya* 'Similarity of appearance' with god Śiva.

attains the world of Rudra. He should have faith and devotion for ever. O goddess, the man should always read devoutly and make others read so.

114. A prayer greater than this, there never had been before nor will ever be. Neither the Yakṣas, nor the Piśācas, neither the goblins nor Vināyakas (spirits creating impediment) shall bring about any obstacle in the house of that person where this prayer is kept.

115. O lady of lotuslike eyes, the greatness of this prayer has been mentioned by me to you as I am delighted. It is destructive of multitudes of sins. It is accompanied by the merit of holiness. It is sung by the four-faced lord himself.

116. After recounting this story endued with the fruits of meritorious deeds to the goddess, the lord whose matted hair has been fixed with thc moon and who is fond of Guha (Kārttikeya) went to Kailāsa cave on the back of his Bull. He was accompanied by Umā.

117. This story that dispels sins has been heard by me from Prajāpati. It is recounted to you.

After learning this entirely along with all the characteristics, the excellent Brāhmaṇa proceeds to the region of the sun.

CHAPTER TWENTYSIX

The Origin of the Liṅga-Image of Śiva[1]

The Sages said :

1. "We wish to hear completely about the greatness of Mahādeva, the lordship of that noble soul and the details of his excellence in supremacy."

---

1. The story of how the Liṅga of god Śiva appeared is told in different Purāṇas like Liṅga, 17; KP II 38; Vā.P.55. The Liṅga of Śiva is not the phallus

Sūta said :

2. "This has been declared by Viṣṇu formerly in the course of his conquest of the three worlds after binding Bali, the lord of the three worlds, of great prowess.

3-5. The consort of Śacī (Indra) was delighted when the Daityas were destroyed. Thereafter, all the Devas came to see the eternal lord. They came to the place where the lord of cosmic form abides near the milk ocean. The Siddhas, the Brāhmaṇa sages, the Yakṣas, the Gandharvas, the groups of divine damsels, the serpents, the divine sages, the rivers and the mountains approached the great soul and the supreme Being, Hari and began to eulogise him.

6. "You are the supporter and the maker (of the universe) O Lord, you create the worlds. It is due to your grace, that the three worlds attain ever-lasting welfare.

7-8. All the Asuras have been defeated. Bali has been imprisoned by you".

On being thus addressed by Devas (gods), Siddhas and the great sages, Viṣṇu, the supreme Man, replied to the Devas.

"O excellent Devas, let this be heard. I shall explain the reason.

9-10a. I have attained *Siddhatva* (state of a great Siddha) due to the grace of that lord who is the creator of all living beings, who is the personification of the destructive principle and who is the lord and cause of Time, by whom the worlds and I have been created along with Brahmā, by means of his Māyā.

10b-12a. Formerly, when the three worlds had been swallowed (enveloped) and merged in the darkness and all was unmanifest, and while I, with all the living beings within my belly, lay there alone, I had a thousand heads, eyes and feet and had the conch, discus and the club in my hands, I was lying on the pure expanse of water.

---

but a column of fire, the beginning or the foot and top of which could not be probed by gods Viṣṇu and Brahmā. The Liṅga-worship is a Purāṇic transformation of Vedic fire-worship.

12b. In the meantime I espied the lord of unlimited lustre, from afar.

13. He resembled a hundred thousand suns. He shone by means of his own splendour. He was a four-faced person (*Puruṣa*) of great Yogic power and golden lustre.

14. He was a lord wearing a skin of black antelope, and he was adorned with a *Kamaṇḍalu* (waterpot). This excellent person (Brahmā) reached me in a trice.

15-16. Then Brahmā who is (reverently) bowed to by the worlds, spoke to me :—"Who are you ? Whence have you come ? Why do you stay here ? Tell me, O lord. I am the creator of all worlds. I am selfborn. I have faces all round."

On being addressed thus by Brahmā, I spoke to him :—

17-18. "Indeed I am the creator of the worlds and the annihilator as well again and again."

Conversing thus, we desired to conquer each other. We saw a flame blazing to the north of us. O sinless ones, on seeing that flame then we were surprised.

19-20. At the splendour and power of the lustre of Śiva, we remained with palms joined in reverence. We saw the mass of splendour increasing in size. It was excessively miraculous. Brahmā and I hastily rushed towards that massive flame. That circular mass of flames stood up piercing heaven and earth.

21. In the middle of that massive splendour, we saw the extremely resplendent Liṅga of the size of a mere span. It was unmanifest (?) yet endowed with extensive lustre.[1]

22. That (Liṅga) in the middle was neither of gold nor of silver nor was it made of rock. It could not be specified. Nor could it be contemplated upon. It was visible and invisible again and again.

23. It was richly endowed with thousands of sparks. It was surprisingly mysterious. It was endued with great refulgence and it was increasing in size tremendously.

---

1. The identity of Rudra and Agni (the fire-god) is stated in ṚV. II. 1.7, the Śatapatha Br. III 3.1.10; VI 1.3.10; the Taittarīya Br. I. 1.5. 8-9., The Tāṇḍya Br. XII 4.24.

24. Clusters of flames spread everywhere. It was frightful to all living beings. It was extremely terrible in its features. It appeared to pierce heaven and Earth.

25. Then Brahmā told me,— "You go quickly beneath. Let us find out the end of this noble-souled Liṅga.

26. I shall go upwards until its end is seen."

After making this stipulation, we went upwards as well as beneath.

27. Thereupon, I went far below for a thousand years, but I could not find its end. I became frightened thereby.

28. Similarly, Brahmā went upwards, but he too did not reach its extremity. He too returned along with me to that vast expanse of water.

29. We were surprised and frightened of that great soul. We were deluded by the Māyā of that great Being. Our consciousness got lost and we stayed there (helplessly).

30. Thereupon, we meditated on the lord with faces on all sides, the imperishable lord who is the source of origin and the cause of dissolution of all the worlds.

31. We made obeisance, with palms joined in reverence, to the trident-bearing Śiva (*Śarva*), the lord of extremely terrific voice, of terrible features and curved fangs, to that great unmanifest lord.

32. "Obeisance to you, O lord of worlds and Devas. Salutations unto you, O lord of Bhūtas, O highly noble soul.

Obeisance to you, O lord who have achieved permanent Yogic powers. Hail to you, O Lord established over the universe.

33. You are Parameṣṭhin (the highest deity), the supreme Brahman, the imperishable great region; you are the eldest one. You are Vāmadeva, Rudra, Skanda and Lord Śiva.

34. You are Yajña; you are Vaṣaṭkāra; you are Oṁkāra; you are the subduer of enemies; you are Svāhākāra, the obeisance, the consecration of all holy rites.

35. You are Svadhākāra, Yajña, holy rites and observances, the Vedas, the worlds, the Devas—the lord alone is everything all round.

36. You are the quality of sound of the firmament; you are the source of origin and cause of dissolution of all living

beings, you are the quality of smell in the earth, the quality of taste in the waters and the colour in *Tejas* (fiery element), you are the great lord.

37. O lord of the Devas, you are the quality (called) touch in Vāyu (wind); you form the body of the moon.

38. O Lord of the Devas, you are knowledge in the intellect; you are the seed of Prakṛti.

39. You are the annihilator of all the worlds; you are Kāla identical with the god of Death, the cause of destruction. You sustain the three worlds, O Lord, you alone create them.

40. With your eastern face you assume the form of Indra; with your southern face you withdraw the worlds again.

41. With your western face you are stationed in Varuṇa undoubtedly. O excellent one among the Devas, with your northern face you are Soma.

42-45. In one way or in many ways, O Lord, you are the source of origin and cause of dissolution of the worlds. O Lord, from you are born these viz.: the Ādityas, the Vasus, Rudras, Maruts, the Aśvins, the Sādhyas, the Vidyādharas, the Nāgas, the Cāraṇas, the ascetics, the Vālakhilyas and others who have performed good holy rites and many others.

O lord of Devas, from you are born these viz.: Umā, Sītā, Sinīvālī, Kuhū, Gāyatrī, Lakṣmī, Kīrti, Dhṛti, Medhā, Lajjā, Kānti, Vapus, Svadhā, Tuṣṭi, Puṣṭi, Kriyā, Sarasvatī, the goddess of speech, Sandhyā and Rātri (Night).

46. O Lord endowed with the potential strength and influence of ten thousand sets of ten thousand suns, obeisance be to you, O lord, as white as a thousand moons. Obeisance be to you who hold *Vajra* (thunderbolt) and Pināka bow. Obeisance be to you, O lord, with arrows and bow in your hands.

47. Obeisance to you, O lord, whose limbs are embellished with *Bhasma* (sacred ash). Hail to you, O lord, the destroyer of Kāma's body.

Salute unto you, O lord Hiraṇyagarbha; obeisance unto you, O lord of golden raiment.

48. Bow to you, O lord of golden womb. Obeisance to you, O lord of golden navel; Hail to you, O lord of golden

semen. Obeisance be to you, O lord, mysterious with a thousand eyes.

49. Obeisance be to you, O lord of golden colour. Salute to you, O lord of golden hair; obeisance be to you, O lord of golden heroism* (?); obeisance be to you, the lord who distributes gold.

50 Obeisance be to you, O lord and master of gold; Bow to you, O lord with the sound of gold. Obeisance to you, O lord with the Pināka in your hand; salute to you, O bluethroated Śaṅkara".

51. On being eulogised thus, the lord of great intellect appeared before us. The lord of Devas, the source of origin of the Universe, who had the lustre of ten million suns.

52. Mahādeva of great lustre became filled with pity. He spoke to us as if he was about to swallow the sky with a thousand crores of mouths.

53. His neck was like a conch-shell in shape. His belly was well shaped He was bedecked in different kinds of ornaments. His limbs were variegated on account of different jewels. He wore different kinds of garlands and had applied different kinds of unguents.

54. The lord had Pināka in his hand; he held the trident; he was worthy of being worshipped by the Devas; he had serpents as the sacred thread; he was the cause of freedom from fear unto the Devas.

55. At that time, he burst unto a laughter, the sound of which was similar to that of *Dundubhi* (a big drum) and was comparable to the rumbling sound of the cloud. The sound filled the whole universe.

56-57. We two were frightened at that great sound. Then Mahādeva said,—"O excellent ones among the Devas, I am delighted. Both of you see the great Yogic power. May all fear be eschewed. Both of you are eternal and are formerly born of my limbs.

58. This Brahmā, the grandfather of the worlds is my right hand. Viṣṇu who is never defeated in any battle, is my left hand.

* Vā.P.55. *hiraṇya-cīra* 'of golden dress or garments'.

59-60. I am pleased well with both of you. I shall give unto you the boon as you please".

Then, delighted in our minds we bowed down at the feet of the lord.

We said to Mahādeva who was standing in front of us with grace.

"O lord of the Devas, you are delighted; if a boon has to be bestowed by you, let us be devoted to you for ever."

The Lord of gods said :

"O highly fortunate ones, let it be so. Create subjects extensively".

After saying so, the lord vanished there itself.

61. Thus the potentiality of that intelligent lord has been recounted to you. This is the greatest knowledge. The unmanifest one is termed Śiva (Auspicious).

62-63. Only those with the vision of knowledge see this subtle Being who cannot be contemplated upon. We shall make obeisance to that lord of the Devas. "O Mahādeva, Obeisance be to you, O Maheśvara, Salute be to you."

Sūta said :

64. "After hearing this, all the Devas went to their respective abodes, paying homage and respects unto Śaṅkara the great soul.

65. He who recites this hymn unto the lord, the great soul, obtains all desires and gets rid of all sins.

66. All this was narrated to them by Viṣṇu, the powerful one, due to the grace of Mahādeva, about the eternal Brahman. Thus everything regarding the power of Maheśvara has been described to you.

CHAPTER TWENTYSEVEN

Śiva cursed by Dāruvana sages :[1] *Their repentance and Prayer : Installation of Śiva Liṅga—The Injunction Regarding Ash-bath*

The sages said :—

1. Recount once again, O Sūta of great intellect, the greatness of Mahādeva. We are eager and curious to listen to it.

2. How did the lord assume a loathsome form in the forest Dāruvana resorted to by the groups of divine sages? The great sages gained wisdom thereby.

3. On knowledge that it was Mahādeva, they became excited and confused. In order to propitiate him they worshipped him but Bhəva (Lord Śiva) did not become pleased with them.

4. All these activities of the lord of the Devas may kindly be recounted to us in number as they took place. You are the most excellent one among intelligent persons."

Sūta said :

5. "Let this righteous activity be heard while I recount it, O alert ones. It is, due to his compassion towards the devotees, that this had been carried out by the lord of the Devas.

6. (This happened) O Brāhmaṇas, formerly on the splendid and auspicious peak of the Himalayas in the Kṛta-yuga. There is a forest of Devadāru trees which is beautiful and full of many trees and creepers.

7-9. Many sages perform austerities here and carry on holy ascetic rites.[2] Some of them had only *śaivāla* (moss) for

---

1. This story how and why Śiva was cursed by sages in the Dāru-Vana and how they subsequently adopted the Śiva Liṅga for worship is narrated in the LP, KP, VĀ. P, mentioned above. The Dāru-Vana mentioned here is in the Himalayas (vide V 6 below) and not in Maharashtra as given in De 53-54.

2. VV. 7-9 illustrate the different vows observed by sages while performing penance.

their food. Some of them lay within water. Some of them had the ethereal space (for their stay). Some of them supported themselves on the tips of their big toes. Some had their teeth serve the purpose of *Ulūkhala* (threshing Mortar, i.e. they ate the grains of corn chewing them with their teeth); others were *Aśmakuṭṭas* (who pounded their grains on rocks before eating). Some remained seated in heroic postures (*Vīrāsana*). Others followed the way of life of the deer. All those sages of great intellect spent their time in severe penances.

10-12. Then the lord came to that forest in order to confer grace on them. His limbs were grey due to the application of *Bhasman* (ashes). He was naked. He had hideous features. His hairs were dishevelled and ugly. His teeth were terrific. His hands eagerly got hold of a firebrand. His eyes were reddish brown. His penis and scrotum resembled red chalk. His face was beautified by reddish white colour.

13. At some places he laughed boisterously and terribly. At some places he showed surprise and began to sing. At some places he began to dance expressing amorous sentiment. At some places, he began to cry again and again.[1]

14. Deluded and enchanted by him the wives of the sages immediately prevented him from dancing. After coming to the hermitage as a guest, he began to beg again and again.

15. He created a wife unto himself, similar in form and bedecked in ornaments. He roared and bellowed like a bull and brayed like a donkey.

16. He began to befool them making all the embodied ones laugh. Thereupon, the sages became angry. They were over-whelmed by fury.

17. Fascinated by his deluding power (Māyā) they approached him in order to curse him. "Since you sing (bray) like a (donkey) you will become a donkey.

---

1. These verses describe the Pāśupata way of behaviour or penance. *Vide* Pāśupata Sūtra's (with Kauṇḍiṇya's Com.) Ch. III sūtras 1-19. Pāśupatas are instructed to behave in such a way whereby the practitioner of the Vrata is insulted (*avamataḥ*). The strange behaviour of Śiva described in this and subsequent verses is found prescribed in *Pāśupata-Sūtras*.

18-19. Or you will be Rākṣasa, Piśāca (Evil spirit) or a Dānava." As they pleased, those infuriated sages cursed him with different kinds of curses. They cursed that lord of the universe but the powers of austerities of all of them were repelled and made futile against Śaṅkara.

20. Just as the stars in the sky do not shine on account of refulgence of the sun so also their splendour (power of penance) (became ineffective) on Śaṅkara.

21. It is heard that the full-fledged Yajña, the cause of all prosperity of Brahmā, the noble soul, met with destruction on account of the curse of sages.

22. On account of the curse of Bhṛgu, Viṣṇu of very supreme prowess and splendour had to take ten births and was made miserable for ever.[1]

23. Formerly, the penis of Indra along with his scrotum, O sages conversant with Virtue, was made to fall down on the earth by the infuriated sage Gautama.[2]

24. The Vasus were forced to stay in the womb on account of a curse. It is on account of the curse of sages that Nahuṣa was turned into a serpent.[3]

25. It was by Brāhmaṇa that the ocean of milk was rendered unfit to be drunk. Dharma (God of Death) was cursed by the noble-souled Māṇḍavya.[4]

26. These and many others underwent much torment excepting Maheśvara, the lord of the Devas with uneven (three) eyes.

27. Thus, enchanted by him, they did not recognize Śaṅkara. Thereupon, all those sages spoke to each other.

---

1. VR VII 51.11-16 states that Bhṛgu cursed Viṣṇu as he killed Bhṛgu's wife Pulomā.

2. This punishment was meted out to Indra for his adultery with Gautama's wife Ahalyā, *vide* VR I.48 17-28.

3. Mbh. Udyoga. 17, 14-18 states how Nahuṣa was cursed by Agastya when he goaded him with his foot to carry his palanquin quickly to Śacī's palace.

4. The sage Māṇḍavya was wrongfully impaled by god Yama. He therefore cursed him to be a Śūdra. (And he was born of Vidura)—Mbh. Adi. Ch. 107.

28. "This is not the right code of conduct laid down for us householders. Nor is it the rite of those engaged in the vow of celibacy or the forest-hermitages.

29. This is not seen as the Dharma of recluses. This is great injustice and misdemeanour whereby this person is deluded, O Brāhmaṇas.

30. Make his Liṅga drop down. This is not the Dharma (a code of conduct) of sages and ascetics.[1] Speak sweet words. Resort to (at least) one Garment.

31-33. When the Liṅga is abandoned (dropped) by you, you will be accorded due worship.

On hearing these words of the sages, lord Śaṅkara, the destroyer of the eyes of Bhaga, said in polished speech, as though he was laughing boisterously.

"This Liṅga of ours cannot be made to fall down forcibly by all the gods beginning with Brahmā. How then be the other ascetics. O excellent Brāhmaṇas, I shall make this Liṅga fall down."

34-36. They uttered the sentence "Stay in the hermitage or go away".

On being spoken to thus, lord Mahādeva became delighted in the activities of the sense-organs. Even as all of them were observing, the lord vanished there itself.

When the lord vanished and Bhava (God Śiva) was transformed into a Liṅga, there was no appearance of any living being in the range of the three worlds. Everything was agitated and nothing shone.

37. The sun did not shine; the fire became devoid of lustre. The stars and the planets became contrary (to their normal state).

38. The *Kratus* (sacrifices?) of the sages who had plenty of resources and who were engaged in activities conducive to the birth of children and who used to approach their wives only at the permitted period after the days of menstruation, did not function properly.

---

1. The sages were obviously ignorant of the Pāśupata way of life.

39. Without the sense of My-ness (*mamatva*) and devoid of egotism, they tried to perform the holy rite once again. (But) all their potentiality and all their splendour became lost.

40. At that time their mind did not become concentrated in Dharma (holy rites etc.). All of them gathered together and went to the region of god Brahmā.

41. After going to the abode of Brahmā and on seeing the Lotus-born deity, at his abode all of them fell at his feet and narrated the account about Śiva.

42. "He is formidable and frightful. His hair is stiff and rough. His teeth are terrific. His hands are eager to get hold of an owl* (?)

43-44. His penis along with the scrotum is red and embellished (painted) with red chalk. He was always (found) remaining at the sides of our daughters-in-Law and daughters, particularly those who had their babies (?) with them. (He was found) staying near them with an unnatural desire. Taking him to be a mad fellow, we insulted him.

45. He was scolded and beaten. His Liṅga (? penis) was taken out. It is to alleviate his anger that we have sought refuge in you.

46-48. We do not know this matter (thoroughly). Explain it to us, O grand-father''.

On hearing these words of the sages Lord Brahmā meditated and found out that it was *Śarva* (god Śiva). Then with great concentration, he replied thus:—

"This is lord Mahādeva. He should be known as the great lord. His great region is not attained easily. Heis the lord of the gods, sages and manes.

49. At the end of thousand Yugas, when there is the annihilation of all embodied beings, this lord Maheśvara becomes Kāla (God of death) and destroys (everything).

---

* Probably *ulmuka* 'fire-brand' and not *ulūka* as in the text. In V.11 above he is stated to have a firebrand in his hand.

50. He alone creates all subjects singly and by means of his own vigour. He alone is the discus-bearing lord (Viṣṇu) whose chest is characteristically marked by Śrīvatsa.

51. He is called Yogin in the Kṛta Yuga and Kratu in the Tretā Yuga. In the Dvāpara, he is remembered as Kālāgni and as Dharmaketu in the Kali age.

52. Three forms of Rudra should be known and realized by learned men. The *Tamas* form is Agni, the *Rajas* form is Brahmā and *Sattva* is Viṣṇu, the illuminator.

53. One form of his is remembered as having the quarters for his garment (i.e. naked). It is named Śiva. It is in him that the Brahman endowed with Yoga resides.

54-55. Hence, O leading Brāhmaṇas, after subduing your anger and controlling sense-organs propitiate the lord Īśāna, the imperishable lord, the lord of the Devas. After making a replica of the Liṅga of the great soul in the same form as was seen by you, resort to Lord with the trident in his hand.

56. Thereupon, you will see the lord of the Devas who can rarely be seen by ignorant and foolish persons who have not mastered their own selves. On seeing him, all ignorance and evils shall be destroyed."

57. Thereupon, they circumambulated Brahmā of unmeasured vigour. Becoming devoid of all grief, they returned and settled in the forest of Devadāru (Himalayan cedar) trees once again.

58-59. They began to propitiate the lord in the manner described by Brahmā in the various dry lands, on the mountains of variegated forms, in the caves and on the sandy banks of rivers splendid and variegated.

Thus when a year elapsed completely and the spring season arrived, the lord came to that forest assuming that very same form.

60. The great God entered that penance-grove and forest wherein many trees and creepers had put forth flowers, where that part of tract had been resonant with the drone of swarms of bees and which was filled with the sweet notes of the cuckoo.

61-66. Then all those sages eulogised him with great mental purity and concentration and worshipped him with waters, different kinds of garlands, incense and fragrant scents. Those highly fortunate ones worshipped him in the company of their wives, sons and attendants. With gentle words they spoke thus to Girīśa.

"It behoves you to forgive all our actions (of omission and commission) whatever has been perpetrated mentally, verbally and physically due to our ignorance of the lord of the Devas. O Śaṅkara, the conduct of life of Brahmā and other Devas is mysteriously esoteric, elaborate, inscrutable and difficult to comprehend. We do not know how to welcome you. We do not know at all any of your movements. O Mahādeva, O lord of the universe, you are as you are, obeisance be to you. Only noble-souled ones eulogise you, the lord of the Devas, the great lord.

67. Obeisance be to Bhava, Bhavya (splendid one), Bhāvana (sanctifier) and Udbhava (source of origin). Hail to the lord of spirits, the lord of infinite strength and virility.

68. Bow to the lord of tawny-complexioned body the destroyer, the imperishable one, the changing one. Obeisance to the lord, to the supporter of the current of Gaṅgā water. Bow to the lord who is the support; salutations to the soul of good qualities.

69. Obeisance to Tryambaka (the three-eyed lord). Hail to the lord who wields the excellent trident. Bow to you (identical with) Kandarpa. Obeisance be to you the Supreme Soul.

70. Obeisance to Śaṅkara, the bull-bannered one. Hail to the lord of Gaṇas (groups of goblins, the attendants of Śiva). Obeisance to Kāla with the staff in his hands; obeisance to the lord with the noose in his hands.

71-73. Obeisance to the lord who is the main deity in the Vedic Mantras; and to you of hundred tongues. Whatever is there in the world, the past, the present, the future, the mobile and immobile beings—all the visible worlds have originated from your person. O Śambhu, welfare unto you, protect us. Therefore be pleased with us. Whatever man does, whether out of ignorance or knowingly, it is the lord alone who does it by means of his Yogic Māyā."

74-76. After eulogising thus with delighted minds, the sages requested the lord: "Being endowed with the power of penance, we may see you as before. May your Liṅga be stationed in the normal posture as before.

Obeisance to the *Digvāsas* (the naked one) having garland-like clusters of Kiṅkiṇīs (bells in the trinkets).

Salute to the hideous one, to the terrible one, to the lord of frightful face. Obeisance to you who are devoid of form, who have excellent form and who have multiforms.

77. Obeisance be to Kaṭaṁkaṭa (golden-formed one), obeisance to Rudra; obeisance to Svāhākāra. Hail to you, the embodiment of all vital airs; Salute to you the lord with the Guṇas for his bodies.

78. Obeisance to *Durgandha* (foul-smelling one), to *Sugandha* (fragrant one); Salute to the lord with the trident in his hands; Obeisance to lord Śrīkaṇṭha with the dark-blue tuft. Hail to Nīlakaṇṭha, the lord who has applied the ashes in the cremation ground for unguent.

79. Obeisance to the lord identical with the trio of Guṇas. Hail to you the *Viśva* (one identical with the universe), the *Vedhas* (Creator), Bow to the lord who resides always in the cremation ground; Obeisance to the lord of the form of the *Preta* (Departed Soul ?)

80. You are Brahmā among the Devas[1] and Nīlalohita among the Rudras. The soul of all living beings, you are called Puruṣa by the Sāṁkhyas.

81. You are the great Meru among the mountains and the Moon among the stars. Among the sages you are Vasiṣṭha and Vāsava (Indra) among the Devas.

82. You are Oṁkāra among the Vedic Mantras, Jyeṣṭhasāman among the Sāman Mantras. You are the lion among the beings of the forest. You are the supreme Īśvara.

---

1. God Śiva is the best one among all gods etc. Cf. Bh. G. for such a list of excellences and every such excellence is His part :

Yad yad vibhūtimat sattvaṁ....
mama tejoṁśasambhavam / Bh. G. X 41.

83-86. You are the Bull among the domestic animals. You are the lord worshipped in all the worlds. Although you exist in all ways and manners, we see you alone in the beings that come up in front of us as narrated by Brahmā.

Lust, Anger, greed, distress and arrogance, we wish to check these, O Parameśvara (be pleased).

When the Mahāsaṁharaṇa (the great ultimate annihilation) arrives, fire is created by you, O lord, who are of self-governed spirit, by pressing the hand against the forehead. At that time all the worlds are surrounded all round by flames, on account of that fire.

87-88. Hence, all these are on a par with the fire. There are many hideous fires. All the living beings, mobile and immobile, all animals are burned by the fire originating from you. O lord of Devas, be the saviour of all of us as we are being burned.

89-91. For the welfare of all the worlds you sprinkle (with nectar) all the living beings; O lord of great fortune. O Maheśvara, the onlooker of auspiciousness. Command us O lord, we shall carry out your behest. We are unable to find any possible limit to your millions and millions of forms. O lord, obeisance unto you".

Thereafter, the lord and Master said these words :

92-93. "No learned man shall speak insultingly unto those persons who are devoted to my *Bhasman* (holy Ashes), who have burnt all their sins by means of ashes, who carry out everything they say, who have control over their sense-organs and who are Brāhmaṇas engrossed in meditation. No one who desires welfare both here and hereafter, shall transgress them nor shall they speak words unpleasant to them.

94. The man of deluded mind who censures them, censure Mahādeva. He who worships them always worships Śaṅkara. Act like this. Welfare unto you all. You will obtain (achievement of) spiritual power from me."

95. After understanding the unparalleled and excellent holy rite that is destructive of the great darkness (of ignorance) and that had been recounted by Śiva, those people got rid of their fear, greed, delusion and anxiety. They all fell (at his feet), simultaneously and bore (them) by means of their heads.

96-97. Then those delighted Brāhmaṇas began to perform the ablution of lord Maheśvara who assumed his usual Prākṛtika form by means of very pure scented water mixed with Kuśa grass and flowers. They began to sing with various kinds of esoteric Huṅkāras in sweet notes :—

98. "Obeisance unto you, O lord with the quarters for your garments (i.e. naked); Bow to the lord wearing Kiṅkiṇīs (small tinkling ornaments or bells) ; Salutation to the lord half of whose body is female. Obeisance to the lord who promulgated Sāṁkhya and Yoga.

99. Bow to the lord dark in colour, with the clouds for his vehicle; Obeisance to the lord wearing the hide of an elephant as his garment. Salute to the lord wearing the skin of an antelope as the upper garment. Obeisance to the lord having a serpent for his sacred thread."

100. Obeisance be unto Śaṅkara who has well constructed and wonderfully variegated ear-rings. Bow be to you with well-wreathed garlands for ornaments. Hail to you with the excellent hide of a lion for garment, O lord wielding a huge axe".

101. When the Liṅga was installed once again with a desire for the welfare of all the worlds, those excellent sages devoted to the duties of the different castes carried them out.

102. Then the great God who was pleased, replied to those sages :—"O sages of excellent holy rites, I am pleased with your penance. Choose the boons."

103-105. Then those sages viz. Bhṛgu, Aṅgiras, Vasiṣṭha, Viśvāmitra, Gautama, Atri, Sukeśa, Pulastya, Pulaha, Kratu, Marīci and Kaśyapa, all of them endowed with great penance, bowed down to Mahādeva and said these words :—

O lord, we wish to understand these—Ash-bath, nakedness, Vāmatva (left-handed ritual), Pratilomatā (contrary action) and *Sevyāsevyatva* (state of being worthy of being served and of being unworthy of being served)".

The Lord said :—[1]

106. "I shall explain this to you. I shall mention the

1. VV. 106-128 describe Pāśupata Vrata according to the author of this Purāṇa.

entire story (i.e. details) now. I am Agni accompanied by Soma. Soma has resorted to Agni.

107. They say that all the worlds have resorted to the fire made and unmade (i.e. artificial and natural). The whole world, mobile and immobile, is burned many times by fire.

108. Everything can be achieved through *Bhasman*. It is excellent and sacred. He (the devotee) sprinkles the living beings after assimilating the power and essence of ashes.

109. It is only after performing the holy rites in fire that one will perform the rite of *Tryāyuṣa* (trebling the span of life). One is rid of all sins through *Bhasman* (ashes) which is my vigour.

110. *Bhasman* is so called because it illuminates (everything) auspicious and renders it fragrant. It is glorified as *Bhasman* because it instantaneously destroys all sins.

111. The Pitṛs should be known as *Ūṣmapās* (Imbibing heat); the Devas are born of Soma (the Soma juice or the moon). The entire universe consisting of the mobile and the immobile beings is constituted by Agni and Soma.

112. I am Agni of great splendour. This my Ambikā, is Soma; Agni, Soma and I form ourselves the *Puruṣa* with *Prakṛti.*

113. Hence, O highly fortunate ones, *Bhasman* is spoken of as my vim and vigour. The position is this that I retain my own vigour by means of my own body.

114. Ever since then, it is through *Bhasman* that safety is assured in the lying-in-chambers. It is through *Bhasman* that protection is sought in the world in inauspicious circumstances.

115. A devotee whose soul is sanctified by means of Ash-bath, who has conquered anger and who has subdued his sense-organs does not go back (i.e. is not born again) after coming near me.

116. The holy rite Pāśupata is (not inferior to) Yoga; the holy rite of Kāpāla is based on Yoga. This Pāśupata rite is laid down before. It is most excellent.

117. All the remaining *Āśramins* (persons of various stages in life) have been created afterwards by the self-born lord (Brahmā). This creation which is of the nature of bashfulness, delusion and fear, has been evolved by me.

118. Deities and the sages are born only naked. Others, the human beings in the world, all of them are born without any garment.

119. Even the persons who are covered with a silken garment are (no better than) naked, should the sense-organs be unconquered. They are well hidden (covered) if they are duly subdued. It is not the garment that is the real reason (about nudity and non nudity).

120. Forgiveness, fortitude, non-violence, absence of attachment to all (worldly things) and equal indifference to both honour and dishonour—these constitute the excellent covering garment.

121-124. He who smears his limbs (body) with the *Bhasman* and renders them grey in colour, he who mentally meditates on *Bhava* (Śiva), he who takes his bath with *Bhasman*, (becomes free from sins). Even if a person commits thousands of misdeeds and takes an ash-bath, the *Bhasman* burns all the sins, just like fire that burns a forest by means of its refulgence. Hence, if a person exerts himself always and takes Ash-bath three times a day, he attains *Gāṇapatya* (the state of being a follower of Gaṇapati). After performing all kinds of *Kratus* (sacrifices), after taking in the excellent nectar if the people meditate on Mahādeva, if they merge themselves (in him) and are sanctified by identifying themselves with him, they shall attain immortality (*Mokṣa*) through the northern path.

125-126. Those who, through the Southern Path, resort to the cremation ground, attain all these supernatural powers viz.—*Aṇimā* (minuteness), *Mahimā* (greatness) *Laghimā* (lightness), *Prāpti* (ability to reach things), *Garimā* (heaviness), the fifth quality, *Prākāmyam* (freedom of will), *Īśitva* (Masterliness), *Vaśitva* (ability to control) and *Amaratva* (immortality).

127-129. Indra and other Devas performed *Kāmika* (conducive to the attainment of desires) holy rites and became persons of well-known splendour after attaining great *Aiśvarya* (prosperity and power).

All of you be free from arrogance and delusion and devoid of passion; let your conduct be free from the defects of *Tamas* and *Rajas*. Understand this excellent holy rite that attacks all sins. Perform this vrata which is a great favourite of Paśupati (Śiva).

If anyone reads this with purity, faith and control of the sense-organs he shall become purified in soul and rid of all sins. He goes to the world of Rudra.

CHAPTER TWENTYEIGHT

Meeting of Pururavas and Pitṛs
Performance of annual obsequies on the New Moon Day

The sage said :—

1. O Sūta ! King Pururavas, the son of Ilā, used to go to the heaven on the New Moon day in every month. How was it ? How did he propitiate the Pitṛs (Manes).

Sūta said :—

2. O Śāṁśapāyani, I shall narrate his power. I shall narrate the contact of the noble-souled son of Ilā with the sun as well as with the moon.

3-5. I shall tell you about the increase and the decrease in the size of the moon that has its essence within, during the two fortnights, the bright one and the dark one. I shall state the decision in regard to one with the Pitṛs (*Pitṛmataḥ*) as well as to one belonging to the Pitṛs (*Pitṛyasya*). I shall narrate the acquisition of nectar from the moon as well as the propitiation of the Pitṛs; I shall mention the sight of the Pitṛs viz. the Kāvyas, the Agniṣvāttas and the Saumyas. I shall mention how Pururavas propitiated the Pitṛs. I shall mention all these in due order as well as the Parvans.

6. When the sun and the moon come into contact with the star, they stay in Amāvāsyā (New Moon) for a night in the same zone.

7. Then during every new moon day, he (Pururavas) goes to see the sun-god and the moon-god, his natural and paternal grandfathers.

8. After paying respects to them, he waits there biding his time. He waits for the exudations of nectar from the following moon, for the sake of the Pitṛs.

9. With a desire to perform the monthly Śrāddha, Pururavas, the learned son of Ilā, worships Soma (the Moon) Pitṛmān (one with the Pitṛs), after resorting to the heaven.

10-11. He considers both *Kuhū* (the New Moon merged with the 1st Tithi of the next fortnight) and Sinīvālī (New Moon mixed with the 14th Tithi). He worships Kuhū when there are two *Lavas** of it as balance. He worships Sinīvālī in accordance with the magnitude of the digit (of the moon). After worshipping it, he bides his time and surveys.

12-14. He imbibes the nectar oozing out from the moon for the sake of satisfaction for the whole month, by means of fifteen exudations of the nectar. During the dark fortnight when his arms get burned by (the Sun's) rays** (he pacifies them) by means of honey exuding from the moon immediately. During the fortnights when there are no winds***(?)the leading king propitiates the Pitṛs in the heaven, in accordance with the injunction pertaining to the rite for Pitṛs.

15. He propitiates the Pitṛs viz. Saumyas, Barhiṣads, Kāvyas and Agniṣvāttas.[1]

---

* *Lava*—a minute division of time (=the sixth part of twinkling of the eye).

** Here Bd.P.V.13a reads:

kṛṣṇa-pakṣe bhujām prītyā dahyamānaṁ tathāṁśubhiḥ /

This is obscure (to say the least). For this line Vā.P.56.12a reads:

kṛṣṇa-pakṣe tadā pītvā duhyamānam tathāṁśubhiḥ /

'Then, in the dark half of the month, having drunk (nectar) as it was being milked by the rays in that manner'.

***Bd.P. 14. a reads *nirvāteṣvatha pakṣeṣu* 'In windless fortnights' is meaningless. Vā. P. 56.13a reads instead: *nirvāpaṇārthaṁ dattena* 'given as oblation to (for the propitiation of) Pitṛs.

1. In Śatapatha Br. II 6. 1.7, those who performed a Soma sacrifice are *Somavantaḥ Pitaraḥ* (probably Saumyas here-of); those who offered cooked oblations like *Caru* were Barhiṣadaḥ Pitaraḥ; those who offered no sacrifice

*Ṛtam** (means) what is mentioned as Agni. It is considered to be Saṁvatsara.

16. The *Ṛtus* (seasons) were born of it (i.e. Saṁvatsara—the year). The *Ārtavas* were born of the Ṛtus. The *Ārtavas* are what are called *Ardhamāsas* (half months or fortnights). (Hence) the *Pitṛs* are the sons of *Ṛtus*.

17. The *Ṛtus* are grand-fathers. The *Māsas* (months) and *Ayanas* (transits of the sun) are the sons of *Abda* (year). The Devas are the great-grand-fathers; the (group of) five years are the sons of Brahmā.

18. The *Saumyas* should be known as born of the moon (*Somaja*). The Kāvyas should be known as the sons of Kavi (Śukra). Upahūtas are remembered as Devas. *Somajas* are remembered as *Somapās* (Imbibers of Soma)·

19. *Ājyapās* (Imbibers of oblated ghee) are remembered as Kāvyas. The classes of *Pitṛs* are three. They are of three classes namely Kāvyas, Barhiṣads and Agniṣvāttas.

20-22. Those who are householders as well as *Yajvās* (performers of sacrifices) are certainly *Ṛtus* and *Barhiṣads*. Those who are householders but are not *Yajvās* (performers of sacrifices) are the *Ārtavas* and *Agniṣvāttas*. The Kāvyas are Aṣṭakāpatis (lords of Aṣṭakas or the eighth day of the lunar fortnights for three months in which Pitṛs are to be propitiated). Now understand the five *Abdas* thereof.

Their *Saṁvatsara* is indeed Agni and Sūrya (the Sun) is *Parivatsara*. Soma (the Moon) is mentioned *Idvatsara* and Vāyu

---

but were consumed by fire in cremation after death were Agniṣvāttāḥ Pitaraḥ. Cf. Vā. P. 30. 6-7.

Later, during the Smṛti period, the classes of Pitṛs increased and had different connotations. Thus here in VV. 18-23 *Saumyas* are sons of Soma and imbibers of Soma. Householders performing sacrifices are *Ṛtus* and *Barhiṣads*.The non-performers of sacrifices are *Ārtavas* and *Agniṣvāttas*. It adds one more division viz. *Kāvyas*, the sons of Kavi (Śukra?) who imbibe ghee vide VV. 72-73 below.

For more details of this classification vide *infra II.* iii 10 VV. 53, 75, 93 and 96.

* The reading *ṛturagnis tu* in Vā P. 56.14.a is preferable to *ṛtamagnis tu* hereof, as *ṛtu* (seasons of the year) are considered as Pitṛ (vide *Taittirīya Brāhmaṇa* I.4.10.8.

is *Anuvatsara.* Rudra is *Vatsara* unto them. Those five *Abdas* constitute a Yuga.

23. Those (*Pitṛs*) who imbibe the nectar in the heaven every month on the new moon day, are remembered as Kāvyas Ūṣmapās and Divākīrtyas.

24-25. As long as Pururavas was alive, he propitiated them with the nectar, since it exudes from the moon every month and it delights them, it is nectar unto the Somapāyin Pitṛs, (those who imbibe Soma—the moon). Thus it is called Saumya Amṛta (nectar pertaining to the moon), *Sudhā* and *Madhu* (honey).

26. Thirtythree Devas (who are called) *Cchedanas** (Those who cut off ?) drink the fifteen digits of the moon gradually in the dark fortnight, (after turning them) into watery form.

27-30. After drinking the nectar for half a month, they go away on the Caturdaśī (fourteenth) day.

On being drunk thus by all the Devas, the moon reaches a point on the New Moon day when it remains with only a fifteenth part. On the New Moon day, it is developed by Suṣumnā duly.[1] Then, for a period of two *Lavas*, the Pitṛs drink the nectar. With a single ray (i.e. the Suṣumnā) the sun develops the moon when it becomes reduced on being drunk. Again the *Somapāyins* drink it. When all the digits are exhausted (the sun) develops the moon once again.

31. Day by day, in due order, a part (a digit) of the moon is developed by the Suṣumnā. The black digits become reduced and the white ones develop it.

32. Thus the body of the moon developed by the vigour of the sun, appears sparkling, white and perfectly circular on the full Moon day.

33. Thus, such is the achievement of the Moon during the two halves, the dark and the bright ones. It is in this manner that the Moon is Pitṛmān (one with the Manes). He is remembered as being *Idvatsara.*

---

* Probably a misprint for *Chanda-jāḥ* 'born of *Chandas*, Veda or prosody'. Cf. Vā. P. 56.25a.

1. Vide *Supra* ch. XXIV, VV. 67-68.

34. He is shining and resplendent with his fifteen exudations of nectar.

Henceforth, I shall recount the *Parvans* (days of changes of the moon) and the *Sandhis* (meeting points) of *Parvans.*

35. Just as there are knotty joints in the Sugarcane and bamboo, so also there are dark and bright *Parvans* in the lunar fortnights.

36. The differences between the full Moon and the New Moon are the knots and joints. The lunar days beginning with *Dvitīyā* constituting the fortnight are the *Parvans.*

37. It is on the first of the fortnights that the rite of *Anvādhāna* is performed. Hence, the *Pratipat* is at the beginning (the first) of all Parvans.

38. The period of two *Lavas* in the evening at the beginning of *Anumati* (the 15th day—the Pūrṇimā mixed with the 14th *Tithi*) is called *Dvilava.* When the Pūrṇimā is mixed with the *Pratipad*—the next Tithi, the period of two Lavas on that Full moon night* should be known as *Aparāhṇa.*

39. The period of evening after Aparāhṇa that has elapsed on the first day of the dark half, is also accepted as part of Paurṇamāsī (Full Moon?)

40-41. When the sun is stationed at a deviation of half meridian (?) line, at a distance of a Yuga (Yoke) and when the meridian of the moon has risen by the distance of a Yoke (Yuga) that period is called Vyatīpāta. This is because (the sun and the moon) glance at each other after the elapse of the full Moon (period) and at that time they are on a par with each other.[1]

42. On seeing that period indicated by the sun, (the worshipper) moves towards enumeration (?) That is the period for Vaṣaṭkriyā. The period is laid down immediately.

43-44. The junction at night in the full fortnight of the full moon is also *Pūrṇimā* (full Moon). Hence, during the night

---

* *rākāyāḥ* (of the Rākā) of Vā.P.56.35 for *rākāyām* here-of is preferable.

1. The text is a bit obscure but *Sūryasiddhānta* XI. 1-2 defines Vyatīpāta more clearly: "When the moon and the sun are on opposite sides of either solstice and their minutes of declination are the same, it is Vyatīpāta, The sum of their longitudes is half a circle i.e. 180°. Normally there are 13 *vyatīpātas* in a year.

of full Moon, the moon becomes very reddish or (pleasing (?) *Virajyate*).

Since during the after-noon when the *Vyatipāta* is full, the moon and the sun in full-fledged form glance at each other, it is called Pūrṇimā.

45. Since the Pitṛs along with the Devas approve of it, the period previous (?) to the Pūrṇimā (i.e. the 14th Tithi with which it is mixed) is remembered as *Anumati.*

46. The full Moon day is called *Rākā* because at that time the moon shines very splendidly in the sky. Wise people say that it is *Rākā* because of the delightful nature (*Rañjanāt*) of the Moon.

47. When the moon and the sun stay in the same star together (*amā*—close to, near by) on the fifteenth night from *Rākā* (the full moon day) it is regarded as Amāvāsyā.

48. After ending or separating (?) that Amāvāsyā day, the sun and the moon see each other after coming together. When this happens it is called *Darśa* (the New Moon day).

49. (Defective Text upon 59).

On the *Amāvāsyā* (New Moon) day the period is of two Lavas in the junction of the 15th and the 1st day of a lunar fortnight. It is of the duration (of pronouncing) two letters Ku-hu. There are three periodic changes of the moon.*

50. The period when the moon vanishes is Amāvāsyā and it functions from the midday. The moon reaches the sun in half a day and the night.

51-52.** Along with the sun it goes to the *Sāmudra* period which is in between *Kuhu* and *sinīvālī* in the morning. The periods of contact are two. Invariably it occurs a Midday (?).

53. On the *Pratipat* day of the bright half, when the discs of the sun and the moon are being separated, it is the time for *Āhuti* (oblating of ghee into fire) and the *Vaṣaṭkriyā* of

---

* *amāvāsyā* which mixed with the *pratipad* of the next fortnight is called *Kuhu.*

** The text is defective and obscure. *saṅgama* in V.51b is probably *Saṅgava.* 'the second division of the day'. Vā.P.46b (if taken for 51a hereof) reads *sūryeṇa sahasā muktaṁ gatvā Prātastanotsavau.*

Darśa (the New Moon). Amāvāsyā should be known as the *Ṛtumukha* (the face of the season) of this Parvan.

54. When the moon wastes away during the dark half, Amāvāsyā is a Parvan by day time. That is why the sun is eclipsed (*Gṛhyate*—is caught) during the day time on the Amāvāsyā day.

55-56. It is eclipsed during the day. Therefore, Amāvāsyā becomes reduced by day (?). The names of the days of the lunar fortnight have been fixed by the scholars in accordance with the increase of the digits of the Moon of watery nature. Then both the moon and the sun reveal themselves.

57. By that path alone it (? the moom) comes out of the solar sphere gradually. The moon touches (remains in contact with) the sun for the whole of the day and night except for a period of two *Lavas*.

58. That period of *Darśa* is the time for *Āhuti* and *Vaṣaṭkriyā* offering of oblation with the utterence vaṣat. The period comes to an end (within which) the cry *Ku-hū* is uttered by a cuckoo.

59. Amāvāsyā measured by that time is declared as *Ku-hū*. The magnitude of Sinīvālī is that period of the moon which remains after the moon has decreased in size.

60-61. The sun enters the Amāvāsyā. Therefore, it is remembered as *Sinīvālī*. The period for these except *Ku hu* is a period of two *Lavas for Anumati*, Rākā and *Sinīvālī*. *Ku-hu* is remembered as having (only the time necessary for the cuckoo to utter) *Ku-hu*.

62. When, in the middle of Pūrṇimā the Vyatīpāta (deviation) of the moon and the sun has come together, it is accepted as *Pratipat*. It is a period of Parvan extending to the *Mātrās*. That is also the period in the middle of *Ku-hu* and *Sinīvālī* which is called *Sāmudra* (spot or mark) (?).

63-67. (Partly defective text). The period of Parvan in the sphere of the sun and the fire and the moon is on a par with the digits (*Kalāsama**— (?) when the digits are equal).

---

* *Kalāśrayaḥ* 'dependent on Kalās' in Vā P. 56.58.

Thus in the bright half, during the night, at the joints of the parvans the glorious moon in a perfect circle is eclipsed. Since the moon is replenished, the Pūrṇimā is on the fifteenth digits added on gradually day by day. Hence, fifteen digits (are acquired) by the moon and the sixteenth digit is its own.

Hence, the (complete) wastage of the waters (?) of the moon takes place on the fifteenth night.

Thus, there are the pitṛs, Devas, Somapās, Somavardhanas, Ārtavas and Ṛtus. The flourishing and prosperous Devas worship them.

Henceforth, I shall describe the Pitṛs who are the partakers of the monthly Śrāddhas.

68-70. (I shall also describe) their movement and the acquisition of the Śrāddha along with its principles.

It is not possible to understand the movement, to and fro, of the dead persons even by means of well-known austerities. How then can it be understood by means of the physical eye ?

These *Laukika* (worldly) Pitṛs are remembered after the Devapitṛs (divine Manes).

The Devas are Saumyas, Kāvyas, Ayajvans and Ayonijas.[1] All those Pitṛs are Devas. The real Devas make them speak.

71. The human Pitṛs are those other than they and they are remembered as *Laukikas* namely father, grandfather and the great-grandfather

72. Those who perform Yajñas by means of Sāman Mantras are remembered as *Somavants*. Those who perform *Haviryajñas* are remembered as *Barhiṣads*.

73. The *Homins* (those who perform *homas*) who perform Yajñas on behalf of *Ayājyas* (those unworthy of Yajñas) are remembered as *Agniṣvāttas*. The *Sāyujyagas* (those who attain the salvation of complete identity) are also remembered among them by the Brāhmaṇas on account of the similarity in *Dharmas* (holy rites).

---

1. As per Vā. P. 56-64, these classes of Pitṛs are not born from a womb (*ayonija*)

74. Those who are well-versed in the paths of the holy duties pertaining to their *Āśramas* (stages in life) and are endowed with faith in rituals do not become weary and exhausted in the end (i.e. at the times of death).

75-78. If the devotees are engaged in these holy rites till their death in seven ways viz. penance, celibacy, Yajña, progeny Śrāddha, learning and charitable gifts, they go to heaven and rejoice there along with those Devas, Pitṛs, Sūkṣmajas (subtle-borns) and *Somayājins* (those who perform Soma sacrifices). They perform worships like the Pitṛs. If water libation is offered by the members of their families and their kinsmen, (the Pitṛs known as) *Somalaukikas* partake of monthly Śrāddhas and become contented. These (Pitṛs) who partake of monthly Śrāddhas are *Manuṣyapitṛs* (Human Manes).

79-86. There are some Pitṛs other than these. They are entangled in births due to their Karmans. They only have dropped off from the duties of the Āśramas; those who are devoid of Svadhā and Svāhā; wicked souls with bodies pierced; those who have become ghosts in the abode of Yama; those who bewail their evil actions after reaching the place of torture; long-lived ones; extremely dried ones; those with moustaches; those without garments; those who are overwhelmed with hunger and thirst; those who run about here and there; those who wish to approach rivers, lakes, tanks and wells; those who are desirous of taking away others' foodstuffs; those who are being taken away to different places; those who are being made to fall in different places; those who undergo tortures again and again in the following hells viz. *Śālmala, Vaitaraṇī, Kumbhī-pāka, Karambhavālukā, Asipatra-vana* and *Śilā-Sampeṣaṇa* due to their own previous actions. These miserable Pitṛs remaining there do not perish. If three Piṇḍas (Balls of rice) are given to them on Darbha grasses not by the left (i.e. by the right) by their kinsmen on the ground by reciting their names and Gotras (lineage) they delight those Pitṛs who are stationed in the places of ghosts.

87. Those who do not reach the place of torture, those who fall and drop down in five ways attain the state of

immobile beings. At the end of that they are born in low families on account of their own actions.

88-91. They are born in wombs of different forms in the animal kingdom or they are born in a manner unapproved in religious texts. If they offer Śrāddha in the different Births by means of those articles of diet which they themselves subsist by, that Śrāddha becomes fruitful. Wherever the creature lives, it acquires food in accordance with what had been offered (as Śrāddha previously) at the proper time, duly to deserving persons.[1]

Just as the calf finds out its mother-cow even when the cows are lost (i.e. when many cows are tethered together) so also the Mantra takes to the Pitṛs the food-stuff offered in the Śrāddha.

It is in this manner that Śrāddha duly and faithfully offered by means of Mantras is not fruitless.

92. Kumāra (god Skanda) recounted these different things after seeing them with his divine eyes. He is conversant with the departures and arrivals of the dead ones as well as the acquisition of Śrāddha by them.

93. They are remembered as Bāhlīkas, Uṣmapās and Divākīrtyas. The dark fortnight is their day and the bright fortnight is the night for their sleep.

94. Thus these Pitṛs are Devas and the Devas are the Pitṛs. The Ṛtus (seasons), Ārtavas and Ardhamāsas (half months) are remembered as Pitṛs mutually.

95. Thus these Pitṛs, Devas and human Pitṛs become pleased when the holy rites are accompanied by faith. When they are pleased the descendants also are pleased.

96. Thus this search for and investigation into the nature of the Pitṛs who imbibe Soma (has been completed). It is this principle of the Pitṛs that has been decisively recounted in the Purāṇas.

97-100. The period of the Full Moon and the New Moon and the place of torture have been succinctly recounted to you. This is the eternal creation.

---

1. VV. 88-91 justify the performance of Śrāddhas.

The Universal form of creation has been mentioned only partially. It is impossible to enumerate in full. It should be trusted faithfully by one who wishes for prosperity.

Indeed, this creation of Svāyaṁbhuva Manu has been begun by me and narrated in detail and in accordance with the sequence.

What more shall I describe to you ?

CHAPTER TWENYNINE

Cycle of Yugas : Characteristics of Yugas[1]

The sage said:—

1. I wish to hear about the nature and principle (or reality) of those sets of four Yugas, which were before in the Svāyambhuva Manvantara.

Sūta said:—

2. What I have already described in the context of (the description of) the Earth etc, the set of four Yugas is among them. I shall recount it. (All of you listen and) understand.

3-4. There are six aspects to be mentioned in regard to the set of four Yugas. viz. Yuga, the difference of Yugas,

1. Though this Purāṇa followed the vedic tradition and regarded a Yuga-period as consisting of five years (vide *Supra* ch. 21.131-132 and Note thereon), here the author follows Manu 1.61-74, 79-86. According to him the 1st Yuga, *Kṛta* extends over 4000 years of gods with a twilight period (*sandhyā*) of 400 Divine (of god's) years before its actual advent and a transitional period to the next Yuga (Sandhyāṁśa) of 400 celestial years. The three other Yugas viz Tretā, Dvapara and Kali consist respectively of a period of 3000, 2000 and 1000 divine years preceded by and followed by *Sandhyā* and *Sandhyāṁśa* each extending over a period of 300, 200 and 100 gods' years. This theory is adopted by Purāṇas e.g. KP. I. chs 51 and 53, NP. I. ch. 41, Mbh. Vana chs 149, 188, VP. I. 3, Vā. P. chs 21, 22, 57, 58.

Yugadharma (peculiar characteristics of the Yuga), *Yuga-Sandhi*, (the junction of Yugas), *Yugāṁśaka* (the part of the Yuga) and the *Yugasandhāna* (joints of two Yugas). I shall narrate these factually in details. I shall enumerate every thing and I shall indicate the exact number (where necessary).

5. After calculating the human year by means of worldly reckoning, I shall mention the set of four Yugas calculating the same by means of human years.

The smallest unit of times is equal to the time taken for a winking.[1] The time for the utterance of a short syllable should also be understood the same.

6. Fifteen *Nimeṣas* make one *Kāṣṭhā*. Thirty *Kāṣṭhās* make a *Kalā*. Thirty *Kalās* shall be a *Muhūrta*. The day and the night together consist of thirty *Muhūrtas* and they are equal to each other.

7-8a. It is the sun who divides the human and worldly day and night. There, the day is meant for holy rites and other activities and the night is intended for sleep.

8b-9. A night and a day of the Pitṛs make a (human) month. Their further division is as follows: The dark fortnight is their day and the bright fortnight is their night fot the purpose of sleep. Thirty human months make one month of Pitṛs.

10. Three hundred and sixty human months make one year of the Pitṛs.

---

1. VV. 5-21 give the divisions of Time adopted in calculating Yugas. The smallest unit of time is the period required for winking of the eye and is called *Nimeṣa*:

15 Nimeṣas=Kāṣṭhā; 30 Kāṣṭhās=Kalā
30 Kalās=Muhūrta; 30 Muhūrtas=Day and night
30 days=A Month;=One day (and night) of Pitṛs
30 Human months=1 Month of Pitṛs
360 Human months=1 Year of Pitrs
Human *Uttarāyaṇa* (6 months)=Day of the Devas
Human *Dakṣiṇāyana* (6 months)=Night of Devas
1 Human year=a complete Day (day and night) of Devas
30 Human years=a month of Devas
360 Human years=One year of Devas
3030 Human years=1 Saptarṣi year
9090 Human years=1 Dhruva year
360,000 Human years=1000 Years of gods.

11-12a. A hundred years according to human calculation are considered to be equal to three years and ten months of the Pitṛs.

12b-13. What is remembered as one human year according to worldly calculation is one day and night of the Devas. It has been so decided in the scriptural texts. The divine day and night make one year. Their further division is as follows:

14. The northern transit (of the Sun) is the day and the southern transit is the night (of Devas). The further calculation in regard to the divine night and day is as follows:

15-16. Thirty human years are remembered as a divine month. A hundred human years should be understood to be equal to three divine months and ten divine days. This is remembered as the divine reckoning. Three hundred and sixty years according to human reckoning are glorified as one divine year.

17. A year of the seven sages (Great Bear) is considered to be equal to three thousand and thirty human years.

18. The year of Dhruva is remembered as equal to nine thousand and ninety years according to human calculation.

19. Thirty six thousand years according to the human reckoning should be known as equal to a hundred years. This is remembered as divine reckoning.

20-21. Three hundred and sixty thousand human years constitute a thousand divine years—so say the people who are conversant with numbers and calculation.

22. It is thus that the sages sang about the divine calculation. Now (I shall narrate) the reckoning of the number of Yugas according to the divine calculation.

23. Wise persons and sages have said that there are four Yugas in Bhārata subcontinent.[1] They are Kṛta, Tretā, Dvāpara and Kali.

24. The first one is Kṛtayuga by name. Thereafter, Tretā is mentioned. Then Dvāpara and Kali. One shall reckon these as the Yugas.

---

1. It is strange that Yugas should be restricted to India (Bhārata) only.

25-28. They say that Kṛta Yuga consists of four thousand years. The *Sandhyā* (junction or transition period) consists of so many (i.e. four) hundred years. The part of the junction (with the next Yuga or *Sandhyāṁśa*) is equal to the *Sandhyā* period.

In the other three Yugas also along with their *Sandhyās* and *Sandhyāṁśas* the thousands and the hundreds function under the same principle.

The extent of Tretā and Dvāpara is three thousand and two thousand years in due order. Three hundred and two hundred years constitute the *Sandhyās* and the *Sandhyāṁśas* are also equal to them. Excellent Brāhmaṇas say that Kali Yuga consists of a thousand years. Its *Sandhyā* is one hundred years and *Sandhyāṃśa* is equal to *Śandhyā*.

29. *Yugasaṅkhyā* (the total number of years in all the four Yugas together) is mentioned as twelve thousand (divine) years for the four yugas viz. Kṛta, Tretā, Dvāpara and Kali.

30. In this connection the years are found to be as follows in accordance with the human calculation:[1] I shall mention the number of years in the Kṛta Yuga. Understand it.

31. The Kṛta Yuga consists of one million four hundred and forty thousand human years.

32. The duration of the Tretā Yuga is one million and eighty thousand human years.

33. The duration of the Dvāpara Yuga is seven hundred and twenty thousand human years.

34. Similarly, the duration of the Kali Yuga is three hundred and sixty thousand human years.

---

1. According to this Purāṇa the period of Yugas is as follows:

Yuga	*Years*
Kṛta	1440,000
Tretā	1080,000
Dvāpara	720,000
Kali	360,000
Total	3600,000 Years

with *Sandhyā* and *Sandhyāṁśas* 4320,000 years.

35-36. (Partially defective text).

Excluding the periods of *Sandhayās* and *Sandhyāṁśas* the duration of the four Yugas is three million six hundred thousand human years.

Including the *Sandhyās* and the *Sandhyāṁśas* the duration of the four Yugas is four million three hundred and twenty thousand years according to human reckoning.

37. Thus the sets of four Yugas numbering seventyone are called Manvantara.

38-40. Understand the number of years in the Manvantara. There are three hundred and six million seven hundred and twenty thousand years according to human reckoning in a Manvantara. It is not more. This reckoning of Manvantara is remembered by Brāhmaṇas conversant with calculation. Thus the duration of a Manvantara has been recounted along with the Yugas.

41. The natural* (?) Kṛta Yuga is endowed with four thousand years (?). I shall mention the balance of Tretā as well as Dvāpara and Kali.

42. No matter can be mentioned in two ways simultaneously (?) Though it has come traditionally in due order, these two Yugas have not been recounted to you before.

43-46. It was not recounted because I was too much engrossed in the description of the line of sages.

In the beginning of the Tretā Yuga,[1] Manu and the seven sages expounded the various Dharmas.

The seven sages expounded the following holy rites viz. Śrauta Dharma (the holy rites mentioned in Śrutis) recommended by Brahmā, such as concerning taking a wife and performing Agnihotra. They expounded matter mentioned in Ṛksaṁhitā,

---

* Probably *Prathamam* 'The first' as in Vā.P. 58.38.

1. VV. 43-92 describe the *Yuga-dharma* of the Tretā Yuga: Vedic Mantras and Siddhis of the previous Kalpa which were 'lost' at the end of that Kalpa manifested themselves to sages. The Vedas formed only one undivided Saṁhitā. God Brahmā (re-) established the duties of various castes and stages in life (Varṇāśrama-dharma). The institution of kingship was firmly rooted. It was a covetable picture of a happy society. Cf Mt. P. Ch. 142.

Yajussaṁhitā and Sāmasaṁhitā. These are the holy rites characterised as Śrauta Dharma.

Svāyambhuva Manu expounded the traditional holy rites characterised by customs and conventions. These rites are connected with the conduct of life of the people of different castes and stages of life. He expounded them along with truthfulness, celibacy, learning and austerities.

47-48. In the first Tretā Yuga, those Mantras alongwith *Tāraka* (i.e. *Oṁkāra*) and other examples manifested themselves without any conscious effort or previous knowledge, unto the seven sages and Manu. That is because of the penance performed by them and their saintly endeavour.

49-50. Those *Siddhis* (spiritual powers and achievements) which appeared before the Devas in the first Kalpa, of their own accord (appeared before these also i.e. seven sages and Manu). When the original *Siddhis* ceased to exist, others began to function. Thousands of those Mantras which existed in the Kalpas gone by manifested themselves in their intellect once again.

51. The Ṛk, Yajus, Sāman and Atharvan Mantras were uttered by the seven sages and Manu expounded the Smārta Dharma (Dharma as laid down in Smṛtis).

52. In the beginning of Tretā, the undivided compact Vedas alone were the bridges (i.e. the sole authority) unto Dharma. But owing to the contraction in the period of longevity they are abandoned in the Dvāparas.

53. It is by means of their penance that the sages study the Vedas during Dvāpara, etc. The Vedas are devoid of beginning and end. They are divine. They have been evolved by the selfborn lord before.

54. Though they are the same in meaning, righteousness, holy rites and ancillary subjects, they undergo changes in every Yuga.

55. The Kṣatriyas have *Ārambhas* (enterprises) as their Yajña (sacrifice); the Vaiśyas have Havis (offerings of ghee etc.) for Yajña; the Śūdras have service for Yajña and excellent Brāhmaṇas have Japa (chanting of Mantras) for Yajña.

56. Then, in the Tretā Yuga, people of all castes were

joyous (because) they were well-protected by Dharma. They regularly performed holy rites, and were happy and prosperous.

57. Kṣatriyas obeyed the Brāhmaṇas. The Vaiśyas obeyed the Kṣatriyas. The Śūdras obeyed the Vaiśyas. The people co-operated with one another.

58. Their activities were auspicious; so also were their castes and stages of life. They were pure in the thoughts of the mind, in the utterance of words and in their physical activiry.

59-60. In the Tretā Yuga, the initiation of all activities was never fruitless. It became fulfilled. In the Tretā Yuga, span of life, intelligence, strength, beauty, health and piety were common to all. At that time, Brahmā established different castes and stages in life.

61. Again, the subjects out of delusion kept up those Dharmas(but) with mutual antagonism. They then approached Manu.

62. Svāyambhuva Manu, the Prajāpati (lord of the subjects) saw the reality of situation. After meditation, he begot two sons of Śatarūpā.

63. They were Priyavrata and Uttānapāda. They were the first kings. Thereafter, kings were born. They wielded the staff of Law and Order.

64. Those kings were called *Rājans* because they delighted and pacified the subjects. Those with hidden sins could not be controlled by those kings.

65. Yama, king of Dharma and son of the Sun-god is remembered as their chastiser. The classifications of castes are said to have been begun in the Tretā.

66. It was then that Mantras were gathered together by the sages who were the sons of Brahmā. It was only then that the Yajñas were initiated by the gods.

67-68. In the Svāyambhuva Manvantara, the Yajña was formerly initiated by the Devas by means of all requisites, gathered by Yama and Śukra along with Viśvabhuj and Devendra of great prowess. Truthfulness, chanting of Mantras, penance and charity constitute Dharma in the Tretā.

69. At the end of a thousand Righteous activities, the Dharma of nonviolence begins to function. It is then that heroes are born with great strength and span of life.

70. They had renounced punishments. They were extremely fortunate and highly righteous. They were expounders of Brahman. Their eyes were extensive like the petals of a lotus. They had broad, wide chests and their limbs were well-knit together.

71. The sovereigns of the world in the Tretā Yuga were capable of agonizing even lions; they were extremely vigorous. Their mode of walking was like that of intoxicated elephants. They were great wielders of bow (great experts in archery).

72-73. They were fully equipped with all good characteristics. They were *Nyagrodhaparimaṇḍalas*. The word *Nyagrodha* denotes the two arms. Hence, *Nyagrodha* means *Vyāma* (Extended arms). He whose height extends as much as a Vyāma, he whose girth and height are equal, should be known as *Nyagrodhaparimaṇḍala* (a well-built man).

74. The following seven things viz. a discus, a chariot, a jewel, a spouse, a treasure, a horse and an elephant—these are considered to be the seven jewels of emperors.[1]

75. They say that the following seven are the inanimate jewels of the sovereign over the world, viz. a discus, a chariot, a jewel, a sword. The excellent shield is the fifth, the flag and the treasure.

76. (The seven jewels of an Emperor) having life are mentioned as follows : The Queen, the family priest, the commander-in-chief, the chariot-maker, the minister, the horse and the elephant.

77. These jewels are divine ones. They have been (naturally) acquired by the noble-souled ones. These fourteen (jewels) should be assigned to all Emperors.

---

1. VV. 74-77 describe two lists of seven 'jewels' of an emperor (*Cakravartin*). Here 14 jewels are mentioned. A similar list of royal jewels is found in Pāli literature. The representation of the 2nd cent B.C. of a *Cakravartin* at Jagayyapetta shows these 'jewels' and one more feature—at the touch of *Cakravarti's* hand above (towards the sky) it shows gold coins.

78. In all the Manvantaras of the past and future, emperors are born on the Earth from a part of Viṣṇu.

79. Emperors are born in the Tretā Yuga of all the Manvantaras of the past, present and future.

80. The following four shall be very wonderful and excellent in regard to those kings :—viz. strength (or army), Dharma (virtue, piety), happiness and wealth.

81. Wealth, dharma, love, fame and victory are acquired by the kings on a par with one another and without coming into conflict.

82. They over-power even the sages by means of Aṇimā (minuteness) and other *Aiśvaryas*, the power of lordship, learning and penance.

83. (They overpower) Devas, Dānavas and human beings by means of strength and austerity.

They are also born with superhuman characteristic features present in their own bodies.

84-86. The hairs are soft and glossy; the foreheads are high; the tongue is one that wipes off clean. The lips and eyes have the lustre of copper; (their chests) are marked with Śrīvatsa scar; the hairs are lifted up.

The arms extend as far as the knees; the hands are copper-coloured. They are slim in the hips; their girth is as much as the extended arms. They have the shoulders of the lion and they urinate like lions.

Their gait is like that of lordly elephants; they have large chin-bones; they have the lines of wheel and fish on the soles of the feet and those of conch and lotus in the palms.

87-89. The kings are eightyfive thousand in number and they shine without ageing.

The movements of the sovereigns in four viz. the sky, the sea, the subterraneous regions and in mountainous region, are unobstructed.

Sacrifice, charity, penance and truthfulness are mentioned as the Dharmas specially significant in the Tretā.

At that time Dharma (Righteousness) begins to function with the classification of castes and stages of life. Daṇḍanīti (Polity, administration of law and order) functions for the establishment of the bounds of decency.

90-92. All the subjects are delighted and well built. They are free from ailments. Their minds are full (i.e they are joyous).

It is remembered that there was only one Veda with four feet (parts) in the Tretā Yuga. At that time men lived upto three thousand years, endowed with sons and grandsons. They used to die in due order. This is the characteristic feature of Tretā Yuga. Understand the Tretā Sandhyā (the transition from Tretā Yuga or junction). The characteristic features are reduced by one-fourth in the Sandhyā from the main Yuga and still further reduced by one-fourth in the *Sadhyāṁśa* from the *Sandhyā*.

CHAPTER THIRTY*

The Inauguration of the Sacrificial Cult
Fall of King Vasu for Denunciation of Sacrifices

Śāṁśapāyani said :—

1. How could Yajña begin to function formerly in the Svāyambhuva Manvantara, at the beginning of the Tretā Yuga. Narrate it factually to me.

2-4. When the *Sandhyā* (the period between two Yugas) elapsed along with the Kṛta Yuga, when (the time unit) called Kāla [kalā] began to function at the advent of Tretā Yuga, when the creation of rain had taken place and (the plants and) the medicinal herbs had grown, when the practice of cultivation and agriculture had been fully established, when the people devoted to the stage of life of a householder established the classification of castes and stages of life with keen insight, then how was Yajña initiated after gathering together all the requisites ?"

---

*This Chapter corresponds to Ch.58.76 ff. of Vā.P.

5. On hearing this Sūta said :—

Let this be heard, O Śāṁśapāyani, how in the beginning of Tretā Yuga, Yajña started functioning.

6-9. I shall recount in the proper order (how Yajña began) formerly in the Svāyambhuva Manvantara.

When the *Sandhyā* the transitional-period (or junction) elapsed along with Kṛta Yuga, when the period called Kāla began to function at the advent of Tretā Yuga, when the creation of rain had taken place and (the plants and) the medicinal herbs had grown, when the practice of cultivation and agriculture had been fully established, when the people became devoted to the life of householders and after establishing the classification of the castes and stages of life, they arranged the *mantras* into a well-knit compendium, they included those Mantras in holy rites (for the sake of welfare) here and hereafter. At that time lord Indra (the enjoyer of the universe) initiated the Yajña.

10. (They started the Yajña) alongwith all the gods and with all the requisites gathered together. The great sages came to his horse-sacrifice which was being lavishly performed.

11-16. All those who had come asked him even as he was performing the Yajña with the animals worthy of being sacrificed.

When the Ṛtviks (sacrificial priests) were busy with their ritualistic fire-worship as the activities concerning the performance of Yajña; when the priests (authorised in) singing the Sāman Mantras had begun their sweet notes; when the leading Adhvaryus (sacrificial priests) had quickly started their proceedings; when all the flocks of the animals (procured for and) worthy of being sacrificed had been cut and struck, when the *Havis* offerings were being poured into the fire by Brāhmaṇas performing Agnihotra; when all the Devas the partakers of the Yajña, had been invoked in the due order—those Devas who are of the nature of *Indriya* (the presiding deities of sense-organs) were the partakers of Yajña—they worshipped those Devas who existed at the beginning of the Kalpa—the great sages, the Adhvaryus, rose up at the time of squeezing and crushing (of the Soma juice). On seeing the miserable flocks of animals, the great sages collectively asked Indra—' "What is the procedure of your Yajña ?[1]

17. This is highly unrighteous and sinful. It (this sacrifice) has been spread (performed) with a desire for rites involving violence to life). In your Yajña, O excellent god, the killing of animals is involved.

18. An evil thing has been started for the destruction of Dharma on account of this injury to the animals. This is not Dharma; it is Adharma (sin). Violence is not called as Dharma (Righteous).

19. If your honour wishes to perform the Yajña in accordance with the scriptures, perform the Yajña by means of Dharma that does not infringe established institutions. Perform the Yajña according to the injunctions laid down (in scriptures).

20-21. O excellent god ! (sacrifice should be performed) with sacrificial seeds which are kept for a maximum period of three years and which do not put forth sprouts. In them (such seeds described above) no violence (to life) exists (is involved). O highly intelligent one, this is the Dharma laid down formerly by Brahmā".

Thus Indra, the enjoyer of the Universe, (was asked) by the sages who perceived reality.

22. Then a great argument took place between Indra and the great sages—" By what means should the Yajña be performed—by mobile (living) beings or immobile articles ?"

23. After stating the principle the great sages became dejected on account of the argument. After coming to terms with Indra, they asked Vasu who was moving about in the firmament.

24. "O king of great intellect, how (what) is the procedure for Yajña found out by you. O lord, son of Uttānapāda, explain and dispel our doubts".

25. On hearing their words, Vasu, without considering the pros and cons recollected the Vedas and Scriptural texts.

1. VV. 16-21 record the Brahmanical protest against animal-sacrifices. They state that the seeds which are 3 years old and incapable of germination should be used instead of animals in sacrifice.

He then explained the principle of Yajña.

26. "Sacrifice should be performed with whatever is duly brought" said the king. 'Sacrifice should be performed by means of animals worthy of being sacrificed or by means of seeds and fruits.

27-29. Violence is but natural to a sacrifice—such is my (opinion) as well as what is mentioned in philosophical texts and scriptures. Just as the Devatās, so also the Mantras, are symbols of violence. This is said by great sages endowed with austerities over a long period, through their philosophical texts and Tāraka and other (Mantras). This has been said on the basis of their authority. Hence, it behoves you all to achieve it provided those Mantras and statements are considered authoritative by you, O Brāhmaṇas, so, let the Yajña be continued and allowed to function. Otherwise, your words will be otherwise (false)".

30. After being answered to in this manner, those saints with souls united with Brahman of unified souls, realized the inevitability and hence restrained their speech.

31. Immediately after saying this, the king entered Rasātala (nether worlds). After being a traverser of the upper regions Vasu (now) came to be a traverser of the netherworlds.[1]

32. By means of that statement he had been a resident of the (nether) surface of the world. King Vasu who tried to dispel doubts in regard to Dharma, went down.

33. Hence, even though one may be conversant with many things, one should not express anything by way of clarification of doubts when alone and single-handed. Dharma has many an opening. Its way is subtle and it goes a long way.

34. Hence, nothing definite can be stated by anyone in the matter of Dharma including the Devas and the sages but excepting Svāyambhuva Manu.

35. Hence, nonviolence has been declared by great sages

---

1. The fall of king Vasu for supporting animal sacrifices showed how that institution of animal sacrifice became condemned at the time of this Purāṇa.

as the gateway to Dharma.[1] Thousands and millions of sages have gone to heaven by means of their own austerities.

36-38. Therefore, the great sages do not praise either charity or Yajña. By giving roots and fruits or greens and vegetables gleaned by them or waterpot in accordance with their capacity, many ascetics have become well-established in the heavenly world.

Non-harassment, absence of greed, penance, mercy to the living beings, control of sense-organs, celibacy, truthfulness, tenderness, forgiveness, fortitude—these are the roots of the eternal Dharma, but they are very difficult to achieve.

39-41. It is heard (traditionally) that many sinless Brāhmaṇas, Kṣatriyas and others have achieved spiritual power by means of penance. They are Priyavrata, Uttānapāda, Dhruva, Medhātithi, Vasu, Sudhāman, Virajas, Śaṅkha, Pāṇḍyaja, Prācīnabarhiṣ, Parjanya, Havirdhāna and other kings. These and many others have gone to heaven by means of their austerities. They are saintly kings of great inherent strength whose reputation has been firmly established.

42. Hence, by all reasons, penance is superior to Yajña. It is due to his penance that this whole universe had been formerly created by Brahmā.

43. Hence, Yajña does not follow it (penance) anywhere. This (world) is regarded as based on penance.

Articles (of sacrifice) and Mantras are the bases of Yajña. Penance is of the nature of non-intake of food.

44. One attains the Devas by means of Yajña and Vairāja by means of penance. Brahminical holy rites (are achieved) by means of renunciation and the victory over Prakṛti through Vairāgya (absence of passionate attachment).

45-48. One attains *Kaivalya* (salvation) through knowledge. These are declared as five goals.

Thus great argument took place between the Devas and the sages in connection with the functioning of the Yajña formerly during Svāyambhuva Manvantara.

Thereafter, on seeing him (Vasu ?) struck down by means of the power of Dharma, all of them ignored the words of Vasu

1. VV. 35-48 establish the superiority of Jñāna mārga over Karmamārga, including animal sacrifices.

and went away as they came. When the groups of sages departed, the Devas concluded the Yajña. It was thus that Yajña was initiated in the Svāyambhuva Manvantara. Thereafter, this Yajña has been modified along with the Yugas.

CHAPTER THIRTYONE

Narration of the Four Yugas : Castes and Stages of Life

Sūta said :—

1. Henceforth, I shall recount the position of the Dvāpara Age once again[1]. When Tretā Yuga passes by, Dvāpara Sets in.

2. The Siddhi that the subjects had in the Tretā Yuga becomes defunct along with the subjects, when Tretā Yuga elapses at the beginning of Dvāpara.

3. In Dvāpara the mixture and combination of the castes begins to take place among the subjects. All activities are affected adversely (and get inverted).

4. The main activity in Dvāpara is declared as a combination of *Rajas* and *Tamas* with all these viz. the emphasis on Yajñas*, administration of justice, pride, arrogance, forgiveness and strength.

5. The Dharma that had been in existence in the first Kṛta Yuga continues to function in Tretā Yuga. After becoming agitated and intensely affected in Dvāpara, it becomes extinct in the Kali Yuga.

6. In that Yuga, there is utter destruction of (the classification of) the castes. Similarly, the different stages of

1. This chapter depicts the state of the society, religion, religious texts etc. in the Dvāpara Age. The deterioration and confusion of social, religious and other conditions provide a back-ground to the Chaos in the Kali Age.

* Vā. P. 58.4 reads *yācñā vadhaḥ paṇo* 'Begging, killing, gambling' instead of *yajñāvadhāraṇam* in this text.

life get jumbled and mixed up. The Śruti and Smṛti come to be at variance with each other in that Yuga.

7. Owing to the difference between Śruti and Smṛti no definite conclusion can be arrived at. Because of the absence of definiteness, there is no (clear-cut) principle of Dharma.

8-10. Owing to the absence of (a specific) Dharma, there is difference of opinion even among friends. Owing to mutual difference and confusion in the points of view there is no definite conclusion such as "This is Dharma. This is not Dharma."

The confusion in the points of view results from ambiguity and uncertainty of the causes, inconclusiveness in regard to the effects (or decisions) and difference of opinion among the people.

Hence, utter confusion and contradiction is brought about in the scriptural texts by persons with different points of view.

11. It is laid down that there is only a single unified Veda with four feet (i.e. sections, books) in the Tretā Yuga. In view of the fact that there is reduction in the span of life, the Veda is distinctly classified in the Dvāpara age.

12-13. The Saṁhitā texts of Ṛk, Yajus and Sāman are recited by the great sages differently with changes in the settings (arrangements) of Mantra and Brāhmaṇa portions and alterations in the notes, accents and letters. Changes are brought about due to the changes in the (presiding) sages and Mantras and confusion in the view-points. They are similar in certain places and altered utterly in certain places due to difference in the points of view.

14. The Brāhmaṇas, Kalpa-Sūtras and Mantra Pravacanas (different scriptural texts) and other texts as well have a similar plight. Others follow these but some oppose it and stand apart.

15. They begin to function in Dvāpara Age and recede during the Kali Yuga.

There was only one *Ādhvaryava* (Yajur Veda) but later it split into two.

16-18. By means of common and contradictory matters, the whole scriptural text has been confounded.

With the schools of *Ādhvaryava* (Yajur Veda) confused and confounded in various ways, with alternative readings in Atharva, Ṛk and Sāman Mantras, there was a lot of unrest (confusion) in Dvāpara. They had many divisions and sub-divisions and alternatives. They began to function in Dvāpara and became extinct in Kali.

19. Effects of these contrary happenings take place in Dvāpara—effects such as absence of rain, then death and sickness and other calamities.

20. On account of miseries verbal, mental and physical, they have despondency and absence of interest in worldly matters. Due to despondency and dejectedness, they begin to ponder over modes of relief from misery.

21. Through the ponderings they attain disinterestedness in worldly affairs and absence of attachment. Through this detachedness they begin to see defects. Through the sight of defects there is the possibility of *Ajñāna* (ignorance) in Dvāpara.

22. To those *Ajñānins* (ignorant persons) in the first Svāyambhuva Manvantara in the Dvāpara Yuga, enemies of the scriptural texts crop up.

23. There are uncertainties and indecisive alternatives in the science of Āyurveda, in the Aṅgas (ancillary subjects), in the Jyotiṣa (Astronomy and Astrology) in the Arthaśāstra (Economics) and in Hetu-Śāstra (Science of dialectics).

24-26. There are similar alternatives in the Bhāṣyas (commentaries) and Vidyās (learning) of the Prakriyā Sūtras and Kalpa Sūtras (scriptural texts). There are different Smṛti-śāstras (Law Codes etc.) and there are separate *Prasthānas* (Schools and Systems). These occur in the Dvāpara Yuga because of the difference of opinion among men.

It is with very great difficulty that agricultural and other professions flourish (due to the efforts) mental, verbal and physical. In the Dvāpara, it is preceded by great physical strain of all living beings. There is greediness (in the people). The professional activity is primarily commercial. There is no definiteness in the principles.

27-28. There is the composition of scriptural tracts based on Vedas (but) there is mixing and mingling of Dharmas. The discipline of the classification of castes and stages of life come to nought. Lust and anger flourish in Dvāpara. Passion, greed and murder begin to prevail in Dvāpara. It is in Dvāpara that Vyāsa[1] classifies the Veda into four sections.

29-30. When Dvāpara comes to a close, its *Sandhyā* (twilight or transitional period between Dvāpara and Kali Yugas) too functions in the same manner. The characteristic feature of Dvāpara, devoid of good qualities becomes established. In the same manner the *Sandhyāṁśa* also functions.

(Now) Understand (the details) of Kali Yuga[2] on the basis of what remains of Dvāpara.

31-33. The acceptance (of characteristic features etc.) of the Kali age is based on the residue of the *Sandhyāṁśa* of Dvāpara. Violence, jealousy, untruth, Māyā (deception) and murder of ascetics—these are the characteristic features of Kali age. (Of course) the subjects achieve (certain things) and that is the entire Dharma. Dharma declines. It is doubtful whether agricultural activities flourish despite the activities, mental, eulogistic and physical. There are fatal sicknesses in the Kali age and there is the perpetual headache of hunger and fear.

34. There is terrible fear of drought. There are calamities in all the countries. In the Kali age, the Smṛti has no authority (i.e. is not regarded as an authority) over the people.

35. In the Kali age, the subjects die at various ages Some one dies even as a child in the womb. Another dies in the prime of youth. Some people die as old men while some people die during their childhood.

1. Vyāsa, 'arranger' (of Vedic Mantras into different Saṁhitās) is a designation. Every Dvāpara has a different Vyāsa. Purāṇas mention 28 Vyāsas.

2. Almost all Purāṇas depict a gloomy picture of the Kali Age. Vide Mbh. *Vana* ch. 188, 190, Br. P. chs 229-230, Mt. P. 144. 32-47, Bh.P. XII. 1-2, VP. VI.1. It appears that that was probably the state of the society when these Purāṇas came to be written, though unfortunately much of that description applies even today.

36. There is danger and fear unto the subjects owing to wrongly performed sacrifices, negligent studies (of the Vedas), evil actions, misleading religious texts and the faults in the holy rites performed by the Brāhmaṇas.

37. Violence, deception, malicious jealousy, anger, envy and intolerance occur in men in the Kali age. There is passion and greediness everywhere in every creature.

38. After reaching the Kali Yuga a great excitement is aroused At that time, the maximum age is when a thousand years are completed* (?)

39. The twice-born people neither study the Vedas nor worship by Yajñas. Men are annihilated, the Kṣatriyas and the Vaiśyas in due order.

40. At that time, the kings are mainly Śūdras who set in vogue all sorts of heresies. The subjects become devoid of good qualities.

41. Alliances and associations of the Śūdras and *Antya-yonis* (Lowest-born) with Brāhmaṇas take place in the Kali Yuga, in regard to bed, seats and food-stuffs.

42. Span of life, intellect, strength, beauty and prestige of the family dwindle down and become extinct. The Śūdras take to the conduct of life of the Brāhmaṇas and the Brāhmaṇas behave and act like Śūdras.

43. Thieves adopt the customs and conventions of kings, and kings behave and live like thieves. When the close of the Yuga is mminent, it is only these servants who survive.

44. At the close of the Yuga, O excellent sage, the women become false and unfaithful. They misbehave. They become addicted to liquor and meat and become deceitful.

45. At the close of the Yuga, O excellent sage, the faithful wives do not survive. Beasts of prey flourish and the cattle decrease.

46. Know that at the close of that Yuga, good people turn back and keep aloof. Dharma of great consequence rooted in the pious act of charity, is very rare then.

47. Dharma in which there is no strict adherence to the system of four stages of life (but slackness therein) will prevail.

* This line is not found in Vā.P.56.37 which is otherwise identical with this verse.

In some places the land will yield but very little but in some other places it may be excessively fruitful (fertile).

48. The kings will not be protectors but the enjoyers of their share in the offerings (taxes etc.). At the close of the Yuga, they will be eagerly devoted to the act of protecting themselves.

49. Kings will cease to be protectors. Brāhmaṇas will be dependent on Śūdras. All excellent twice-born ones will make obeisance to the Śūdras.

50. The common people begin to sell boiled and cooked rice; the Brāhmaṇas begin to sell the Vedas. Young women begin to sell their bodies when the close of the Yuga is imminent.

51. In this Kali age, even excellent Brāhmaṇas become the sellers of the benefits of their penance and performance of sacrifices. Many people will turn into ascetics.

52. They say that the close of the Yuga is then, when the lord (Indra) begins to shower mysteriously in diverse ways. In the basest of the Yugas, everyone will become a trader.

53. People will begin to sell merchandise through false weights and measures. The whole society will be surrounded by hunter-like people and heretics of evil habits and conduct of life.

54. When the close of the Yuga is imminent, men will be in a minority and there will be majority of women. People will be begging of one another many times.

55. When the Yuga wanes away there will not be anyone who helps in return for another's help. There will not be any one who does not injure and spoil others, whose words are not harsh; who is straight-forward and who is not malicious.

56. When the close of the Yuga sets in, its characteristic feature is apprehension of danger etc. Then the earth will be void without wealth.

57, Rulers will not be protectors though they are (expected) to be protectors. They will take away jewels (and valuables) of others and molest their men's wives.

58. People will be lustful in their minds. They will be evil-minded, base and fool-hardy, addicted to criminal and reckless acts. They will be roguish with all good activities

destroyed. They will keep their hairs loose and untied. They will not be sympathetic.

59-63. At the close of the Yuga, men less than sixteen will be begetting and women less than sixteen will be giving birth to children.

When the close of the Yuga is imminent Śūdras with perfectly white sparkling teeth wearing ochre-coloured robes, with clean shaven heads will subdue their sense-organs and practice piety.[1]

There will be thieves stealing plants and corn, clothes and garments. Some thieves will rob other thieves. There will be a robber taking away valuables from another robber.

When knowledge and holy rites have disappeared, when the whole world has become inactive (in religious matter), worms, rats and serpents will be attacking and harassing men.

Welfare, health and capability will permanently be difficult to obtain.

Countries afflicted by hunger and fear will be eagerly waiting for Kauśikas (persons who can find out hidden treasures). Affected by misery, the maximum span of life will be only hundred years.

64. In the Kali Yuga, all the Vedas are seen and not seen (i.e. not read and understood clearly). Yajñas afflicted only by sins and evils, become spoiled.

65. After the advent of the Kali age, many types of heretics crop up. They may be Buddhists wearing ochre-coloured robes, Jainas, Kāpālikas and others who sell the Vedas. Still others are those who sell holy centres of pilgrimage.

66. There are others who are the enemies of the system and discipline of the castes and stages of life. All these heretics are born when the Kali Age steps in.

67. Then Śūdras become experts in interpreting affairs concerning religious activities and they study the Vedas. Kings

1. Probably a reference to Buddhist *bhikṣus*. There appears to be a dominance of Buddhism when this Purāṇa was written. This is confirmed in VV. 65-66 infra.

born of Śūdras' wombs begin to worship and perform horse-sacrifice.

68. Then the subjects accomplish something either by killing women, children and cows or by killing one another or by robbing one another.

69. The conduct and activity in the Kali age is declared as a *Tāmasa* activity because of too much of affection for sinful deeds. People are short-lived with constant narrations of their own misery. Their bodies are short and lives too are short owing to sickness.

70. At that time the practice of killing children in the womb comes into vogue due to enmity. Hence, span of life, strength and beauty become reduced after the advent of Kali Yuga.

71. At that time, men attain Siddhi within a short time. Blessed and excellent twice-born ones will practise piety and devotion at the close of the Yuga.

72-73. These excellent Brāhmaṇas practise the holy rites laid down in the Śrutis and Smṛtis. They practise without any malice or envy.

In the Tretā, the Dharma practised for the whole of the year bears fruit. It is declared that the same Dharma practised for a month in Dvāpara bears fruit. The intelligent devotee practising the same for a day, attains the desired fruit in the Kali Yuga.[1]

This is the condition in the Kali age. Understand (the state of affairs) in the Sandhyāṁśa (the transitional period between two Yugas).

74-76. Siddhis prevalent during the *Sandhyās* of Yugas become reduced to three-fourths in the following Yugas. Siddhis prevalent in the Yugas become reduced to three-fourths in the following *Sandhyās*. The characteristics of the *Sandhyās* become stabilised in the *Sandhyāṁśas* after being reduced to three-fourths.

Thus when the period of *Sandhyāṁśa* at the end of (a set of four) Yugas arrives, (the lord appears) as their chastiser.

1. This is a relieving feature of the Kali age.

He rises up for the purpose of slaying the wicked Bhṛgus. He is called Pramati[1] and he belongs to the Lunar race.

77-80. In the previous Svāyambhuva Manvantara, he had been born of a part of Mādhava (Viṣṇu).

For a full period of twenty years, he wandered over the Earth taking with him an army along with horses, chariots and elephants. Surrounded by hundreds and thousands of Brāhmaṇas wielding weapons, he killed all the Mlecchas all round alongwith all those kings, the heretics born of Śūdra women. The lord exterminates those heretics. Everywhere he kills all those who are not scrupulously religious.

81-84. The lord who was strong and who annihilated all the Mlecchas slew these also—People who were born of parents of different castes, those who depended on them, the Udīcyas (Northerners), Madhya Deśyas (Persons of middle lands), Parvatīyas (Mountain-dwellers) Prācyas (Easterners), Pratīcyas (Westerners), those who walk about on the ridges of the Vindhya mountains, Dākṣiṇātyas (Southerners), Draviḍas along with Siṁhalas (Ceylonese), Gāndhāras, Pāradas, Pahlavas, Yavanas, Śakas, Tuṣāras, Barbaras, Cīnas (Chinese), Śūlikas, Daradas, Khaśas, Lampā-kāras, Katakas and different tribes of Kirātas. The powerful lord wielding the discus slew all these barbarous people.

85-86. Invisible to all the living beings, he wandered over the whole earth. The lord was born of a part of lord Mādhava. In the former birth he was very valorous and he was well known by the name of Pramati. In the first Kali Yuga, he was born in the Gotra of the moon.

87. He began (the victorious march) when he was aged thirty-two. For twenty years he continued to slay men and all other living beings everywhere.

88-89. Annihilating every thing by his ruthless activity, he made only seeds to remain on the earth. He managed to subdue the Vṛṣalas who were generally sinful, by making them angry

1. This incarnation of Viṣṇu re-established order at the end of Kali Age. Elsewhere (in Mt. P.) he is said to have been born in the Lunar race in the Kali Age in Cākṣuṣa Manvantara. See VV. 85-86 below.

with one another on sudden provocations. Thereafter, in the region between the Gaṅgā and the Yamunā, he established his camp of rest along with his followers.

90. Thereafter, when the Kalpa elapsed, he went back to his eternal abode along with his army after exterminating Mleccha kings by thousands.

91-92. When the period of *Sandhyāṁśa* arrived towards the end of the Yuga, only a few subjects remained here and there. They were unfortunate fellows with planets adverse to them. Many of them were greedy and they collectively struck and injured one another.

93. There was anarchy. When the close of the Yuga was imminent, the subjects were afflicted by mutual fear.

94. They were agitated and bewildered. They left their houses, wives and relatives. They never cared for their lives. (They were not hopeful about their ability to survive). Even without reason, they became very miserable.

95. When the Dharma based on Śruti and Smṛti became extinct, the people killed one another, devoid of bounds of decency, affection, shame and friends and allies.

96. When virtue ceased to exist, the people were afflicted and they were reduced to a size of twentyfive (as against 52 *Aṅgulas* in height). Agitated and distressed they found their sense-organs out of gear. They had to forsake their children and wives (and run away).

97. People oppressed by drought had to abandon their agricultural activities. They were miserable. Leaving their own native lands they began to stay in the bordering districts.

98. They were compelled to resort to rivers, marshy places, near the seas and mountainous regions. Extremely miserable, they sustained themselves by means of meat, roots and fruits.

99. They used to wear leaves, bark-garments or hides of antelopes. They observed no holy rites. They had abandoned their families. They had fallen off from the systematic discipline of the castes and stages of life. They had been adopting the terrible practice of *Saṅkara* (mixing of castes by means of

indiscriminate inter marriage etc.). They had reached such a plight. Only a very few such people survived.

100. They were oppressed with old age, sickness and hunger. Owing to misery, they reached a stage of abject dejectedness. From this dejected state, they reached the state of pondering over the same. Pondering took them to a state of equanimity.

101. Through the state of equanimity, they had the realisation of the Ātman. Through this knowledge, they acquired piety and devotion. Thus those who survived the last stage of the Kali age, acquired tranquility and control of sense.

102. When the close of the Yuga was undergoing transformation, they became quiescent as though they were asleep or inebriated day and night after making the mind enchanted (and insensible).

103-106. Owing to the power of the inevitable future, the Kṛta Yuga set in. When the holy Kṛta Yuga began to function, the subjects pertaining to the Kṛta Yuga were born of those who survived from the Kali Yuga. Those Siddhas who remained then, began to move about invisibly. They established themselves there along with the seven sages. The Brāhmaṇas, the Kṣatriyas, the Vaiśyas and the Śūdras were those, who were remembered as seeds. (They were intended to be the nucleus for the succeeding generation). At that time they became identical with those who were born in (the closing stages of) Kali. They were devoid of any difference. The seven sages recounted Dharma to them as well as to others.

107. That (Dharma) is equipped with the conduct of life of the different castes and stages. It is of two types : *Śrauta* (as laid down in the Vedas) and the *Smārta* (as laid down in the Smṛtis). The object in the Kṛta age remained thus as persons with holy rites.

108. When the Dharmas of *Śrauta* and *Smārta* varieties had been pointed out to the people of Kṛta Yuga, some of them remained till the close of the Yuga for the sake of establishing Dharma.

109-110. The sages remain in authority over the whole of the Manvantara. The grasses of the forests are burned by the forest fires but their roots are unaffected. Just as fresh shoots of grass grow from these roots so also the people of Kṛta Yuga grow from the people of the Kali age.

111. Thus there is an uninterrupted series of Yugas, with the connection of a Yuga with another unbroken, till Manvantara comes to a close.

112. Happiness, span of life, strength, beauty, virtue, wealth and love—these are reduced to three-fourths in each of the succeeding Yugas.

113. The achievement of piety of the Yugas becomes reduced in the *Sandhyāṁśas*. Thus is the *Pratisandhi* (transition between the two Yugas) that had been mentioned by me (before), O Brāhmaṇas.

114-119. By means of this alone should all the sets of four Yugas be reckoned.

This repetition of sets of four Yugas multiplied by a thousand constitutes what is called a day of good Brahmā. The night too is declared as extending to this much period. Here there is straight-forwardness and state of being insentient in all living beings till the end of the Yuga.

This alone is remembered as the characteristic feature of all Yugas. The sets of four Yugas multiplied by seventyone and gradually transformed is called Manvantara.[1] Whatever occurs in one set of four Yugas happens in the others also in the same manner and in the same order.

In the same manner, differences also are produced in every creation. They are restricted to thirty-five and they are remembered as neither less nor more. So also the Kalpas have the same characteristic features as the Yugas. This alone is the characteristic feature of all the Manvantaras.

120. Just as the repetitions of the Yugas had come into vogue since a long time owing to the intrinsic nature of the Yuga, so also the living world (world of living beings) being transformed through decrease and increase does not remain (the same permanently).

---

1. 71 sets of four Yugas constitute a Manvantara. The verses that follow constitute an elucidation of *Dhātā yathāpūrvam akalpayat*. (The creator arranged or created everything as before.)

121-124. Thus the characteristics of all the Yugas, past and future in all the Manvantaras have been mentioned succinctly. Know that, by means of the (discription of) a Manvantara, all the other Manvantaras have been explained and also one Kalpa is described by means of (the description of) another. Similarly in the future ones, inference should be carried out by one who knows. In all the Manvantaras past and future, all the beings are of equal identifications in regard to names and forms.

125. The Devas of eight classes who are the lords in this Manvantara, the sages and the Manus—all these are equal in regard to the purpose (served by them).

126-127. Thus the lord always evolves the classification of castes and stages of life in the former Yugas and arranges the intrinsic features of the Yugas.

The classifications of castes and stages of life, the Yugas and the Siddhis of the Yugas have been recounted as necessary consequence. Now, understand the creation of the *Sṛṣṭi* (Creation of the living beings).

I shall mention the situation in the Yugas in detail and in due order.

CHAPTER THIRTYTWO*

Yugas and Classes of People : Lineage of Sages[1]

Sūta said :

1. Learn from me the different subjects viz. Asuras, Serpents, Gandharvas, Piśācas, Yakṣas and Rākṣasas, that are born in (different) Yugas.

---

* This chapter corresponds to Vā.P.Ch.59.

1. This chapter records the belief that there has been a continuous deterioration in height or physical built and other capacities of all the subjects of creation, be they gods, men or serpents. Archaeological excavations have not substantiated this belief.

2-4. Understand in which Yuga their nativity takes place and how long do they live.

The Piśācas, the Asuras, the Gandharvas, the Yakṣas, the Rākṣasas and the Serpents who are born in the Kṛta Yuga have their height and girth equal.

The height of the joyous divine beings is ninety-six Aṅgulas according to the measure of their own figures. It has become so due to the nourishment (?) It is taken as their natural measure.

5-7. Human beings existing in the *Sandhyāṁśaka* are shorter by seven times seven Aṅgulas than the height of the Devas and Asuras (?)

The height of Devas and Asuras in hundred and fifty eight Aṅgulas is remembered by those born in the Kali age.

It is remembered by persons born in Kali (that their height) from head to foot is eightyfour Aṅgulas of their own fingers.

8. This height of human beings becomes reduced in the *Yugāṁśaka* (transitional period between two Yugas) in all the Yuga periods past and future.

9-10a. Man is regarded to be eight spans high with his own fingers as unit.

He who is nine spans high from head to foot and has arms extending as far as the knees is worshipped even by the Devas (gods).

10b-11a. By means of the same activity* (?) the increase and decrease in the different Yugas of the height of cows, horses, elephants, buffaloes and immobile beings, should be understood.

11b-12a. The hump of the cattle is seventy-six Aṅgulas high. The height of elephants is declared as hundred and eignt Aṅgulas in full.

12b. The height of trees is remembered as a thousand Aṅgulas without forty Aṅgulas and fifty Yavas.**

---

* For *Karmaṇaitena* here-of, Vā.P/59-10 reads *Krameṇaitena* 'in this serial order.'

** One Yava=1/4 Aṅgula.

Therefore the height of trees $=1000-40+12\frac{1}{2}=947\frac{1}{2}$ Aṅgulas.

13-14a. The constitution of the bodies of the Devas is similar to that of the body of human beings. It is realised, if we ponder over reality.

The body that has nothing else to excel it in intellect is called the body of the Devas. So also that which has something to excel it is called human body. Thus have been described the living beings divine and human.

14b-15. The body of Devas is said to be endowed with the excellence of intelligence. Similarly, the body of human beings is also possessed of excellences (of intelligence and others).

16-19. The beings—animals, birds and immobile ones—are useful ones. For example—the cows, the goats, the sheep, the horses, the elephants, the birds and the trees—these are useful in holy rites. Hence, they are worthy of Yajñas in every respect. They are born in the abodes of gods. Hence, they are of the same form.

The auspicious forms of the Devas are such as could enjoy as they wished. They became happy with those charming beings mobile and immobile and befitting their own forms and magnitude. Henceforth, I shall narrate the remaining ones called as *sats* and *Sādhus* (good ones).

20. The word *Sat* indicates the Brahman.[1] Those who possess it are called *Sants* due to their similarity with the *Brahman*.

21 Those who neither become angry nor are too overjoyed in regard to those ten objects of (ten) sense-organs (i.e. five pertaining to the sense-organs and five to the organs of physical activity) and eight varieties of causes—are called *jitātmans* (those who have conquered their own selves).

22. Inasmuch as Brāhmaṇas, Kṣattriyas and Vaiśyas are engaged in general religious rites as well as in special rites, they are the twice-born castes.

23. One who adheres to the religious duties prescribed for one's caste and stage of life and one who is happy in practis-

1. VV. 20-26 give the characteristics of saints, sādhus and knowers of Dharma.

ing the path to heaven (?) is called a knower of Dharma (*Dharmajña*) due to his knowledge of the Dharma as enjoined in Śruti (Vadas) and Smṛtis.

24. A religious student who works for the welfare of his preceptor is called *Sādhu* (good one) because he strives for the achievement of learning. A house-holder is called *Sādhu* because he gathers together the requisites for his house-hold.

25. A *Vaikhānasa* (forest-hermit) is declared as *Sādhu* because he achieves power of penance in the forest. The striving recluse is remembered as *Sādhu* because he accumulates and achieves Yogic power.

26. Thus the religious student, the householder, the forest-dwelling hermit and the recluse are all called as *Sādhus* because they achieve the Dharmas of their respective stages of life.

27. Neither the Devas nor the Pitṛs, neither the sages nor the human beings understand the point "This is Dharma—This is not", because of different points of view (?)

28. The words Dharma and Adharma mentioned here refer to the rites.[1] Auspicious rite is remembered as Dharma. Inauspicious rite is declared as Adharma.

29. The root √*Dhṛ* is used in the sense of Dhāraṇa (Holding, Sustaining) and (Dharma means that which sustains us). In the sense of *Adhāraṇa* (non-sustenance) and *Amahatva* (Non-greatness) the word Adharma is mentioned.

30. That Dharma which takes us to what we desire (and what is good for us) is taught by the preceptors. It is also taught by the preceptors that Adharma has adverse and undesirable fruits.

31. They call these persons Ācāryas[2] (preceptors) viz.—old men devoid of greadiness, Self-possessed persons devoid of arrogance and straight-forward persons who have been educated and well disciplined.

---

1. VV. 28--30 and 33-36 explain the concept of Dharma and what is Śrauta and Smārta Dharma? A detailed elucidation of various virtues constituting Dharma are given in VV. 43-57.

2. VV. 31-32 mention the qualifications of an Ācārya (preceptor).

32. He himself practices (Dharma). He establishes the code of good behaviour and he gathers together (and masters) the various scriptural texts—he is therefore, called *Ācārya*.

33-34. Two types of Dharma have been laid down by Brāhmaṇas conversant with Dharma viz. *Śrauta* and *Smārta*.

Śrauta Dharma pertains to marriage rites as well as (adoption of) Agnihotra worship.

The *Smārta Dharma* pertains to the conduct of life of people of different castes and stages of life, *Yamas* (controls of the sense-organs) and *Niyamas* (observances). After learning from the previous persons (or after instructing the previous ones) the seven sages expounded the *Śrauta Dharma*.

35. The Ṛk, Yajus and the Sāman constitute the Śruti. They are the limbs of the Veda. It was after remembering the code of conduct of life in the previous Manvantara that Manu expounded his Smṛti.

36. Hence, *Smārta Dharma* is declared as the Dharma that differentiates the castes and stages of life. These different types of Dharma are called *Śiṣṭācāra*.

37-39. The word *Śiṣṭa* is derived from the word *Śeṣa* (Remainder). They call what remains by the word *Śiṣṭa*.

Those righteous persons who survived in the Manvantara and continued to stay were Manu and the seven sages. They remained there for sustaining the worlds. Those who remain for the sake of Dharma are called Śiṣṭas. In every yuga, this Dharma has been practised very well by the *Śiṣṭas* (survivors) viz. Manu and others who have already been referred to by me before.

40. The study of the three Vedas, agricultural operation, administration of justice, performance of sacrifice, special duties of the people of different castes and stages of life are practised by *Śiṣṭas* again and again.

41-43a. Since they have been practised by the previous persons they are *Śiṣṭācāra* and righteous activity as well.[1]

The following eight meritorious activities also are characteristically *Śiṣṭācāra* viz. charitable offerings, truthfulness, auste-

---

1. VV. 37-43 give a peculiar definition of Śiṣṭas and explanation of *Śiṣṭācāra*. The identification of *Śiṣṭācāra* with Dharma is in V. 57. Manu XII.109 and Vasiṣṭha. VI. 143 define *śiṣṭācāra* differently.

rity, knowledge, learning, sacrifice, renunciation (of the world) and departure from one's household and sympathy. Since the *Śiṣṭas* (the remaining ones, or the well-disciplined ones), Manu and the seven sages practise these in all the Manvantaras, they are, therefore, declared as *Śiṣṭācāra*.

43b-44. It should be known that a Dharma is called Śrauta if it is traced to the Śruti. It is called Smārta if it is traced to the Smṛti. That which refers to sacrifice and Vedas, is called Śrauta Dharma and that which concerns the activities and duties of the people of different castes of life is called Smārta.

I shall mention the characteristic features of Dharma with regard to each part.

45. This is the characteristic sign of truthfulness viz. After seeing an event and on being asked, he (a person) does not conceal the fact and states it exactly as it has happened.

46. Celibacy, chanting of Mantras, vow of silence and observance of fast—these constitute the form of *Tapas* (Penance). It is extremely terrible and very difficult to achieve.

47. The collection of sacrificial materials, *Havis* (ghee) offerings, Ṛk, Sāman and Yajur Mantras, Ṛtviks (sacrificial priests) and *Dakṣiṇās* (monetary gifts and fees) is called Yajña.

48. The perfect vision of impartiality between oneself and all living beings whether for welfare or distress—is remembered as *Dayā* (Mercy, Sympathy).

49. If a person, on being scolded or struck does not scold or strike in retaliation either verbally, mentally or physically—this attitude is remembered as *Titikṣā* (forbearance) and Kṣamā (patience).

50. Refraining from taking other man's belongings well protected by their owners but abandoned in their excitement, is glorified as *Alobha* (absence of greed).

51. Non-indulgence in sexual intercourse, absence of thought thereof, avoidance of prattling about it, receding from all activities (connected with it is *Brahmacarya* (celibacy). It is called a penance without any vulnerable point.

52. If man's sense-organs do not function falsely either for his own sake or for others' sake that is the sign of *Śama* Quiescence and Restraint of passions).

53. If a person is obstructed (and hence disappointed) in regard to the object of sense-organs (i.e. five sense-organs and five organs of action) or eight-fold causes, but he does not become infuriated, he is considered to be *Jitātman* (one who has conquered his own self).

54. If a person feels that he must give away unto a deserving person whatever is desired most by him, or the money that has come down to him duly and justly, that is the characteristic sign of *Dāna* (charitable offering).

55-56a. *Dāna* is of three types, *Kaniṣṭha* (base) *Jyeṣṭha* (superior) and *Madhyama* (middling). Among them, that which is conducive to salvation is the superior one. That which is only for the sake of achieving ones' own selfish ends is the base one. Sharing (of one's possessions) with all living beings out of sympathy is the middling.

56b-57a. The Dharma regarding the discipline of the four castes and stages of life is laid down by the Śrutis and Smṛtis. What is not antagonistic to *Śiṣṭācāra* (the practice of well-disciplined cultured people) is also Dharma, approved by good learned men.

57b-58. Absence of hatred toward what is not liked by one, approval of what is (desirable and) desired, and turning away from pleasure, excessive agony and distress is *Viraktatā* (absence of passion).

Relinquishing of all committed actions along with the omitted ones is called *Sannyāsa* (Renunciation).

59-61a. (Defective Text). Giving up of both auspicious and inauspicious activities is called *Nyāsa* or (Relinquishment. Unmanifest particular things are Vikāras (Transformations) in the matter of insentient objects (?) Perfect understanding of the distinctness of the sentient and the insentient, is called *Jñāna* (Knowledge). These are remembered as the characteristic features of different parts of Dharma by sages conversant with the principles of Dharma, in the previous Svāyambhuva Manvantara.

61b-62. I shall describe unto you the procedure of Manvantara as well as *Cāturhotra and Cāturvidya* (Holy rites).

Different Śruti is assigned to different Manvantara.

63-65a. Ṛk, Yajus and Sāman (are assigned to different Manvantaras) in the same manner as deities are assigned. In spite of the procedure of annihilation of all living beings, *Śatarudriya*, the procedure of *Hotra* as well as *Stotra* (Hymn, Prayer) function as before.

The *Stotra* is of four types : *Dravyastotra* (Eulogy of materials), *Guṇa-Stotra* (Eulogy of quality) *Phala-stotra* (Eulogy of fruit) and the fourth one *Ābhijanaka-Stotra* (Eulogy of Abhijanas).

65b. In all the Manvantaras, Brahmā sets in motion the four types of *Stotras* in regard to the Devas even as they come into being. Thus the origin of the collections of Mantras is of four types.

66-68. As the sages perform the severe and extremely difficult penance, the Mantras of different Vedas—Atharva, Ṛk, Yajus and Sāman appear before them severally in the same manner as in the previous Manvantaras. They appear in five ways viz.—owing to non-contendedness, owing to fear, owing to misery (pain), owing to happiness and owing to grief.

69. These Mantras appear before the sages casually because of the (supreme) vision of the sages named *Tāraka* (that which redeems). I shall state the *Ṛṣitva* (state of sagehood) of the sages along with the characteristics.

70. Among the past and future ones, it is said (that) there are five types of sages. Hence, I shall recount the origin of the sages.[1]

71-73. When the Guṇas were in (a state of) equilibrium, when there was the annihilation of everything, when there was no classification of the Vedas, when everything was full of darkness and it could not be indicated or specified particularly (the *pradhāna*) unintelligently functions for the sake of *Cetana* (Sentient one). It functions through the intellect of the sentient one and through consciousness (?) Both of them function like

1. The following verses (VV 71-73) describe the process of evolution of the universe to explain how sages (the Seven Sages—*Saptarṣis*) came into being in a new Kalpa.

the fish and the water. The *Sattva** (? *Tattva*) presided over by the sentient one functions in the nature (Guṇas).

74. On account of the cause, its effect functions in the same way. The object functions due to the subject. The *Artha* (meaning) functions due to its (state of possessing an Artha).

75. Within the time (?) when it should take place the *Bhedas* (differences) of the nature of *Karaṇa*** (sense-organ) become realised. Then *Mahat* and other principles manifest themselves gradually.

76. The *Ahaṁkāra* (Ego) was evolved out of *Mahat* and from it the *Bhūtas* (Elements) and the *Indriyas* (sense-organs) were born. The different *Bhūtas* were mutually born out of the elements.

77-82. The effect and the cause*** (sense-organs) suddenly get transformed itself. Just as the sparks and particles come out of the fire-brand simultaneously, so also the *Kṣetrajñas* (Individual Souls) come out of their Material cause at the same time.

Just as the glow-worm is suddenly seen in blinding darkness so also the transformed (Kṣetrajña) from the unmanifest shines like the glow-worm. It is great and embodied. The (all) knower became stationed there itself at the entrance to the *Dvāraśālā* (Hall of entry) where the great and embodied one was present. Beyond the vast expanse of darkness, the *Mahat* is perceived on account of its disparity. The Śruti says— "He stationed himself there. The learned one (the knowing one) was stationed at the end of *Tamas* (darkness)".

When it (the *Avyakta*) transformed itself, *Buddhi* (Intellect) appeared in four ways viz. *Jñāna* (Knowledge) *Vairāgya* (Absence of attachment), *Aiśvarya* (Prosperity, masterliness) and

* Vā. P. 59.66b reads *tattvāni* 'the principles'.

** The obscurity of the verse is due to the reading *Karaṇātmaka*. If emended as *Kāraṇātmaka* as in the identical verse in Vā P. 59.68a, it means 'differences of the nature of cause' became explicit etc.

*** Karaṇa emended as Kāraṇa as in Vā P.59.69c. The word *Karaṇa* 'Sense-organs' obscures the meaning implied in the next line.

Dharma (Virtue). These should be known as conducive to the final emancipation of man.

83-86. He is called *Mahātman* (the great Soul) by good people, because it is the transformation of the body* (?)

Since he lies within the body, he is called *Puruṣa*. Due to his knowledge of the *Kṣetra* (field, body) he is called *Kṣetrajña*. Since he lies within intelligently he is of the nature of consciousness. The non-sentient *Vyaktā-Vyakta* (manifest-cum-nonmanifest) is encompassed for the sake of achievement (?).

Thus the *Kṣetrajña* (individual Soul) is *Vivṛtta* (transformed one) and it is equipped with the knowledge of the *Kṣetra* (field, i.e. the body).

Simultaneously with *Vivṛtti* (transformation) the *Ṛṣi* himself excessively activises (*Param arṣayate*) *Avyakta* (the unmani fest one). Therefore, it has the *Paramarṣitva* (the state of being a great sage).

87. It is from the root √ṛṣ that means "to go" that the name has been derived at the outset. It is considered that it has *ṛṣitā* (the *ṛṣi*-hood) as it is self-born.[1]

88-90. They are born of God himself, they are the mental sons of Brahmā.

Since on being born, the great *Mahat* principle was surrounded by them, since those self-possessed persons went round the *Mahat* principle by means of their good qualities, hence they are called *Maharṣis*. They are the supreme viewers (seers) of the *Buddhi* (Intellect). They are the sons of *Īśvaras* (gods) both mind-born as well as bosom-born. They go beyond (or get under control) *Ahaṁkāra* (Ego) and penance. Hence they are *Ṛṣis*.

91. Hence, the seven sages are called sages because they see the principle of *Bhūtādi* (*Ahaṅkāra*). The *Ṛṣikas*, the sons of sages, are those born of the womb after sexual intercourse.

92. The *Tanmātras* (subtle elements) and *Satya* (the reality) are also realised by those sages of great prowess. Hence, those seven sages are the seers of the ultimate truth.

---

* A comparison of Bd.P. VV. 75-85 hereof with Vā P.39.69-77 shows that the lines in the Bd. P. are confused and disconnectedly mixed up. Hence the obscurity.

1. VV. 87-90 give the derivation of the term 'ṛṣi' and 'maharṣi'

93. They are the sons of Ṛṣikas. They should be known as sons of sages since they realise (*Ṛṣanti*) the *Ṛta* (The great truth of the cosmos) and the particularities (*Viśeṣas*) factually.

94-95.[1] Hence, those seven sages also are called sages because they see the vast extent of the Śruti. The following are the five classes of sages having the knowledge of the particular Ātmans viz. (1) *Avyaktātman* (the Unmenifest Ātman) (2) *Mahān Ātman* (the Soul called *Mahat*) (3) *Ahaṁkārātman* (the *Ātman* of the cosmic Ego) (4) *Bhūtātman* (the *Ātman* of the living beings or elements) and (5) *Indriyātman* (The *Ātman* of the Sense-Organs), listen to them by their names.

96-97. Bhṛgu, Marīci, Atri, Aṅgiras, Pulaha, Kratu, Manu, Dakṣa, Vasiṣṭha and Pulastya. These ten were mentally born of god Brahmā. They are themselves masterly and powerful ones. Since they are considered as supreme as well as sages they are Maharṣis.

98-100. The following sages are the sons of *Īśvaras*. Understand them. Kāvya (Śukra), Bṛhaspati, Kaśyapa, Cyavana, Utathya, Vāmadeva, Apāsya, Uśija, Kardama, Viśravas, Śakti, Vālakhilyas and Arvata. These sages are said to have attained the state of sages by means of penance. Understand *Ṛṣikas*, the sons of sages born of womb.

101-103. Vatsara, Nagṛhū, Bharadvāja, Dīrghatamas, Bṛhaduktha, Śaradvata, Vājaśravas, Śuci, Vaśyāśva, Parāśara, Dadhīca, Śaṁśapa, Rājā (King) Vaiśrvaṇa—these are called *Ṛṣikas*. They attained sage-hood on account of their truthfulness. They are remembered as Īśvaras, Ṛṣis and Ṛṣikas.

104-106.[2] All these are the composers (seers) of Mantras. Understand them entirely; Bhṛgu, Kāvya (Śukra), Pracetas,

1. VV. 94-103 give the various divisions of Sages as *Maharṣis*, *Ṛṣikas*, *Īśvaras*.

2. VV. 104-122 give the list of the Sages who are composers or seers of Mantras. They are divided according to their families viz. that of Bhṛgu (19) Aṅgiras (34) Kaśyapa (6) Vasiṣṭha (7) Kuśika (13). Three Brahmiṣṭhas (viz. Agastya, Dṛḍhāyu and Vidmavāha), two Kṣatriya Kings (viz. Manu and Pururavas), three Vaiśyas (viz. Bhalandana, Vatsa and Saṁkila). It may be noted that these seers of Mantras are Brāhmaṇas, Kṣattriyas and Vaiśyas and their number is 93 and not 90 as given in V.122.

Ṛcika, Ātmavān, Aurva, Jamadagni, Vida, Sārasvata, Ārṣṭiṣeṇa, Yudhājit, Vītahavya, Suvarcas, Vainya, Pṛthu, Divodāsa, Bādhyaśva, Gṛtsa and Śaunaka. These nineteen sages are Bhṛgus (i.e. the descendants of Bhṛgu). They are expounders of Mantras.

107-111. The following are the thirty-three excellent members of the family of Aṅgiras viz. Aṅgiras, Vaidyaga, Bharadvāja, Bāṣkali, Ṛtavāka, Garga, Śini, Saṅkṛti, Purukutsa, Māndhātā, Ambarīṣa, Yuvanāśva, Paurakutsa, Trasaddasyu, Dasyumān, Āhārya, Ajamīḍha, Tukṣaya, Kapi, Vṛṣādarbha, Virūpāśva, Kaṇva, Mudgala, Utathya, Sanadvāja, Vājaśravas, Ayāsya, Cakravartin, Vāmadeva, Asija. Bṛhaduktha, Dīrghatamas and Kakṣivān.

112-114. All these are composers of Mantras. Understand the Kāśyapas. (Sages of Kaśyapa group) : Kāśyapa, Vātsara, Naidhruva, Raibhya, Asita and Devala—these six are the expounders of Brahman.

Atri, Arvasana, Śyāvāśva, Gaviṣṭhira. Āvihotra, Dhīmān and Pūrvātithi—these are called Atris. They are great sages and composers of Mantras.

115-116. Vasiṣṭha, Śakti, Parāśara, the fourth one Indrapramati, the fifth one Bharadvasu, the sixth one Maitrāvaruṇi and the seventh one Kuṇḍina—these seven members of the family of Vasiṣṭha should be known as expounders of Brahman.

117-122. Viśvāmitra, (the son of Gādhi), Devarāta, Udgala, Madhucchandas the learned, the other sage Aghamarṣaṇa, Aṣṭaka, Lohita, Kata, Kola, Devaśravas, Reṇu, Pūraṇa and Dhanañjaya—these thirteen righteous persons should be known as the excellent members of the Kuśika family.

Agastya, Dṛḍhāyu and Vidhmavāha—these three sages are Brahmiṣṭhas (fully engrossed in the meditation on Brahman and having excellent penance and of excellent reputation.

Manu the son of Vivasvān (Sun) and King Pururavas the son of Ilā, these two excellent Kṣatriyas should be known as expounders of Mantras.

Bhalandana, Vatsa and Saṁkīla—these three are composers of Mantras and are remembered as the most excellent ones among Vaiśyas.

Thus the Mantras composed by the sages are said to be ninety. The sages are Brāhmaṇas, Kṣatriyas and Vaiśyas. Understand the *Ṛṣiputras* (sons of sages).

CHAPTER THIRTYTHREE

Characteristics of Sages and of Mantras

Sūta said :—

1. The sons of Ṛṣikas should be known as the sons of the sages. They are the expounders of the Brāhmaṇas. (Scriptural texts). Understand them by names.

2-4. The *Śrutarṣis* (sages distinguished by knowledge of the Vedas)—the most important among them—are mentioned briefly.[1] They are Bahvṛca, Bhārgava, Paila, Sāṅkṛtya, Jājali, Sandhyāsti, Māṭhara, Yājñavalkya, Parāśara, Upamanyu, Indrapramati, Māṇḍūki, Śākali, Bāṣkali, Śokapāṇi, Naila, Paila, Alaka, Pannaga, Pakṣaganta (and others). The Śrutarṣis are eighty-six in number.

5-6. These Brāhmaṇas are the most important among Bahvṛcas who are distinguished for their knowledge of Vedas.[2]

---

1. This is a confused statement of the traditional learners of *Bahvṛc* an epithet of the ṚV as it consists of the biggest number of Ṛks. Bh. P. XII. 6-54-60 gives a somewhat different genealogy of the Teachers of ṚV. In this Purāṇa the genealogy of Vedic Teachers from Paila is given *infra* Ch.34.24-33. Mahidāsa's Comments on CVS accepts the academic genealogy of Sages of the Ṛgveda though many names in our text are not included here. Our text states that there are 86 *Śrutarṣis* out of whom selected Ṛgveda Scholars are mentioned in VV.2-6 here.

2. The lines in the printed text appeared to be mixed up. Bh.P.XII.6 quoted in the Com. of Mahidāsa on Śaunaka's CVS. states that Vaiśampāyana was taught Yajur-Veda by Vyāsa. That the Yajur-Veda had 86 branches (bhedas) is accepted in our text as 86 *Śrutarṣis*. And a few selected sages have been named in the Yajur-Veda group.

Vaiśampāyana,[1] Lauhitya, Kaṇṭhakāla, Avaśāvadha(?) Śyāmāpati, Palāṇḍu, Ālambi and Kamalāpati. Their disciples and the disciples of their disciples constitute the eighty-six *Śrutarṣis.*

7-8. O Brāhmaṇas, these Brahmanical sages are called Adhvaryus of the Caraka Branch of Black Yajurveda[1] :—Jaimini, Bharadvāja, Kāvya, Pauṣyañji, Hiraṇyanābha, Kauśilya. Laugākṣi, Kusumi, Lāṅgalī, Śālihotra, Śaktirāja and Bhārgava.

9-11. The preceptor of those who sing Sāman Mantras is King Pururavas, the son of Ilā.[2] Forty-six other sages, together with their disciples are also *Śrutarṣis.*

Kauśīti, Kaṅkamudga, Kuṇḍaka, Parāśara, Lobhālobha the pious-souled, Brahmabala, Kranthala, Madagala and Mārkaṇḍeya who is conversant with Dharma—these ninety should be as *Hotravad Brahmacārins* (? i.e. Religious students performing Homas).

12-14a. After the expounders of Mantras and Brāhmaṇas, the Adhvaryus of the Caraka branch of Black Yajurveda (are to be understood).[3] Calūbhi, Sumati, Deva-vara, Anukṛṣṇa, Āyus, Anubhūmi, Prīṭa, Kṛśāśva, Sumūli and Bāṣkali—these are prominent Adhvaryus of Carakādhvaryakas. They are Brahmacārins (celibate ones) worthy of being paid obeisance.

14b-17a. Śuka the learned son of Vyāsa, Lauki, Bhūriśravas, Somāvi, Atunāṇtakya (?), Dhaumya and Kāśyapa, The forest-dwellers viz. Ilaka, Upamanyu, Vida, Bhārgava, Madhuka, Piṅga, Śvetaketu, Prajādarpa, Kahoḍa, Yājñāvalkya, Śaunaka, Anaṅga and Niratāla—these are *Madhyama Adhvaryus.*

17b-20. The following are the ladies capable of expounding the Brahman : Aditi the mother of the Devas, Jalāpā, Mānavī, the two splendid celestial damsels viz. Urvaśī and

1. The list of the 12 Carakas in the CVS is totally different from that given in this Purāṇa. Thus CVS states the 12 classifications of Carakas as follows : Caraka, Āhvaraka, Kaṭha, Prācya-Kaṭha, Kapiṣṭhala-Kaṭha, Cārāyaṇīya, Vārāyaṇīya, Vārtāntaveya, Śvetāśvatara, Aupamanyava, Pātāṇḍanīya and Maitrāyaṇīya.

2. This is not known to CVS.

3. VV. 12-170 give a list of prominent Adhvaryus of Caraka Branch of Black Yajurveda.

Viśvayoṣā, Mudgalā, Anujīvā, Tārā of great fame, Prātimedhī, Mārgā, Sujātā, Mahātapā (of great penance), Lopāmudrā who is conversant with Dharma and Kauśītikā. The celestial damsels are of approved beauty.

Thus the important children of the sages have been mentioned by me.

21-22. They are the founders of the branches of Vedic Schools. Therefore, they are regarded as sages. They are known by these names also—Īśvaras (Masters), expounders of the Mantras, Ṛṣis and Ṛṣikās. The sons of the sages are the expounders of *Kalpas* (Ritualistic texts) and of Brāhmaṇas, along with the sons of Īśvaras, Ṛṣis and Ṛṣikas.

23-32. Similarly, understand the statements as to their visions of the Mantras.[1]

The Mantra, which is that which is equipped with command (? authoritative) is *advaita* (non-dualistic), that has deep resonant sound is *Dipta*. The Mantra named *Liṅga* (Symbol) is perfectly direct perception. What is called *Paridāna* (Devotion) is that which has become the soul of all living beings.

They know that the statement which indicates the meaning mentioned in the *Nirukta* (semantics, one of the ancillary subjects of the Vedas) as *Svāyambhuva*. Whatever is associated with some Mantra is along with the case endings of substantives (?)

That which is directly spoken is considered to be the statement of Ṛṣis. It mostly consists of different words from the *Nigamas* (Vedas) and Nipātas (Particles, indeclinables, exceptional forms of words).

That which is a great statement is remembered as the statement of Ṛṣikas.

That in which the words are not very clear, that in which there are many doubts is the statement of Ṛṣiputras. All of them are lamentations (or all lamentations also are such).

That which mainly consists of *Hetu* (Reason) and Dṛṣṭānta (example) is (called) *Citraśabda* (one with diverse words).

1. VV.23-32 explain many technical terms such as Mantra, Nirukta, Nipāta, Hetu, Dṛṣṭānta and others. The statement of Ṛṣis is in Vedic, those of Ṛṣikas are great, clear or emphatic while those of Ṛṣiputras are dubious.

That which has no sense, that which is not praised by anyone and that which is feeble—this statement is Mānuṣa (human).

(Persons) well-known as Miśras attained the status of the sages on account of their prowess. For the sake of prosperity they are born of different castes (?) by means of drawing and attraction (?) They have the knowledge of the past, present and future. They cure the misery of birth.

Those statement of Miśras is capable of activising the strength of the preceptor.

The who are composers of scriptural texts, those who go every-where, due to their greatness, and those who possess the intensity of very great penance are considered as sages. They are Bṛhaspati, Śukra, Vyāsa and Sārasvata.

33-35. Vyāsas are those who compose scriptural texts. They are remembered as Vedavyāsas. Since, although they are born later (i.e. younger in age), they are superior to the earlier ones in their intellect; since they are richly endowed with prosperity, they are, therefore, remembered as Ṛṣis (sages).

In the matter of the conception of a sage neither the period nor the age is the authoritative criterion.

A (younger) person is some times seen superior-most in intellect, since even a boy who is elderly (i.e. mature) in intellect is a learned sage.[1]

36. They call this Ṛk Mantra : viz. the same foot in the middle is used with the full complement of words and their end is properly distributed.

37. They call this Yajus Mantra : viz. the Mantra is not measured by means of syllables in the foot but by means of *Karaṇa* (Rhythmical pause) and its end possesses syllables in excess.[2]

38-39. The following seven adjuncts of a Sāman Mantra are called *Sapta Vindhyas*[3] viz. (1) Hrīmkāra (2) Prastava

1. This Subhāṣita glorifying wisdom and intelligence as superior to the age is found in Pāli and Prakrits also. The word '*bala*' here is a misprint for '*bāla*'.

2. This applies to Yajur-mantras in prose and not to metrical ones.

3. *Vindhya* is a technical term indicating a part of a Sāma Stanza. The parts are enumerated in VV 38-39. *Prastava* is beginning of the hymn, *Prati-*

(beginning) (3) Praṇava Oṁkāra) (4) Gīta (Song) is the fourth one (5) the fifth one is Prati-Hotra. (6) They call the sixth one *Upadrava* (7) *Nidhana* (? end). Without Hrīṁkāra and Praṇava it is called Pañcavindhyā.

40-41. (Defective text) On saying "Brahmaṇe Dharma" (Dharma is for the sake of the Brahman), that which is implied and indicated then is considered Āśāsti (Blessing). Paridevanā is lamentation. Narration of a question out of anger or hatred—this is laid down as the characteristic sign of the Mantra among all Vidyās.

42-43. Mantras characterised as Ṛk, Yajus and Sāman are said to be nine types:—*Mūrti* (form), *Nindā* (censure), *Praśaṁsā*, (praise), *Ākrośa* (scolding), *Toṣa* (contentedness), *Praśna* (question), *Anujñā* (permission) and *Ākhyāna* (narrative and modes of blessing).

I shall mention the different types of Mantras falling into twentyfour classes.

44-46. The following are the twentyfour types of Mantras :

(1) *Praśaṁsā* (Praise) (2) *Stuti* (Eulogy) (3) *Ākrośa* (Rebuking) (4) *Nindā* (Censure) (5) *Paridevanā* (Lamentation) (6) *Abhiśāpa* (Curse) (7) *Viśāpa* (Revocation of a curse) (8) *Praśna* (Question) (9) *Prativacas* (Reply) (10) *Āśis* (Blessing) (11) *Yajña* (Sacrifice) (12) *Ākṣepa* (Reviling) (13) *Arthākhyāna* (Narration of the meaning) (14) *Saṁkathā* (Conversation) (15) *Viyoga* (Separation) (16) *Abhiyoga* (Attack) (17) *Kathā* (Story) (18) *Saṁsthā* (Situation) (19) *Vara* (Boon) (20) *Pratiṣedha* (Denial) (21) *Upadeśa* (Advice) (22) *Namaskāra* (Obeisance) (23) *Spṛhā* (Desire) and (24) *Vilāpa* (Lamentation).

Thus the twentyfour types of Mantras are mentioned.

47-48. Ten modes or formations of the Brāhmaṇas, which had been laid down formerly by the sages conversant

---

Hotṛ is the response or supporting tune by the assistant *Hotṛ*, *Upadrava* is the fourth of the five parts of a Sāman Stanza. (Sāyaṇa on Ṣaḍaviṁśa Br.). According to that Brāhmaṇa, a Sāman Stanza has five parts. Hriṁkāra and *Oṁkāra* appear subsequent additions.

with the principles of Yajña, are as follows—*Hetu* (Reason) *Nirvacana* (Specific explanation) *Nindā* (Censure) *Praśasti*, (Praise) *Saṁśaya* (Doubt), *Nidhi* (Deposit) *Purākṛti* (Previous action), *Purākalpa* (Previous Kalpa), *Vyavadhāraṇa-Kalpanā* (Conception of ascertainment), *Upamā* (Comparison).

49. This is the characteristic feature of a "Brāhmaṇa" in regard to persons of all (vedic) branches.

Hetu is derived from the root *Hati* (√*han*-). It kills what is spoken (argued) by others.

50. Or it can be derived from the root *Hinoti* meaning "to go" when the meaning has been arrived at. *Nirvacana* means determination of the meaning of a statement.

51. Preceptors call it *nindā* where there are words of censure in finding fault.

Praśasti is derived from the root (√*śaṁs*-) *Śaṁsati* with the preposition *Pra*. *Praśasti* or *Praśaṁsā* means praise on account of good qualities.

52. "This is this. This is not this". Where there is indecision like this, there is *Saṁśaya* (Doubt). "This should be done like this". This is called *Vidhi* (Rule, Mode).

53. "This is the utterance of so and so (Lit. of others and others)". This is mentioned by learned men as *Purākṛti* (? Precedent). This object that is completely out of view (in distant past) is called *Purākalpa* (A story of the past).

54-56. The word '*Purā*' indicates what has gone by. If due to its being over in the days of yore the story of the past is decisively fixed by means of *Mantras*, *Brāhmaṇas*, *Kalpas* (Ritualistic texts) and *Nigamas* (Vedas) of pure expanse it is called *Vyavadhāraṇa Kalpanā* (conception of ascertainment). "Just as this, so also that", "This is like that" this is called *Upamā* (comparison). This is the tenth characteristic feature of the Brāhmaṇa.

Thus, at the outset, the characteristic feature of the Brāhmaṇa has been laid down by learned men.

57-58. The commentary of that Mantra as pointed out by the Brāhmaṇas who know it, has been mentioned word by word. The application of Mantras is duly laid down in the holy rites. The word *Mantra* is derived from the root *Mantrayati* and *Brāhmaṇa* (scriptural text) is derived from the word Brāhmaṇa (*Bṛṁhaṇa* ?)

Those who know Sūtra (aphorism) say that it must be brief with very few words, unambiguous, full of meaning and comprehensive. It must not contain any unwanted interpolation. It must be free from blame.

CHAPTER THIRTYFOUR

Vyāsa and the Line of his Disciples
Controversy between Yājñavalkya and Śākalya

Vāyu said :—

1. On hearing his words, the sages asked Sūta thereafter "How were the Vedas classified once again, O highly intelligent one, recount that to us."

Sūta said :—

2. In the Dvāpara Yuga that had gone before in the Svāyambhuva Manvantara, god Brahmā said to Manu :—"O highly intelligent one, protect the Veda.

3. The Yuga has changed, O dear one. The twice-borns have become deficient in energy and vigour. All of them have been duly enveloped by the defects of the Yuga.

4. Due to the Yuga, its extent is seen to have been reduced. What has been spoken in the Kṛtayuga has been reduced to a ten-thousandth part.

5. The vigour, the splendour and the strength—everything has become very much diminished. Everything perishes. The Vedic rites have to be performed. Let there not be the destruction of the Veda.

6. If Veda meets with destruction, the Yajña (institute) will be destroyed. When the Yajña is destroyed the Veda will (automatically) be destroyed. Then everything perishes.

7. The original Veda had four feet and it extended to a hundred-thousand (*mantras*). Again the Kṛṣṇa (the black Yajurveda) was ten times that (in extent). Indeed the Yajña was the yielder of all desires."

8. On being told thus, Manu who was engaged in what was conducive to the welfare of all the worlds, said "So be it." Then the lord divided the Single Veda of four feet into four divisions.

9-10. It was at the instance of Brahmā as well as with a desire for the welfare of all the worlds (that he divided the Veda). Therefore, I shall narrate to you all the classification of the Vedas in accordance with the current Manvantara. It is by adopting the mode of inferring what is beyond perception by means of what is (actually) perceptible, that we decide things of the past. O excellent ones, understand that.

11-13. In this Yuga, Vyāsa, the son of Parāśara, the scorcher of enemies, who was well known as Dvaipāyana was the eternal part of Viṣṇu.

12. Urged by Brahmā, he began to recount the Veda in this Yuga. For the purpose of (preserving the continuity of) the Vedas, he took four disciples viz. Jaimini, Sumantu, Vaiśampāyana and Paila the fourth one. There was a fifth (disciple) also along with these viz. Lomaharṣaṇa.

14-16. With due formality, he accepted Paila as the listener (i.e. disciple) unto the Ṛgveda, O Brāhmaṇa, Vaiśaṁpāyana as the expounder of the Yajurveda; he accepted Jaimini as the disciple for the Sāmveda and the meaning (of its mantras). Similarly, he accepted Sumantu, the excellent sage, as the disciple for the Atharvaveda. The saintly lord accepted me as the disciple for Itihāsas, Purāṇas and Kalpavākyas.

17. The Yajurveda was one and whole. He divided it into four. There was *Cāturhotra*[1] (four types of sacrificial duties) therein, and he ordained Yajña thereby.

18. He ordained *Ādhvaryava* (the work of the priest Adhvaryu) by means of Yajur-Mantras and the *Hautra* (the

1. For duties to be performed by four Chief Priests viz. Hotṛ, Adhvaryu, Udgātṛ and Brahmā in a sacrifice, *vide* the next verse.

work of the priest Hotṛ) by means of Ṛk Mantras; he performed *Audgātra* (the work of the priest Udgātṛ) by means of Sāmaṇ Mantras and the duty of Brahmā (the presiding priest) by means of Atharvan Mantras.

19-20. Thereafter, by picking out the Ṛk. Mantras, he composed the Ṛgveda. By selecting Hotṛka Mantras, the lord of the Universe composed the Yajurveda. He composed Sāmaveda by means of the Sāman Mantras and thereby he got the work of Udgātṛ performed. He performed all the rites of the king by means of the Atharvaveda.

21. By means of narratives and subsidiary narratives, folksongs, utterances from Kalpa texts etc. Vyāsa who was an expert in the meanings of the Purāṇas composed the Purāṇa Saṁhitā.

22. Whatever remained he included it in the Yajurveda and associated Yajña with it. This is the definite conclusion in the scriptural texts that it (came to be called) Yajurveda on account of *Yajana* (Sacrifice).

23-24a. Since the feet (of mantra verses) are excessively long, the Yajur Mantras are very intricate. This Veda with excessive vigour is utilised by a hundred Ṛtviks who have perfectly mastered the Vedas. It is with this that the horse-Sacrifice is fully developed.

24b. Taking up the Ṛk-Mantras, Paila classified them into two groups.[1] After composing two Saṁhitās the eminent

---

1. VV.24b-33 describe the divisions of the Ṛgveda along with the principal teachers thereof

Paila

Indra-Pramati (4 branches) — Bāṣkala

(1) Bodhyā
(2) Agnimātṛ
(3) Pārāśari
(4) Yājnavalkyā

Māṇḍukeya (complete Ṛgveda)

Satyaśravas

(Cont.)

preceptor handed them over to his two disciples—one to Indrapramati and the other one to Bāṣkala.

26. The excellent Brāhmaṇa, Bāṣkala composed four Saṁhitās and taught his disciples who were eagerly engaged in serving him and who were desirous of his welfare.

27. The four Saṁhitās are as follows : The first branch is Bodhyā; the second branch is Agnimātṛ; the third one is Pārāśarī and the last one is Yājñavalkyā.

28. Indrapramati, the excellent sage taught one (undivided) Saṁhitā. He taught the highly fortunate and famous Māṇḍukeya.

29-30. That sage of great fame taught his eldest son Satyaśravas. The renowned sage Satyaśravas taught his son Satyahita. Satyahita taught his son Satyaśrī who was noble-souled and who was eagerly devoted to truthfulness and piety.

31. Satyaśrī had three disciples who had great brilliance, were learned, and were eagerly devoted to the clear grasp of the scriptural texts.

32-33. Śākalya was the first among them. Another one was Rathītara and the third one was Bharadvāja the son of Bāṣkala—these were those who made the Śākhās (of that Veda) function (and flourish).

Śākalya (also known as) Devamitra was haughty and arrogant on account of his knowledge. O Brāhmaṇa, he was slain during the Yajña of Janaka.

Śāṁśapāyana enquired :—

34-35. How was that sage who was haughty and arrogant on account of his knowledge slain during the horse-sacrifice of Janaka? How did the argument begin? Why did it start at

---

(Cont.)

|
Satyahita
|
Satya-śrī
|

Śākalya or Devamitra	Rathītara	Bharadvāja (Son of Bāṣkala)

all? With whom was the argument done ? Mention all these as they had happened as it is known to you.[1]

Sūta said :—

36. There was a great assemblage (of learned men) during the horse-sacrifice of Janaka. Many thousands of sages came there.

37-38. All of them were desirous of watching that Yajña of the saintly king Janaka. On seeing the Brāhmaṇas who arrived, he had his curiosity aroused—"Who is the most excellent Brāhmaṇa among these ? How can I come to that decision ?" After thinking thus, the king hit upon an intelligent plan.

39-41a. He brought the following articles (as gift) viz. A thousand cows, plenty of gold, villages, jewels and maid-servants. The king then announced to the sages, "O sages of excellent fortune, I bow down my head unto all of you. The wealth that has been brought here is for the most excellent one among you. O excellent Brāhmaṇas, know that my wealth is for you."*

41b-45. On hearing the words of Janaka and on seeing the most valuable wealth, those sages well-versed in the Vedas became greedy. They were desirous of seizing the same.

They challenged one another in their height of arrogance due to Vedic knowledge, with their mind dwelling on the riches displayed. They began to quarrel and claim thus—"This wealth (ought to) be mine. This is mine and not yours". Another said : "Say, why do you swagger".

Owing to the fault of wealth, they began to argue in various ways.

---

1. The story how Śākalya lost his life as a result of his discomfiture in his disputation with Yājñavalkya is based on the dispute recorded in the *Bṛhadāraṇyaka Upa* III.8. 12-26. The difference between the stories is that in the *Bṛhad-Upa* it was after Gārgī that Śākalya accepted Yājñavalkya's challenge.

This is a good picture of disputations held in royal courts, the appointment of referees and the methodology of disputations in ancient India.

* For *me vittaṁ vittaṁ dvijottamāḥ* / of the text Vā.P.60.38b (identical verse) reads: (*tasmai tad upanītam*) *hi vidyā-vittaṁ dvijottamāḥ* / 'This is brought as the prize for scholarship' etc.

But there was another scholar there who was a great seer and also the son of god Brahmā, called Yājñavalkya. He was endowed with great splendour; he was a great ascetic and was the most excellent among those who had realized Brahman. Yājñavalkya who was born of a part of Brahmā, proclaimed loudly :

46. He said to his disciple who was the most excellent among the knowers of Brahman, "Take this wealth, O dear one and take it home. There is no doubt about it that this is mine.

47. I am the sole arguer in all arguments. No one else is equal to me. If any learned man is not pleased (with this) let him challenge me without delay."

48. Then the vast expanse of the ocean-like crowd of Brāhmaṇas became agitated like an ocean in the deluge. Thereupon, Yājñavalkya who was absolutely calm and normal said smilingly :

49. "O learned men, do not get angry. All of you are speakers of truth. Let us speak (i.e. argue) in accordance with our capacity, trying to understand each other".

50-51. Thereafter, their arguments were accepted with many words and thousands of splendid meanings originating from subtle vision (of Branches of Philosophy). There were examiners engaged by the king. They were endowed with good qualities, embellished with places of spiritual learning both of the worldly matters as well as in the Veda (i.e. they had competence in secular as well as religious topics for discussion).

52. The arguments between the noble-souled scholars began for the purpose of winning the wealth. All the sages were on one side and Yājñavalkya was on the other.

53. Thereafter, all those sages were individually asked by the intelligent Yājñavalkya. They did not reply. (They were unable to reply).

54. After conquering all the sages, that (sage) of great intellect, a mass of Vedic wisdom, suddenly spoke to Śākalya, the originator of arguments.

55. "O Śākalya, speak out what is relevant. Why do you remain (silent) meditating. The stake has been deposited

by the Yajamāna (i.e. the King on whose behalf they are to perform sacrifice etc.) and has been taken away and held by me".

56. On being attacked thus, his face and eyes became red like copper due to anger. In the presence of the sages he spoke to Yājñavalkya accompanied by his man (i.e. the disciple*).

57. "Slighting us as well as other excellent Brāhmaṇas like blades of grass, you wish to seize for yourself the gift of wealth of great value, as a prize for learning".

58. On being spoken thus by Śākalya, Yājñavalkya said to him,—"Know that the strong point of Brahmiṣṭhas (persons engrossed in the meditation on Brahman) is the vision (insight) of the principles of learning and objects of reality.

59. Love or desire has its association with wealth. Hence we love wealth. Brāhmaṇas are *Kāmapraśnas* (those who can ask whatever they wish). Hence, we speak out the question as we please.

60-61. This is the reward of the saintly king. Hence, the gift of wealth has been taken away by me".

On hearing these words (of Yājñavalkya), Śākalya became extremely infuriated. In order to ask the question as he pleased, he spoke these words to Yājñavalkya—"Now reply to me factually whatever question (I am pleased to ask) pointed out by me."

62. Then a great argument took place between those two knowers of Brahman. More than a thousand questions were put then by Śākalya.

63. Even as the other sages listened—Yājñavalkya replied everything. Śākalya had no further argument or question. Yājñavalkya spoke to him.

64. "Answer at least one question put by me, O Śākalya as I please.

In this disputation with the stake of (the wealth offered

---

* For *sa-puruṣam* of the text, Vā P. 60.51b reads *taṁ paruṣam* (spoke harsh words to him)—a better reading.

by Janaka as bait) or instantaneous death here (if you fail to reply*).

65. Which is well associated with the subtlest of knowledge—Sāṅkhya or Yoga? which is more important, the path of spirituality or the path of meditation?"[1]

66. Then the question was put forward by the intelligent Yājñavalkya. Unable to know it (and reply), Śākalya had to court death.

67-68. Thus, it is remembered that Śākalya became distressed in the course of his explanation of the question.

Thus a great dispute took place among (the sages) seeking wealth. There were arguments between the sages and Yājñavalkya.

Yājñavalkya took away the gift of wealth after establishing his own fame. Surrounded by his disciples (that learned sage) of great self-control went home.

CHAPTER THIRTYFIVE

The Legend of Yājñavalkya's receiving the Veda from the Sun-God :[2] Legend of Vyāsa : Description of Svāyambhuva Manvantara

Sūta said :—

1. Śākalya (otherwise known as) Devamitra, an intelligent noble-soul, a leading Brāhmaṇa who was the foremost

* Vā P. 60.58b reading is more explicit:

śāpaḥ paṇo'sya vādasya abruvan mṛtyum āvrajet.

1. The last question of Yājñavalkya to Śākalya in the *Bṛhad. Upa* was about *Aupaniṣada Puruṣa* and not about the superiority of the path of Sāṅkhya (spiritual wisdom) or Yoga (path of meditation) as in this Purāṇa.

2. The Legend that Yājñavalkya received a new Veda (the white Yajurveda) from the Sun-god is as old as the Mbh. Śānti 318.6-12. But this chapter in the Mbh. does not mention his guru's order to recant the Yajurveda learnt by Yājñavalkya from him due to his insolence and uncharitable remarks about his class-mates' capacity to perform that penance.

among those who were conversant with the Vedas, composed five Saṁhitās.[1]

2. He had five disciples viz. Mudgala, Gokhala, Khalīyān, Sutapas and the fifth his dear (child) Śaiśireya.

3. The excellent Brāhmaṇa (?) expounded three Saṁhitās viz. Śāka, Vaiṇa and Rathītara. He composed a fourth (work) the Nirukta.

4. He had four disciples viz. Paila, Īkṣalaka, Śatabalāka the intelligent and Gaja, O excellent Brāhmaṇas.

5. Bharadvāja, son of Bāṣkala, expounded three Saṁhitās. He had three noble-souled disciples endowed with good qualities.

6. They were, Tvāpanāpa the intelligent, Pannagāri the wise one and the third one Ārjava. All of them were praiseworthy, of holy observances due to the power of penance.

7. They were devoid of passion. They had great splendour. They were perfect masters of the Saṁhitās.

Thus have been described the *Bahvṛcas* by whom the Saṁhitās were made to function.

8-9. The disciple of Vaiśampāyana composed Yajurveda. Eightysix splendid Saṁhitās[2] were expounded by him. He gave

---

1. In continuation of note 1. p. 333 the spiritual or academic genealogy of Paila from Śākalya onwards is as follows:

Śākalya

Mudgala | Gokhala | Khaliyān | Sutapas | Śaiśireya

Composition of three Saṁhitās and the Nirukta

(Son of Śakalya)

Paila | Īkṣalaka | Śatabalāka | Gaja

Bāṣkala

Bharadvāja (expounded 3 Saṁhitās)

Tvāpanāpa | Pannagāri | Ārjava.

2. Cf. *yajurvedasya ṣaḍaśīti bhedā bhavanti* CVS P. 31.

them to his disciples and they grasped them in accordance with the injunctions. One of them, Yājñavalkya of supreme power of penance, was excluded[1] (? by the preceptor).

10. There were eightysix disciples, the propounders of diverse Saṁhitās and there were three different kinds in every one of them.

11. The three kinds in the splendid last variety of Veda are the (1) Northern (2) of the middle region and (3) the eastern one.

12-13. Śyāmāyani became the leader of the *Udīcyas* (Northerners). Āsuri is remembered as the first founder of (the Vedic branch) of the middle region. Ālambi is the foremost among the *Prācyas* (Easterners). There are (thus) the three regional heads.[2]

Thus the *Carakas*, the Brahman expounders of the Saṁhitās have been described.

The sages said :—

14. Why are they (called) *Carakādhvaryus*? Tell the reason factually. What is the (rite) observed (by them)? For what reason did they attain the status of *Caraka*.

Sūta said :—

15. The sages had some work to do, O excellent Brāhmaṇa. After reaching the top of the Meru, they conferred with one another as follows :

16. "If any excellent Brāhmaṇa does not turn up here within seven days, he shall (have to) perform (expiation for) Brāhmaṇa-slaughter (*Brahma-Hatyā*). This is proclaimed as our stipulated condition."

17. Thereafter, all of them excepting Vaiśaṁpāyana went to the place where the assemblage had been fixed. (They attended along with all the members of their groups).

---

1. It is not clear whether Yājñavalkya was not taught Yajurveda or was made to vomit it and hence became Veda-less one. In other words, Vaiśaṁpāyana must have taught Yajur-Veda to Yājñavalkya.

2. As stated in the footnote on Ch. XXIII, the list of Carakas is different in the CVS.

18. At the instance of the Brāhmaṇas, he performed (the atonement for) *Brahma-Hatyā*. After calling together all the disciples he said :—

19. "Perform (the expiation of) *Brahma-Hatyā* on my behalf, O excellent Brāhmaṇas. All of you gather together and utter the words conducive to welfare, as desired.

Yājñavalkya said :—

20. "I shall perform it single-handed. Let these sages stand by. Purified by my own penance, I shall lift it up with my power".

21. On being told thus, he (Vaiśampāyana) became angry and expelled Yājñavalkya. He said "Return to me every thing that has been learned by you".

22. On being told thus, (the sage) the most excellent one among the knowers of Brahman, vomited out the Yajur Mantras that had perceptible forms and had been smeared with blood.

23. Thereafter, the Brāhmaṇa meditated upon the sun-god and propitiated him. The Veda that had come up went over to the sun and stayed there.

24. The sun-god who was pleased with him gave unto Brahmarāti (i.e. Yājñavalkya who had the fund of Vedic knowledge) those Yajur Mantras that had gone up to the Solar sphere.

25-27. Mārtaṇḍa (the Sun) gave those Yajur-Mantras to the intelligent Yājñavalkya who had assumed the form of horse.[1] (Some) Brāhmaṇas study those Yajur Mantras by some means or the other. The Mantras had been given to (Yājñavalkya) who had assumed the form of a horse. Hence, those Brāhmaṇas became *Vājins*. Those by whom (the expiation for) *Brahma-Hatyā* had been observed are remembered as Carakas because they had performed (*Caraṇāt*) the atonement. The disciples of Vaiśampāyana are detailed as *Carakas*).[2]

---

1. As contrasted with the Mbh and other Purāṇas, here it is Yājñavalkya who assumes the form of a horse and not the Sun-god, while receiving the new Veda.

2. The Brāhmaṇas who performed penance for warding off the sin of Brahma-hatyā of their guru are called *Carakas*—a popular etymology.

Thus these Carakas have been recounted. Now understand the Vājins.

28-30. There are fifteen Vājins. They are the disciples of Yājñavalkya viz. - Kaṇva, Baudheya Madhyandina, his son, Vaidheya, Addha, Bauddhaka, Tāpanīya, Vatsa, Jābāla, Kevala, Āvaṭī, Puṇḍra, Vaiṇoya and Parāśara.[1] These are mentioned as Vājins. They are fifteen excellent men. The branches of Yajur Mantras should be known as one hundred and one.

31. Jaimini taught his son Sumantu.[2] Sumantu taught his son Sutvan.

---

1. Cf. the list of disciples of Yājñavalkya in CVS. p. 32 as that list somewhat differs from the list in the Bd. P.

2. VV. 31-55 give the genealogy of Sāmaveda Teachers. It is different from that in CVS. Our text gives it as follows:

Jaimini
|
Sumantu
|
Sutvan
|
Sukarman (studied 1000 Saṁhitās)

(One thousand disciples, one per Saṁhitā (But these were killed by Indra as noted in CVS. p. 43)

Pauṣyañji (Studied 500 Saṁhitās)

King Hiraṇyanābha alias Kauśalya (Studied 500 Saṁhitas and Eastern Sāmagas)
Prince Kṛta

(Udīcya (Northern) Sāmagas)
|
Laugākṣi | Kuśumi (Kuthumi in Vā.P.) | Kuśīdī | Lāṅgali)

School of Laugākṣi
|
Nāḍāyanīya | Tāṇḍiputra | Anovaina | Susahas | Sunāman

School of Kuśumī
|
Aurasa | Parāśara | Nabhirvitta

Kauthuma, son of Parāśara had six followers—Lāṅgalas alias Śālihotras viz. Hālini, Jyāmahāni, Jaimini, Lomagāyani, Kaṇḍu and Kohala, these expounded 6 Saṁhitās.

32-33. Sutvan taught his son Sukarman. Sukarman quickly studied a thousand Saṁhitās and expounded them to a thousand disciples who had the splendour of the sun. As they were studying during the days (when they should not be studied) Indra slew them.

34. Thereafter, for the sake of his disciples he performed Protest fast unto death (Prāyopaveśana). On seeing him furious, Indra granted him a boon.

35. "You will have two disciples of great vigour and unequalled splendour. Let those two extremely intelligent (disciples) study the thousand Saṁhitās.

36-38. O excellent Brāhmaṇa, these highly fortunate gods (Devas) have become furious".

After saying this to Sukarman of great fame, the glorious Vāsava (Indra) saw that the anger of the Brāhmaṇa had calmed down and (so) the lord vanished suddenly. His disciples were

---

King Hiraṇya-nābha

Prince Kṛta
Composed 24 Saṁhitās (taught one to each student)

Senior disciples

1. Rāḍi
2. Rāḍavīya (Mahāvīrya in Vā.P.)
3. Pañcama
4. Vāhana
5. Talaka
6. Māṇḍuka (Pāṇḍaka in Vā P.)
7. Kālika
8. Rājika
9. Gautama
10. Ajabasta
11. Soma-rājāyana
12. Puṣṭi
13. Parikṛṣṭa
14. Ulūkhalaka.

Junior Disciples

1. Śālī (Vaiśala in Vā.P.)
2. Aṅgulīya
3. Kauśika
4. Śālimañjarī
5. Pāka (Kāpīya in Vā.P.)
6. Śadhīya
7. Kānini
8. Pārāśarya

It may be noted that the number of disciples is 22, to make it 24, we must add their teachers Hiraṇya-nābha and Kṛta.

Lastly this Purāṇa differs considerably from the CVS in names of teachers of the Sāmaveda (vide CVS, pp. 43-46).

(1) The intelligent and highly excellent Brāhmaṇa Pauṣyañji and the second one (2) Hiraṇyanābha alias Kauśalya who was a king. Pauṣyañji taught half a thousand (i.e. 500) Saṁhitās.

39. The splendid disciples of Pauṣyañji were known by the name Udīcya Sāmans. Kauśilya studied five Saṁhitās called Sattvas* (?)

40. The disciples of Hiraṇyanābha are remembered as Prācya Sāmagas. The four disciples of Pauṣyañji were Laugākṣi, Kuśumi, Kuśīdi and Lāṅgali. Now understand the different branches of these.

41. The different branches of (the school of) Laugākṣi are - Nāḍāyanīya, Tāṇḍiputra (son of Taṇḍi), from him a fine scholar named Anovaina, Susahas son of Sakoti, and Sunāman. Understand these as the members of the different branches of the school of Laugākṣi.

42-44. Kuśumi had three disciples viz. Aurasa, Parāśara and the brilliant Nābhivitta. Thus, the Kausumas are remembered of three types.

Śauriṣu and Śṛṅgiputra (son of Śṛṅgi)—these two observed holy rites for a long time.

Rāṇāyanīya and Saumitri were experts in Sāma Veda. Śṛṅgiputra of great penance expounded three Saṁhitās.

45. Vaina, Prācīnayoga and Surāla were excellent Brāhmaṇas. Kauthuma Pārāśarya (son of Parāśara) expounded six Saṁhitās.

46. Āsurāyaṇa and Vaiśākhya were devotedly attached to the elderly Vedic scholars.

The intelligent Patañjali was the son of Prācīna Yoga.

47. The branches of (the school of) Kauthuma, son of Parāśara are remembered as six. Lāṅgala (otherwise known as) Śālihotra expounded six Saṁhitās.

48. Hālini, Jyāmahāni, Jaimini, Lomagāyani, Kaṇḍu and Kohala—these six are remembered as the followers of Lāṅgala.

49. These were the disciples of Lāṅgali and Saṁhitās

---

* *Sattvāni pañca* in the text is wrong, as Kauśalya studied five hundred Saṁhitās. Vā. P.61.35 correctly reads *Śatāni pañca*.

were founded and promulgated by them. One alone, a prince Kṛta (was made) the disciple of Hiraṇya-Nābha.

50. He composed twentyfour Saṁhitās. The foremost among bipeds expounded them to his disciples. Understand their names.

51-55. Rāḍi, Rāḍavīya, Pañcama, Vāhana, Talaka, Māṇḍuka, Kālika, Rājika, Gautama, Ajabasta, Somarājāyana, Puṣṭi, Parikṛṣṭa and Ulūkhalaka (were the elder ones). The younger ones were Śālī, Aṅgulīya, Kauśika, Śālimañjarī, Pāka, Śadhīya, Kānini and the virtuous soul Parāśarya—Thus the Sāmagas have been recounted.

Among all the Sāmagas, Pauṣyañji and Kṛta are declared as the most excellent ones. They were expounders of Saṁhitās.

O Brāhmaṇas ! Sumantu divided Atharvan into two and gave them to his disciples.[1]

56-58. He gave Kabandha the black (Atharvan Mantra). That scholar Kabandha classified it into two even as he listened to it and passed them on, one to Pathya and the second to Devadarśa. That lordly sage classified it into four. Devadarśa's four disciples were Moda, Brahmabala, Pippalāda and Śaulkāyani was the fourth one. He was conversant with

1. VV. 55-62 give the list of branches and teachers of the Atharva Veda. It is different from the information in CVS, pp. 46-49. The genealogy in this Purāṇa is as follows:

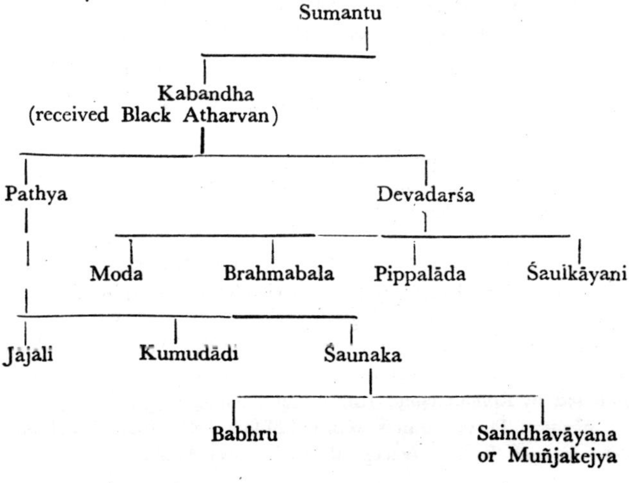

Dharma and he was established (and engrossed) in penance. All these four disciples of Devadarśa were firm observers of holy rites.

59. Know that the further excellent classification of Pathyas is three-fold. (The disciples were) Jājali, Kumudādi and the third one is remembered as Śaunaka.

60. Śaunaka divided the Saṁhitā into two and handed over one to Babhrū. The intelligent sage transferred (taught) the second Saṁhitā to (a disciple) named Saindhavāyana.

61-62. Saindhava (otherwise known as) Muñjakeśya split into two the Saṁhitā already divided into two.

The excellent divisions[1] of Atharvan Saṁhitā are as follows :- Nakṣatrakalpa, Vaitāna, the third one Saṁhitā-Vidhi, the fourth one the Kalpa of Aṅgiras and the fifth one Śāntikalpa.

63-65. O excellent sages, Khaḍga* (?) expounded the Purāṇa along with me.[2]

The following are said to be my disciples who cling closely to the Purāṇas viz. Ātreya, the intelligent Sumati, Kāśyapa, Akṛtavraṇa, Bhāradvāja, Agnivarcas, Vasiṣṭha, Mitrāyu, Sāvarṇi, Somadatti, Suśarman and Śāṁśapāyana. Three Saṁhitās were composed by three of them.

66. Kāśyapa, Sāvarṇi and Śāṁśapāyana are the composers of Saṁhitās. My Saṁhitā shall be the fourth one. These four are the original (purāṇa) Saṁhitās.

67. All of them have four Pādas (feet/sections). All of them have the same import. In the alternate reading, they are futile in the same way as the branches of the Vedas.

---

1. The divisions of the Atharva Veda are five : (1) Nakṣatra-Kalpa, (2) Vaitāna, (3) Saṁhitā-Vidhi (4) Aṅgiras-Kalpa (5) Śānti-Kalpa. Probably (2) is the Vidhāna-Kalpa and (3)is the Saṁhitā-Kalpa as in the CVS, p. 46.

* This reading is meaningless. Vā P.61.55 reads *ṣaṭśaḥ* (*kṛtvā*)' dividing in six parts'. O excellent sages ! Having divided in six parts the Purāṇa has been assigned by me (to my pupils).

2. VV.63-69 sum up the position regarding the Purāṇa tradition entrusted to Romaharṣaṇa, the Sūta. Although he had six disciples, the Purāṇas were composed by Romaharṣaṇa (the original Saṁhitā), Kāśyapa, Sāvarṇi and Śāṁśapāyana. These Purāṇas consisted of four *Pādas* (parts) each and of 4000 verses in each Purāṇa (except that of Śāṁśapāyana).

68-69. All of them comprise four thousand verses except Śāṁśapāyanikā. Laumaharṣaṇikā is the original one. Kāśyapikā is the next one. Sāvarṇika is the third one embellished with straight-forward statements and themes. The Śāṁśapāyanikā Saṁhitā is embellished by impressive and inspiring themes.

70.[1] There are altogether eight thousand and six hundred Ṛk Mantras. There are fifteen, ten and ten more Ṛks (35 i.e. altogether 8635).

71-73. [2]Along with the Vālakhilya and Suparṇa hymns they are stated to be seven* (?)

The Sāman Mantras altogether are eight thousand and fourteen. The Sāmagas sing this along with the Āraṇyakas and "Ho-Ha" **.

The Ādhvaryava consists of twelve thousand verses[2] and Yajur Mantras. Vyāsa composed as many Yajur and Brāhmaṇa Mantras along with *Grāmya* (rural), Āraṇyaka (Forest) and recitation of sacred texts (scriptural divisions).

74. Henceforth, there is the qualifying adjective Pūrvā (former) for the Kathās (Stories) (?). The Ṛk, Brāhmaṇa and Yajus are remembered as containing *Grāmya, Āraṇyaka* Mantras (?).

75. So also the additional hymns known as *Khilas* and *Upakhilas* of the disciples of Hari-dru. Similarly, the additional

---

1. VV. 70-72 : According to this text the Ṛgveda consists of 8635 Ṛks, but actually the number is 10552 of the Śākala Saṁhitā according to Satvalekar's Svādhyāya Maṇḍal edition—a figure supported by (V.S. p. 17. The Sāma Veda is said to be of 8014 mantras, though actually the present Sāma Saṁhitā consists of 1810 mantras out of which only 75 are of Sāma, the rest belong to the ṚV. The CVS. com., however, supports our Purāṇa as follows:

Aṣṭau Sāmasahaṣrāṇi sāmāni ca caturdaśa.

2. The number of mantras of Ādhvaryava is given as 12000 Yajur mantras, (12330 in Svādhyāya maṇḍal edition).

* The text is obscure. Vā P. 61.62b reads,

vālakhilyāḥ sahapraiṣāḥ sa-savarṇāḥ prakīrtitāḥ /

'Vālakhilyas along with Śāvarṇas and with assistant Priests'—But there, this line is a continuation of previous two lines which are identical with V. 70 hereof.

** *Sahomam* 'along with homa' in Vā P. 61.63.

Mantras of Taittirīyas are remembered as *Parakṣudras* (every short verses like Kṣudra sūkta).

76. In the Veda of Vājasaneyakas, the total number of Ṛk Mantras is reckoned as one thousand nine hundred. The Brāhmaṇa portion is four times that.[1]

77. The total number of Yajur Mantras and Ṛks is eight thousand eight hundred and eighty, along with Śukriya (Sāmas belonging to Pravargya and) *Khila* (Additional) Mantras according to) Yājñavalkya.

78-81. Similarly, listen to (the number of verses) of Cāraṇa Vidyās (a school of Atharva Veda) along with its extent (number).

The total number of Ṛks (according to various Śākhās) is said to be six thousand twenty-six.[2] Yajur Mantras, it is said, are somewhat more than this.

There are eleven thousand ten Ṛks.

There are ten thousand and eighty Ṛks.

There are one thousand and thirty Ṛk Mantras according to the authorities.

This much is the extent of Ṛk Mantras.

Another thing about Atharvan Mantras. It is the conclusion that according to Bahvṛcas the Atharvan Mantras are five thousand.

82. It should be known by the sages that there are a thousand more excepting twenty (i.e. nine hundred and

---

1. This verse is a quotation from Kātyāyana as per com. of CVS, p. 39. The number of verses in Vājasaneyi Saṁhitā is 1900 as per our text and Kātyāyana. But V. 77 states that the total no of Yajur mantras, ṚKS along with Śukriya (i.e. Vājasaneyi Saṁhitā Ch. 36-40 or the Pravargya section of Sāman verse and Khila mantras is 8880 according to Yājñavalkya.

2. VV 78-81 give the extent of the Atharva Veda. According to our text the number of Ṛk (mantras) in the Atharva is 6026 but the Svādhyāya Maṇḍal edition gives 5977 mantras. I believe the plural *Cāraṇa-Vidyānām* in V. 78a should be interpreted to include the nine schools of the Atharva Veda such as Paippala, Śaunaka, Dānta and others mentioned in CVS. But the CVS, later states that the five Kalpas viz. Nakṣatra, Vidhāna, Vidhi-Vidhāna, Saṁhitā and Śānti each consists of 500 (*Pañca-Śatāni*) mantras, but the total of these is given twelve thousand (CVS, pp 46-47). It appears that our Purāṇa writer gives traditional round figures without verifying (and counting the mantras in) the original Saṁhitās.

eighty). What is said here is in accordance with Aṅgirasas.[1] They have Āraṇyakas also.

83. Thus, the number is reckoned. The different branches are mentioned. The originators of the branches and the causes of difference (are also mentioned).

84. There are differences of branches (of Vedic schools) in all the Manvantaras in this manner. The Śruti (as uttered by) Prajāpati is eternal. These are remembered as their alternative recensions.

85-86. On account of the fact that the Devas are not eternal, the Mantras originate, again and again.[2] The differences among the Śrutis during Dvāpara Yugas have been recounted.

Thus, after classifying the Vedās and handing them over to his disciples, the godly excellent sage went to the forest for performing penance.

87-89a. These different schools of Vedic branches have been evolved by his disciples and the disciples of his disciples.

There are fourteen Vidyās (Lores) viz. the six Vedāṅgas (Ancillary subjects), the four Vedas, the Mīmāṁsā and Nyāya Vistara (Logic), Dharmaśāstra and Purāṇa (Mythology).

Four more lores viz. *Āyurveda* (Medicine), *Dhanurveda* (Science of archery) *Gāndharva* (Musicology), these three together with *Arthaśāstra* (Economics, Political economy) constitute (along with the former ones) the eighteen lores.[3]

---

1. The old name of the Atharva veda was Atharvāṅgirasa. The Atharvan mantras were auspicious while the Aṅgiras mantras pertain to black magic. According to this Purāṇa the number of such mantras (including those in the Brāhmaṇa portion) is 980.

2. It is a pet theory of our author that Devas are not eternal but *mantras* are so, and they manifest themselves again and again in the new world-order on new creation of the universe.

3. Traditionally there are fourteen *vidyās* (lores or sciences) but by adding four subsidiary Vedas, they are regarded as eighteen. CVS, p. 47 gives the following relations between vedas and upavedas.

Veda	*Upaveda*
The Ṛgveda	The Āyurveda (Science of medicine)
The Yajurveda	The Dhanurveda (Military Science)
The Sāmaveda	The Gāndharvaveda (Music)
The Atharvaveda	The Artha Śāstra (Economics, Politics, Administration, Architecture.

89b-90a. It should be known that Brahmarṣis are the earliest ones, thereafter the Devarṣis and then the Rājarṣis.[1] Thus the sources of origin of the sages are three.

90b-91. Expounders of Brahman (or Veda) are born in the five families viz.—Kāśyapas, Vasiṣṭhas, Bhṛgus, Aṅgirasas and Atris.

Since they approach (ṛṣanti) Brahmā, they are remembered as Brahmarṣis.

92-95. The Devarṣis are the sons of Dharma, Pulastya, Kratu, Pulaha, Pratyūṣa, Deva (Prabhāsa as per Vā.P.) and Kāśyapa. Know them by name.

The Devarṣis (divine sages) Nara and Nārāyaṇa are the sons of Dharma; the Vālakhilyas are the sons of Kratu; Kardama is the son of Pulaha; Kubera is the son of Pulastya; Dala is the son of Pratyūṣa; Nārada and Parvata are the sons of Kāśyapa.

They are remembered as Devarṣis because they approach the Devas.

96. The kings born of the family of Manu, the family of Pururavas, the scions of the families of Ikṣvāku and Nābhāga—these should be known as Rajarṣis (saintly kings).

97. Since they approach the subjects befriending and delighting them, they are called Rājarṣis.

Brahmarṣis devoid of impurities are remembered as those who are well established in the region of Brahmā.

98. The splendid Devarṣis should be known as those who are well established in the world of the Devas.

All Rājarṣis are considered to be those (who are) well established in the world of Indra.

99-103. I shall tell the characteristics of those who, on account of their nobility of birth, penance and ability to utter (compose and recite) *mantras*, are proclaimed as Bramharṣis (Brahmanical sages), divine sages (Devarṣis) and Rājarṣis (Royal sages).

They have the knowledge of the past, present and future; they invariably utter the truth; they are self-contented, self-

1. VV.89-103 define the terms Brahmarṣi, Devarṣi, Rājarṣi, enumerate their names and describe their powers, competence etc.

enlightened and famous on account of their penance; they are able to realise everything even while in the womb; they compose and recite Mantras, are able to go everywhere on account of their masterly super-power; they are Devas, Brāhmaṇas and Kings—those who have acquired all these are considered to be sages.

Seven of them with seven characteristic good features are remembered as the seven Sages.[1]

104-106. They are long-lived; they compose Mantras; they have divine vision acquired from Īśvara (God); they have started their own lineage; they are perpetually engaged in the enlightenment and can perceive things directly; they have six holy rites; they are modest householders; they deal with every one impartially, faultlessly and in a manner that they cause good religious acts. They sustain themselves by means of tasty exudations prepared by themselves and not all base; they are intelligent householders; they live deep inside the forests.

107. In Kṛta and the other Yugas, at the very outset the establishment of the four castes and stages of life is carried out by all of them.

108. In the early years of the advent of Tretā-Yuga again, these seven sages introduce and establish the division of social classes (*Varṇas*) and stages of life everywhere.

109-110. Heroes and warriors are born again and again in their lineage. The father begets a son and the son later on becomes a father(?). Thus the line continues without a break till the end of the Yuga. The number of these householders is said to be eighty eight thousand.

111. These (householders) resort to the Pitṛyāna to the South of Aryaman (Sun). They take wives unto themselves and perform Agnihotra sacrifices and they are remembered as causes of progeny.

112. The householders are innumerable. They resort to cremation grounds. Eightyeight thousand of them are placed in the Northern path.

1. VV. 104-108 describe the special qualifications and characteristics of Saptarṣis (Seven Sages) as it is their job to create law, order and dharma at the beginning of a Yuga and establish a well organised society.

113. They are the sages with sublimated sexual impulses and it is reported that they have reached heaven. Composers of Mantras and Brāhmaṇas are born at the end of the Yuga.

114-115. Thus, they are repeatedly reborn in the Dvāpara Ages. They are the composers of Kalpa texts (Ritualistic Texts) and different scriptures and treatises on Ārṣa-Vidyā* (Lores pertaining to the Sages).

Vedic rites are put into practice by them again and again in the Dvāpara Yugas in the Vaivasvata Manvantara.

116. The vedas were classified twenty-eight times by the great sages.[1] During the first Dvāpara, the Vedas were classified by the self-born lord himself.

117. During the second Dvāpara, Prajāpati was the Vedavyāsa (classifier of the Vedas). In the third Dvāpara, Uśanas was the classifier and Bṛhaspati (was such arranger) in the fourth.

118. Savitṛ was the classifier in the fifth Dvāpara; lord Mṛtyu is remembered (as the Vyāsa) in the sixth Dvāpara. Indra (did the same) in the seventh and Vasiṣṭha in the eighth.

119. Sārasvata in the ninth, Tridhāman in the tenth; Trivarṣā in the eleventh and Sanadvāja (was the Vyāsa) thereafter (i.e. in the 12th).

---

1. As mentioned before, *Vyāsa* is the designation of the sage who classifies the mass of Vedic mantras in four Saṁhitās in Dvāpara Yuga. The list of such Vyāsas is given in VP. III 3, Bh. P. I.4. 14-25, KP I. 52. The following were the 28 Vyāsas in each of the various Dvāpara Yugas according to our Purāṇa. 1. The Self-born god (Svayambhū) 2. Prajāpati, 3. Uśanas, 4. Bṛhaspati, 5. Savitṛ, 6. Mṛtyu, 7. Indra, 8. Vasiṣṭha, 9. Sārasvata, 10. Tridhāman 11. Trivarṣā, 12. Sanadvāja, 13. Antarikṣa, 14. Dharma, 15 Traiyāruṇi, 16. Dhanañjaya, 17. Kṛtañjaya, 18. Ṛjīṣa, 19. Bharadvāja, 20. Gautama, 21. Uttama, 22. Haryavana, 23. Vena. 20. Vājaśravaṇa 25. Somamukhyāyana, 26. Tṛṇabindu, 27. Tataja, 28. Śakti, 29. Parāśara 30. Jātukarṇa 31. Dvaipāyana, 32. Future Vyāsa V Drauṇi (Aśvatthāman).

It is strange that 31 Vyāsas should be mentioned instead of the prescribed no. 28. Moreover, there are discrepancies in the lists of Vyāsas in other Purāṇas. For example KP. I.52 gives the following different names of Vyāsas 11. Ṛṣabha, 12. Sutejas, 14. Sucakṣus, 22. Nārāyaṇa, 24. Vālmīki.

* *bhāṣya-vidyās* 'Commentatorial Lores' in Vā P. 61.3.

120. Antarīkṣa (was Vyāsa) in the thirteenth; Dharma in the fourteenth; Traiyāruṇi in the fifteenth and Dhanañjaya in the sixteenth.

121. Kṛtañjaya in the seventeenth; Ṛjīṣa in the eighteenth; after Ṛjīṣa, Bharadvāja was the Vyāsa and Gautama (was so) after Bharadvāja.

122. After Gautama it was Uttama; Haryavana is remembered (as Vyāsa) thereafter; Vena was after Haryavana and Vājaśravas is remembered (as Vyāsa) thereafter.

123-124. Somamukhyāyana was after Vājaśravas and Tṛṇabindu thereafter. After Tṛṇabindu it was Tataja; Śakti is remembered (as Vyāsa) after Tataja; Parāśara (was so) after Śakti. Jātūkarṇa came thereafter and Dvaipāyana is remembered (as the Vyāsa) thereafter.

125-126. Thus twentyeight Vedavyāsas are the ancient ones. In the future Dvāpara, when Dvaipāyana Vedavyāsa passes away, Droṇi of great power of penance, shall become Vedavyāsa. In the future also there will be the classifications of branches (of Vedic Schools).

127-128. Brahmā had acquired Brahman (Vedic knowledge) that is imperishable by means of penance. Holy rite is also acquired by means of penance and fame by the holy rite. Again, truthfulness is acquired by splendour and the imperishable Bliss is acquired by truthfulness. The pure, immortal Brahman, the imperishable Bliss, is enveloped and pervaded by Satya (Truth). Brahman alone is called Amṛta (nectar immortal).

129. It is eternal, determined as this one-syllabled *Om* alone. It is designated as the Brahman on account of its greatness or (inconceivable) vastness and its quality of firmness.

130. Obeisance to that Brahman that is established in Praṇava (i.e. Oṁkāra); that is remembered again and again as Bhūr, Bhuvaḥ, Svaḥ in the Vedas—the Atharvan, Ṛk, Yajus and Sāman.

131. Obeisance to that excellent Brahman that is designated as the cause of annihilation and origination of the Universe and that is the esoteric secret beyond Mahat.

132. It is unfathomable, unlimited and imperishable or inexhaustible. It is the source of origin of delusion of the Universe. It gets the aims of human life realised through illumination and activity.

133. It is the firm support of those who have the knowledge of Śāṅkhya system; it is the goal of those who have perfect control over their minds and sense-organs; it is mentioned as *Avyakta* (unmanifest one); the Brahman is the eternal material cause Prakṛti.

134. It is indicated and extolled as (by means of the following terms): *Pradhāna* (chief), *Ātmayoni* (source of the origin of the self), the mysterious secret Being or Consciousness; *Avibhāga* (undivided), *Śukra* (pure), *Akṣara* (imperishable) and *Bahudhātmaka* (that which appears as multiformed).

135. Perpetual and repeated obeisance unto that Supreme Brahman. In the Kṛta Yuga (as) there is no religious rite, how can there be persons who have not done their religious duties?

136-142. Whatever is done once in the world, that which is committed and omitted, what should be heard and what is heard, whether good or bad, what should be known and pondered over, what should be touched and eaten, what should be seen or heard or smelt somehow (is Brahman itself).

What is shown by it is understood by the Devarṣis. Who is competent to seek and find out what has not been pointed out? It is God alone who has declared all things, everything and every one. Whenever anything is done by anyone, he identifies himself with it.

What is done here before, is not spoken about by another. When something is done by some-one, somewhere and somehow, it is done by it alone (i.e. Brahman). The act (merely) appears to be that of the doer.

Virakti (Absence of passion), Atirakti (too much of passion), knowledge and ignorance, pleasure and displeasure, *dharma* and *adharma* (virtue and evil), happiness and sorrow, death and immortality, the state of being above, below or at the sides—all these belong (to that Brahman) that is the cause of the unseen (destiny).

143-144. They belong to the self-born lord, the eldest Brahmā *Parameṣṭhin* (the highest Deity). During the Tretā Yugas, again and again it becomes understandable to every one. What is to be understood as one (the State of being a Single Veda) is divided and classified during Dvāpara Yugas again and again. Brahmā communicated these Vedas at the beginning, during the Vaivasvata Manvantara.

145. Sages are repeatedly born in the Yugas again and again. They compose various Saṁhitās as they are born of each other.

146. Eighty-eight thousand Śrutarṣis are remembered. So many Saṁhitās are repeated again and again.

147. In every Yuga, those Śākhās are classified again and again by those who resorted to cremation grounds and the Southern path.

148. In all the Dvāpara Yugas, the Saṁhitās (are classified) by the Śrutarṣis. These Śākhās are in vogue again and again in their *Gotras* (families).

149-150. The Śākhās are the same and the composers too are the same. This is true till the end of the Yugas. In the same manner should be understood everything in all the Manvantaras of the past and the future.[1]

151. There are classifications of Śākhās in all the Manvantaras. They have passed by in the past Manvantaras; they exist in the current Manvantara. Whatever is going to take place will take place in the future Manvantaras. The succeeding one should be understood by means of the preceding one, and both should be understood by means of the current one.

152-153a. The decisive (knowledge) regarding the Manvantara is in the same manner. Thus the Devas, the Pitṛs, the sages and the Manus go up along with the Mantras and return along with them.

---

1. This purāṇa repeatedly emphasises the belief that everything takes place in the manner by the same persons as in the previous Manvantara vide *ṚV* X.190.3 *Dhātā yathā-pūrvam akalpayat*. There is little that is absolutely unprecedented and new.

153b-156. All the gods go to and from Janaloka again and again for ten Kalpas. When the time for return arrives, they come into contact with the inevitability of death. Thereafter, they perceive birth full of defects and preceded by ailments. So they return. Their return at that time is due to their seeing the defects. Thus they move to and fro ten times in the course of many Deva Yugas. From the Janaloka they go to Tapoloka, from where they do not return.

157. Thus thousands of Deva-Yugas have passed by. They face death in the Brahmaloka along with the sages.

158. It is not possible to describe them in detail and in due order because time has no beginning and numbers (are endless).

159-163. Manvantaras have elapsed along with the Kalpas, Sages, Pitṛs and the Devas. They are created at the due period. The Yugas come and go. In this manner hundreds and thousands of Kalpas and Manvantaras have gone by along with the subjects. At the end of a Manvantara there is annihilation and at the end of annihilation there is creation. It is impossible to describe in due order the creation and annihilation of the Devas, Sages, Pitṛs and Manvantaras even in the course of hundreds of years.[1]

Understand the number of years of Manvantara in human reckoning.

164-166. The extent of Manvantaras has been calculated by persons who are experts in calculation. Every Manvantara extends to three hundred and six million seven hundred and twenty thousand years without the extra years (of Sandhyās and Sandhyāṁśas). This calculation of Manvantara is in accordance with human reckoning. I shall mention the Manvantara in accordance with the divine reckoning of years.

167-168. In accordance with the divine reckoning the Manvantara comprises of eight hundred and fifty two thousand years. Fourteen times this period is called *Ābhūtasamplava* (the annihilation of all living beings). A thousand sets of four Yugas are proclaimed as a day of Brahmā.

1. This is another way of stating the eternal nature of time.

169-170. After that all the living beings become burned by the rays of the sun. Keeping Brahmā at the head and accompanied by the Devas, Sages and the Dānavas, they enter lord Nārāyaṇa, the most excellent among the gods. It is he who creates all living beings again and again, at the beginning period of all Kalpas.

171. Thus this is considered to be *Sthiti Kāla* (period of Sustenance) along with the Devarṣis. Understand the *Prati-Sandhi* (Intervening periods) of all Manvantaras.

172. What is called Yuga has been recounted by me before, O sinless ones. The period comprising of Kṛta, Tretā etc. is declared as Catur-yuga (a set of four Yugas).

173. The lord has said that the period of Manu's reign consists of seventyone sets of four Yugas along with the extra years (of the Sandhyās and Sandhyāṁśas).

174. Thus, the characteristic feature of all the Manvantaras past and future has been described by means of the present (current) one.

175. Thus, the creation of Svāyambhuva Manu has been recounted to you. I shall mention its Pratisandhi as well as that of the other.[1]

176. A Manvantara duly repeats itself as before along with the sages and the Devas on account of the inevitability of events.

177-179a. The lords of the three worlds, the seven sages, the Devas, the Pitṛs and the Manus who had been in existence earlier in this Manvantara, realise the imminence of their death at the time when the period of Manvantara along with the extra years becomes complete. They know that their reign has come to an end. On realising this, they become sad and all of them are eager to go to Maharloka.

179b-180. When that Manvantara comes to a close, when the period of existence is complete, those Devas may stay on for the period of a Kṛta Yuga. Then the future lords of the Manvantara are born.

---

1. VV. 176 ff. describe the *pratisandhi*—the transition from one Yuga to another and from one Manvantara to another.

181-186a. So also the Devas, the Pitṛs, the sages and Manu.

When the Manvantara comes to a close, when, similarly, the Kali Yuga also comes to an end, the Kṛta Yuga sets in even when the *Kaliśiṣṭas* (Persons who survive the final stage of Kali) are present.

Just as the continuity of the Kṛta Yuga is remembered as preceded by Kali Yuga by learned men, so also the beginning of Manvantaras is preceded by the ends of Manvantara.

When the previous Manvantara has come to a close and another one has begun, at the beginning of the Kṛta Yuga, the seven sages and Manu who have survived, remain there biding their time. Their sages who have become exhausted wait for the (incoming) Manvantara in order to celebrate the advent of the new Manvantara and for the sake of progeny.

When the creation of rainfall begins they begin to function as before.

186b-189. When mutually opposed pairs start functioning, when the medicinal herbs have begun to grow, when the subjects devoid of abodes have begun to stay here and there, when the agricultural activities have begun, when piety and virtue have subsided, when the whole world is devoid of gaiety, when the mobile and the immobile beings are ruined (i.e. those that had been ruined before had not been revived), when (the whole society) beginning with the villages and ending with the towns has become devoid of the discipline of classification of castes and stages of life, those righteous men, the seven sages and Manu who have survived from the previous Manvantara, remain ready for their progeny.

190-191. Even as they perform penance extremely difficult to be performed for the sake of progeny, the Devas, the Asuras, the Pitṛs, the sages, the serpents, the ghosts and goblins, the Gandharvas, the Yakṣas and the Rākṣasas are born as before on the death of the earlier persons.

192. Then those who have survived among them viz. the seven sages and Manu begin to expound the behaviour and conduct of life of good men at the beginning of the Manvantara.

193-194. Men begin to perform holy rites along with the Devas. By means of the vow of celibacy they repay the debts unto the sages. By means of progeny they repay the debts unto the Pitṛs, and by means of sacrifice they repay the debts unto the Devas. They abide by the Dharma consisting of the discipline of conduct for (different) castes for a hundred thousand years.

195. After establishing the three Vedas, the process of agricultural operation, administration of justice, pious rites, duties and the practice of all castes of stages of life and after building hermitages (for penance), they thought of departing to the heaven.

196. When the earlier Devas were thus eager to proceed to heaven all of those gods who established themselves perfectly in religion stayed perfectly virtuous.

197. When the Manvantara has passed by, they leave off all their abodes and go along with Mantras to the Maharloka that is free from ailments.

198. They had returned from their authoritative positions. They had acquired mental Siddhis. With perfect control over their sense-organs, they remain waiting for the total annihilation of all the *bhūtas* (i.e. the end of the universe).

199-200. Then, when the earlier Devas have passed away, when the abodes of the Devas have become vacant in all the three worlds, other Devas who are heaven-dwellers become present here. Thereafter, those who are endowed with the power of penance fill their (vacant) abodes.

201-202. They possess truthfulness, virtue, vow of celibacy and learning. The passing away of the seven sages, of Manu, of the Devas, and of the Pitṛs, of the past and future (has been mentioned) from the beginning. There is no break in the line of their progeny till the termination of the Manvantara.

203. It is in this same manner that the *Sthiti* (continuance in life) of those persons is also in the same order as before in all the Manvantaras till all the living beings are annihilated.

204. The characteristic feature of the transitional stage of the previous Manvantaras of the past and future has been mentioned by Svāyambhuva (son of the self-born lord) i.e. (by what is mentioned about the Svāyambhuva Manvantara).

205. The achievements (happenings) of the future Manvantaras depends upon the past Manvantaras. Thus, the unbroken line of progeny continues till the annihilation of all living beings.

206. (Defective Verses). The changes of the Manvantaras are invariably continuous in the Maharloka. The people of the Mahar and Jana worlds proceed to (and establish in) Satya-Loka.

207. By the vision of the (future) happenings there and by the knowledge of the evident manifoldness, those who are established in Satya Loka remain steady there on account of its permanence when there is a change in the period of transition of Manvantaras.

208. With the changes of the Manvantara, they leave the Satya-loka in ultimate end (?). Then on account of earnest devotion and abandonment of *Viṣayas* (objects of sense) they enter lord Nārāyaṇa alone.

209. In all the repeated changes of the Manvantaras that have been functioning for a long time, the world of living beings does not remain (still or the same) even for a moment. It is due to the characteristic feature of the Fate that the world of living beings undergoes change by way of decrease and increase.

210-211. Thus are the Manvantaras of those Manus of righteous souls and divine vision who are eulogised by the sages. Obtain these directly as composed by Vāyu, by means of a happy mixture of detailed explanation and brief condensation. The Manus have divine power. All the Manvantaras contain saintly kings, divine sages, Brahminical sages, Devas, and serpents. The Manvantaras are duly endowed with the lord of Devas, Seven Sages, Lord of the subjects and Pitṛs.

212-215. It is meritorious to glorify the Īśvaras (Gods). They are born of noble and liberal-minded families. They have great fame. They have flourished on account of their excellent intellect. They are honoured and worshipped on account of their reputation, lustre and renown.

This (story) is conducive to the attainment of the heaven, it is very holy; it is a great esoteric secret; it is conducive to the birth of a son. This excellent story should be recited during the great Parvan days. It quells misery and it bequeaths longevity.

May the lord of subjects endowed with Yogic power bestow Siddhi on me, because I have glorified succinctly the famous progeny of Aja (the unborn Lord Brahmā) that is holy and that mainly consists of kings, divine sages (or Devas and Sages) and Manu.

Thus the Svāyambhuva Manvantara has been recounted in detail and in due order. What shall I describe again ?

CHAPTER THIRTYSIX

The Lineage of Manu : Manvantaras[1] *Milking of the Earth*

Śāṁśapāyana said :—

1. I wish to hear about the remaining Manvantaras[1] in the proper sequence and also about the rulers of the Manvantaras as well as those whose leaders are Śakra (Indra) and (other) Devas.

---

1. The description of Manvantaras is one of the five essential Characteristics of a Purāṇa. Purāṇas like Bh. P. VIII. 1.29, NP. I.40.17-37, VP.III. Chap. 1 and 2, KP. I.51, Vā. P. 62 describe the various *uvuvantaras*. Each Manu presides over the world for seventy-one cycles of four Yugas. He has his separate set of Indra, gods, Saptarṣis etc. There is a general agreement of Purāṇas about the names of the first seven Manus (including the present one viz. Vaivasvata). But there are some differences in the names of future Manus but most of them are bracketed under a common name Sāvarṇi such as Dharma Sāvarṇi, Rudra Sāvarṇi etc. Our Purāṇa, however, gives some different names such as Raucya, Bhautya of the future Manus.

Sūta said :—

2. Understand even as I recount succinctly and in detail about those Manvantaras which have gone by and which are yet to come.

3-5. The following six are the Manus of the past viz. Svāyambhuva Manu at the outset; then Svārociṣa Manu, then Uttama, Tāmasa, Raivata and Cākṣuṣa. I shall mention the eight (Manus) of the future (four of whom are) Sāvarṇi, Raucya, Bhautya and Vaivasvata. I shall narrate these (later on) before Vaivasvata Manu. The five Manus of the past—know them to be *Mānasas* (Mental Sons).

6-7. I have already recounted to you the Manvantara of Svāyambhuva Manu. Henceforth, I shall mention succinctly the creation of the subjects by the second noble-souled Manu Svārociṣa.[1] In the Manvantara of Svārociṣa the Tuṣitas were the gods.

8-12. So also the scholars Pārāvatas. Thus two groups are remembered.

The sons of Kratu (also known as) Svārociṣ were born of Tuṣita. The Pārāvatas were Vāsiṣṭhas (? Sons of Vasiṣṭha). Two groups are remembered (each consisting of) twelve. These twentyfour Devas are considered as *Chandajas*.

The Tuṣitas are—Divasparśa, Jāmitra, Gopada, Bhāsura, Aja, Bhagavān, Draviṇa of great strength, Āya of powerful arms, Mahaujas of great virility, Cikitvān who was well-known, Aṁśa and Ṛta the twelfth among them. These are glorified as Tuṣitas.

1. Just as in the 1st Manvantara, Svāyambhuva (the son of god Brahmā) was the presiding Manu, Yāmas were the gods, Yajña, the incarnation of Viṣṇu officiated as Indra and the seven sages were Marīci, Atri, Aṅgiras, Pulaha, Kratu, Pulastya and Vasiṣṭha were the Saptarṣis, VV. 6-20 describe the 2nd Manvantara in which Svārociṣa was the Manu, the twelve Tuṣitas and 12 Pārāvatas were the gods (Devas), Vipaścit was the Indra and the seven sages (the descendants of the seven sages of the previous Manvantara) viz. Ūrja, Stamba, Prāṇa, Ṛṣabha, Datta, Niścala and Arvarivān were the Saptarṣis and Caitra, Kimpuruṣa and other nine sons of Manu Svārociṣa.

Thus we find such sets of gods, sages, Indra etc. in each Manvantara in the following verses.

It may be noted that there are some variations in the names of these gods and sages in different Purāṇas.

These were the sons of Kratu. They were *Somapāyins* (Imbibers of the Soma juice).

13-15. The Pārāvatas were as follows :

Pracetas the shining one, Viśvadeva, Samañja, the famous Ajihma, Arimardana, Āyurdāna, Mahāmāna, Divyamāna, Ajeya of great fortune and grandeur, Yavīyān (younger one) of great strength, Hotṛ and Yajvan. Thus the Pārāvatas, have been recounted. Thus these were the Devas in the Svārociṣa Manvantara.

16. The twentyfour gods were the *Somapās* (Imbibers of Soma juice) then. Their Indra then was Vipaścit, well-known all over the worlds.

17-18. The seven sages were—(1) Ūrja son of Vasiṣṭha, (2) Stambha son of Kaśyapa, (3) Prāṇa son of Bhṛgu, (4) Ṛṣabha son of Aṅgiras, (5) Datta son of Pulastya, (6) Niścala Ātreya son of Atri and (7) Arvarīvān son of Pulaha.

19-20. The following are declared as the nine sons of Svārociṣa Manu, viz. Caitra, Kimpuruṣa, Kṛtānta, Vibhṛta, Ravi, Bṛhaduktha, Nava, Satu and Śruta. They were the perpetuators of the line of lord Manu. They have been thus enumerated in the Purāṇas. This is the second Manvantara.

21. These four viz. Manu, the seven sages, the Devas and the Pitṛs—constitute the root (the basis) of a Manvantara and their descendants are the subjects.

22. The following is the conclusion in the scriptural texts—The deities are the sons of the sages; the Pitṛs are the sons of the Devas, and the sages are the sons of the Devas.

23. The Kṣatriyas and the Vaiśyas (were born) of Manu and the Brāhmaṇas of the seven sages. Thus the Manvantara has been recounted succinctly and not in details.

24-25a. The details of the Śvārociṣa Manvantara should be known from that of the Svāyambhuva Manvantara. It is not possible to describe it in details even in hundreds of years, on account of the repeated multiplicity of the subjects in every family.

25b-27a. In the third Manvantara of Uttama,[1] five

1. VV. 25b-41 describe the 3rd Manvantara called Uttama.

groups of Devas are mentioned. I shall mention them. Understand.

They are Sudhāmans, Vaśavartins, Pratardanas, Śivas and Satyas. Each of these groups consists of twelve Devas.

27b-28. The twelve Sudhāmans are called (1) Satya, (2) Dhṛti, (3) Dama (4) Dānta (5) Kṣama (6) Kṣāma (7) Dhvani (8) Śuci (9) Iṣa (10) Ūrja (11) Śreṣṭha and the twelfth one Suparṇa by name.

29-31. The Vaṁśavartins (Vaśavartins) are mentioned as follows : Sahasradhāra, Viśvāyu, the two Samitāras, Bṛhat, Vasu, Viśvadhā, Viśvakarman, Mānasa, Virājasa, Jyoti and Vibhāsa.

The Pratardanas are glorified. They are—Avadhya, Avarati, lord Vasu, Dhiṣṇya, Vibhāvasu, Vitta, Kratu, Sudharman, Dhṛtadharman, Yaśasvija, Rathormi and Ketumān.

32-33. There are twelve other (Devas) worthy of partaking of their shares in the Yajña viz. Haṁsasvara, the liberal-minded Pratardana and Yaśaskara, Sudāna, Vasudāna, Sumañjasa, Viṣa, Yama, Vahni, Yati, Sucitra and Sutapas. They are to be known as Śivas.

34-36. Understand the names of the Satya group of gods as they are viz. Dikpati, Vākpati, Viśva, Śambhu, Svamṛḍīka, Divi, Varcodhāman, Bṛhadvapus, Aśva, Sadaśva, Kṣema and Ānanda. These twelve Devas who are worthy of partaking of their shares in the Yajña are recounted as Satyas.

Thus these were the gods in the Manvantara of Uttama.

37. They were the sons of Uttama, the Prajāpati, the Aṅgiras (?). The Indra (leader) of those Devas was well-known by the name Suśānti.

38. Vasiṣṭha had seven sons well known as Vāsiṣṭhas. All those were the seven sages in the Manvantara of Uttama.

39-40. Uttama the noble-souled Manu had thirteen sons viz. Aja, Paraśu, Divya, Divyauṣadhi, Naya, Devāmbuja, the unequalled Mahotsāha, Gaja, Vinīta, Suketu, Sumitra, Sumati and Śruti.

41. These were the progenitors of the race of Kṣatriyas. This is the third Manvantara. Thus the creation of Uttama has been recounted along with that of Svārociṣa.

42-43. Understand the creation of Tāmasa[1] in detail and in due order. In the fourth Manvantara of Tāmasa, the Manu, the sets (of Devas) proclaimed are viz. Satyas, Surūpas, Sudhīs and Haris. Those Devas in the Manvantara of Tāmasa were the sons of Pulastya.

44-48. Each of those sets of Devas consisted of twenty-five (Devas). (Defective text) In that Manvantara the Indriyas (? sense-organs) are remembered as the Devas. It is through the sense-organs that people understand things. The sages affirm (about the sense-organs). They have their testimonies. *Manas* (the Mind) the eighth one (?) is that at the head.

Śibi of great exploits, is the Indra of those Devas. O excellent ones, understand those seven sages who were in that Manvantara. They were—Kāvya the son of Aṅgiras, Pṛthu the son of Kaśyapa, Agni the son of Atri, Jyotirdhāman the son of Bhṛgu, Caraka the son of Pulaha, Pīvara the son of Vasiṣṭha and Caitra the son of Pulastya.

49-50. The following were the sons of Tāmasa, the Manu viz. Jānujaṅgha, Śānti, Nara, Khyāti, Śubha, Priyabhṛtya, Parīkṣit, Prasthala, Dṛḍheṣudhi, Kṛśāśva and Kṛtabandhu.

Understand the groups of Devas mentioned in the fifth (? second) Manvantara of Svārociṣa.*

51-54. They were Amitābhas, Ābhūtarayas, Vikuṇṭhas and Sumedhas.

Variṣṭhas were the splendid sons of Variṣṭha the Prajāpati**(?).

There were fourteen very brilliant Devas in each of the four Gaṇas (sets of gods).

The following fourteen are remembered as the Devas called Amitābhas in the Svārociṣa (Cāriṣṇava in Vā. P.) Manvantara viz. Ugra, Prajña, Agnibhava, Prajyoti, Amṛta, Sumati, Virāva (? Vāvirāva), Dhāman, Nāda, Śravas, Vṛtti, Rāśi, Vāda and Śabara.

---

1. VV. 42-50 detail the fourth Manvantara Tāmasa.

* Some misprint, as the order of Manvantaras is confused here.

** Vā. P. 62-46 reads "the sons of Cariṣṇu" for 'Variṣṭhas' hereof.

55-56. They know that the names of the set (called) Ābhūtarayas are as follows :—Mati, Sumati, Ṛta, Satya, Edhana, Adhṛti, Vidhṛti, Dama, Niyama, Vrata, Viṣṇu, Sahas, Dyutimān and Suśravas.

57-60. Vṛṣa, Bhettṛ, Jaya, Bhīma, Śuci, Dānta, Yaśas, Dama, Nātha, Vidvān, Ajeya, Kṛśa, Gaura and Dhruva. These have been glorified as Vikuṇṭha (class of gods).

Understand the (gods called) Sumedhas. They are Medhas, Medhātithi, Satyamedhas, Pṛśnimedhas, Alpamedhas, Bhūyomedhas the lord, Dīpti-Medhas, Yaśo-Medhas, Sthiramedhas, Sarvamedhas, Sumedhas, Pratimedhas, Medhajas and Medhahantṛ.

61-62. Vibhu of great exploits and manliness was their Indra.

In the Raivata[1] Manvantara the seven sages were—Devabāhu the son (or descendent) of Pulastya; the descendant of Kaśyapa named Sudhāman; Hiraṇyaroman the descendant of Aṅgiras, Vedaśrī the descendant of Bhṛgu, Ūrdhvabāhu the descendant of Vasiṣṭha, Parjanya the descendant of Pulaha, and Satyanetra the descendant of Atri.

63-64. The sons of Raivata were :—Mahāvīrya, Susambhāvya, Śatyaka, Harahā, Śuci, Balabandhu, Nirāmitra, Kambu, Śṛṅga and Dhṛtavrata.

This is the fifth Manvantara.

65. Svārociṣa, Uttama, Tāmasa and Raivata—these four Manus are considered as belonging to the family of Priyavrata.

66-67. In the sixth Manvantara[2] viz. Cākṣuṣa Manvantara, the five sets of Devas are remembered viz. Ādyas, Prasūtas, Bhāvyas, Pṛthukas and the Lekhas of great majestic lustre. All of them were heaven-dwellers. They are called after the names of their mothers (?).[3]

---

1. VV. 51-65 describe what is generally known as Raivata Manvantara but is wrongly called Svārociṣa in this text. Vā. P. calls this Cāriṣṇava Manvantara. It is in VV. 61-62 that our text corrects itself and calls this as Raivata Manvantara.

2. VV. 66-81 give the outline of the 6th—Cākṣuṣa Manvantara.

3. Does the author want to suggest the existence of matriarchical society in the 6th Manvantara?

68. They were the grandsons of Āraṇya (?) the Prajāpati, who was the son of Atri. Each of these groups is remembered as comprising of eight Devas.

69. Antarīkṣa, Vasu, Havya, Atithi, Priyavrata, Śrotā, Mantā and Anumantā—these are glorified as Ādyas.

70-72. Śyenabhadra, Śvetacakṣus, Mahāyaśas, Sumanas, Pracetas, Vanenas, Supracetas and Muni of great inherent strength—these are mentioned Frasūtas.

Vijaya, Sujaya, Mana, Syoda (?) (Udyāna in Vā. P.) Mati, Parimati, Viceta's and Priyaniścaya—these Devas are remembered as Bhāvyas.

Understand now the Pṛthukas.

73-74. Ojiṣṭha, god Śakuna, Vānahṛṣṭa, Satkṛta, Satyadṛṣṭi, Jigīṣu, Vijaya and Ajita of great fortune—these are the heaven-dwellers (named) Pṛthukas. I shall mention the (group of gods called) Lekhas also by name. Understand.

75-76. Manojava, Praghāsa, Pracetas of great fame, Dhruva, Dhruvakṣiti, Acyuta of great vigour, Yuvanas and Bṛhaspati—(thus) the Lekhas have been gloriously recounted. Manojava of great virility became their Indra then.

77-78. The following were the seven sages in the Cākṣuṣa Manvantara viz. Uttama the son (descendant) of Bhṛgu; Haviṣmān the son of Aṅgiras; Sudhāman the son of Kaśyapa; Virajas the son of Vasiṣṭha; Atināman the son of Pulastya; Sahiṣṇu the son of Pulaha and Madhu the son of Atri.

79-80. The following ten were the sons of Cākṣuṣa Manu born of Naḍvalā viz. Ūru, Pūru, Śatadyumna, Tapasvin, Satyavāk, Kṛti, Agniṣṭut, Atirātra, Sudyumna and Abhimanyu the tenth. This is the sixth Manvantara.

81. His creation is reckoned on the basis of Vaivasvata Manvantara the current one. Thus the Manvantara of Cākṣuṣa Manu (has been recounted) in detail and in the due order.

The sages said :—

82. Whose successor and heir was Cākṣuṣa? In whose family was he born? Recount factually unto us all other persons born of his family.[1]

1. VV. 82-102 trace the genealogy of Cākṣuṣa Manu from Atri Uttānapāda Dhruva etc.

Sūta said :—

83. Listen to the succinct account, O Brāhmaṇas of the creation of Cākṣuṣa in whose family was born Pṛthu the valorous son of Vena.

84-86. There are other lords of subjects (such as) Dakṣa, the son of Pracetas.

Atri, the Prajāpati, accepted Uttānapāda as his son. Since the Prajāpati was a king, he became his adopted son. He was given in adoption by Svāyambhuva Manu to Atri for some reason, after the advent of the sixth future Manvantara of Cākṣuṣa. With this as introduction I shall recount it, O Brāhmaṇas.

87-88. Sūnṛtā, the beautiful lady of excellent hips, the daughter of Dharma, gave birth to the four sons of Uttānapāda. That lady, well-known by the name Sūnṛtā, was the splendid mother of Dhruva. That lady of sparkling smiles was born of Lakṣmī, the wife of Dharma.

89-90a. Uttānapāda begot the sons Dhruva, Kīrtimān, Āyuṣmān and Vasu. He begot two daughters of sparkling smiles viz. Svarā and Manasvinī. The sons of these two ladies (have already been) mentioned.

90b-93a. In the first Tretā Yuga, the grandson of Svāyambhuva (Manu), Dhruva of great virility, performed a penance without taking in food for ten thousand years according to the divine reckoning. He was desirous of (and prayed for) acquiring great fame. Praying for great fame, he practised all the Yogic rites. Brahmā who was delighted with him, bestowed on him the excellent abode among the luminaries. It is divine and devoid of rising and setting, till the total annihilation of all living beings.

93b-95. On seeing his great grandeur and prosperity, Uśanas, the preceptor of the Daityas and the Asuras sang this verse :—

'O ! How wonderful is the power of his penance'! O (how commendable is) his learning ! O (how great is) the holy rite, whereby the seven sages stand by, after keeping this Dhruva above them.

The heaven is attached to Dhruva. He is the master and lord of the heaven.

96. Bhūmi (the queen of Dhruva) gave birth to the two kings, Sṛṣṭi and Bhavya, (the sons of) Dhruva.

Lord Sṛṣṭi, told his own shadow, "Become a woman".

97. Since he was a man of truthful speech, the shadow became a woman immediately with a divine body. She was embellished with divine ornaments.

98. Sṛṣṭi begot of Chāyā (His spouse, the shadow) five sons devoid of sins viz. Prācīnagarbha, Vṛṣabha, Vṛka, Vṛkala and Dhṛti.

99-100. Suvarcā, the wife of Prācīnagarbha, gave birth to a son named Udāradhī who was Indra in his previous birth. This lord attained the status of Indra by practising Yogic feats for the period of a Manvantara, by taking food once at the end of a thousand years.

101. Bhadrā gave birth to Divañjaya, the son of Udāradhī. Varāṅgī gave birth to Ripu (the son) of Divañjaya who was a conqueror of his enemies.

102. Bṛhatī gave birth to Cakṣus with all splendour (as the son) of Ripu. Manu, the great scholar, who made the race of Brāhmaṇas and Kṣatriyas function, was his son. Puṣkariṇī (otherwise known as) Vāruṇī gave birth to Cākṣuṣa Manu.

The sages said :—

103. Wherefore is the daughter of Prajāpati, O sinless one, is called Vāruṇī ? Mention this along with the underlying fact. Indeed, you are an adept in detailed narration.

Sūta replied :—

104. Udaka, the son of Araṇya, attained the status of Varuṇa. Therefore, she was known as Vāruṇī. She became well-known thus, on account of her brother.

105. Ten splendid sons were born of Manu and Naḍvalā, the daughter of Viraja, the Prajāpati. They were of great vigour and vitality.

106-107a. They were Ūru, Pūru, Satyadyumna, Tapasvin, Satyavāk, Kṛti, Agniṣṭut, Atirātra, Sudyumna (these nine) and Abhimanyu the tenth. These were the sons of Manu and Naḍvalā.

107b-108. Āgneyī gave birth to Ūru's six sons of great splendour viz. Aṅga, Sumanas of good reputation, Gaya, Śukra, Vraja and Ajina.

Sunīthā gave birth to a single child of Aṅga (named) Vena.

109. There was a great commotion on account of the fault and crime of Vena. For the sake of a progeny, the sages churned his right hand.

110-112. When his hand was churned, the handsome Pṛthu was born. After producing his son Pṛthu of famous valour, the sages said—"O subjects (be) joyous. This is your king. He is born with an armour, wielding a bow. He appears (as if) burning on account of his splendour. This king will bestow sustenance on you all". Pṛthu, the son of Vena, the ancestor of all Kṣatriyas protected all the worlds then.

113. That king was the first among those who were crowned and anointed after the Rājasūya sacrifice. Two clever bards Sūta, Māgadha were also born for the purpose of eulogising him.

114-115. This cow (viz. the earth) was milked by that intelligent great king (for the sake of) vegetables for the subjects who were desirous of sustenance. He was accompanied by the Devas, the groups of sages, the Pitṛs, the Dānavas, the Gandharvas, the groups of celestial damsels, the serpents, the Puṇyajanas (the demons and goblins), the mountains, the trees and the creepers.

116. Being milked in the different vessels, Vasundharā (the Earth containing rich deposits) yielded them milk as desired by them. The subjects sustained their lives thereby.

Śāṁśapāyana requested[1] :—

117-121. O sage of great noble rites, recount the birth (and life- tory) of Pṛthu in detail, how formerly the Earth was

1. The story of Pṛthu and his milking of the earth is a Purāṇic transformation of the Vedic conception of milking of the Virāj cow. The *Virāj Sūkta* (AV. VIII 10) forms the basis of the Purāṇic legend. This purāṇic legend records the right of the sages (public leaders) to do away with a wilful tyrant. This Pṛthu, the son of Vena is a Vedic king and is recorded to have worship-

milked by that noble-souled (Pṛthu), how (he was accompanied) by the Devas, the Nāgas (serpents) the Brahmanical sages, the Yakṣas, the Rākṣasas, the Gandharvas and the celestial damsels formerly, how and by what means (he milked them). Even as we ask, tell us about their different special vessels, the milker, the milk, as well as the different calves used by them. Tell us in due order the special types of milk (yielded by her). For what reason was the hand of Vena churned formerly by the infuriated great sages of yore? Mention that reason unto us.

Sūta Narrated

122. I shall recount to you, O Brāhmaṇas, the birth of Pṛthu, the son of Vena. Listen to it with concentration and purity of mind, O excellent Brāhmaṇas.

123. This *Brahman* (i.e. the story as sacred as the Vedas) should not be communicated to one who is not pure, to one who is a sinner, to one who is not a disciple, to one who is antagonistic and under no circumstances to one who does not observe holy rites.

124-125. The origin of Pṛthu the son of Vena is conducive to the acquisition of wealth, fame, longevity and merit. It is on a par with the Vedas. It is an esoteric secret mentioned by the sages. If any person who is free from jealousy listens to this story or recounts this to others after making obeisance to the Brāhmaṇas, he will never have an occasion to repent over his omissions and commissions of acts.

126. There was a king named Aṅga. The lord was on a par with Atri and was born of the family of Atri. He was a Prajāpatī and a zealous protector of Dharma.

---

ped the Aśvins in his sacrificial chambers (AV. XX. 140.5). The milking of *Virāj* cow by Pṛthu with the earth as a milking pail and Vaivasvata Manu as the calf is recorded in AV. VIII 10.24 (but here Cākṣuṣa Manu is made the calf see V. 202).

The whole episode is a development of an ancient Vedic legend and has been depicted in various Purāṇas as in Bh. P. IV. 18, Mbh. *Śānti* 59.98-128 Mt. P. ch. 10. 1-35, Vā. P. 62. 103-197 (to mention a few). The different motifs introduced here show how social order was established by Pṛthu who was the first crowned and anointed king. The ideal kingship and the happy condition of subjects here is covetable even today.

127. Vena was his son. He was not very much devoted to pious activities. This lord of the subjects was born of Sunīthā the daughter of Mṛtyu.

128. That Vena was the son of the daughter of Kāla (god of death). Hence, on account of a (hereditory) default of his maternal grandfather, he turned his back on Dharma (Virtue) and carried on his activities in the world as he pleased.

129. That king brought to a standstill (prohibited) holy rites and devout practice. Transgressing the (injunction of the) Vedas, and scriptures he became engaged in sinful activities.

130. He was devoid of practice of self-study of the Vedas and the chanting of Vaṣaṭkāra. While he was ruling over the kingdom, the gods never drank the Soma juice in great *Yajñas*.

131. "No Yajña should be performed. No monetary or other gifts should be offered", this was the cruel solemn declaration of that Prajāpati, when his (utter) ruin was imminent.

132. (He declared) "I should be worshipped and honoured in the Yajña by the gods and the twice-born ones. Yajñas should be performed (unto me) and Homas should be offered on my behalf (i.e. with me as the object of worship)".

133. As he exceeded the bounds of decency (because) he had many heroic acts to his credit, all the great sages with Marīci as their leader spoke to him then.

134. "O king, we are going to initiate a religious rite lasting for a hundred years. Do not commit any sinful deed. This is not the eternal Dharma.

135. You are born in the family of the god of death. Undoubtedly you are a Prajāpati. Formerly, you had entered into a contract stipulating, "I shall protect the subjects."

136-139. As all those Brāhmaṇa sages said thus, Vena, of evil intellect, laughed and said—"Who else is an expert on account of the things understood by me? Who else is the creator of the *dharma* whom (whose words) should I listen to (obey)? Who is equal to me on the Earth in regard to heroism, power of penance and truthfulness? You are all slow-witted souls. Certainly, you do not know me factually. I am the source of origin of all the worlds and particularly of all righteous acts. If I so wish I may burn the entire Earth or flood it with water. I may create or swallow (destroy) it. No doubt need be entertained in this respect".

140. Vena was thus defiled excessively on account of his ignoble behaviour. When he could not be dissuaded from his arrogance, the great sages became infuriated.

141. Even as he was struggling, the extremely infuriated great sages seized him by means of both the arms. They twisted and churned the left hand of that very powerful king.

142. It is reported that at the outset an extremely short person was born of that hand that had been crushed and churned. He was dark in colour too.

143. He was extremely frightened. With all his sense-organs in utter confusion, he stood there with joined palms. On seeing him distressed and bewildered they said—"Niṣīda" (sit down).

144. He became a person endowed with endless exploits and established the community of Niṣādas (tribal people, hunters). Moreover he created the Dhīvaras (fishermen) originating from the sins of Vena.

145. Other tribal people who have their abodes on the Vindhya, viz. the Tamburas, the Tuburas, the Khaśas and others with special interest in sinful activities—Understand them as persons born of the sins of Vena.

146. Again the infuriated great sages whose anger had been aroused, churned the right hand of Vena as though it was the *Araṇi* (the piece of wood used to kindle the sacred fire by means of attrition).

147. Pṛthu was born of that hand that resembled a lotus. He was called Pṛthu because he was born of the big (*Pṛthu*) palm of hand.

148-150. He shone with his body (as if) blazing like fire. He wielded the primordial bow of loud report named Ajagava. For the sake of security and protection, he held arrows and the coat of mail of great lustre. When he was born all the living beings everywhere became extremely delighted. They approached the great King. Vena went to heaven (like a) saintly king on account of the birth of a noble-souled good son.

151-152. That tiger among men was saved from the hell named *put* by his noble son. Rivers and the seas took gems and jewels as well as water for the sacred sprinkling (at the time) of coronation and all of them approached him. Lord Grandfather (god Brahmā) came along with Aṅgiras and the immortal ones (gods).

153-154a. All the living beings, both mobile and immobile approached the ruler of men, the son of Vena, the protector of the subjects, of great splendour, with Supreme sovereignty* and sprinkled him with the sacred water.

154b-155a. That great king was anointed (as a sovereign) by gods, the sons of Aṅgiras. Valorous Pṛthu, the son of Vena, was the first (primordial) king of great fortune.

155b. His subjects had been antagonized by his father but they were conciliated and kept satisfied by him.

156-159. Thenceforth, he was named Rājā (king) on account of his *Anurāga* (Affection, love). When he wished to march against the ocean, the waters became stunned and paralysed. Even the mountains crumbled down. But (none of his) flagstaffs got broken. The Earth bore rich harvest without being ploughed. The cows yielded plenty of milk as desired by everyone (or yielded everything desired). There was honey in every cluster of flowers.

At the very same time, while he was performing a sacrifice, while the Soma juice was extracted, Sūta was born of the *Sautya* day (i.e. the day on which the Soma juice was extracted). After he had been born thus, Māgadha (bard) was born.[1]

160. He was born while the Sāmagas (those who sing the Sāman hymns very well) were singing and when Śubhāṇḍa** (?) pertaining to the Viśve-Devas had arrived. Hence he is called Māgadha.

---

* Rājarāja or Kubera is inappropriate in the context. Hence the emendation—*rāja-rājyena* is adopted from Vā.P.62.135.

1. VV. 156-173. As usual the author gives the popular etymologies of Sūta and Māgadha, and records the duties allotted to them. The relation between Māgadhas and their home-land Magadha is clear but not so about Sūta and Anūpa (south Malwa).

** misprint for *srug-bhāṇḍa* 'vessel containing wooden ladles' vide Vā.P. 62.141.

161-162. The *Havis* offerings of Bṛhaspati got mingled with those of Indra. He invoked Indra by means of the *Daiva* (divine) Mantra. It was then that Sūta was born. Thereby a default occurred there and therefore an expiation too in the holy rites (became due). For the Havis offering of the preceptor got mixed and therefore over-powered by the Havya of the disciple.

163-165. On account of the (mingling) activity of the lower and the upper, the progeny became one mixed in caste as in the case of one born of the womb of a Brāhmaṇa lady from a source of origin belonging to a lower caste viz. from a Kṣatriya. The Sūta has similarity with the previous earlier one and hence it is mentioned that he has the same duties as the previous one (i.e. the Brahman). It is the middle dharma of Sūta, the duties of Kṣatriyas. (He has these duties also) viz. looking after and maintaining chariots, elephants and horses. Practice of medicine is the lowliest duty. It was for the sake of eulogising Pṛthu that both of them were called there by the great sages.

166. All the sages told those two—"Let this king be eulogised. This is a job befitting you and this ruler of men is a deserving person".

167-168. The Sūta and Māgadha thereafter said to all those sages,—"We shall please the Devas and the sages by means of our activities. But we do not know anything about the performance, characteristic features and reputation of this king. Wherefore can we eulogise him ? Then the brilliant Brāhmaṇas spoke:

169. "This (king) is always devotedly engaged in his duty. He is truthful in speech. He has perfect control over his sense-organs. He is habituated to the wise pursuit of knowledge. He is liberal-minded and charitably disposed. He is never defeated in battles.

170-173. Those two (i.e. Sūta and Māgadha) were engaged by the sages (with the following instructions) viz. "Let him be eulogised for his future activities".

Sūta and Māgadha eulogised him by composing songs about the past achievements of that powerful king Pṛthu. At the end of that encomium, Pṛthu the lord of the subjects was highly pleased. He gave the land of Anūpa (South Malwa) to Sūta and Magadha to Māgadha. Ever since then the rulers of the Earth are eulogised by Sūtas and Māgadhas. They are awakened (in the morning) by Sūtas, Māgadhas and bards through words and expressions of benediction. On seeing him the subjects were extremely delighted. The great sages said :—

174. "This ruler of men, the son of Vena, shall offer you means of sustenance". Thereupon, the subjects eagerly rushed to the highly fortunate son of Vena.

175-176. "Give us the means of sustenance as per promise by the great sages". On being approached (and requested) thus by the subjects, the mighty ruler with a desire for the welfare of the subjects, seized his bow and arrows and rushed at the Earth. Thereupon, afraid of the son of Vena, the Earth assumed the form of a cow and began to flee.[1]

177-179. Taking the bow with him, Pṛthu pursued her (i.e. the Earth in the form of a cow) as she ran. Afraid of the son of Vena, she went to Brahmā's world and other worlds as well (but eventually) saw the son of Vena in front of her with the bow in his raised hand. He was shining brilliantly on account of the refulgent sharp arrows. He never failed in his aim (in hitting the target). He was noble-souled with great yogic power. He could not be assailed even by the immortal ones. Unable to get succour from elsewhere, she resorted to the son of Vena himself.

180-181. She who was worthy of always being honoured by the three worlds, joined her palms in reverence and said to the son of Vena :—"You are not able to see any sin in killing a woman. How can you sustain the subjects who had been nurtured and brought up by me ? O king, all the worlds are stationed in me. This universe is being supported by me.

182-183. The subjects who have been nurtured by me should not perish for my sake, O king. It does not behove you to kill me. You wish to do something conducive to the

---

1. See note 1, p. 370 above. As stated therein, this is an elaboration of a Vedic legend.

welfare of the subjects. O protector of the Earth, listen to these words of mine. All enterprises begun methodically with proper means become fruitful.

184. Even after killing me, O king, you cannot protect the subjects (If you kill me, you will become incompetent to protect the subjects). I shall be present within. O lustrous one, get rid of your anger.

185. O protector of the Earth, they say that females, even from among the lower categories of animals, should not be killed. It does not behove you to abandon righteous behaviour, in the case of living beings".

186. On hearing these diverse statements of the Earth the magnanimous noble-souled king controlled his anger and spoke to the Earth thus :—

187. "If anyone were to kill one or more for the sake of one whether it be himself or another, then his action is sinful.

188. But O gentle, splendid lady, in case many flourish happily when a single person is killed, there is neither major nor minor sin in the act of his killing.

189. Therefore, O Vasundharā (Earth), I will kill you for the sake of subjects, if you do not carry out my request that is conducive to the welfare of the world.

190. If you turn your face against my behest, I will kill you presently with a single arrow. Establishing my prestige thus, I shall myself sustain the subjects.

191. In compliance of my instructions, O the most excellent one among the up-holders of Dharma (piety), enliven and nourish the subjects perpetually. Indeed, you are capable of it. There is no doubt about it.

192. Adopt also the status of my daughter. In that case I shall withdraw this terrific-looking arrow which I have raised up for slaying you".

193. Thereupon the Earth who had been told thus, replied to the son of Vena :—

"Undoubtedly O ! King, I shall carry out all these behests.

194. Find out that calf unto me whereby I shall pour out milk out of affection. O the most excellent one among the upholders of Dharma, make me flat and level everywhere so that the milk that flows out shall spread everywhere equally".

Sūta said:—

195-200. Thereupon, he removed the heaps or collections of rocks everywhere. The son of Vena removed with the tip of his bow all the mountains that had risen up. In the Manvantaras that had gone by, the Earth had been uneven. (Now) all her uneven parts became even naturally. In the previous creation when the surface of the Earth was uneven, there had been no distinction between cities and villages. There were no plants or crops. There was neither agriculture nor breeding of cattle. There was no market place or trade route. Such had been the condition formerely in the Cākṣuṣa Manvantara. All these had been possible (or created) (only) in the Vaivasvata Manvantara.

The subjects lived in those places wherever there was level ground. Initially the diet of the subjects consisted of fruits and roots.

201. We have heard that at that time their sustenance was maintained with great difficulty. Everything was made available in this world even since the days of the son of Vena.

202. After adopting Cākṣuṣa Manu as the calf, lord Pṛthu milked plants and vegetables from the Earth on its own surface.

203. Those virtuous subjects began to sustain themselves by means of that food ever since then. It is heard that the Earth was once again milked by the sages.

204-206. Soma (The Moon) was the calf in their case. Bṛhaspati (Jupiter) was the milkman. Gāyatrī and other (Vedic) Metres carried out the function of the Utensil (milk-pot). Penance and the eternal Brahman (Vedas) was their milk (the yield).

Again it is heard that the Earth was milked by the groups of Devas with Purandara (Indra) as their leader, taking up (with him) a golden vessel. Maghavan was the calf and lord Savitṛ was the milkman. Ūrjā (Power, energy, Procreative energy) and honey was the milk. The deities sustain themselves by means of that.

207-209a. It is heard that the Earth was again milked by the Pitṛs by means of a Silver Vessel. The yield was Svadhā and it was conducive to their immediate contentment. Yama the valorous son of Vivasvān was their calf. The powerful god Antaka (the god of death) was the milkman of the Pitṛs.

209b-212a. It is heard that the Earth was once again milked by the Asuras with an iron vessel and the all round yield was the power of Māyā (deception, illusion). Virocana, the extremely famous son of Prahlāda, was the calf unto them. Ṛtvikdvimūrdhā (?) the son of Diti was their milkman. With the (different types of) Māyā for their milky yield all the Asuras became Māyāvins (experts in making use of Māyā). Those persons of great virility sustain themselves by means of Māyā. That is their great source of strength.

212b-215a. After adopting Takṣaka as their calf, it is heard, that the Earth was once again milked by the serpents, with a pot of ground (or bottle-gourd) as their vessel and poison as their milk. O excellent Brāhmaṇa, Vāsuki, the valorous son of Kadru, was the milkman unto those *Nāgas* and *Sarpas* (different varieties of Serpents). Those terrible beings sustain themselves by means of that alone (i.e. poison). They are excessively poisonous. They have that as their food. They are active on account of it. That is their source of vigour. They solely depend on it.

215b-217. In a pot not annealed properly, the Earth was once again milked by the Yakṣas and the Puṇyajanas after adopting as their calf Vaiśravaṇa who was fond of Antardhāna (becoming invisible). The milkman was Rajatanābha who was the father of Maṇidhara. The son of Yakṣa was extremely resplendent and he was endowed with great reputation. He had perfect control over (his sense-organs). This is perfectly true because they sustain themselves by means of it (? i.e. becoming invisible).

218-220a. The Earth was once again milked by Rākṣasas and Piśācas. Their milkman was Kubera. That of Brāhmī was Brahmā* The powerful Sumālī was the calf. The milky yield was blood. The Earth was milked in Kapāla-Pātra (skull-vessel). *Antardhāna* (the power of becoming invisible) was milked by the Rākṣasas. In all respects the Rākṣasas sustain themselves by means of that milk.

220b-222a. Then the Earth was milked by the Gandharvas and the groups of celestial damsels with lotus as their vessel. They made Citraratha their calf. The milky yield was pure fragrant scent. Their milkman was Vasuruci[1]. (Viśvāvasu in Vā. P the splendid son of a sage (? of Muni), the extremely powerful king of the Gandharvas, the noble-souled one resembling the sun.

222b-224a. It is heard that the sparkling goddess Vasundharā (Earth) was again milked by the mountains.** The milky yield was as follows : the medicinal herbs having embodied forms and different types of precious gems and jewels. Himavān was the calf and Meru the great mountain was the milkman. The vessel was a mountain itself. Hence, the mountains are all well-established.

224b-227. It is heard that the Earth was once again milked by the trees and the creepers after taking up as their vessel the (leafy cup of) Palāśa tree that grows again and again when cut down or burnt. The Plakṣa tree, the tree of prolific blossoms, was the calf of these famous ones (i.e. trees and creepers). It yielded the milk they desired.

The Earth was thus a milch cow that yielded everything they desired. It made the living beings flourish. She

* This is obscure—Vā. P. 62 reads *Brahmopetas tu dogdhā* 'Rākṣasa called Brahmopeta was the milkman'.

1. Mt. P. 10. 25 reads here Vararuci for Vasuruci as the milk-man and Nāṭya Veda was the milk:

Dogdhā Vararucir nāma nāṭya-vedasya pāragaḥ /

In other words a new discoverer or inventor is the milkman and the contribution to that science or lore is the milk.

** Kālidāsa in *Kumāra-sambhava* I.2 has ditto echoed this.

alone was the *Dhātrī* and *Vidhātri* (one who created and laid down rules and shaped the destiny), the *Vasundharā* (one who holds riches) was the supporter (of every one). We have heard that the Earth (of such potentialities), the source of origin of all the worldly things mobile and immobile, the foundation of the Universe, had been milked by Pṛthu for the welfare of worlds.

CHAPTER THIRTYSEVEN

Cākṣuṣa Manvantara ; Dynasty of Vaivasvata Manu

Sūta said :—

1. As per traditional report, the Vasudhā (the Earth) was extended here with oceans as its limits. It is glorified in songs as Vasudhā because it holds (within its bowels) riches (*Vasu*).

2. Formerly, it was completely inundated with the *Medas* (fat, suet) of (the demons) Madhu and Kaiṭabha. Hence by etymological derivation it is called *Medinī* by the expounders of the Brahman.

3. Thereafter, on its attainment of the status of the daughter of the intelligent king Pṛthu, the son of Vena, it came to be cited as *Pṛthivī*.

4-5. The division of the Earth also was formerly accomplished by Pṛthu. The Earth consisting of a series of towns and mines (of various natural products) and inhabited by the people of four castes was protected by that intelligent king. King Pṛthu the son of Vena, was a person of such power and influence, O excellent Brāhmaṇas.

6-12a. He is worthy of being bowed down to and honoured by entire living beings all round.

Pṛthu alone is worthy of being offered of obeisance by Brāhmaṇas of great dignity and splendour, and experts in the

Vedas and the Vedāṅgas (ancillary subjects of the Vedas), since he is ancient and had Brahman as the source of origin.

Pṛthu, the primordial king, the valorous son of Vena, should be bowed down to by the highly fortunate kings who seek great reputation.

Pṛthu alone, who was the first formulator of Military service, should be bowed down to by warriors in the battlefield desirous of obtaining victory in the war.

The warrior who glorifies king Pṛthu and then proceeds to the battlefield returns safely from the terrible battle and attains glorious fame.

The saintly king of great fame, Pṛthu alone, should be bowed down to by Vaiśyas too who strictly abide by the duties and activities befitting the Vaiśyas, since it was he who had offered them sustenance.

Thus the different types of calves, milkmen, milk and the vessels—all these have been recounted by me in due order.

12b-15a[1]. At the outset, the Earth was milked by the noble-souled Brahmā after making the wind god the calf. The seeds on the surface of the Earth were the milky yield.

Thereafter, in the Svāyambhuva Manvantara (the Earth was milked) after making Svāyambhuva Manu the calf. All types of plants were the milky yield.

Thereafter, when the Svārociṣa Manvantara arrived, the Earth was milked after making Svārociṣa, the calf. The plants and food-grains were the milky yield.

15b-16a. In the Uttama (Manvantara) the earth was milked by intelligent Devabhuja* after making Manu the best calf and the (milk-yield was) all crops.

16b-17a. Again during the fifth Manvantara called Tāmasa, the earth was milked again by Balabandhu after makiny Tāmasa (Manu) as the calf.

17b-18a. It is reported that when the sixth Manvantara of Cāriṣṭava (Cāriṣṇava in Vā. P.) arrived, the Earth was milked by Purāṇa for the calf Cāriṣṭava. (cāriṣṇava).

* Vā P. 63.15 reads *Devabhujena* 'by Devabhuja' instead of *Devānujena* hereof.

1. VV. 12b-20 give the list of persons who "milked" the earth in each Manvantara. In a way each "milking" represents advancement in human civilization.

18b-19a. When the Cākṣuṣa Manvantara arrived, in that Manvantara, the Earth was milked by Purāṇa (?) after making Cākṣuṣa, the calf.

19b-20a. When the Cākṣuṣa Manvantara had elapsed and the Vaivasvata Manvantara arrived, the Earth was milked by the son of Vena. How it was milked has already been recounted to you by me.

20b-22. The Earth was thus milked in the previous Manvantaras by these viz.—the Devas and others, the human and other living beings too. A similar situation should be understood in the Manvantaras of the past as well as of the future. The Devas reside in heaven throughout a Manvantara.

Now listen to the progeny of Pṛthu. Two very valiant sons were born to Pṛthu. They were Antardhi and Pāvana.

23-24. Śikhaṇḍinī gave birth to Havirdhāna (the son) of Antardhāna (same as Antardhi).

Dhiṣaṇā, the daughter of Agni (Āgneyī) gave birth to six sons of Havirdhāna—viz. Prācīna-Barhis, Śukla, Gaya, Kṛṣṇa, Praja and Ajina. Lord Prācīnabarhis was a great Prajāpati (Lord of the subjects, or sovereign ruler).

25. On account of his strength, learning, penance and virility, he was the sole monarch of the Earth. His Darbha grasses had their tips towards the East.[1] Hence, he was known as Pracīnabarhis.

26. After a great penance, that Prajāpati married Savarṇā the daughter of the ocean.

27 Savarṇā, the daughter of the ocean, gave birth to ten sons of Prācīnabarhis. All of them were masters of the Science of archery. They were called Pracetas (collectively).

28. Performing pious rites (collectively) without being separated from one another, they underwent severe penance for ten thousand years lying down within the waters of the ocean.

29. While they were performing the penance, the trees

1. Cf. Vp. I 14.4. This speciality is attributed to the king's performance of many sacrifices.

encompassed the Earth that was not being protected. Then there was the destruction of subjects.

30. This happened when the Cākṣuṣa Manvantara passed by. The whole firmament became enveloped by the trees and hence the wind was unable to blow.

31-32. For ten thousand years, the subjects were unable to carry on their activities. On hearing about it all, those Pracetas equipped with the power of penance, became infuriated and they created wind and fire out of their mouths. The wind uprooted the trees and dried them up.

33-35. The fire burned them. Thus there was a terrible destruction of trees. On coming to know of the destruction of the trees and when a few trees remained, King Soma (the Moon god) approached these Pracetas and said—" Now that you have seen the purpose realised, O Kings, sons of Prācīnabarhis, get rid of your anger for the continuity of the world. The trees will grow on the Earth. Let the fire and wind be calm.

36. This fair-complexioned daughter of the trees has become the crest-jewel of all women. This girl has been held (and nurtured) in the womb by me, as I had already known the future events.

37. She is Māriṣā by name, and has been created by the trees themselves. Let this girl who has been nurtured in the womb of Soma (the Moon-god) be your wife.

38. With half of your splendour and with half of mine, the scholarly Prajāpati, Dakṣa will be born of her.

39*. He is on a par with fire. He will make these subjects flourish once again, the subjects who have been mostly burned down by the fire of your splendour".

40. Thereafter, at the instance of Soma, those Pracetas controlled their anger and as per religious procedure accepted from the trees, the girl Māriṣā as their wife.

---

* *Alternatively* :

On account of the fire consisting of your fiery brilliance, he (Dakṣa) will be just like fire. But he will make the subjects multiply and flourish again—the subjects most of whom are consumed by fire.

41-42. Thereafter, they mentally impregnated Māriṣā. Prajāpati Dakṣa was born of Māriṣa as the son of all the ten Pracetas. He had excessive splendour on account of the part of Soma (the Moon god). He was vigorous. In the beginning Dakṣa created subjects mentally and later on (he created them) through sexual intercourse.

43. After mentally creating the mobile and immobile beings and the bipeds and quadrupeds, Dakṣa created women.

44. He gave ten daughters to Dharma; thirteen to Kaśyapa and twentyseven (daughters) who were suitable for passing (calculation) of the time (i.e. the Constellations) to (the Moon) god.

45-46. After giving (the daughters) to these, he gave four others to Ariṣṭanemi; two to Bāhuputra and two to Aṅgiras. He gave one daughter to Kṛśāśva. Children were born of them. This is sung about as the Sixth Manvantara of Cākṣuṣa Manu.

47-48. The Vasus, the Devas, the birds, the cows, the Nāgas (Serpents, elephants), the Daityas and the Dānavas, the Gandharvas and the *Apsaras* as well as other species were born of Vaivasvata Manu, the seventh among Manus, who was Prajāpati (a patriarch or Lord of the Subjects). It was only after that, that the subjects were born of sexual copulation. The creation of the former subjects, it is said, was through thought, (will), sight, and touch.

The sage asked :—

49-51. Formerly, the auspicious origin of the Devas, the Dānavas, the Devarṣis (divine Sages) and the Noble-souled Dakṣa was narrated by you. The birth of Dakṣa from the vital airs of Brahmā was mentioned by you. How did the Dakṣa of great penance attain the state of being the son of the Pracetas again? O Sūta, it behoves you to clarify this doubt of ours. He was the son of the daughter of Soma (Moon). How did he become his father-in-law?

Sūta explained :—

52. Creation and annihilation, O excellent ones, do happen perpetually among the living beings. The sages and those

people who possess *Vidyā* (Learning) do not become confused in this matter.

53. All these, Dakṣa and others, are born in every Yuga. They are annihilated again. A learned man does not become confused in this matter.

54. The state of being elder or yonder also was present in them, O excellent Brāhmaṇas. But penance alone was weighty. Prowess was the reason thereof.

55. He who comprehends this creation of Cākṣuṣa consisting of the mobile and immobile beings, shall become one endowed with progeny. He shall cross the life-span. He will be honoured in the heaven (after his death).

56-57. Thus the creation of Cākṣuṣa has been succinctly recounted. Thus these six types of creation, of the nature of the Manvantaras beginning with Svāyambhuva and ending with Cākṣuṣa, have been concisely narrated in the due order. These are the creations as described by wise men who were excellent Brāhmaṇas.

58-60. Their detailed explanation should be understood through the creation of Vaivasvata (Manvantara). All these creations of Vivasvān are neither deficient nor superfluous as regards health, longevity, magnitude, virtue, wealth and love. He who reads this without jealousy attains all these good qualities. I shall narrate (the creation of the noble-souled Vaivasvata the current Manu, both succinctly and in detail. Understand it even as I recount.

CHAPTER THIRTYEIGHT

Vaivasvata Manvantara : *The Mārīca Creation*

Sūta said :—

1. During the Seventh Manvantara of Vaivasvata Manu, the Devas and the great sages were born of Kaśyapa, the son of Marīci [1]

1. This explains the Title "The Mārica Creation".

2. The following are remembered as the eight groups of Devas : (1) Ādityas (2) Vasus (3) Rudras (4) Sādhyas (5) Viśvedevas (6) Maruts (7) Bhṛgus and (8) Aṅgiras.

3-4. The Ādityas, Maruts and Rudras should be known as the sons of Kaśyapa. The three sets (of gods) viz. Sādhyas, Viśvedevas and Vasus are the sons of Dharma. The Bhṛgus are the sons of Bhṛgu and the Devas (called) Aṅgiras are the sons of Aṅgiras. In this Vaivasvata Manvantara, these are considered to be *Chandajas* (born of Chandas).

5. All these too will meet death after the efflux of time. Thus the current splendid creation should be known as that of the son of Marīci.

6-8. At present, their brilliant Indra is Mahābala (greatly powerful) by name.

The Indras of all the Manvantaras of the past, present and future should be known as having equal (similar) characteristic features. All of them are the lords (of everything) past, present and future.* All of them are bountiful and crested (eminent) and wield the thunderbolt in their hands. All of them have severally performed a hundred sacrifices.

9-12. There Indras have overpowered all living beings whether mobile or immobile in the three worlds, by their Dharma (and other special reasons), by their brilliance, penance, intelligence, might, learning and exploit. I shall explain to you in details why (and how) these mighty ones are the dominant lords and masters of *Bhūta*, *Bhavya* and *Bhavat*, (try to) understand me as I recount. It is remembered by the Brāhmaṇas that *Bhūta*, *Bhavya* and *Bhavat* are the three worlds. This *Bhūrloka* (Earth) is remembered as *Bhūta*; the *Antarikṣa* (Atmosphere) is remembered as *Bhavat*. The Diva (Heaven) is remembered as *Bhavya*. I shall mention their means (of derivation).

13. While meditating upon the names (i.e. what names should be given to the worlds), this (name viz. *bhuḥ*) was uttered at the outset by god Brahmā. As the word *Bhuḥ*

* See VV.12-20 below for the special meaning of *bhūta*, *bhavat* and *bhavya*.

was spoken at the outset the *Bhūrloka* (Earth) came into existence.

14-15. The root *Bhū*—is remembered as one meaning 'existence'. It also means 'appearance of the world'. Hence this first world became *Bhūrloka* because of its 'coming into being', (*Bhūtatva*) as well its being visible (Darśana). It is remembered by the Brāhmaṇas as 'Bhūr' because of its being *bhūta*. After this had come into being, the second word *Bhavat* was uttered by Brahmā.

16. The word *Bhavat* is used when something is being produced. *Bhuvarloka* (atmosphere) is mentioned by this word because of its being produced (*Bhavana*.)

17-20. The atmosphere (*antarikṣa*) being *bhavat* (is the process of being produced). The second world is, therefore, called *Bhavat*.

When the second world had been produced the word *Bhavya* was uttered by Brahmā. Therefore, that world became *Bhavya* world. The word *Bhavya* is considered in the case of what has not yet come into existence (or happened). Hence this *Bhavya* is remembered by the name *Tridiva* (Heaven). The Earth is remembered by the word *Bhū*. The *Antarikṣa* (Atmosphere)is remembered as *Bhuvaḥ*. The heaven is remembered as *Bhavya*, *This* is the decision in regard to the (names of the three worlds. Three *Vyāhṛtis* (utterances) took place (while) speaking about the three worlds.

21-22. There is a root viz. *Nath*—This root is remembered by persons who know (grammar) in the sense of 'protection'. Since they are the protectors of the three worlds namely the *Bhūta*, *Bhavya* and *Bhavat*, they are declared as Indras by Brāhmaṇas. Devendras are the Chief ones and the meritorious ones.

23a. In the Manvantaras those who are the Devas are participants in (the oblations etc. in) sacrifices are called the protectors of the three worlds by the Brāhmaṇas.

23b-25. The Yakṣas, the Gandharvas, the Rākṣasas, the Piśācas, the Serpents and the human beings are remembered as (effects of the) glory of the Devendras. The Devendras are the elders, protectors, kings and the Pitṛs (Manes). The excellent gods protect these subjects righteously. Thus the characteristic features of the Devendras have been succinctly recounted.

26-29. I shall mention the seven sages who have currently resorted to the heaven. They are (1) The intelligent sage Viśvāmitra of great penance, who was the son of Gādhi and who belonged to the family of Kuśika. (2) Jamadagni, the valorous son of Aurva and the scion of the family of Bhṛgu. (3) Bharadvāja of great reputation who was the son of Bṛhaspati. (4) The righteous and scholarly sage named 'Śaradvān' who was the son of Utathya and who belonged to the family of Gotama. (5) The holy lord Atri son of the Selfborn lord is the fifth one. He is (otherwise known as) *Brahmakośa* (having Brahman as the protective covering). (6) Vasumān the son of Vasiṣṭha is well known in the world. He is the sixth one (7) Vatsara born of the family of Kaśyapa.

These seven sages are honoured by good men.

30-33. These seven sages enumerated now exist in the present Manvantara.

The following nine are the righteous sons of Vaivasvata Manu : Ikṣvāku, Nṛga who was impudent, Śaryāti, Nariṣyanta, Nābhāga who was famous, Diṣṭa, Karūṣa, Pṛṣadhra and Pāṁśu who is remembered as the ninth. They have been glorified as very religious. This present Manvantara is the Seventh one.

Thus, O Brāhmaṇas, the Second Pāda (quarter) has been recounted by me in detail and the proper order. What more shall I recount.?